EFFECTIVE FINANCIAL

MANAGEMENT IN

PUBLIC AND

NONPROFIT AGENCIES

EFFECTIVE FINANCIAL

MANAGEMENT IN

PUBLIC AND

NONPROFIT AGENCIES

A PRACTICAL AND INTEGRATIVE APPROACH

Jerome B. McKinney

QUORUM BOOKS

NEW YORK • WESTPORT, CONNECTICUT • LONDON

Library of Congress Cataloging-in-Publication Data

McKinney, Jerome B.
  Effective financial management in public and nonprofit
agencies.

  Bibliography: p.
  Includes index.
  1. Finance, Public. 2. Corporations, Nonprofit—
Finance. I. Title.
HJ197.M35 1986 658.1 ′5   86-624
ISBN 0-89930-154-1 (lib. bdg. : alk. paper)

Library of Congress Catalog Card Number: 86-624
ISBN: 0-89930-154-1

First published in 1986 by Quorum Books

Greenwood Press, Inc.
88 Post Road West, Westport, Connecticut 06881

Printed in the United States of America

The paper used in this book complies with the
Permanent Paper Standard issued by the National
Information Standards Organization (Z39.48-1984).

10 9 8 7 6 5 4 3 2

CONTENTS

FIGURES

TABLES

PREFACE

Public and other not-for-profit financial management has been going through profound changes during the past decade. Strong inflationary pressures, high interest rates and rising costs of materials have driven up the prices that must be charged for goods and services. This occurred at a time when the public was demanding more and better services while demonstrating an unwillingness to pay higher taxes or fees. Accordingly, there is a strongly held view that public and other not-for-profit agencies can and must find new ways to cut costs while improving efficiency, effectiveness, and accountability.

Even more so than in the past, effective management of financial resources will be critical to the success and survival of public and other not-for-profit agencies. While the non-financial manager will not be expected to be an accountant/bookkeeper or an auditor, any lack of familiarity with the concepts of accounting and other financial processes will limit the manager's ability to monitor and evaluate fiscal activities. This text is written to be understandable to those who are not "experts" but those who are or may become managers.

A major shortcoming in the financial management field has been the lack of integrated financial management systems that tie together the fiscal side (budgeting, financing and controlling) and the substantive management side (planning, programming and evaluating) so as to facilitate the unimpeded flow of required information to the appropriate responsibility centers. This book is written to fill that vacuum, providing integration and practicality.

Among the benefits that this volume provides are the following: (1) it combines budgeting and financial management in one volume; (2) it permits easy adaptation to both public and not-for-profit agencies; (3) it balances theory with practice; (4) it includes understandable descriptions of technical subjects; (5) it shows how to think about resource needs and translate them into effective budgets; (6) it shows how to develop, implement, and maintain control over expenditures; (7) it provides a step-by-step approach for the development and use of critical measurement indicators for important functions; (8) it discusses such infrequently examined topics as cash, risk, internal control, fiscal health and fraud, waste, and abuse management; (9) it shows how to obtain and use financial advisory services; and (10) its simplicity of style makes it a useful book for the novice as well as the experienced reader.

The author thanks his graduate assistants, David Miller and David Reimer, Professor Aman Khan of Florida International University for his early critical review of the project, and students and practitioners who exchanged ideas and examples. Special thanks go to Marcel Dennot for his tireless assistance with the graphic designs and to Professor Lawrence Howard for his continued encouragement. I also owe thanks to Charlie Lyons and Sally Flecker for their editing and the Graduate School of Public and International Affairs of the University of Pittsburgh for secretarial support.

EFFECTIVE FINANCIAL

MANAGEMENT IN

PUBLIC AND

NONPROFIT AGENCIES

CHAPTER 1

UNDERSTANDING FINANCIAL MANAGEMENT

The pursuit of virtually every collective public purpose has financial implications. Undertakings that have no cost seldom have many benefits. Financial management plays an indispensable role in the achievement of an organization's objective. It is the fuel that gives life and substance to the engine of public administration. Financial management is the only activity that touches every employee in an organization. The continuing upward spiral of inflation, the rising cost of governmental programs, and citizens' demands for more cost-effective delivery of goods and services are forcing managers of public and other not-for-profit organizations to make creative use of their limited financial resources. This is happening at a time when taxpayers not only are showing an unwillingness to support more services but are making an unmistakable demand to prune or cut back existing services.

This chapter gives the reader a broad overview of the components and processes involved in financial administration. The discussion is presented in five sections. The first presents a definition of financial management, showing how it is emerging as a critical force in everyday management. The second compares public and private financial management, indicating their similarities and differences and the way articulated objectives are pursued. The third discusses the organizational framework in which financial administration[1] takes place. Next, the duties of financial managers are briefly examined, and the roles of accountability and improved financial management are introduced. The final section of the chapter contains an overview of the book.

DEFINING FINANCIAL MANAGEMENT

Public financial management is the process wherein a governmental unit or agency (1) employs the means to obtain and allocate resources and/or money, based on implied or articulated priorities; and (2) utilizes methods and controls to effectively achieve publicly determined ends. Two important elements are emphasized: efficient raising of resources, and wise and accountable use of funds to achieve the highest quality end products possible. Though the definition does not stress time and uncertainty (and the literature seldom articulates these concepts), both have particular importance to the field of applied public financial management. So defined, financial management is viewed not as a staff specialty concerned only with controlling government or agency funds but as an integral part of management.

In general terms, financial management comprises three main activities: (1) It determines the scope and content of fiscal policies. This is a process in which an agency, a community, or relevant political leaders set forth programs and provide the appropriation or resources required to accomplish their objectives. (Issues such as employment, inflation, borrowing, taxation, and revenue raising are considered and resolved.) (2) It establishes general guidelines and standards to ensure that funds are spent honestly and wisely to achieve publicly determined purposes. (3) It provides organizational structures and controls to effectively carry out fiscal duties and responsibilities.[2] Traditionally, the main financial management components include budgeting, taxation (revenue raising), accounting, treasury management, purchasing, and auditing.

In Figure 1.1, the integrated approach to financial management incorporates an additional set of components, including planning, programming, and evaluating functions. The box below Figure 1.1 clarifies what is meant by each of these six processes.

Integrative Role. The critical and integrative role that financial management plays linking the core management and financial processes in the everyday operation of organizations can be seen in Figure 1.1. For simplicity, the combination of the two processes may be seen as a set of sequential steps: planning, programming, budgeting, financing, controlling, and evaluating.

The first of the basic management processes depicted in Figure 1.1 involves the articulation of the goals and objectives to be pursued (planning). Their feasibility for implementation is determined, and the selection of appropriate activities to realize the planned goals is made (programming).

The first action on the "financial process side" is the budget (or expenditure plan), which allocates available resources based on these programmed activities and priorities. Once the expenditure plan has been developed, financial resources are sought to execute the plan (financing). In order to

Figure 1.1
Financial Management's Integrative Role

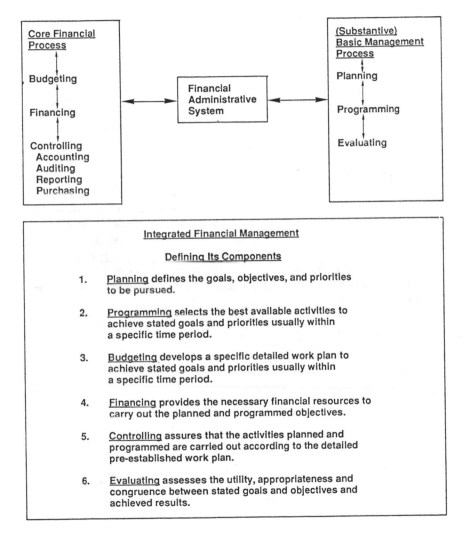

Core Financial Process
↑
Budgeting
↑
Financing
↑
Controlling
Accounting
Auditing
Reporting
Purchasing

Financial Administrative System

(Substantive) Basic Management Process
↑
Planning
↑
Programming
↓
Evaluating

Integrated Financial Management

Defining Its Components

1. Planning defines the goals, objectives, and priorities to be pursued.

2. Programming selects the best available activities to achieve stated goals and priorities usually within a specific time period.

3. Budgeting develops a specific detailed work plan to achieve stated goals and priorities usually within a specific time period.

4. Financing provides the necessary financial resources to carry out the planned and programmed objectives.

5. Controlling assures that the activities planned and programmed are carried out according to the detailed pre-established work plan.

6. Evaluating assesses the utility, appropriateness and congruence between stated goals and objectives and achieved results.

monitor the progress of activities as they move through the execution stages, and thereby ensure that the planned, programmed, and financial objectives are being carried out according to targets and expectations, a system of control is created. Whenever it is determined that progress is not meeting expectations, interventions can be made to redirect the activity toward its target.

Returning to the management side, it can be seen that evaluation is the final action in the process. This activity determines whether the articulated goals and objectives have been achieved.

Traditionally, financial management has given little attention to the basic management processes of planning, programming, and evaluation. Instead, it has dwelled on the core financial processes, especially the budgeting and controlling activities. However, because of the continuing competition for declining financial resources, the basic management processes are destined to receive more attention. Planning, programming, and evaluating require policy makers to look, understand, and reflect before they leap into enacting unwise policies. This changing emphasis will be discussed later in this volume.

Changing Orientation in Financial Management. The financial crises experienced by cities such as New York and Cleveland have led to increased interest in financial management at all levels of government, particularly at the local level. While the traditional emphases on control and compliance (conforming activities to laws, rules, and procedures laid down by the purchasing, accounting, auditing, and budget systems) are still important, new critical concerns have emerged. These concerns can be stated as a series of questions, including the following:

1. What indicators would permit us to assess the fiscal health of a governmental unit?
2. What is the most effective approach for forecasting revenue and expenditures?
3. What are the best methods for effecting cutback management while balancing the needs and demands of the community?
4. What methods are used to evaluate the adequacy of financial management systems in (a) permitting managers to anticipate financial problems, and (b) allowing managers to solve them before they reach critical limits?

PUBLIC VERSUS PRIVATE FINANCIAL MANAGEMENT

As in the public sector, virtually every key decision made in a private firm has financial implications. Managers ask questions such as the following: In an attempt to make the best financial decision, how can risk and the potential return on an investment be balanced? Is there sufficient cash or access to funds to meet daily needs and maturing obligations? What should be the firm's credit policy toward its customers, and what privileges should particular customers be granted? What are the potential sources of funds that may be used to finance investments?

Many of the concepts, objectives, and techniques employed in one sector are also utilized in the other (as shown in Figure 1.2). First of all, both the public and the private sector are concerned with financing ongoing operations and effectively managing the flow of funds. Second, in seeking debt funds both sectors must go to the same financial markets. Third, large public sector purchases require competitive bidding, although this is true to a lesser extent than in the private sector. Fourth, both sectors have systems of employee pension plans. Finally, both have unions that require contract negotiations and wage/salary administration, although unionization is a greater factor in the private sector.

Major differences between the private and public sectors relate to what the final objectives are and the way resources are raised. Ideally, the ultimate objective of public sector financial decision makers is to maximize the production and delivery of goods and services. The emphasis is on the provision to the community of socially beneficial services, a large portion of which are distributed on the basis of need. Business decision makers seek to maximize profit and/or wealth for their stockholders.

The private sector depends on the contribution of investors in order to obtain funds to conduct business. The public sector imposes taxes to meet its objectives. These tax resources are typically extracted based on some measure of ability to pay. There are no equity shares that can be traded or sold.

In pure public or non-profit agencies where the provision of services is based entirely on need, no individual charges or costs are paid by recipients of the services. Pure public or non-profit agencies produce collective or indivisible services and/or goods, such as defense, from which individual recipients cannot be excluded from simultaneous enjoyment—hence the impossibility of pricing.

In between the conceptual poles of purely public and purely private lies a host of quasi-public agencies and organizations. The services of such quasi-public or non-profit agencies are provided on a break-even or partial cost recovery basis (e.g., school lunches, parking facilities, and sewage treatment). However, there are cases where public policy requires that individuals with incomes below a particular cut-off point be exempted from paying for the provision of services.

Finally, non-government/non-profit agencies experiencing heavy deficits will suffer the same fate as businesses unless the leadership of these organizations can find sympathetic ears among corporate managers and/or publicly elected officials.

ORGANIZING FOR FINANCIAL ADMINISTRATION

Particularly at the state and local level of government, checks and balances and separation of powers (functions) have dominated the way finan-

Figure 1.2
Comparing Objectives: Public/Non-Profit and Private Organizations

ACTIVITY	OBJECTIVE	
	Public/Non-Profit Organization	Private
Resource allocation	Budget and political process	Market and pricing system
Resource application	Optimal use-provision of goods and services to meet stated objectives	Optimal use in terms of higher return on investment
Expenditure/ Expense	Wise usage of funds to achieve policy objectives	Wise usage of funds to maximize return on investment
Finance	Less integrated with management	Usually integral part of top management
Managing and determining source of funds	From taxation and borrowing; political officials with financial manager's advice; raising additional funds at least cost; ensuring liquidity position to enable entity to meet current maturing obligations and to deliver appropriate goods and services.	From earnings, equity, and borrowing according to financial plans; ensuring liquidity position to meet current and maturing obligations to achieve profit and wealth maximization
Determining organizational structures	Provision normally is made by legislative or by funding sources; lesser functions determined by practice, convention and financial necessity to better provide goods and services	Usually by practice, industry, rationality or pragmatic necessity to achieve greater profits
Production of goods and services reporting	Dollar accountability (fiscal-stewardship) and operational accountability of managers	Operational accountability of managers

cial administration is conducted in the United States. The view that honesty can be promoted by dividing powers among independently elected officers has led to the election of many fiscal officials. Though this view is widely held and the practice is still prevalent, there is little evidence to show that it produces competent and creative officials. On the contrary, it has sometimes led to fragmented, decentralized, uncoordinated, and ineffective financial systems.[3] This has generated a number of problems, including the following: (1) inability to act quickly; (2) competition over policy space and responsibility for financial activities; and (3) multiple clearances and conflicting advice from financial decision makers.

While the form that a *decentralized financial decision-making model* may take varies, financial activities are typically administered by separate officers who are appointed or elected. In each case a board or individual other than the chief executive is given some powers over these officials with insufficient supervisory authority to bring   about integration of the financial management system.

The complexity of modern government and the need to respond quickly to citizens' demands has led to a movement away from the decentralized financial model to the *centralized* one (see Figure 1.3). This model is closely allied with the hierarchical decision-making approach and the integrated model of decision making. Both models locate power at the top of the hierarchy, from which authority flows downward and responsibility and accountability flow upward. In this centralized organization, supervisory powers to direct financial officials reside in one individual, typically appointed by the chief executive of the governmental unit. This arrangement promotes policy integration, minimizing divided responsibility and making it more likely that plans will be executed according to policy intentions.

Three major guidelines have been suggested by Moak and Hillhouse in organizing for financial administration:[4] (1) standards for effective leadership, (2) guidelines for the efficient and effective use of resources, and (3) ways for ensuring accountability to citizens.

The first of these guidelines, pursuit of effective leadership, requires that the chief executive be judicious in his/her delegation of responsibility. This would aid in achieving an appropriate span of control in the administration of financial activities. To facilitate this objective, staff with the capacity to develop alternative financial plans must either be available or be trained; a system of controls to assure that articulated policies are executed as planned and programmed must be developed. To promote honesty and integrity, due cognizance should be given to the segregation of duties to make the occurrence of errors and collusion among employees difficult. Additionally, efforts should be made to provide technical assistance to operating managers.

The efficient and effective application of financial resources requires, first, that provision be made for the specialization and division of labor

Figure 1.3
Suggested Division of Large Non-profit Organizations

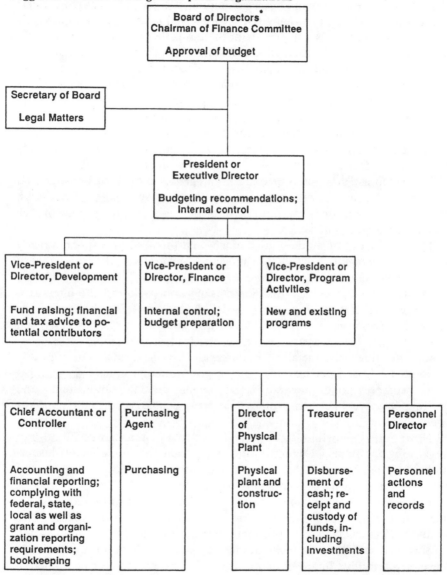

* All activities are ultimately the responsibility of the board
  of directors.

Source: John H. Engstrom and Timothy O'Keefe, "Staffing: The Financial Function," in Tracy D. Connors and Christopher T. Callaghan, eds., *Financial Management for Non-profit Organizations* (New York: AMACOM, division of American Management Association, 1982), p. 184. With permission of the publisher.

regarding the main financial functions. There is also strong need for coordination, i.e., grouping of related financial activities. This facilitates the establishment of "responsibility centers" to permit comparison of standards with achieved results. To ensure that resources are used as planned, a monetary and non-monetary control system is developed to monitor the expenditures and amount of goods or services produced from one time period to the next.

Because of the demand for responsiveness and the need to fix blame or approbation for job performance in governments, concern for accountability (Moak and Hillhouse's third guideline) has particular significance in financial management. This requires that clear lines of authority be set up to identify the duties of executing officers. It is important that a system of financial controls leading directly to the chief executive be established. The identification of financial duties and the institutionalization of executive controls set in place the structure needed to obtain an integrated financial reporting system for the organization.

In addition to the internal control system, responsiveness to public concerns typically requires that a system be established which permits citizens to appeal arbitrary financial rules and regulations. Perhaps the means most widely employed to promote accountability of financial activities is the use of the independent post-auditor.

DUTIES OF FINANCIAL MANAGERS

Financial management duties and roles have traditionally been looked upon as mainly a staff specialty function which provides support and advice to line managers.[5] This compartmentalized approach, though still present in some organizations, has given way to the integrated practice in which the financial manager acts as an integral part of the management decision-making team.

The major functions of financial managers include the following:

1. *Financial planning.* This involves (a) participation in short- and long-range planning and evaluation of various courses of action; (b) interpretation of the financial implications of legislation and regulations; (c) preparation of procedural manuals and instructions to facilitate compliance with such regulations; and (d) definition of programs and activities.

2. *Budget preparation and expenditure control.* The manager provides (a) guidance and assistance in the preparation and submission of budgets; (b) establishment of expenditure classification control; and (c) management of cash requirements.

3. *Accounting system and procedures.* The manager (a) develops the accounting system to permit incorporation of budgeting and internal controls in order to meet agency and other mandated needs; (b) develops appropriate cost accounting systems to accommodate agency needs and undertakes special cost and work mea-

surement studies when necessary to assist in alternative decision making; (c) advises operating heads on how best to use the accounting system; and (d) periodically reviews agency accounting, budgeting, financial, and statistical reporting systems and procedures, making improvements where required.

4. *Reporting for financial management control.* The manager develops agency information systems for reporting financial and other relevant data to operating and supervisory management. This information should indicate variances between budget and actual performance.

5. *Maintenance of asset control system.* The manager establishes control procedures for safekeeping of assets such as inventories, cash, materials, and equipment.

6. *Financial liaison.* The manager develops and maintains effective liaison with officials (e.g., state auditors general) as well as other agencies whose regulations may require changes in agency financial regulations.

7. *Staff training.* The manager advises and participates in the development of staff training.

8. *Analysis of fiscal health.* The financial manager must be able to analyze fiscal conditions. The manager must constantly be aware of answers to questions such as: Can the unit of government or agency pay its own way? Can the unit pay for services and avoid large tax or fee increases? Proper attention to these questions requires the evaluation of the community's fiscal condition. This requires having reliable information on local infrastructure such as roads, bridges, sewers, etc., and on the extent of unfunded obligations for pension liabilities.

The financial manager is expected to sort out key factors affecting the fiscal condition of the community. For example, can the community maintain an economic base to meet expenditure demands and revenue expectations? Can the community maintain existing service levels? In addition, the manager must be able to determine the causes of fiscal distress and be able to measure its extent.

It can be seen that the financial manager is a key player in maintaining the viability of an agency. The manager is expected to assist in developing plans and options for keeping and attracting businesses. In the case of an agency, the manager must develop, maintain, and/or expand revenue sources. He/she acts as a negotiator in union contracts and with community groups seeking goods and services that involve use of monetary resources. Finally, the manager acts as a controller in all financial activities.

Accountability and Improved Financial Management. Clients and constituents are demanding improved goods and services at a time when resources are declining at all levels of government. Taxpayers are resisting tax increases. Donors are demanding results for their contributions. Demands are being made that public managers and not-for-profit organizations utilize available resources wisely. Additionally, there is a concern that systems be devised to facilitate greater accountability for the expenditure of public money.

Accountability will require that managers at all organizational levels know specifically to whom and for what they are accountable. This will necessitate that objectives be clearly articulated. Operations must be planned and programmed, indicating explicitly what is to be done; what the (allowable) resources are; what methods will be employed; what the required performance is; and how results will be measured and evaluated. All of this requires that greater emphasis be given to program planning.

In program planning, each manager has a responsibility to allocate resources in order to achieve the organization's objective with maximum efficiency and effectiveness. Program planning involves prioritizing both the objectives sought and the tasks to be performed in order to achieve them. If fewer resources are allocated to the manager than are anticipated, he/she will need to decide what will be pruned or dropped and what combination of resources will be required to achieve the objective.

To improve the utilization of resources and to avoid a "hit or miss" or "seat of the pants" approach to decision making, those concerned with financial management are expected to assist, engage in, and provide guidance for both short-range and long-range financial planning. Elements such as the following must be set forth: (1) clear identification of objectives; (2) proposed plan(s) of action to achieve those objectives; (3) expected results for each unit of time in the plan; (4) alternative plan(s) of action; and (5) measures to judge efficiency and effectiveness in meeting the objectives.

ORGANIZATION OF THE TEXT

The first two chapters of this volume provide the reader with an understanding of the scope, nature, and function of modern financial management, stressing the changing focus and the important role of accounting.

Resource management functions are examined in chapters 3 through 7. Successful practices and techniques in revenue administration, purchasing, cash management, and debt and risk management from across the United States are evaluated. While some attention is given to theory, the major focus is on how the systems work, indicating their potentials and possible restraints.

Chapters 8 through 18 discuss the management control process as a means of achieving accountability. The reader is shown how linkage may effectively be achieved among the accounting, auditing, reporting, and monitoring systems in financial management. How indicators can be developed and used to control day-to-day operations and permit a close watch on community fiscal health is also covered.

Chapters 19 and 20 explore special concerns such as fraud, waste, and abuse (FWA), and the advising functions which are important to the modern financial manager.

NOTES

1. The terms *management* and *administration* are used interchangeably throughout this volume.

2. Jerome B. McKinney and Lawrence C. Howard, *Public Administration: Balancing Power and Accountability* (Oak Park, Ill.: Moore Publishing Co., 1979), pp. 345-47.

3. Lennox L. Moak and Albert M. Hillhouse, *Local Government Finance* (Chicago: Municipal Finance Officers Association, 1975), p. 26.

4. Ibid., pp. 35-36.

5. These are the individuals who are responsible for direct delivery of goods and services to the clients and constituents for which an agency has been created. These persons are also known as doers, as opposed to staff people, who are known as advisors.

CHAPTER 2

ACCOUNTING: IMPORTANT ROLE IN FINANCIAL MANAGEMENT

In both public and private organizations, accounting has served as a major mechanism of management control. It is important to note that the structure of financial analysis is dependent predominantly on accounting information. It is by means of accounting information that the consequences of the various options available to management are revealed. Management can use accounting information as a control and monitoring tool to assess performance and take corrective action. In public and not-for-profit agencies, decision makers should therefore have an understanding of the accounting process as well as its strengths and weaknesses. While it is not required that decision makers be accountants, an understanding of the function and structure of accounting systems is necessary for effective fiscal planning and management. To be of maximum use, the accounting system should have a flexible account structure which provides data not only for appropriated expenditures, but also for (1) program elements or activities to aid in budget analysis and presentation, (2) special project details, (3) major organizational and geographical divisions, (4) a common data base to facilitate performance measurement, and (5) determination of full cost of intended programs and activities.

The purpose of this chapter is to give the reader who is unfamiliar with accounting a general overview of the accounting process and its practice. Those who desire a more extensive and detailed introduction to this subject are directed to any of the standard introductory texts.[1]

DEFINING ACCOUNTING

Accounting is an instrument of the controlling process directed at collecting, summarizing, recording, ordering, reporting, and analyzing financial resources and transactions of an organization. Accounting keeps track of what an organization (e.g., a governmental unit, hospital, club, or family) is doing and facilitates standardizing, monitoring, and using data in an organization. Accounting reduces all transactions into common denominator–money terms, allowing for comparison of two or more activities which otherwise would be difficult to compare. In a way, it makes it possible to compare apples and oranges. Accounting is thus a common language which keeps track of transactions that occur within an organization and with other organizations. The accounting system is retrospective in that it records information relating mainly to an organization's past fiscal condition.

There are a number of fundamental objectives that an effective accounting system should seek to satisfy. They include the following:

1. *Control.* As the basic element of the financial control structure, accounting is the most important means for ensuring that public expenditures are limited to the purposes and amounts legally authorized.

2. *Accountability.* The accounting system maintains a set of procedures to ensure that officers and employees are held responsible and accountable for the safeguarding of money and property entrusted or assigned to them. A system of internal controls must be maintained to permit the continual review of commitments in an effort to promote confidence and integrity in the system.

3. *Internal and external reporting*
   a. Internal reporting relates to the use of accounting information in the planning and control of routine operations in the organization.
   b. External reporting relays the state and condition of the organization to other administrative officers, government regulating agencies, various constituencies/client groups, creditors, and the general public.

4. *Information.* The accounting system facilitates the provision of information to appropriate officials, bond raters, and creditors in the form, frequency, and timeliness desired. Information is the single most important product, especially in local governments, where accounting is the only system that provides comprehensive, detailed, and comparable information on the activities of all agencies. The accounting system provides information to assist management in the formulation of long-range policy plans and strategies. This latter aspect is at present more of a hope than a reality in most governments and not-for-profit agencies.

Financial Accounting. The major objective of financial accounting is the preparation of a financial statement. The financial statement offers a measurement of past and current financial status to internal and external users[2] (bond holders, taxpayers, the press, creditors, bond raters, the general public, and other interested groups) in conformance with generally accepted accounting principles (GAAP) as they apply to government and not-for-profit organizations. Financial accounting focuses on the recording of financial transactions. By means of a predetermined code or chart of accounts, financial transactions are systematically recorded in accounting ledgers (books containing the summary of account). The data from these ledgers are used periodically to produce required fiscal statements. The statements provide monetary information and are used for budget preparation, internal control, and adherence to legal and other external reporting requirements.

Managerial Accounting. The provision of information to aid internal management in improving the effectiveness of programming, decision making, and control is the concern of managerial accounting. Attention is focused on the organization of information to enhance decision making related to activities, operations, programs, or responsibility centers. Distinguishing features of managerial accounting include the following:

- It is future oriented.
- It provides data for internal use and management decision making.
- It is eclectic in that it is not bound by generally accepted accounting principles and emphasizes relevance and flexibility of data selection, including data from other disciplines.
- It places emphasis on non-monetary data, unlike financial accounting.
- It uses variance reports to analyze deviations from planned performance.
- It encourages cost consciousness with its emphasis on performance standard and unit cost as they relate to responsibility centers. A responsibility center is a section or division of an organization (for example, purchasing and maintenance) for which an individual is assigned responsibility and given control over resources to achieve one or more purposes (objectives) as part of the overall goal(s) of an organization.
- It promotes, through its cost approach, linkage between management control and program, and performance and zero-base budgeting.

Cost Accounting. The assemblage and recording of all cost elements related to a project or a unit of work is the responsibility of cost accounting. Expressed another way, "it is an art of determining the cost of a product, service or activity."[3] Cost accounting, as noted earlier, is the connecting link between financial and managerial accounting. Financial accounting provides the historical data which may be used in costing out options for management decision making. Figure 2.1 shows how a cost accounting system may be used strategically to aid management decision making. Cost information can be used to enhance planning, budgeting, controlling, evaluating, pricing, and reporting. There are a number of important uses for governmental cost information, including the following:

- *Budgeting* provides the basic costing data for preparing the budget, planning, and making decisions regarding resource allocation.
- *Cost efficiency analysis* provides information to assess the efficiency of programs and activities.

Figure 2.1
The Costing Matrix

	Direct Cost	Marginal Cost	Fixed Cost	Unit Cost	Variable Cost	Avoidable Cost	Life-cycle Cost	Total Cost
Eliminate Service			X		X	X		
Reassign Personnel					X	X		
Reduce Service	X	X			X	X		
Improve Productivity		X		X				
Contract Out						X		
Civilianize the Delivery	X					X		
Substitute Equipment			X	X		X	X	
Charge for Service		X						X
Status Quo	X							X

Source: Joseph T. Kelley, *Costing Government Services: A Guide to Decision Making* (Washington, D.C.: Government Research Center, 1984), p. 36.

- *Life-cycle costing* furnishes the total cost associated with a long-lived asset, including acquisition, operation, and maintenance costs over the life of the equipment less any resale value.

- *Avoidable cost* accounts for the amount of expense that would not occur if a given decision were implemented.

- *Contracting-out decision* provides a basis to determine if an activity should be completed in-house or contracted out.

- *Fee determination* facilitates the development of fee schedule and reimbursement costs.

- *Reporting* adds greater cost consciousness to financial statements, as fund accounting does not permit cost and performance analysis.

- *Opportunity cost* shows the maximum value of benefits forgone by selecting one option over another. Opportunity cost is useful when choices must be made between alternative courses of action. For example, if a governmental unit wishes to contract out its garbage collection rather than continue to do it in-house, opportunity cost is considered.

- *Differential costs* present the amount of increase or decrease in revenue or expenses that is expected to result from a particular course of action as compared to an alternative. It may also be viewed as the difference between incremental costs at two different levels of activity.

- *Full cost* offers another way of presenting total cost or "absorption cost."

Cost Behavior. It is important to be able to discern the behavior of various kinds of costs as they relate to managerial decisions. Costs may be categorized according to their behavior patterns at different levels of activity. Based on the changes of total cost generated by a change in activity level, there are four basic cost relationships, as shown in Figure 2.2:

- *Fixed cost* is one that remains constant regardless of the variation in volume of activity. Since the expense does not change as the number of units or products increases, the cost per unit decreases. Yearly rent and insurance premiums are good examples of fixed cost.

- *Semi-fixed cost* is also known as "step" cost. It is fixed for a given level of activity, but it increases to higher plateaus as activity increases. Supervision is a good example. An additional supervisor is expected to be taken on when the volume of work reaches a specific level of activity.

- *Variable cost* is one which tends to fluctuate according to the variation in the volume of the activity. Variable cost increases or decreases directly in proportion to the change in the level of activity. For example, the materials cost for making license plates increases or decreases depending on the number of units produced.

- *Semi-variable cost* is a cost that has both fixed and semi-variable characteristics. The predominant element of the cost is variable, but it has some element of fixed costs at either the lower or higher range of activity. The guaranteed minimum wage is a good example of fixed cost at the lower end of activity. Social Security, unemployment taxes, maintenance, and salary plus commission represent examples of fixed cost at the higher level of activity.[4]

Figure 2.2
Cost Behavior Patterns

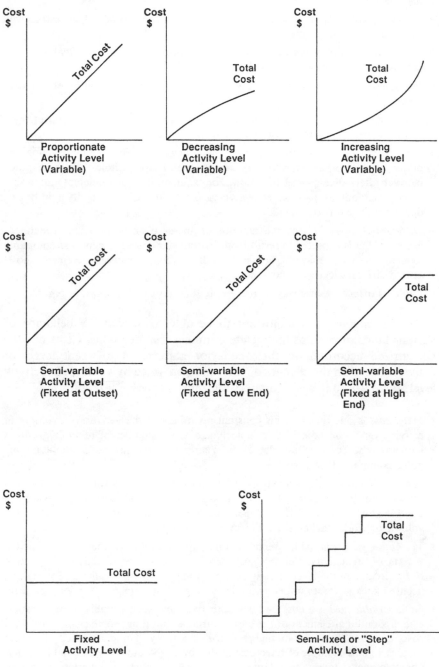

Responsibility Centers/Accounting. These two concepts are intertwined in theory and in practice. Responsibility accounting is the mechanism used to provide performance information to the individual directly responsible for a particular activity or function (viewed in this context, unit, section, department, and division are considered responsibility centers). The reporting of results is made possible, permitting the identification and fixing of responsibility for significant variances from planned performance. It permits management to take timely and corrective action. It is particularly noteworthy that responsibility accounting assigns responsibility to those individuals who have influence over day-to-day costs, minimizing the potential for buck passing. In a county health department, for example, the costs of sanitation, inspection, communicable disease control, environmental control, and community mental health may be reported separately. The county health director, then, could hold each unit accountable for the results in its respective responsibility area.

In responsibility accounting, appropriated funds are made available to specific organizational units within an agency. Each unit is responsible for the resources entrusted to it. The responsible unit official may authorize commitment of expenditure and is ultimately accountable for the actions taken and the results achieved. The resources made available are stipulated in the budget and must be recorded in the accounts. Each commitment, payment, or refund must be recorded in the accounts. Thus, at any given time, the amount allocated less the recorded transaction provides the balance available for use. Responsibility costs in monetary terms are costs incurred by and on behalf of a responsibility center over a period of time.

Anthony and Young suggest the following procedures in determining and allocating costs:[5]

- Determine the object or unit of goods or services for which cost is being sought. For example, a cost object for a hospital may be a patient day and for a university a student year. A university may choose to use different cost objects, such as the cost for a classroom or laboratory hour.

- Determine the responsibility cost center (an area over which management is held accountable for inputs and outputs and over which a reasonable degree of control is exercised) from which the cost is to be collected.

- Determine the direct costs (traceable to a specific cost object or cost center) and indirect costs (applicable to more than one cost object or responsibility cost center).

- Allocate service support center costs to the mission (the main purpose for which an agency exists) as shown in Table 2.1. The basis or technique for allocating or apportioning those service center costs is the one that is most appropriate, based on the agency or individual's experience. It may be the square feet of area occupied by the mission cost center, or the hours of service rendered by the service cost center.

Table 2.1
Matrix Showing Responsibility Centers and Programs

Responsibility Centers	Alcohol Detoxification	Drug Rehabilitation	Trauma Center	Renal Dialysis
Mission Centers				
Routine exam	No. days	No. days	No. days	No. days
Surgery	-	-	No. procedures	-
Laboratory	No. tests	No. tests	No. tests	No. tests
Radiology	No. procedures	No. procedures	No. procedures	No. procedures
Outpatient Care	No. visits	No. visits	No. visits	No. visits

Service Centers	
Housekeeping Dieting Laundry Administration Social Services	Cost distributed to mission centers and programs to determine their full costs.

Four types of responsibility centers are common, especially in the private sector. (1) The *cost center* (also known as an *expense center*) is the smallest area of responsibility for which costs or expenses are collected; it does not measure the monetary value of the responsibility center's output. (2) A *revenue center* is charged with the responsibility of achieving some pre-determined output expressed in monetary terms or revenue. (3) A *profit center* measures the monetary value of the input (expenses) incurred and the output (revenue) produced. The difference between expense and revenue equals profit. (4) The *investment center* measures not only the profit generated but also the amount of capital employed, providing the basis for determining the return on investment (ROI). Of the four types of centers, the cost/expense center is the most widely used in public and not-for-profit organizations.

BASIC ACCOUNTING CONCEPTS AND PRINCIPLES

Accounting principles are built on a number of important concepts. Accountants apply these concepts in their day-to-day accounting activities (recording, classifying, summarizing, and interpreting data) as a matter of habit, seldom making specific reference to them. The following are the major concepts and principles of accounting:

- *Money as a measure*. Accounting recognizes only those activities that can be quantitatively expressed in monetary terms; this gives accounting the power to express heterogenous activities in a common language. It permits items owned by an agency, such as receivables, equipment, and inventories, to be aggregated as one total. A possible shortcoming is that it cannot measure quality improvement in the service delivery or morale of an organization.

- *The entity concept*. Accounting reports are required for each economic or legal organization that uses a body of resources to achieve a common operating goal. A useful distinction is that the accounting system recognizes transactions only as they affect the business, not the individuals who manage the organization.

- *The going concern concept and periodicity*. The assumption is made that a business will continue in existence for an indefinite period. Assets are thus valued according to what is expected to happen to them in the normal course of operations. An implicit assumption is that accounting is a means whereby an organization's value is enhanced over an indefinite time horizon. To determine how well managers are performing their resource-enhancing objective, an arbitrary time period such as a calendar year or a twelve-month fiscal period is identified as the required time to present reports on the organization's accomplishment.

- *Consistency*. The ability to make comparisons is an important requirement in the analysis and use of financial data. In the accumulation and presentation of financial data, the principle of consistency requires that an enterprise follow the same generally accepted accounting practices in the recording and reporting of financial data in succeeding periods. When an independent auditor finds exceptions to these practices he must report such inconsistencies.

- *Conservatism and the cost concept.* Given two equally acceptable alternatives, the accountant will typically accept that option which tends to portray an entity in the least optimistic financial position. If given the choice between two or more equally acceptable asset values to record, the one with the least value will be accepted. Similarly, the larger of two acceptable liability options will be chosen. The guiding principles relating to recognition of expense and income suggest that, when in doubt, it is better to overstate expense and understate revenue. The operating view is to anticipate losses but not gains. It is particularly noteworthy that this does not justify deliberate misinterpretation of the operating results of an enterprise unit.

- *Matching.* Under this principle accountants attempt to match all expenses or expenditures incurred with the revenues generated in the achievement of objectives for a specific period of time. The main aim is to permit evaluation of the effort-achievement relationship. The matching of effort (expenses) with achievement (revenue) in determining operating profit or loss is difficult in the not-for-profit sector because of the problems in assigning value to service achievements.

- *Duality concept.* This is a central guiding norm and strength of the accounting system. The principle requires the identification of the source from which the available resources of an organization are received. The concept generates the following equation: assets = liabilities + equity (or funds). It matches assets with liabilities and funds, providing the system with internal checks, relating every inflow with an outflow of an entity.

Generally Accepted Accounting Principles. Until 1984 there were two primary authoritative sources of generally accepted accounting principles (GAAP) applicable to state and local government: (1) American Institute of Certified Public Accountants (AICPA), *Audit of State and Local Governmental Units* and related interpretations; and (2) Municipal Finance Officers Association (MFOA), *Governmental Accounting, Auditing, and Financial Reporting* (1980) and National Committee on Governmental Accounting (NCGA), *Statement #1, Governmental Accounting and Financial Reporting Principles* (1979). As of 1984, accounting and financial reporting standards for state and local governments are set by the Governmental Accounting Standards Board (GASB), established by the financial Accounting Foundation. In the private sector, this is paralleled by the Financial Accounting Standards Board (FASB), which has the responsibility for setting standards for business organizations. GAAP is applicable to the general purpose financial statements of entities or activities in the public sector, such as hospitals, colleges, universities, utilities, and pension plans. Organizations in the public sector are subject to FASB standards except in those instances where GASB has issued pronouncements applicable to such entities or activities. Existing standards established by AICPA and NCGA will remain in effect until amended or superseded by GASB.

Non-governmental not-for-profit agencies rely on AICPA pronouncements and a variety of authoritative bodies from which they obtain guidelines for accounting. In the hospital field, the American Hospital Association sets accounting standards; in the not-for-profit human service organizations, the United Way acts as an authoritative body (see its *Accounting and Financial Reporting Manual*).

BASIS OF ACCOUNTING

Basis of accounting identifies when revenues, expenditures, expenses, transfers, and liabilities are to be recognized. Stated another way, a basis of accounting is the procedure that is used for indicating specific points in the transaction cycle when resource inflows and outflows are to be recognized. Basis of accounting indicates when to record the measurement of income, expenditure, commitment, liability, or transfer. There are three bases that are generally found in practice: the cash basis, the accrual basis, and the modified cash accrual basis.

Cash Basis. This approach measures and records changes in an entity's books only when cash is paid out or received. Because many non-profit enterprises predominantly provide socially desirable services, they typically measure only inflows (revenue) and outflows (expenditures) of spendable resources. Likewise, profit-oriented entities that provide services in exchange for fees often use the cost basis of accounting, emphasizing the points of cash receipt and disbursement as opposed to the points where resources are earned and used (accrual basis). Most individuals maintain their finances on the cash basis.

Accrual Basis. The accrual basis presents the recognition and recording of all revenues in the period earned, all expenses or expenditures in the period incurred or consumed, all assets in the period purchased, and all liabilities in the period owed or incurred. The General Accounting Office (GAO) notes the following requirements for accrual accounting:

(1) Expenditures accrue when charges are incurred (i.e., when services are performed, property is received, amounts become owed for which no performance is required, irrespective of the time when payment is made and invoice and/or property is received.

(2) Revenues due are recorded when earned; money received in advance of government's performance is recorded as a liability.

(3) Expired costs or resources consumed constitute the measure of performance of an activity or unit of work and should be accumulated by major organizational segments, budget activities, programs or responsibility centers.[6]

The accrual concept places emphasis on earning and at the point where resources are consumed, rather than on inflow and outflow, as in the cash basis. Accrual acounting is an example of the matching principle—revenues are matched with expenses for a specific period of time.

Though accrual accounting is widely practiced in the private sector and in proprietary operations in the not-for-profit sector, difficulties are encountered when attempts are made to apply it to most governmental and not-for-profit agencies. Some revenues, such as property taxes, can be accrued (with reasonable allowance for uncollectible revenues) in those cases where tax-payers are obligated to pay given amounts when the tax is levied. There are, however, revenues, such as permits and fees, that are not measurable until the cash is actually collected because there is no reliable way to determine how much will be collected. The same can be said about the collectibility of fees in public and not-for-profit agencies when goods and services are distributed to clients on a need basis. Liability for long-term debt is an example. While a liability exists on long-term debt at the time of issuance, the liability is not recognized until the period when payment is due because only then are resources required to meet the liability.

Modified Accrual Basis. Under this basis are presented expenditures other than accrued interest on general long-term debt, inventory and disbursements which may be recorded at the time of purchase or when used, and prepaid expenses which are normally recorded or recognized on the accrual basis at the time the liability is incurred. Revenues are recorded when received, and those that are measurable and available for expenditure are accrued to properly reflect the taxes levied and the revenues earned.

Because revenue and expenditure measurement is subject to unique constraints, legal and otherwise, in the not-for-profit sector and especially in governmental units, the modified accrual basis of accounting is used. The modified accrual basis also accords with the principle of conservatism, which is relevant to not-for-profit organizations. The system permits expenditures to be fully stated or perhaps overstated, while the reverse is true for revenue. This procedure enhances the possibility for creating a surplus and reduces the chances for generating a deficit.

Accounting Basis: Advantages and Disadvantages. Before an agency chooses a basis of accounting, it should evaluate the advantages and disadvantages of each. The cash basis is the simplest method to implement and is widely used in small businesses, small governmental units, and other not-for-profit organizations. The cash basis is also the least expensive. In addition, it requires the least accounting knowledge and experience to operate the system. On the negative side, the cash basis provides the least accurate information. For example, revenues and expenses for which cash has not been received or paid are not recognized. Also, it is more difficult for a certified public accountant to express an opinion about the accounting statements.

The accrual basis provides the most accurate picture of the financial position of an agency because the method requires the recording of all transactions affecting the agency whether or not cash changes hands. The accrual basis gives an accurate picture of the organization at any point in time, assuming accurate and up-tp-date records are kept. A disadvantage of the accrual basis is its added cost, because of the extra knowledge, experience, and training needed to implement it. A decision to use the accrual basis should weigh the accuracy to be gained versus the cost of implementing it.

The modified cash basis is a compromise between these two extremes. It increases the accuracy of accounts without all the additional costs associated with the accrual system. The modified basis does, however, require additional personnel because bookkeeping is slightly more complicated than under the cash basis.

In determining which basis of accounting is best for an organization, recognition should be given to the following factors:

- technical knowledge of the available personnel
- sophistication of information required to ensure efficient and effective operation
- comparative cost of the basis
- external reporting requirements
- internal reporting requirements

CONTRASTING PUBLIC AND PRIVATE ACCOUNTING

Not-for-profit organizations, especially government agencies, operate in a different political and economic environment than do business enterprises. Thus governmental accounting standards have developed differently than have business enterprise standards. Despite this, there are many common practices that make governmental and business accounting standards more alike than different. Many of the principles and concepts (e.g., controlling, reporting, concern for relevance, comparability, consistency, and understandability) enumerated earlier have applicability in both the not-for-profit and the private sector. The basic differences between the two sectors can be stated as follows:

1. Not-for-profit agencies, especially those in the public sector, require strict adherence to legal and administrative directives.
2. In the private sector, the income statement (the principal inflow and outflow statement) emphasizes earning and using resources. This inflow and outflow statement shows the extent to which operating objectives have been met, focusing on how resource outflows benefit future periods as well as the current reporting period.
3. Not-for-profit agencies have inflow (revenue) and outflow (expenditure) statements. However, they are concerned with raising and expending resources according to specific budget plans.
4. Not-for-profit agencies are expenditure-oriented rather than expense-oriented. (Expenditure measures the monetary value of resources used in the acquisition of goods and or services.)
5. Emphasis is put on the source of revenues and ways in which they are used. Therefore, not-for-profit organizations are dollar accountability–oriented. Typical is the expression "where got where gone."

6. GAAP takes precedence in private sector accounting. In a public organization, when GAAP and legal requirements conflict, GAAP gives way.

7. Public accounting transactions are guided by an inflexible budget plan, while the private sector employs a flexible budget which changes as the volume of output changes.

8. Private sector accounting records are maintained to show owner's equity in one consolidated account. In the not-for-profit sector there is no equity accounting and funds are based on legal requirements.

9. Not-for-profit accounting emphasizes current funds, with no recognition of capital or fixed assets.

10. Private accounting uses the accrual basis, while not-for-profit accounting typically uses either the cash or the modified cash accrual basis.

PRINCIPAL ACCOUNTING STATEMENTS

All accounting transactions are summarized in three principal statements: the balance sheet, the income statement, and the statement of changes in financial position.

The Balance Sheet. The balance sheet is one of the basic accounting reports indicating the resources controlled by an organization and the ways they are financed. The main purpose of the balance sheet is to show the financial position of an agency at a specific point in time. The financial position shows the available resources (assets) compared with outstanding obligations (liabilities and fund equity) on a particular date. The balance sheet may be compared to a snapshot; with every movement after the snapshot, the picture is likely to change.

The balance sheet for Bright Hospital is shown in Table 2.2. An examination of the format and categories provides a general idea of what a balance sheet is all about.

Two broad categories contained in a balance sheet are assets and liabilities. Assets are things of value that can be owned. They constitute the resources of an organization measured in monetary terms on a specific date (for example, Bright Hospital on December 31, 1986). Liabilities are the debts owed by an organization to others outside the organization (for example, claims which outsiders have against the hospital that must be paid at certain known times in the future). When total liabilities are subtracted from total assets, the difference represents the funds or equity invested by contributors or shareholders.

Inspection of the asset and liability categories reveals that they are subdivided into current and fixed assets and current and long-term liabilities.

Current assets refer to cash or other assets that may reasonably be expected to be converted or realized in cash, sold, or consumed, usually within a year or less, through the normal operation of a business.

Table 2.2
Bright Hospital—Simplified Consolidated Balance Sheet as of December 31, 1986

ASSETS

Current Assets
Cash		305,000
Accounts receivable - patients	$1,200,000	
less uncollectible accounts	20,400	1,179,600
Inventories		134,400
Prepaid expenses		23,000
Total Current Assets		1,642,000

Fixed Assets
Land ($200,000 1986)		250,000
Buildings & equipment	$6,500,000	
less accumulated depreciation	860,000	
Total Fixed Assets		5,640,000
Total Assets		7,532,000

LIABILITIES

Current Liabilities
Accounts payable	$ 170,000	
Taxes payable	6,000	
Salaries payable	150,000	
Current loans	400,000	
Advance payments-third party		
contracts	130,000	
Total		856,000

LONG-TERM LIABILITIES
Long-term loans ($400,000 1986)	$1,400,000	
Bonds ($1,000,000 in 1986)	2,000,000	
Mortgages	350,000	
Fund Balances		2,926,000
		6,676,000
Total Liabilities and Fund Balances		7,532,000

    This balance sheet was simplified for ease in understanding non-profit
institutions typically consisting of several separate divisions, such as current
funds unrestricted and restricted, and fund categories such as construction,
building, land, endowment, or other funds depending on the original source and
disposition of capital funds. Each fund would have a set of self-balancing
accounts.

There is no set number of current assets. They vary according to the type and need of an individual organization. Table 2.2 provides a list of the items frequently found in the current asset subdivision of a balance sheet.

- Cash consists of money in the form of currency, coin, checks, money orders, banker's drafts on hand or on deposit with an official, and bank deposits, free for disbursement at any time.
- Accounts receivable are claims against customers for amounts owed on open accounts or on credit from private persons, firms, or corporations for delivery of goods and services. In Table 2.2 accounts receivable refers to services rendered to patients. In government organizations, accounts receivable does not usually include amounts due from other funds of the same governmental unit. Note that although taxes and assessments receivable are included in the term (receivable) they are reported separately as *taxes receivable* and *special assessments receivable*. In accounts receivable, a provision is made for the uncollectible amount that is likely to prove worthless. This amount is subtracted from the accounts receivable, showing the net amount.
- *Inventories* refer to items or merchandise for sale in the normal course of business. In not-for-profit organizations inventory has at least two different meanings: (1) supplies not for sale but for use in the delivery of goods or services; (2) a detailed list showing quantities, descriptions, and values of property (e.g., desks, cabinets) owned.

Fixed assets represent assets such as land, buildings, machinery, furniture, and other equipment having a nominal life of more than one year. The purchase price of most fixed assets is reduced by a depreciation charge each year. Fixed assets less accumulated depreciation represents the remaining economic and potential productive value of the assets. During each fiscal period the amount allowed for depreciation is included in the income statement as part of the cost of doing business. The depreciation expense may be viewed as an allowance for capital recovery that may be managed to generate sufficient funds to replace the asset at the end of its useful life.

Current liabilities comprise those obligations that will come due in a short period of time (usually a year or less) and will have to be paid out of current assets. Table 2.2 shows the categories that are classified as current liabilities:

- Accounts payable constitutes the claims of vendors or suppliers to the organization.
- Taxes payable is the amount owed but not yet paid.
- Salaries payable represents the salaries that employees have earned but are still owed by the organization.
- Advance payments on third party (insurance company) contracts are payments that have been received for which no services have been rendered.
- Current loans refers to the short-term loans that have been obtained from banks and other financial institutions.

Long-term liabilities comprise the obligations that are not required to be met for at least a year or more. The following are key examples that are usually classified as long-term liabilities:

- Long-term loans are funds borrowed from banks and other financial institutions.
- Bonds are a form of interest-bearing note employed by organizations to borrow money on a long-term basis. They are like long-term loans but have more formal requirements. Typically they are secured by some specific assets, except in the case of governmental units and large corporations, which may float some bonds on their general credit. In addition, bonds may be traded on exchanges, while long-term loans may not.
- Mortgages are long-term loans which are usually secured by some identified fixed assets.

Funds in not-for-profit organizations are resources which are available to obtain goods and services. Examples of funds in not-for-profit organizations are unspent resources from taxes, charges, donations, and endowments, which may be restricted or unrestricted. The presence of restricted funds means that the donor or authorizing body (legislature or board) stipulates the conditions regarding the use of the funds; no such conditions apply on the use of unrestricted funds.

Income statement is a summary of revenues and expenses or expenditures for a specific period of time. In profit-oriented companies, profits are measured by comparing revenues generated in a given period with expenses incurred to produce those revenues in the same time period (this is known as the matching principle). Revenues represent the inflow of assets from the sale of products or the delivery of services to customers or clients. Expenses are the sacrifices made or the costs incurred to produce those revenues. When revenue exceeds expense, net income results. If the reverse is true, the organization or business is said to be operating at a loss. Table 2.3 presents the income statement of Bright Hospital for January 1, 1986, to December 31, 1986.

The income statement typically contains three parts, showing revenues, expenses, and net profit or loss. The revenues in Bright Hospital were generated mainly from inpatient, ambulatory, and auxiliary services.

Not-for-profit organizations that operate on the cash basis simply compare the total funds inflow and outflow and accept the result as an adequate measure of the organization's performance. The use of this approach violates the matching principle if some revenues are earned in one period but are not recognized until the next, when they are physically received. This is true for expenses as well. When the matching of revenues and expenses does not occur, it may distort assessment of performance. This is the main reason why many not-for-profit organizations are moving toward greater use of the accrual concept for measuring income. The accrual concept effectively overcomes the distortion of net income because

Table 2.3
Bright Hospital—Income Statement for the Period January 1, 1986, to December 31, 1986

REVENUES

Income from		
Inpatient services	$4,800,000	
Ambulatory services	400,000	
Auxiliary income	1,100,000	
Total deductions including		
free service	300,000	
Other Revenue: Sale of		
Radiology Equipment	180,000	
Total Revenues (net)		$6,780,000

EXPENSES

Salaries and wages	$4,925,000	
Supplies	80,000	
Depreciation	290,000	
Administrative and general		
expenses	890,200	
Interest	129,800	
Miscellaneous and other		
expenses ($50,000 rate payable)	390,000	
Total Expenses		$6,705,000

NET PROFIT (Excess of Revenues
over Expenses) $ 75,000

it matches revenues with expenses for each given period. Bright Hospital is on the accrual basis. Thus the $75,000 in net income or surplus may not be equated with cash. Net income and cash will be exactly the same only when all expenses incurred are actually paid and when all revenues earned are received in the period for which the income statement is prepared.

The *funds flow statement or statement of changes in financial position* is devoted exclusively to reporting changes in fiscal position for a specified period of time. This statement identifies the sources from which additional investable funds or cash were derived and the uses to which these funds were put. For this reason this statement is known variously as the statement of "funds provided and applied," "sources and uses of funds," or "changes in financial position."

The statement has come into general use because of the need to provide information to decision makers relating to finance and investment activities. Information on sources and uses of funds may be obtained from an analysis of the income statement and the balance sheet. The principal sources (inflow) and uses (outflow) may be summarized as follows:

Sources:

    Net cash revenue from operations for the period

    Additional investment (e.g., donations and endowment)

    Increase in bonds or long-term loans

    Sale of equipment used in operation

Uses:

    Addition to plant and equipment

    Reduction of expenses during period

    Distribution of income

A statement of changes in financial position for Bright Hospital is shown in Table 2.4

ACCOUNTING AND INTERNAL CONTROLS

Internal controls are commonly classified as administrative controls and accounting controls. Internal administrative controls are comprised of procedures and records that assist management in achieving an organization's goals. For example, when poor-quality work occurs in a particular responsibility center, the use of internal controls permits management to better evaluate personnel performance and attempt to improve the quality of the output. Internal accounting controls refer to procedures, records, and reports that have been designed to safeguard assets and to promote the reliability of financial records and reports. For example, guidelines and specific

Table 2.4
Bright Hospital—Statement of Changes in Financial Position for Year Ended
December 31, 1986

Sources

From operations:		
Cash revenue	5,200,000	
Less: cash expenses	5,150,000	50,000
From other sources:		
Sale of operating equipment	300,000	
Long-term loans	400,000	
Bonds	1,000,000	1,700,000
Total cash generated		1,750,000
Uses (cash):		
Purchase of land	200,000	
Purchase of equipment	1,500,000	1,700,000
Increase in cash during the year		50,000

procedures developed to ensure the recording of transactions in accordance with generally accepted accounting principles aid in assuring the reliability of financial records. An important means for safeguarding assets is to limit access to assets to authorized personnel.

The internal control system varies depending on the size of the not-for-profit organization. In organizations where the number of employees is few and the manager of the organization provides direct supervision and oversight, few controls are needed. The situation changes as the complexity and size of the organization increase. This requires that management delegate greater authority, making it necessary to put more reliance on the accounting system.

The following are some broad internal control principles that should be considered:

1. Competent personnel and rotation of duties.
   - Employees should be adequately trained and supervised.
   - Clerical personnel should be rotated periodically from job to job. This broadens understanding and is helpful in uncovering irregularities that may have taken place.
   - Annual leaves and the reassignment of jobs to others during the absence should be enforced.
2. Assignment of responsibility.
   - Clearly defined responsibility is a prerequisite to efficient execution of assigned duties.
   - Overlapping and undefined responsibility areas should be avoided. For example, when two people must be assigned to the same cash register, each should be given a separate cash drawer and a register key.
3. Segregation of responsibility for related duties.
   - Divide related duties or operating responsibilities among two or more individuals to minimize the possibility of error, fraud, and inefficiency. For example, a single individual should not be able to extend credit on account to customers, record the account, and collect the payment.
   - Provide for checks and balances by distributing the responsibility over a number of departments. This requires that the work in a department and its accompanying documents be compared to and agree with those prepared in other departments.
4. Separation of operations and accounting.
   - There should be separation of responsibility for the maintenance of the accounting records from those engaging in business transactions and those with custody of the organization's assets. For example, the employee who handles cash payments should not have access to the journal or ledger, to reduce the possibility of error and embezzlement.
5. Proofs and security measures.

- Various techniques include separate bank accounts, provision for safekeeping of cash and other valuable documents, and encouragement of public observance and acceptance of printed receipts from clerks.
- Fidelity insurance can be used to insure against losses caused by fraud due to shortcomings in the internal control system.
- Independent review of the internal control system should be carried out periodically to determine if the internal control procedures adopted are being followed.

THE FUND ACCOUNTING SYSTEM

The fund is the basic accounting entity for the public sector and, to a lesser extent, for other not-for-profit organizations. In private sector accounting, the entire business or firm is the basic accounting and reporting unit; in government, the fund is the basic unit. The fund is referred to as:

- a fiscal and accounting entity
- a system with a self-balancing set of accounts

It is characterized by:

- recording of cash and all other financial resources, related liabilities, and residual balances and charges therein
- segregation for the purpose of carrying out specific activities or attaining particular objectives, special regulations, restrictions, and limitations

Fund Balance Requirement. Each fund contains a set of self-balancing accounts. When total revenue exceeds total expenditure, the fund has a surplus balance. Especially in local government, each fund is typically required to be balanced. In a number of governmental jurisdictions, negative fund balance may have to be erased by increasing revenues during the succeeding periods.

Types of Funds. There are three main categories of funds: governmental funds, proprietary funds, and fiduciary funds. The nature of the activity accounted for determines the category. The following are brief definitions of the funds used in governmental units:

- The *general fund* accounts for all financial resources except those that are required to be accounted for in another fund. Most revenues are accounted for in the general fund. This is usually the largest fund and is created to carry out the basic purposes (services) for which the governmental unit was established. For example, fire, sanitation, and health would be in the general fund, but the construction of a firehouse typically would be accounted for in another fund. Normally a bond would be floated to finance the building costs and would be subject to certain laws and legal requirements.

- *Special revenue funds* account for proceeds or specific revenue sources (often earmarked) that are restricted to expenditure for specific purposes. Typically, special revenues exclude special assessments, expendable trusts, and major capital projects.

- *Capital project funds* account for financial resources to be used for the acquisition or construction of capital facilities unless the transactions are handled by special assessment, enterprise, or trust funds.

- *Debt service funds* account for monies accumulated for the payment of general long-term debt principal and interest.

- *Special assessment funds* account for funds that are utilized for projects financed from special assessments levied against property owners.

- *Enterprise funds* measure income. They are like "commercial" or non-expendable funds used to account for activities that parallel those of a profit-oriented organization. For example, a publicly owned water or electric utility applying user charges according to services received is similar to a privately operated water utility. The earnings from the enterprise fund may be used for general purposes or other uses when it has been determined that such uses are justified.

- *Internal service funds* account for financing of goods and services provided by one department or agency to other departments or agencies of a governmental unit on a cost recovery basis. A motor pool for which each department makes a contribution would be an example.

- *Fiduciary funds* account for assets (trust and agency funds) held by a governmental unit in a trustee or agency capacity. A bequest left to a city to maintain a park would be an example. Both expendable and non-expendable funds are included in this category. Expendable trust funds account for monies being held that may be totally expended. In the case of non-expendable funds, only the interest earned may be expended; such funds are accounted for like proprietary funds. Since agency funds are purely custodial, they do not require measurement of results of the operation.

Fund Accounting Cycle. The major objective of fund accounting, especially governmental fund accounting, is to show that resources (unrestricted and restricted funds) have been used in accordance with authorized purposes. Accounting records are expected to show data from budgetary authority and transactions relating thereto. Accounting for funds begins as soon as authority has been granted to obtain and expend resources for specified purposes. The boxes below show entries that might be typical of a fund accounting cycle. Tables 2.5 and 2.6 show the ending balance of the City of A as of December 31, 1987.

DOUBLE ENTRY BOOKKEEPING: SOME BASIC MECHANICS

The convention of debit and credit was designed to show increases and decreases affecting a financial entity. For every debit there must be an equal credit and vice versa to maintain an absolute balance or equality at all times.

Table 2.5
City of A—Balance Sheet as of December 31, 1987

Assets		Liabilities, Reserves, and Fund Balance	
Cash	$10,000	Vouchers Payable	$90,000
Taxes Receivable	100,000	Due to Working Capital Fund	10,000
		Reserve for Encumbrances	50,000
		Fund Balance	40,000
Total Assets	$110,000	Total Liabilities, Reserves and Fund Balance	$110,000

Table 2.6

City of A—General Fund Analysis of Changes in Fund Balance for Year Ended January 31, 1987

```
Beginning Fund Balance January 1, 1987        $ -0-
Deduct:  Excess of expenditures and
    encumbrances over revenues for period
    ended January 31, 1987:

Expenditures                  940,000
Revenues                      900,000             (40,000)
Fund Balance                                    $(40,000)
```

Before an entry can be made, all the possible accounts that can be debited or credited for the entity or organization must be known. The following must also be determined: all of the asset accounts (things owned by the organization), such as cash, accounts receivable, inventory, and supplies; all of the liabilities (claims or obligations others have against the organization), such as accounts payable and loans payable; all of the revenue or income accounts, such as taxes, donations, and endowments; all of the expenses/expenditures (expired costs or things acquired or obligations against the organization), such as rent, postage, salaries, insurance, and travel.

General Fund Books			
Transaction	Entry	Debit	Credit
1. Adoption of budget for fiscal year ending Dec. 31, 1986, indicating estimated revenues of $1,000,000 and appropriations of $900,000.	Estimated Revenues Appropriations Fund Balance	1,000,000	900,000 100,000
2. Accrual of income from tax levy.	Taxes Receivable Revenues	600,000	600,000
3. To record the receipt or realization of other taxes.	Cash Revenues	300,000	300,000
4. Collection of taxes previously levied.	Cash Taxes Receivable	500,000	500,000
5. Expenditures made in accordance with appropriations.	Expenditures Vouchers Payable Due to Utility Fund Due to Special Assessment Fund Due to Working Capital Fund	700,000	500,000 90,000 100,000 10,000
6. Estimates of expenditures for orders placed for supplies and equipment	Encumbrances Reserve for Encumbrances	250,000	250,000
7. Liquidation of encumbrances ($200,000) upon receipt of invoices and determination of actual expenditures ($190,000) to record the obligation ($190,000) and approve vouchers to be paid.	Reserve for Encumbrances Encumbrances Expenditures Vouchers Payable	200,000 190,000	200,000 190,000

8. Payment of vouchers and billing.	Vouchers Payable	600,000	
	Due to Utility Fund	90,000	
	Due to Assessment Fund	100,000	
	Cash		790,000
9. To close revenues and estimated revenue accounts at end of fiscal year.	Revenues	900,000	
	Fund Balance	100,000	
	Estimated Revenues		1,000,000
10. To close appropriations, expenditures, and encumbrances at end of fiscal year.	Appropriations	900,000	
	Fund Balance	40,000	
	Expenditures		890,000
	Encumbrances		50,000

Transactions 1-10 in the box above must be posted into a set of books called the ledgers (the place where the summaries of all accounts are recorded on a regular basis, for example, every week or every month). The ledgers are "T" accounts having a debit and a credit side. The "T" accounts for transactions 1-10 are as follows:

A. Balance Sheet "T" Accounts

Cash

③ ,300,000	⑧ 790,000
④ 500,000	10,000
Bal. 10,000	

Taxes Receivable

② 600,000	④ 500,000
	100,000
Bal. 100,000	

Due to Working Capital Fund

Bal.	⑤ 10,000

Due to Utility Fund

⑧ 90,000	⑤ 90,000

Reserve Encumbrances

⑦ 200,000	⑥ 250,000
	200,000
Bal.	50,000

Vouchers Payable

⑥ 600,000	⑤ 500,000
	⑦ 190,000
600,000	690,000
90,000	
Bal.	90,000

Fund Balance

⑨ 100,000	① 100,000
⑩ 40,000	
140,000	100,000
	40,000
Bal. 40,000	

Due to Special Assessment Fund

⑧ 100,000	⑤ 100,000

B. Expenditure/Expense and Revenue "T" Accounts

Expenditures			Encumbrances		
⑤ 700,000	⑩ 890,000		⑥ 250,000	⑦ 200,000	
⑦ 190,000				⑩ 50,000	
890,000	890,000		250,000	250,000	

Estimated Revenues			Appropriations		
①1,000,000	⑨ 1,000,000		⑨ 900,000	① 900,000	

Revenues		
⑩ 900,000	② 600,000	
	③ 300,000	
900,000	900,000	

In order to minimize errors, to facilitate tracking and coordination, and to maintain the account balance, a system known as a chart or code of accounts is used. The following is an example:

1. All assets accounts may be identified as follows:

    22.   Cash

    22.1   Petty Cash

    33.   Accounts Receivable

    33.1   Allowance for Uncollectible Accounts

2. All liabilities and fund balances may be identified as follows:

    40.   Accounts Payable

    41.   Boards

    42.   Long-term Debt

    50.   Fund Balance

3. All revenue and expense and expenditure accounts may be identified as follows:

    60.   Personnel Services

    60.1   Regular Employees

    60.2   Replacement and Overtime

    61.   Contractual Services

    61.1   Utilities

    61.1.1 Fuel

    61.1.2 Water Sewer Fund

    70.   Property Taxes

    71.   Sales Taxes

The number of accounts is limited only by the degree of detail desired by the managers of the organization or enterprise.

Understanding Debits and Credits. According to the system of accounting logic, increases ($+$) in assets are accumulated on the left and decreases ($-$) on the right. By applying this system consistently, the balance in an account can be determined at any given point in time, as follows:

$$\frac{\text{Assets}}{+\ \mid\ -}$$

The system is based on the accounting equation: assets = liabilities + capital, or

$$\frac{\text{Assets}}{+\ \mid\ -} = \underline{\text{Liabilities} + \text{Capital}}$$

In applying the accounting equation logic to liabilities and capital accounts, increases ($+$) are accumulated on the right side and decreases ($-$) on the left side, as follows:

$$\frac{\text{Assets}}{+\ \mid\ -} = \frac{\text{Liabilities}}{-\ \mid\ +} + \frac{\text{Capital}}{-\ \mid\ +}$$

In accounting, the left side of an account is known as the debit side, and the right side is known as the credit side.

So far we have dealt with items found in the balance sheet (assets, liabilities, and capital). Because the accounts in the balance sheet are not closed out at the end of the period, they are referred to as real accounts. The reverse is true for income statement accounts. They are known as nominal accounts and are closed out to the capital account at the end of the period. Thus the debit/credit analysis of revenues and expenses is related directly to capital. Revenue (credit) increases capital where expenses (debit) decrease capital, as shown in the following:

$$\frac{\text{Revenues}}{\begin{array}{c|c} \text{Debit} & \text{Credit} \\ - & + \end{array}}$$

Following the same logic for expenses, increase (debit) in expense produces a decrease in capital, as shown in the following:

$$\frac{\text{Expenses}}{\begin{array}{c|c} \text{Debit} & \text{Credit} \\ + & - \end{array}}$$

By memorizing a few basic rules, the system of debits and credits can be applied:

	To Increase Accounts	To Decrease Accounts
Assets	Debit	Credit
Liabilities	Credit	Debit
Revenues	Credit	Debit
Expenditures/expenses	Debit	Credit
Capital	Credit	Debit

To determine net income/loss or net deficit or surplus (in not-for-profit agencies) all revenues are totaled and all expenditures are totaled and subtracted from revenue for each fiscal period.

BREAK-EVEN ANALYSIS

Break-even analysis is a tool that has been widely used in the private sector. While there are some constraints (for example, the assumption that there is a direct relationship between revenues and outputs, not typically true in most not-for-profit agencies) in applying it to the not-for-profit sector, there are opportunities where it may be employed, especially in those agencies that are client-oriented.

The break-even point is defined as that level of activity where total revenues equal total expenses or expired costs. At this level of operation the organization will neither realize a profit nor incur an operating loss—the ideal operating point for not-for-profit organizations. While break-even analysis can be applied to past periods, it is most helpful when used to aid in future planning, especially if curtailment of operation is an objective.

Break-even analysis assumes that costs can be broken down into variable and fixed componenets. The main purpose of break-even analysis is the determination of the level of output where revenue includes both fixed and variable costs. The break-even point can be calculated by means of a formula or it can be determined from a graphic presentation of the relationship among cost, revenue, and the level or volume of productive capacity. Before the break-even sales volume (known as the equation approach) can be determined, the following data are required: (1) estimated fixed cost and expenses for a given period, such as a year; and (2) total estimated variable cost and expenses for the same period. The second approach is based on the unit contribution margin.

The equation approach is as follows: sales (no. of units × unit price) = variable cost + fixed cost.

Example: Sales price $2 per unit, variable costs $1 per unit, and fixed costs $3,000.

Let x = the units at break-even
$$2x = x + 3000$$
$$x = 3000 \text{ units}$$

In the unit contribution approach, the unit contribution margin (unit price minus variable cost) is available to cover the fixed cost. This approach calculates the number of units necessary to cover fixed expenses.

$$\text{Break-even units} = \frac{\text{fixed costs}}{\begin{array}{c}\text{unit contribution margin}\\ \text{(selling price minus variable costs)}\end{array}}$$

Using information in the above example:

$$x = \frac{3000}{(2x - x)}$$

$$x = 3000 \text{ units}$$

With the information from the example above (the equation approach) a break-even chart can be used to determine the break-even point as shown in Figure 2.3. A break-even chart is developed in the following manner:

Figure 2.3
Break-Even Chart

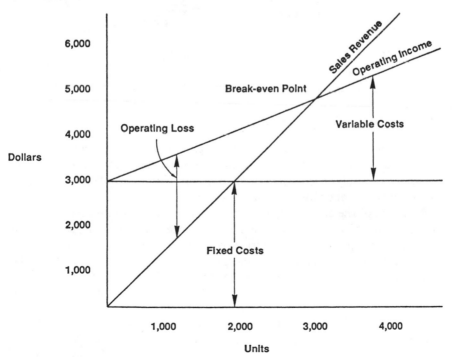

1. The number of units to be produced by an organization is plotted along the horizontal axis, and dollar amounts representing operating data are plotted along the vertical axis.

2. A diagonal line representing sales is drawn from the lower left corner to the upper right corner.

3. A point representing fixed costs is drawn horizontally, paralleling the horizontal axis.

4. The point where sales (revenue) and total costs intersect is the break-even point. The areas representing operating income and operating loss are identified.

Once the various cost components have been determined, break-even analysis can be innovatively applied to a number of not-for-profit organizations where unit cost information is maintained on the delivery of services. The following indicates an application: A state school for the blind knits special floor rugs that are very popular. In order to encourage the development of multiple skills, however, the state sharply reduces its subsidy to the rug making beyond the break-even point. It has been determined that the selling price for the rugs is $40, labor cost is $20, materials cost is $10, and fixed cost is $10,000. What is the break-even point?

$$\text{Contribution Margin} = \text{Selling Price} - \text{Variable Cost}$$

$$\text{CM} = \$40 - \$30 = \$10$$

$$\text{Break-even unit} = \frac{\text{Fixed Cost}}{\text{CM}}$$

$$= \frac{10,000}{10}$$

$$= 1000 \text{ units}$$

CONCLUDING OBSERVATIONS

The importance of the accounting system cannot be overemphasized in public and other not-for-profit organizations. In many governmental units it may be the only mechanism capable of bringing a semblance of coordination to the financial management system.

By means of the accounting system a number of important accountability and control objectives may be achieved. Once the budget is passed, the breakdown of the component parts is recorded by means of a chart or code of accounts directly linking and identifying the division of authority and the responsibility centers in the organization. This operation facilitates responsibility accounting whereby individual units can be held answerable for the appropriated funds made available to them.

Accounting has multiple applications, depending on the objectives being sought for an organization, including accounting for funds, control, and compliance financial accounting. When the emphasis is put on improvement in efficiency and internal decision making, managerial accounting may be effectively applied. When the organization requires the costing out of programs, activities, and special projects, a cost accounting capacity may be developed to generate the data.

Based on the accounting data, balance sheets and income statements can be projected for future operations. Recently, public and other not-for-profit organizations have been employing break-even analysis to aid in making projections.

NOTES

1. See, for example, Roger Hermanson et al., *Financial Accounting* (Plano, Tex.: Business Publications, 1984); Charles T. Hornigen, *Introduction to Management Accounting*, 3rd ed. (Englewood Cliffs, N.J.: Prentice-Hall, 1984); and Edward S. Lynn and Robert J. Freeman, *Fund Accounting: Theory and Practice*, 2nd ed. (Englewood Cliffs, N.J.: Prentice-Hall, 1982).

2. Leo Herbert et al., *Governmental Accounting and Control* (Monterey, Calif.: Brooks Cole Publishing Co., 1984), p. 5.

3. Ibid.

4. Lynn and Freeman, *Fund Accounting*, pp. 627-28.

5. Robert N. Anthony and David W. Young, *Management Control in Non-profit Organizations* (Homewood, Ill.: Richard D. Irwin and Co., 1984), pp. 17, 141.

6. U.S. General Accounting Office, revised, *Title 2, Accounting Manual for Guidance of Federal Agencies* (Washington, D.C.: General Accounting Office, 1978).

CHAPTER 3

REVENUE MANAGEMENT

Governments have the responsibility for providing an array of public and quasi-public goods and services that are expressed through the expenditure process—the governmental budget, identifying who gets what, when, and how much of the available community resources. An important factor to keep in mind is that a budget is simply the other side of the same coin. Thus every expenditure of dollars requires an equal amount of revenues to be withdrawn from the public. This results in a reduction of private consumption and a transfer of private savings to the public sector.

While there are numerous spending categories, typically there are fewer categories that are employed in collecting taxes. Especially in large units of governments and in not-for-profit organizations, revenues are seldom subject to earmarking (that is, they are not designated to be spent for specific programs or activities, such as education or old age pensions) except in those cases where funds are transferred from other governmental units. Also, revenue inflow and sources tend to be relatively stable in contrast to expenditures. For these reasons, among others, revenue raising has seldom attracted a great amount of political attention. Additionally, politicians are loath to talk about revenues because they are extracting resources from the public rather than giving them something, as is the case with expenditure programs. Proposition 13 in California in 1978 departed significantly from this norm because of the success of the tax and expenditure movements during that period.

Unlike expenditure, revenue policies typically have a number of legal constraints. This is true for all levels of government and other not-for-profit organizations. The problem is particularly evident at the local levels of government. Constraints take forms such as uniform assessment, maximum rates, and specified accounting procedures. Other not-for-profit agencies, especially those participating as United Way members, face restrictions on whom they can solicit and the time such solicitations may take place.

This chapter presents the different meanings and concepts of revenue, the economics of revenue raising, and the determination and administration of the revenue plan. Selected methods for forecasting revenues are examined.

DEFINING REVENUE

All levels of government and other not-for-profit organizations classify revenues by sources. These entities also use the term *receipts* synonymously with cash collections, while the term *revenue* is typically equated with accrual of funds (earned but not yet received). Types of revenues vary at different levels of government and among not-for-profit agencies. While the process for assessing, levying, and collecting taxes is similar among government agencies, it differs significantly in other not-for-profit organizations.

Both by law and tradition, there is greater reliance on certain kinds of taxes at different levels of government. For example, real and personal property are viewed almost exclusively as local tax sources. At the federal and state levels the income taxes, corporate and individual, are important.

Meaning of Revenue: Federal Level. The General Accounting Office (GAO) has defined *revenue* as the increase in assets or reduction in liabilities resulting from operations. GAO has identified three important ways by which revenues can be generated:

- when the government performs services for which money is due
- when tangible goods and other tangible property are delivered to purchasers from whom payment is expected
- when the government is owed amounts for which no current performance is required.[1]

At the federal level, the Treasury Department (meaning predominantly the Internal Revenue Service and the Bureau of Customs) is charged with the main responsibility for the collection of receipts. Receipts typically include the following:

- individual income taxes
- corporate income taxes
- social insurance taxes and contributions
- excise taxes
- custom duties
- miscellaneous receipts

Meaning of Revenue and Receipts: State and Local Level. The meanings of *revenue* and *receipts* differ somewhat at lower levels of government.

Revenue may be defined as the inflow or receipt of money by a governmental unit which is not obtained by creating an offsetting liability. Stated another way, revenue consists of total money received by a governmental unit that does not represent a recovery or refund of an expenditure, the cancellation of a liability, or a decrease in assets or contributions from an enterprise or intergovernmental service fund.

Receipts usually indicate cash received unless stipulated otherwise. Note that the above definition of revenue refers to those instances when revenue is recorded on the accrual, modified accrual, or cash basis. Some governmental units and other not-for-profit organizations use the term *revenue receipt* to mean cash. It should be kept in mind that for such organizations revenue is synonymous with the operating income of a governmental unit.

Using the Accrual Basis. If a governmental unit bills property owner A for $2,000 in taxes in 1987 and receives the $2,000 in 1987, this is revenue for 1987. If the governmental unit bills property owner B for $2,500 in 1987 but owner B does not pay until 1988, the $2,500 is revenue for 1987. Both the $2,000 and the $2,500 relate to the 1987 operating activities and to the services furnished for that year and the expenses used for the provision of services. Thus as of December 31, 1987, the $2,500 is an asset, indicated on the balance sheet as accounts receivable or taxes receivable. Revenue is made up of revenue and receipts, generated from a number of sources grouped according to the recommendations of the National Council on Governmental Accounting as follows:

- taxes
- special assessments levied
- licenses and permits
- intergovernmental revenues
- charges for services
- fines and forfeits
- miscellaneous revenues

Sales Revenues. Not-for-profit organizations such as hospitals typically operate on an accrual basis. Thus sales of goods and services for a specific period are revenues for that period. Revenues are generated at the time a patient receives services and is charged, which may not coincide with the time that the patient or a third party was billed or when cash was actually received. (To simplify recordkeeping, some hospitals recognize revenue only when the patient is billed.) In those cases where there is high probability that the patient will not be able to pay his/her bill, revenues are reduced by the amount established as allowance for bad debt.

Membership Dues. When membership dues become payable, they are revenue whether they are paid before, after, or during the membership period. Dues that are unpaid after the period are assets or receivables. At the end of the period, the amount of receivables is reduced for probable bad debt. Life membership is, however, treated differently in most cases. Instead of recognizing only the portion of life membership as it comes due, the total amount is typically identified as revenue at the time it is received.

Pledges. The principles stated above apply to pledges. Future pledges are revenue in those periods to which the pledged contribution applies even if the cash is not received in the same time period. Downward adjustments are made to recognize potential bad debts. Some oppose the recognition of pledges as receivables because they are legally unenforceable. Additionally, uncollectible pledges are too unreliable to allow for the making of reasonable estimates. *Revenue* and *income* are used interchangeably in not-for-profit agencies. More recently, however, *income* has come to mean the amount left over after subtracting all expenses, though the United Way uses the term *revenue* to mean money donated or received from any given source.

Funders' allocation of resources to not-for-profit agencies typically coincides with one of the following practices in making payouts to recipient agencies:

1. A prearranged payment schedule, typically quarterly.
2. Prearranged payments based on actual expense flow, typically biweekly or monthly.
3. Cost reimbursement based on actual expenses.[2]

There are, of course, contributions and special events generating revenues that follow no specific pattern. The funders or contributing organizations have found that they must live with those imposed payment plans.[3]

THE ECONOMICS OF REVENUE RAISING

Functions of government revenue include: (1) generation of resources to finance the delivery of goods and services, (2) income redistribution, and (3) a fiscal policy instrument for managing consumer demands. These activities may be referred to as the revenue, redistributive, and fiscal policy (manipulations of the taxing powers to affect consumer demand) function of taxation.

The decision to pursue one or a combination of revenue functions involves value judgments, that is, determining who will pay and in what amounts. Many questions can thus be raised about the revenue function relating to concerns about the distribution, redistribution, and equity effects of the cost of government services on the taxpayers. The precise *distributional impact* on the incomes of individuals in a given community cannot easily be determined, although estimates of impacts may be derived by a careful study of the components of the tax base and tax rates. It is also important to keep in mind that the tax burden may not fall on the initial tax base object due to tax shifting (ultimate resting place of a tax impact). For example, the property tax on an owner-occupied residence cannot be shifted. But in those cases where the owner rents housing units, the tax can be partially shifted to the renters.

Taxes may affect allocation of resources and economic efficiency by distorting economic decisions of individuals and businesses. When taxes are not related to the provision of goods and services, taxpayers are not in a position to assess the costs and benefits of those goods and services. Lacking such information, taxpayers cannot effectively formulate demands for public services, creating the likelihood of choosing a sub-optimal quantity. This may result in faulty allocation of resources between the public and private sectors. Tax differential rates among different jurisdictions may also have the effect of inducing persons, businesses, and even industries to relocate.

Our discussion suggests that tax/revenue policy has important implications for the stability of the economy. The concern for stability and growth is mainly a national responsibility, though local government units are keenly interested in stability, economic growth, and their taxing capacity. An individual governmental unit by itself has a minimal effect on economic output. But, as noted, where local governmental units provide tax incentives they do induce some businesses to move from one juridiction to another.

Much attention has been devoted in public sector economics to the importance of distributing tax burdens equitably among taxpayers. A number of sophisticated theories and approaches have been developed to aid in explaining the distribution and equity consideration in taxation. In the discussion that follows, two benchmark criteria for evaluating taxes in public finance are discussed: (1) the application of the efficiency criterion, and (2) the application of the equity criterion.

Tax Efficiency. The efficiency criterion accepts the view that different taxes impose varying degrees of distortion on the market economy, creating welfare losses by causing a departure from the pareto optimality (inability to allocate resources to improve the well-being or utility of an individual without making at least one other person worse off). Ideally, one objective of a society's tax system is to minimize the excess burden or welfare cost due to taxation when diverting a given amount of resources from the private to the public sector. The efficiency criterion evaluates a tax on the basis of the amount of excess burden it creates per revenue dollar collected. Those taxes that impose less excess burden are said to be more efficient, from an economic perspective. An effective tax is said to be neutral in that it affects consumption, savings, work, leisure, and other important choices minimally. Ideally, a tax should transfer resources from the private to the public sector without affecting the overall performance of the economy.

Tax efficiency also relates to the way a tax is enforced. This is particularly important because tax equity must mean more than a theoretically rational tax system. Thus there must be equitable enforcement of the tax upon all those subject to it so that no one illegally transfers his/her burden to other taxpayers. Also important for the efficient enforcement of a tax is the convenience, simplicity, and compliance cost to taxpayers in determining their tax liability. These factors ultimately affect the cost of collection and thus the efficiency of the tax.

Horizontal Equity. A tax is viewed as being horizontal if it treats equals equally. For example, two persons in equal economic circumstances before a tax is imposed would be in the same economic circumstances relative to one another after the imposition of the tax. Tax equity suggests that application should not be arbitrary or discriminatory. Horizontal equity requires that taxpayers with the same income should pay identical amounts of tax.

Despite horizontal equity's popularity, it does have some drawbacks. To apply the criterion to a tax system, the point at which two persons have equal economic circumstances or welfare must be ascertained objectively, which is not an easy task. For example, should the size of the family be considered? How are income and wealth to be considered in determining ability-to-pay taxes? Will distinction be made between capital gains and ordinary income?

Vertical Equity. According to the concept of vertical equity, unequals should be treated unequally. The criterion suggests that persons having different taxpaying circumstances or abilities should pay different amounts of tax. In order to judge the degree to which the tax system is vertically equitable, value judgments about the desirable or appropriate way to treat people at different income levels must be made. To facilitate an understanding of vertical equity, the ability-to-pay and benefit principles must be examined.

The *ability-to-pay principle* suggests that all taxpayers should bear "equal sacrifice" (based on their financial capacities) in the payment of taxes. Thus taxpayers with more income would pay more taxes. How large or how small should the differentials be between taxpayers? The tax rates are typically based on three main alternatives: regressive, proportional, and progressive concepts.

If the tax paid as a percentage of income declines as income increases, the tax is considered to be *regressive*, as shown in Figure 3.1. The reverse is true of the *progressive* tax. As income rises, the percentage of taxes paid rises. If the tax paid as a percentage of income remains unchanged as income increases, the tax is said to be *proportional*.

Of the three types of taxes, only the progressive tax is normally viewed as being in accordance with the ability-to-pay principle. This is also partially true for the proportional tax, because the absolute amount of taxes paid increases as income rises despite the fact that the percentage does not

Figure 3.1
Tax Base Relationships in Distributional Equity Terms

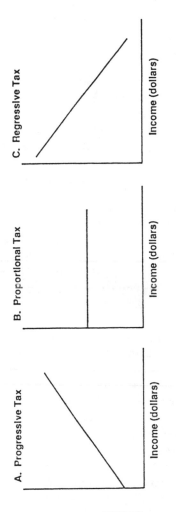

change. Even a regressive tax system may have a degree of progressivity in its application if people with high incomes are required to pay a higher absolute amount of taxes even though the percentage of tax paid to income falls. Only the progressive tax, however, accords with the ability-to-pay principle and distributional equity after taxes.

It should be noted, however, that a particular tax should never be analyzed in isolation from other taxes because it is the combined effect of all taxes that ultimately determines the regressivity or progressivity of a tax system.

The *benefit principle* is viewed as the primary alternative to the ability-to-pay principle. Unlike the ability-to-pay principle, which more directly addresses the concept of equity, the benefit principle addresses the goal of market efficiency. A major advantage of the benefit principle is that it directly relates the revenue and expenditure sides of the budget to each other. Basically, it provides a good approximation of market behavior in the allocation process of the public sector. The operation of the benefit principle permits individuals to voluntarily exchange purchasing power in the form of fees or the acquisition of government-produced goods, permitting individuals to pay directly for the government-produced goods from which satisfaction or profit is derived.

It should be especially noted that equity is suggested by neither the monetary nor the sacrifice benchmark, but by the dual facts that (1) the purchase of the government-produced goods is voluntary, similar to the private market sector; and (2) the payments are made according to the benefit received.

In practice, the benefit approach is restricted because of the inherent nature of collective consumption which typically characterizes the public sector. That is, individuals cannot be excluded from most of the benefits generated by government-produced goods such as defense or police protection. Thus, unless compulsion is involved, requiring consumers to pay, they will benefit as "free riders" and avoid payment. For this reason, many public sector goods that are not susceptible to the market pricing mechanism cannot be provided under the benefit approach. While useful in some cases, the benefit principle is not comprehensive enough in its application to provide the desired benchmark of equity in the distribution of tax burden. It has been found to be applicable in those cases where the government applies the user-charge approach, such as for toll roads and garbage collection.

Among the reasons why these services should be sold (through the application of user charges) are the following:

1. Generation of revenue intake approximating the value of the services produced
2. Motivation to determine whether the service is worth the cost
3. Creation of value consciousness of managers about the service they receive

4. Generation of indicators to assess performance
5. Creation of cost consciousness with respect to value of services exchanged between agencies, minimizing waste and overuse[4]

The Property Tax. This is the major source of revenue for local governments. It accounted for 36 percent of all local revenue and 80 percent of all local taxes in 1982, though states had reduced their reliance on property taxes to approximately 2 percent in 1982. The property tax can be viewed as a tax on wealth levied against the value of property, and based, at least partially, on the ability-to-pay and benefit concepts.

There are a large number of defects associated with the property tax. They include (1) regressivity with respect to income; (2) administrative inefficiency; and (3) creation of distortions in economic decision making.

The property tax is levied on real property and personal property. Real property includes land and improvements to land. Improvement comprises such things as buildings and other structures that are permanently attached or fixed. Personal property consists of tangible and intangible property. Tangible property includes moveable objects such as machinery, inventory, furniture, and automobiles. Intangible property includes items that have no inherent, tangible value. They represent claims to value such as stock certificates and bonds. For tax purposes, property can be categorized and differentiated by class of ownership (e.g., government, religious, and tax free) and by use (e.g., residential, commercial, industrial, and agricultural).

Because of the difficulty of administering personal property taxes, most states have abolished them partially or totally. Each state has its own property tax structure. Once the base has been defined, each governmental unit applies the tax rates to the base. Among typical tax jurisdictions are state, county, municipality, school district, and many other authorities.

There are three steps in the property tax process: (1) assessment, (2) determination of rate, and (3) collection.

Assessment relates to the discovery and valuation of property. It is usually carried out by elected local officials; however, some states may conduct this function for statewide property such as railroads. The quality of the assessment activity is not uniform. The high administrative cost associated with it is a major reason for spacing revaluation at lengthy intervals. Many local units underassess property but then take the opportunity to apply a higher tax rate to generate locally needed revenue.

After the rate is determined, it is applied to assessed value to generate a given amount of revenue. The rate may be expressed in terms of dollars per hundred or thousand dollars of assessed value of property or in terms of mill(s) (1/10 of 1 percent) per dollar of assessed value. A tax rate of $5 per $1,000 of assessed value is also equivalent to 50 cents per $100 or five mills per dollar. The formula used to determine the property tax rate is as follows:

Total budgeted revenue — anticipated
revenues from other sources
The assessed valuation of property
within the governmental jurisdiction

= tax rate to assessed valuation

Collection involves the process of applying the tax rate to each property
in the tax district (assessed value of all taxable properties). Tax bills are calculated and mailed yearly, semiannually, or quarterly. The tax is calculated
as follows:

$100,000   market value determination
× .40   assessment ratio
40,000   gross assessed value
− 10,000   exemption
30,000   net assessed value
× .10   tax rate, 100 mills
$3,000   tax liability
tax rate   = .10
effective tax rate =   3,000   = 0.03
                     ─────────
                      100,000

Economic Effects of the Property Tax. Three criteria are briefly discussed: (1) equity and distribution, (2) allocation and efficiency, and (3)
stability.

On the *equity and distribution* scale, the property tax scores poorly on
both the ability-to-pay and benefit principles of taxation. It relates to the
ability to pay in that property ownership can be equated with wealth and
can be employed to generate income which is an index of ability to pay. The
benefit principle is involved because the owners of the property can avail
themselves of a number of public services that are available directly to
them, such as fire protection. As presently administered, the property tax is
essentially a real estate tax, not a general property tax, and as such does not
accord well with acceptable tax principles. For example, retired persons on
small fixed incomes are subject to higher taxes on the appreciating value of
a home that was purchased many years earlier. Similarly, undeveloped land
which earns no income is taxed as if it were generating income. Another
major distributional problem relates to disparities among governmental jurisdictions due to differences in value of the tax base. Some jurisdictions
have high per capita rates, while others have low rates. Jurisdictions with
low tax bases may not be able to provide the services that citizens may
require. This is a major reason why the California Supreme Court in 1971
held, in *Serano* v. *Priest*, that reliance on the property tax for financing

education discriminated against the poor. While the U.S. Supreme Court overturned this decision in 1973, it acknowledged that the system in most states was inequitable and chaotic.

The property tax produces *allocation and efficiency* distortions for a number of reasons, including assessment practices and effects on locational decisions by businesses and industries that take advantage of specified tax breaks.

Stability is not a strong factor for favoring the property tax because it is relatively income inelastic.

Economic Effects of the Income Tax. In varying degrees, all levels of government levy this tax. The federal government is the most dominant of the three levels. The personal income tax is a prolific revenue source. It is essentially neutral in terms of allocational effects. It acts as a positive economic stabilizer, is easy to administer, and can be adjusted to create equity. On balance, the personal income tax is viewed as one of the better major tax instruments.

Sales Tax Economic Effects. Sales taxes are employed by federal, state, and local governments, with the major use taking place at the state level. At the state level there are two basic types of sales taxes: the general sales tax and the excise tax. Numerous variations are to be found in each. The general sales tax (a percentage of retail sales) is usually based on a broad range of goods and sometimes services. Excise taxes are imposed on specific goods levied as a percentage of sales, based on some specified unit (e.g., a gallon of gasoline).

The general sales tax, also known as the "broad-based," "gross receipts," and "ad valorem" tax, is based on a percentage of the sales value to the seller. Typically the seller quotes the tax rate separately from the price of the goods and it is paid by the customer.

The sales tax is politically appealing and is a productive and steady revenue producer at both the state and local levels of government. The tax is easy to administer, and in some cases local government uses it as a substitute for the unpopular property tax.

The general sales tax has an income substitution effect in that it does raise prices paid by the purchaser or consumer, in essence lowering income. Since all goods are not taxed, it is not easy to generalize about the income substitution effect. Additionally, a number of means have been used to reduce the regressivity of the sales tax, including exemptions on such items as food, medicines, and necessities.

MANAGING THE REVENUE PROGRAM

Besides the structuring of taxes to achieve an equitable and efficient tax system, the fiscal manager must develop and maintain a tax system that will generate sufficient revenues/resources to meet the community's demand for specified amounts of goods and services. A brief summary of general guidelines that should be considered in the development and management of a revenue system follows.

Determining Revenue Needs. Revenue requirement estimates are based on expected or proposed expenditure plans. Ideally, the revenue forecast should be carried out as soon as possible for the ensuing fiscal year to permit evaluation of its adequacy to meet expected needs. When the analysis reveals a gap, the early time lead would permit the design and installation of new or enhanced tax sources. The following factors should be considered in developing the revenue plan:

- inflation rate factor
- political philosophy of policy maker and relevant interest groups
- community growth and development
- expanded and new programs
- population characteristics and trends

Typically, revenue needs in some units of government and not-for-profit agencies are not projected in advance. Instead, the amount of available revenue is surveyed and the agency programs are fitted to them.[5]

Fair and Equitable Distribution of the Tax Burden. As noted earlier, tax rates are based not only on the benefits received principle but also on the ability-to-pay basis. As a tenet of good tax administration, the tax should be uniformly and equitably (non-discriminatorily) applied. No one should be allowed to escape the payment of the tax because of improper assessment, inadequate tax collection procedures, or improper exemption allowance.[6]

Revenue Base and Growth. A tax should have elasticity in that it should be relatively responsive to growth in the economy. The expansion and/or growth in programs made necessary by economic growth should be financed directly from the expanded economic activity in the community. The normal assumption is that growth should always be accompanied by expansion in revenues "if the revenue base is tied to sources which are affected by the growth."[7] Lack of responsiveness of the tax base to economic growth forces governmental units to increase existing taxes or to create new ones. While the revenue system base should be responsive to economic growth, the tax base should not be so structured that it is subject to widely fluctuating cyclical changes in the economy, creating conditions of fiscal instability.

Making It Easy to Comply. This is one of the basic tenets of public administration. Any law or regulation should be administered in a way that motivates or enhances the possibility of voluntary compliance. Thus the tax procedure and administrative system should be developed to promote ease and convenience of compliance. This approach minimizes cost and produces the greatest efficiency in collecting revenue. When the cost of administration and collection is high in relation to better-run tax systems, it may be desirable to revamp the administrative structure.

Revenue Collection and Cash Management. Finding ways to speed up the receipt of revenues is one of the principal objectives of effective cash management—a point that is covered in detail in Chapter 5. Each governmental unit and not-for-profit agency should design revenue programs to generate an adequate amount of cash on a timely basis. The objective is to have sufficient cash to meet maturing obligations and other regular expenditures in order to minimize the need to borrow.

Ideally, a governmental or other not-for-profit agency should devise a revenue collection system that coincides with its expenditure or payment schedule requirements; revenue collection schedules should parallel spending schedules where state or local laws or funding agencies permit. As far as possible, revenue estimates should be provided on a monthly or quarterly basis. Receipts should be maintained on the same basis to facilitate monitoring and tracking of the collection process.[8]

Maintaining Controls over Collections. Basic internal control norms should be observed. The receiving and accounting functions should be separated to minimize the potential for fraud and collusion. Prenumbered written receipts should be required for collection transactions. All receipts should be deposited intact in the agency's bank account. A procedure requiring prompt recording of billed revenues to taxpayers' accounts should be adhered to in order to minimize the possibility of errors and/or misplacement. When the accounts become delinquent, taxpayers should be promptly informed. Especially in small governmental jurisdictions and other not-for-profit agencies where the separation of duties is difficult to achieve due to small staffs, intermittent audits may be necessary to maintain adequate controls.

A number of indices have been developed to assess collection performance. They include the following:[9]

1. The collection index that is used to indicate the progress made in reducing outstanding receivables is calculated as follows:

$$\text{Collection Index} = \frac{\text{Collection made during the period}}{\text{Receivables outstanding at the beginning of the period}}$$

2. Average collection index indicates the average length of time receivables are outstanding. The estimate is obtained by employing the following formula:

$$\text{Avg. Collection Period} = \frac{\text{Net Collection Period}}{\text{Collection Index}}$$

3. Past due index shows the proportion of all accounts either in amount or in number past due. The index is obtained as follows:

$$\text{Past Due Index} = \frac{\text{Total Past Due}}{\text{Total Outstanding}}$$

Managing Delinquent Accounts. Traditionally, there has been a general reluctance by governments to aggressively pursue delinquent accounts, especially in those cases involving unpopular taxes. This attitude has been undergoing an important change in recent years. The demand for more goods and services, resistance to paying greater amounts of taxes, and the pressures of inflation have forced governments to take greater initiative to motivate individuals to pay their taxes.

Increasingly, government officials have been employing new approaches to obtain quicker response from delinquent taxpayers. In some communities delinquent accounts have been farmed out to collection agencies that use procedures similar to those applied in the private sector. In some cases communities publish the names of delinquent taxpayers in the local newspapers. Though this approach has been relatively successful, extreme care must be taken to avoid embarrassment to taxpayers whose names are inadvertently included.

REVENUE FORECASTING

Forecasting has never been in wide use in public and most not-for-profit agencies. The major exception involves the yearly budget in which revenue is forecasted, planned expenditures are projected, and cash flow projections are made in some governmental and other not-for-profit agencies. In the private sector, forecasting has become an accepted practice that has been integrated into the regular decision-making process. The use of forecasting, especially in a number of local governmental units, has been increasing not because of the policy makers' desire for rationality, but because of the opportunity to use the forecast as a political instrument to get program directors and interest group advocates to lower their expectations for expenditure resources. For example, when the forecast is made, advocates for more resources are immediately informed about the constraints and are more likely to limit their requests based on forecasted revenue availability. Depending on the assumptions that forecasters use, the forecasted revenue may be affected upward or downward. These projected figures can then become a guideline or parameter to get budget requests reduced.

Forecasts may be classified in terms of the length of time they cover: (1) The medium-range forecast may be used to tackle such problems as expected budget gap or revenue shortfalls before they become crises. (The medium-range forecasting may extend across a budget period, involving problems such as the possible termination of a federal grant or revenue sharing.) (2) The short-range forecast predominantly involves the development of the annual budget and related revenue forecasts and budget projections. (3) The long-range forecast includes a wider range of internal and external macro-problems that must be examined. The past trends and present conditions of the governmental unit are carefully studied. Such factors as population, age, income structure, and employment (types and patterns) are correlated to determine the governmental unit's tax capacity or capability to undertake the projected expenditures.

Forecasting Methods. What are the appropriate methods that should be used in forecasting revenues? While the answer to this question cannot be completely determined, the degree of accuracy desired, the expertise available, and the available data base would significantly influence the end product. A number of techniques have been suggested. These include the following: (1) best guess or expert approach, (2) time-series components, and (3) least squares (simple regression) method for forecasting.

The *best guess approach* is based upon the use of experts who, because of their education, experience, and previous success, are employed to determine the forecast. Although the experts may use a given formula, approach, or combination of existing methodologies, the methods used are not made explicit. The forecast is given credibility because of their expert reputation.[10] Therefore, it is very difficult to evaluate why the approach is or is not correct.

The *time-series component approach* relies entirely on the recent past as a means of projecting revenues. The approach assumes a continuing direction of the time series. The time-series component approach has been used to make relatively dependable projections of local government revenues. The results produced by time-series analysis "are affected by long-term trends in underlying economic and demographic variables."[11] Such variables are good predictors because they indicate if the economy is moving upward or declining. For example, in a city where the economic activity is sharply declining, the potential revenue intake is likely to follow the same downward path, as in the case of parking meter revenues in Durham, North Carolina in 1976. As the commercial and business activity began to move out of the downtown business district to other areas from 1960 to 1975, parking meter revenues fell from $60,000 in 1960 to just below $20,00 in 1976.[12] (See also Figure 3.2 for Bright City forecast.)

Cyclical factors or wavelike movements occurring irregularly over a number of years affect business activity, which in turn impacts upon revenue. The cycles that impact revenue are interest rate cycles, the business cycle, and stock market cycles,[13] the one having the greatest effect on revenue stability being the business cycle. In view of the potential impact that cycles may have on revenues in general, an understanding of the state of the economy and the phases of the business cycle is most desirable. It is important to note that although the financial manager is not expected to make sophisticated economic forecasts, he/she must be cognizant of the state of the economy on a continuing basis.

Past cycles often provide guidelines. For example, cyclical fluctuations in interest rates tend to influence local government revenues in two ways: they affect borrowing costs paid by governments, and they influence property taxes by affecting the level of new construction.

Seasonal components typically will not be discerned from annual or

Figure 3.2
Parking Meter Revenue Forecast, City of Bright

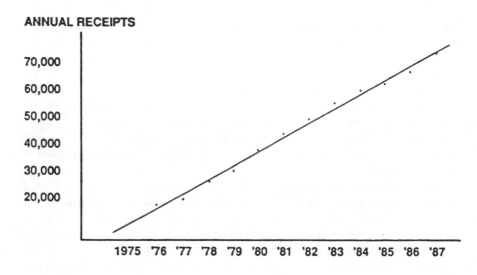

ANNUAL RECEIPTS

cyclical trends. Seasonal variations can be effectively identified by examining monthly time series. An examination of sales tax collections can be used to highlight the impact of the seasonal factor. In examining sales tax collection, it is possible to see that revenues for the month of December usually rise dramatically due to Christmas shopping.

Figure 3.2 for the city of Bright reveals a constant upward trend in parking meter receipts. This pattern is in sharp contrast with what Durham, North Carolina, experienced—a sharp decline due to outmigration of business from central downtown commercial areas between 1960 and 1976. Because the variation from the trend line is small, it suggests that basic trends in determining collection are very significant and that cyclical or other components had minor impact on collections.[14]

Calculating the Trend Line Using the Least Squares Method or Simple Regression. (See Chapter 9.) This permits us to obtain an estimate of the slope and level of the trend and allows us to calculate (see Table 3.1) and plot future trend values. (See Figure 3.3) A degree of caution is advised in

Table 3.1
Least Squares Formula

Let x = time deviation of years from middle year

y = historical level of collection of taxes in dollars

Time series data are as follows:

Fiscal Year	Collections
1980	$150,000
1981	125,000
1982	180,000
1983	220,000
1984	250,000

Year	Actual Collection	Time Deviation of Each Year from Middle	Square of x Deviation		Trend Ordinates (Expected Values)
X	Y	X	x^2	XY	
1980	150,000	-2	4	-300,000	67,000
1981	125,000	-1	1	-125,000	155,000
1982	180,000	0	0	-0-	185,000
1983	220,000	+1	1	220,000	214,500
1984	250,000	+2	4	500,000	273,500
Total	925,000	0	10	+295,000	

Average 185,000

$XY/ X2^2$
Let xy = +295,000
    x =   10
       = 295,000 = $\frac{295,000}{10}$ annual increment = 29,500 annual increment

Figure 3.3
Graphic View of Least Squares Trend Line (Revenue)

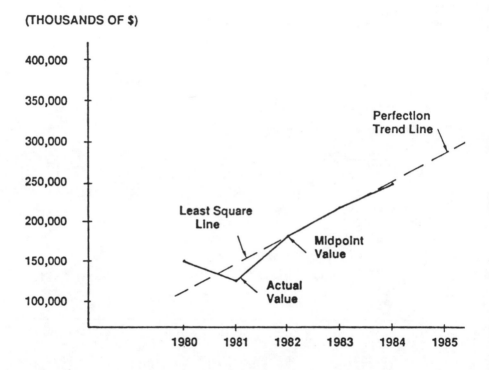

using this method since it rarely produces an exact fit. Indeed, the actual trend may approximate a curved rather than a straight line.

To determine the variation of the actual data from the trend line and to adjust the data for trend, the percentage of trend can be calculated by dividing the actual data for each year by the calculated trend value for the given year and multiply by 100, producing the "percentage trend" as was done in Table 3.2. If there are cyclical component effects, they will show up as high or low percentage of trend value during periods of contraction or expansion. When major irregular component effects are present they will appear as one-time deviations. In Table 3.2 the percentage of trend suggests that 1980 was affected by cyclical factors. Also, the greater the cluster of percentage of trend values around 100 percent, the greater the confidence in

Table 3.2
Calculation of Percentage Trend

Fiscal Year	Actual Collections		Calculated Trend Value			Percentage of Trend
1980	($150,000	÷	$ 67,000)	x	100	230%
1981	(125,000	÷	155,000)	x	100	80
1982	(180,000	÷	185,000)	x	100	97
1983	(220,000	÷	214,500)	x	100	102
1984	(250,000	÷	273,000)	x	100	91

the accuracy of the trend values. This would make permissible the assumption that variations occurring in the actual collection are caused by the underlying trend. When significant variations show up above or below 100 percent, many other factors may be affecting collection, suggesting that caution should be used in interpreting the results.

Forecasting in the Not-for-Profit Organization. In not-for-profit organizations, previous activities are typically used in preparing budgets. The manager responsible for making projections examines past trends and other factors considered likely to affect the revenue outlook. Sub-aggregate factors, such as the number of students, patients, or contact hours with clients or customers, may be used to make revenue projections.

A number of external factors are likely to affect revenue projection. For example, the drop in birth rate may have an effect on elementary school enrollment, resulting in decreased demand for elementary school teachers.

Three types of revenue patterns may occur: regular, seasonal, and random. Regular revenue occurs as anticipated monthly, quarterly, or annual payments. Examples are collections in a church, patient billing, or interest on bank deposits. At a private school, tuition may be received twice a year and fees from sporting events may come in during the summer. Random revenues may come in anytime during the year from charitable institutions, grants, and other special requests.[15]

CONCLUDING OBSERVATIONS

Revenue is the fuel that runs financial management systems. Thus an understanding of it is very important to the financial manager. It is not enough to have knowledge of the technical aspects of revenue raising, involving the economics of taxation, forecasting, and administration. Political implications have become especially important since the enactment of Proposition 13 in California in 1978.

The new desire among taxpayers to pay only necessary taxes and to reduce them when possible has given financial managers and political officials greater incentive to promote efficient collection procedures. Additionally, it has motivated politicians to use revenue forecasting to obtain budget reductions and to seek alternatives to taxing sources, such as greater user charges, to finance government services.

Revenue management in not-for-profit agencies has many similarities to government practices, though there are significant differences in funding sources. Not-for-profit agencies tend to be subject to greater uncertainties about the timing of their revenue inflows.

NOTES

1. See General Accounting Office, *Accounting Principles and Standards for Federal Agencies* (Washington, D.C.: GAO, 1978), pp. 1-25.

2. Robert D. Vinter and Rhea K. Kish, *Budgeting in Not-for-Profit Organizations* (New York: The Free Press, 1984), p. 201; United Way, *Accounting and Financial Reporting* (Alexandria, Va.: United Way of America, 1974).

3. Vinter and Kish, p. 204.

4. Robert N. Anthony and David W. Young, *Management Control in Nonprofit Organizations* (Homewood, Ill.: Richard D. Irwin and Co., 1984), p. 182.

5. See Terry Nichols Clark et al., *Financial Handbook for Mayors and City Managers* (New York: Van Nostrand Reinhold Co., 1985), pp. 36-37.

6. Arthur Mendonsa, *Financial Management in Local Government* (Athens, Ga.: Institute of Local Government, University of Georgia, 1969), pp. 88-89; see also Richard E. Wagner, *Public Finance* (Boston: Little, Brown and Co., 1982), pp. 43-52.

7. Mendonsa, p. 90.

8. Ibid., pp. 90-91.

9. David P. Dolter and Roger Mansfield, "The City as Debt Collector," in *Practical Financial Management*, ed. by John Matzer (Washington, D.C.: ICMA, 1984), p. 71.

10. See Hans Leverbach and James P. Cleary, *The Beginning Forecasters: The Forecasting Process through Data Analysis* (Belmont, Calif.: Lifetime Learning Publications, 1981); and Steven C. Wheelwright and Spyros Makridakos, *Forecasting Methods for Management*, 2nd ed. (New York: John Wiley and Sons, 1978).

11. Charles D. Liner, "Projecting Local Government Revenues," *Popular Government* 43 (Spring 1978): 33.

12. Ibid., p. 85.

13. Ibid.

14. Ibid.

15. James Gaestner, "Revenue Budgets" in *Financial Management for Nonprofit Organizations*, ed. Tracy D. Connors and Christopher T. Callaghan (New York: AMACOM, 1982), pp. 27-28.

CHAPTER 4

PURCHASING AND INVENTORY MANAGEMENT

The magnitude of expenditure for the purchase of goods and services is second only to the expenditure for personnel in most government and other not-for-profit agencies. In 1984 state and local governments' expenditure for the purchase of goods and services exceeded $140 billion. Because of the sizeable allocation of resources to purchasing and procurement, considerable interest has been drawn to the area.

With the new federal drive to reduce or at least slow down the rate of increase in medical-related services, hospitals and other health care and service providers have come under closer scrutiny. The intensity of the surveillance is likely to continue. Regulatory bodies and third party intermediaries (e.g., Blue Cross checks on the reasonableness and validity of cost for the federal government in supported health care programs such as Medicaid) have placed great emphasis on hospital cost containment and efficient purchasing power.

This chapter examines the purchasing function. Emphasis is put on the ways that are used to enhance the administrative structure and to improve the efficiency and effectiveness of the purchasing function.

DEFINING PURCHASING

From a comprehensive perspective, purchasing is concerned in public and other not-for-profit organizations with the acquisition of all goods and services except those provided directly by employees of an organization. This comprises the purchasing of materials, supplies, equipment, furniture, and all other services performed under contract. Included also is the construction of new public works in the provision of services as part of the regular operation of an agency.[1]

SCOPE AND OBJECTIVES OF THE PURCHASING FUNCTION

Purchasing seeks to procure required goods and services to achieve maximum value for the resources expended. Goods and services should be acquired in the appropriate quantity and quality at the place, manner, and time desired at the lowest cost possible. While the overriding purchasing criterion relates to the *lowest cost ultimately possible*, it is critical to understand that quality and price go hand in hand. Prompt delivery of goods and services of inferior quality is counterproductive.

A practice that has gained popularity among some governmental units and other not-for-profit agencies, especially when purchasing long-lived assets, is life-cycle costing. This is used to determine total cost of goods and services. The approach evaluates not only the initial acquisiton cost but also the maintenance, operating costs, energy, productivity potential, and any trade-in or recovery value that may be realized upon disposal.[2]

As a general rule, purchasing seeks to obtain goods and services at the appropriate time and at the best price from competent suppliers. As a universal expectation purchasing in public and other not-for-profit organizations must be free from favoritism and arbitrariness or caprice. Among the duties, responsibilities, and objectives to which a purchasing system should give due cognizance are the following:

- maintaining adequate supplies of materials at all times
- developing qualitative performance measures to aid in evaluating the performance function
- working individually and collectively (with vendors and using agencies) to achieve cost reductions
- conducting comparative cost-benefit studies to determine whether to undertake work in-house or contract out
- automating procedures and processes where it serves to promote efficiency and productivity
- developing and conducting training programs for buyers and supervisors
- employing team buying and other appropriate arrangements that will facilitate more effective performance
- arranging for alternative supply systems and sources to minimize or avoid interruption in the delivery of public goods and services.[3]
- maintaining open lines of communication with the news media

The Purchasing Process. This process comprises the steps concerned with acquisition of goods and services. It is initiated at the time a need is identified and continues until the goods have been received and approved for use or the service has been delivered. While the steps required to carry out the purchasing function vary among governmental units and other not-for-profit agencies, typical activities include the folowing:

- specifying quantities essential to meet necessary requirements
- preparing purchasing requisitions
- selecting source and/or advertising
- soliciting bids
- conducting informal bidding
- analyzing bids
- issuing purchase orders
- following up or expediting (when required)
- receiving and inspecting goods or services
- making payment for goods

In addition to these purchasing activities, the process usually includes provision for stores and inventory control and the clear delineation of responsibility for disposal of scrap, obsolete, or surplus inventory. An important point is that purchasing encompasses far more than the mere processing of orders. Because of the magnitude of resources devoted to purchasing, it plays a key role in helping to reduce agency costs.

CENTRALIZED PURCHASING

Centralization of the purchasing function is widely advocated in both the public and private sector. The widely held view is that centralization is an optimal approach to realizing cost-effective procurement for a large number of activities. It does not permit individual entities to follow their own preferences in the selection of vendors and products and in the purchase of common items in small quantities. When appropriate authority and responsibility are combined with effective management techniques, a centralized purchasing system becomes an instrument accountable to the public and/or clientele for effecting sound procurement policy.[4]

Defining Centralized Purchasing. This may be defined as the concentration of the responsibility and authority for the government-wide or agency-wide purchasing function under the head of a single manager or purchasing agent. In governmental units, authority and responsibility are delegated by statute to the purchasing agent to manage and coordinate purchasing activities.

When Is a Centralized Purchasing Function Needed? To determine this, a number of questions must be asked. What is the anticipated amount of saving to be gained? What are the amounts of poor-quality products being received? What are the needs for standardization and specification? Is there a need for improved bidding procedure? Is there a need for better expenditure control? What are the costs of existing decentralized purchasing and storage systems versus documented benefits? How do the costs and benefits of the decentralized systems compare with the potential benefits from the centralized purchasing system?

How to Establish Centralized Purchasing. Several steps are necessary to effectively accomplish centralized purchasing:

- Obtain full administrative support. In government agencies, political support, including clientele and interest groups, may be critically important.
- Sell the benefits to department heads and other relevant individuals and groups to enlist their cooperation.
- Establish the purchasing department's credibility by carefully choosing the responsibility centers or departments for initial implementation; carefully map out or schedule other departments for joining the system. The process should begin with those departments with which good relations exist and which are more disposed to accommodate change and innovation. However, before centralized purchasing is installed in any of the departments, an assessment of the weaknesses and needed improvements should be conducted.[5]

Once it has been decided to consolidate purchasing activities with a centralized system, a number of activities are required. The basic objectives, responsibilities, and authority of the purchasing function must be determined. It is not enough to establish the scope of authority and responsibility. The regulation should define the degree of accountability desired and how it is to be enforced; a clear delineation of limits should be put on the purchasing agent's delegated responsibilities and authority. With the establishment of the centralized purchasing unit and the appointment of the purchasing agent, the procedures necessary to effectively operate the purchasing function are then developed.[6]

Location of the Purchasing Function. The placement of the purchasing unit varies widely throughout governmental units in the United States. At the federal level, civilian procurement is carried out by the General Services Administration, which is directly responsible to the president. Procurement for the military is done by designated agencies which report to the service chiefs, who in turn have been appointed by the president.

It is interesting to note where the purchasing function is located in Canadian systems. In the Canadian system, "a case can be made for placing the purchasing function under the jurisdiction of the treasurer since purchasing has a greater affinity to finance than to any other central management function."[7] Another model has been emerging in the Canadian local government system, in which the purchasing head reports to a central administrative services group, especially when finance functions are attached to the group, as is the case in Thunder Bay, Ontario.

In a number of places in the United States, such as Chicago, the purchasing office is attached to the mayor's office. As was noted earlier, purchasing accounts for a large portion of expenditure for public goods and services.

As such, it represents an important political investment that can be used to reward political friends and exercise direct financial influence over governmental resources. Thus, to ensure that the purchasing function operates creatively and professionally, due consideration must be given to its placement and authority, the training of its employees, and the mechanisms required for its control.

Advantages of the Centralized Purchasing System. The degree of centralization varies from organization to organization. Thus the benefits to be gained will vary depending on the extent of centralization. When a purchasing system is effectively centralized, it makes possible considerable savings and better maintains a system of internal controls over the procurement function. Among the common benefits that may be realized from a centralized purchasing system are the following:

- It permits lower prices of goods and services: (1) quantity discounts are made possible by consolidating like items to permit bulk buying; (2) due to an increased knowledge of the organization's needs, opportunity to participate in group purchasing is maximized.

- It permits the streamlining of management: (1) better scheduling and delivery of goods and services at the right place and time are facilitated; (2) surplus stocks and shortages are minimized; (3) a systematic disposal policy for dealing with surplus, obsolete, and scrap materials can be maintained; (4) the receiving, storage, and inventory controls are facilitated (for example, fewer orders are processed, reducing recurring cost, inspection time, and recordkeeping); (5) better purchasing practices and greater coordination of purchases are promoted; (6) the opportunity to develop in-house purchasing specialists is enhanced; the chances for attracting high-quality purchasing professionals is increased; (7) the number of employees required to perform purchasing activities is reduced; (8) the receiving process is able to operate in tandem with inventory control. The receiving function is responsible for checking the status of incoming goods to ensure their acceptability in terms of condition, quantity, and proper placement. The receiving activity is charged with the following specific responsibilities: (a) assure that goods and services received have a purchase order on file; (b) examine the goods to determine if they have been tampered with; (c) not any damage in the packing slip and the carrier's way bill in the presence of the carrier or on the form required for that purpose; (d) check the carrier's documentation to compare with the number delivered; (e) forward a copy of the receiving report to the accounting department and to appropriate location for use in central store; (9) the purchasing manager is held accountable for the purchasing function.

- It improves administrative controls through better planning and control, standardization of materials, and implementation of improved funding techniques such as contracting and performance measurement.[8]

Competitive Bidding as an Effective Purchasing Tool. The competitive approach is the most widely acclaimed approach for the acquisition of goods and services, though it is not always used. In fact, at the federal level a significant amount of military procurement is achieved through non-competitive bidding. Typically the competitive approach requires contracts above a specified monetary level to be submitted to competitive bidding or competitive negotiation. Public competitive contracting in state and local governments falls into three categories: (1) competitive sealed bidding (including multi-step bidding); (2) competitive quotation bidding, also known as informal bidding; and (3) competitive negotiation.

Competitive sealed bidding is known by a number of names, including competitive bidding (suggested by the Model Purchasing Ordinance) and formal advertising (the terminology used by the Federal Procurement and Acquisition Regulations). Competitive sealed bidding is the statutory approach employed most frequently at the state and local levels. Purchase by negotiation occurs only when competitive sealed bidding is not feasible or practical. Once it has been determined that a need to purchase exists, central purchasing initiates the sealed bidding procedure with the issuance of an initiation-for-bids (IFB). The IFB is intended to encourage competitors to offer the product or service and to give potential bidders equal opportunity to bid. There are other important norms, duties, and responsibilities that should be clearly set forth, involving (1) controlling the opening and tabulation of bids; (2) public disclosure of bids; (3) acceptance of telephone and telegraph bids; (4) modification or withdrawal of bids; (5) acceptance of late bids; and (6) mistakes in bids. With respect to mistakes, the National Association of State Purchasing Officials has observed, "The essential rule is that no change or correction should be permitted which would prejudice the interest of the public or would be unfair to other bidders."[9]

Multi-step sealed bidding is used in approximately 70 percent of state purchasing. Typically it is used for purchases requiring the provision of complex goods and services (such as a medical records system including personnel training and alternative approaches to performing the work). Multi-step bidding employs the IFB with a two-step approach. Before commencing step one, potential suppliers may request information (a statement is usually attached indicating that no commitment is intended). Step one (the technical proposal) indicates the bidder's experience and resources for delivering the goods or services. Pricing most often comes in the second stage in a sealed envelope. The proposals are opened and evaluated and negotiation about pricing follows.[10] If changes are made in the technical proposal, a revised pricing is allowed. Where a technical proposal is fully acceptable, negotiation is unnecessary and "award is made under sealed competitive bidding."[11]

Competitive quotation is a commonly used method to acquire goods and services where the dollar amounts do not require sealed bids. A kind of informal bidding takes place; potential suppliers provide a listing of their prices, which can be compared with those of competitors to facilitate the best price selection. About 90 percent of the states require competitive quotation.

Competitive negotiation is not a recognized or authorized approach at the state and local levels and has thus been unavailable as a viable alternative procedure except as it may be permitted under emergency conditions.

Competitive Bidding versus Negotiation. While competitive bidding is the preferable procurement approach, it is not always possible to employ it because of the nature of the goods and services involved. A waiver is allowed in cases such as the following:

- sources are limited
- prices are fixed
- services are required to complete ongoing tasks
- products are completed in correctional institutions
- purchase is made from one unit of government to another
- a needed item is available only for a short period
- utility services are purchased
- replacement part is available from only one source

COOPERATIVE PURCHASING

Cooperative purchasing takes a variety of forms. Most often it involves arrangements among two or more governments to purchase goods and services under the same contract. The main objective in cooperative purchasing is to receive a cost reduction by making a volume purchase. The cooperative purchasing method provides a number of benefits:

1. It permits small units of government or agencies to obtain sizeable discounts that would not otherwise be available, permitting significant savings.
2. It eliminates duplicate effort and improves technical support in defining requirements, soliciting, awarding, and administering contracts.
3. Officials can pool collective knowledge regarding when and where to buy and can share the benefits.
4. It can initiate a large enough dividend to encourage suppliers to produce and market new and modified products that are not commercially available.

Cooperative purchasing tends to encourage the sharing of information among purchasing units about where to get the best deals as they relate to the following:

1. new products entering the market
2. alternative products located through value analysis

3. development of cost-effective methods of supplying goods and services
4. equipment repair experience
5. breakthroughs in contracting methods
6. breakthroughs in prices being paid for specific goods and services[12]

Sharing information may also provide valuable insight about the causes of significant price differences of similar items.[13]

It is important to keep in mind that cooperative purchasing will succeed only if it is supported by all participants, especially senior officials of the governmental units or agencies involved. Participation in cooperative arrangements should be based upon the evaluated benefits to be derived by the governmental unit. As a general rule, participants with cooperative arrangements should take turns making the purchase contract, giving all participants an opportunity to benefit from the learning process (except in those cases where the largest participatory unit's lead role permits superior benefits to be gained by all). A key element that must be observed in cooperative purchasing is that once commitments have been made for purchases no back-outs may be allowed. "All participating authorities must accept the group decision."[14]

Permission contracts involve those situations in which a third party (such as a local government which is allowed to enjoy the benefits of a state contract) that is not a participant in a contract is permitted to enjoy the benefits when and if it chooses. The contract price of the main contractor (in this case a state) becomes a "ceiling price against which permissive users of the contract can bargain."[15] The successful bidder of the state purchasing contract permits the third party to use the bid prices as the target bargaining price. Though this practice is unenforceable, it is not typically challenged and is in wide use throughout the United States and Canada.

MEASURING PURCHASING PERFORMANCE

A successful purchasing system requires that the function be operated in an efficient and cost-effective manner. This accountability objective can best be facilitated when realistic and measurable goals and objectives are set and appropriate systems are developed to permit feedback to monitor and control it. This requires that performance be reported periodically and internal and external audits be performed from time to time. Performance measures can provide input information to aid management in assessing how the purchasing duties and responsibilities are being discharged and how performance can be improved. The purchasing system can:

1. aid management to better determine how well the purchasing responsibilities are being met,

2. be used to evaluate performance against set standards or historical indicators,
3. be used to assess the cost-effectiveness of the purchasing function, pointing possibly to cost reduction,
4. be useful in showing time and money savings due to the purchasing agent's actions.

Measurement of the purchasing function is not an easy task because there are no generally agreed upon standards or indicators for evaluating its performance. While indicators have been developed to assess the performance of the purchasing function, caution about their use has been expressed. The first concern is that management tends to give too much emphasis to quantitative indicators, such as savings, and too little to qualitative aspects, such as maintenance of effective levels of inventory and a purchasing manual which clearly defines authority and responsibilities.

The second caution expressed is about reliance on a single indicator to measure performance. Among the shortcomings inherent in the single-indicator approach are the following: (1) it is only a partial performance measure; (2) it is subject to easy manipulation to show improved performance when it has not occurred.[16] Despite the lack of consensus about the appropriateness of indicators as a means for evaluating the performance of the purchasing function, they are used in public and other not-for-profit organizations to assist in such evaluations. Among the indicators that may be used are the following:

1. The ratio of goods and services purchased to the total expenditure of the governmental unit or agency
2. The cost-ratio of making purchases (buying) to total purchases made
3. Volume and percentages of purchases rejected due to defects
4. The average daily value of orders overdue
5. The ratio of price variance to budgeted purchases
6. Administrative savings resulting from blanket use of purchase order
7. The ratio of purchasing employees to total governmental unit or agency employees
8. Reduction in the frequency of rush orders
9. Cost reduction attributable to standardization
10. Cost reduction attributable to value analysis

UNDERSTANDING ECONOMIC ORDER QUANTITY

Because inventory represents a large asset in government and other not-for-profit organizations, it is important that it be managed effectively so that it can make its appropriate contribution to the organization's purpose. This requires that management strive to achieve an optimum inventory balance and recognize the relationships of one inventory item to another.[17] In addition, management must be continually aware of three very important types of costs that are associated with inventory: (1) the inventory carrying cost (e.g., storage, depreciation, and insurance) subsequent to its acquisition; (2) the purchase ordering costs; and (3) the stockout or cost of running out of inventory.

A stockout results in service interruption and dissatisfaction to clientele and/or constituents. In the case of snow and ice removal, a shortage of salt may increase the time necessary to clean the streets. As a first step in minimizing stockout activity patterns, such as the flow and size of inventory orders, the dependability of suppliers and the length of time it takes to receive an order should be determined. Once estimates are made of the cost of stockout, the stockout loss probability factor can be determined. A stockout loss function is shown in Figure 4.1. As the size of the inventory grows, the stockout probability goes down and vice versa. The objective of stockout analysis is to pinpont the time that inventory should be reordered.

While avoidance of an inventory stockout is a desirable objective, inventory must be monitored closely because, as the inventory size rises, the carrying costs (e.g., insurance, storage, spoilage, depreciation or obsolescence, and opportunity costs) rise directly with it. Figure 4.2 gives an idea of the function.

Determination of the stockout or running out cost depends on the specific organization and the kinds of inventory items in question. In the case of a hospital, cost would have to be measured both in terms of tangible cash cost due to the liability of not providing patient care and in terms of intangible costs which are very difficult to measure, such as illness, increased pain, and death.

From the aforesaid, there are several basic decisions that management is required to make. Perhaps the more important are: (1) the size or amount of inventory to order at a given point in time; (2) the extra amount of inventory that will provide safety from stockout; and (3) precisely when to initiate or place an order.

Importance of the Size of the Inventory. If the inventory is larger than can be effectively used, it ties up unnecessary amounts of cash which could be employed for alternative organizational purposes or investment options. The longer the turnover period of the inventory, the greater the likelihood that it will succumb to obsolescence, deterioration, or damage. When the supply of inventory is too low, it creates impediments. Note that these management decisions suggest trade-offs between the different kinds of inventory costs. As the size of the inventory increases, the carrying costs increase, decreasing the chances of an inventory stockout. This in turn decreases the frequency of orders, effectively reducing ordering costs. Figure 4.3 suggests the trade-offs that are involved and the level of inventory that is required to minimize total inventory costs.

Figure 4.1
Estimated Stockout as a Function of Inventory Size

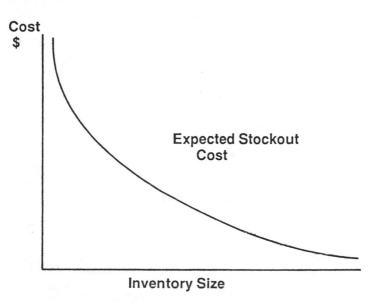

Cost
$

Expected Stockout
Cost

Inventory Size

Figure 4.2
Inventory Carrying Cost as a Function of Inventory Size

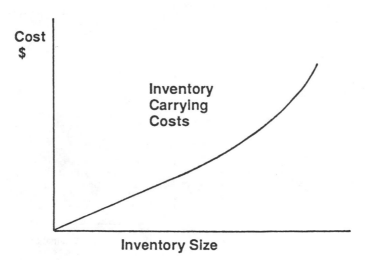

Cost
$

Inventory
Carrying
Costs

Inventory Size

Figure 4.3
Optimum Inventory as a Function of Stockout Costs and Ordering Costs

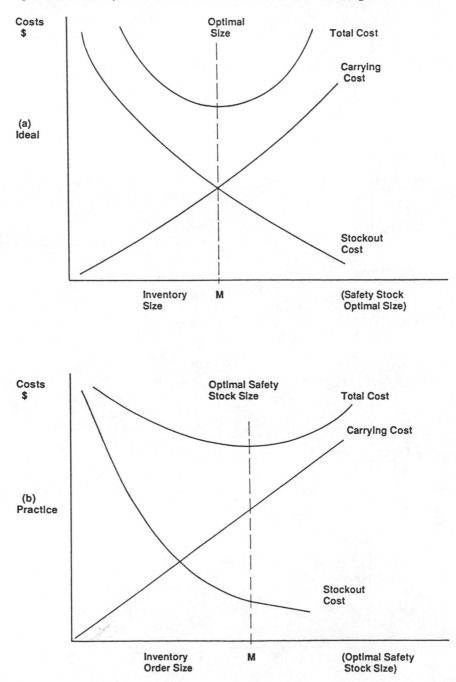

In Figure 4.3, part (b), note that the optimum safety stock is not at the point where carrying costs and stockout cost intersect. The assumption is that optimum stock represents the point of an acceptable stockout loss as opposed to the more ideal situation depicted in Figure 4.3, part (a). The same thinking applies in Figure 4.4, parts (a) and (b). The economic order quantity (EOQ) is not at the intersection of carrying costs and ordering costs. Thus the size of the inventory is smaller than it would be under ideal conditions.

Management's Operation of the Organization. Rush purchase orders reduce efficiency and increase cost. These problems are compounded due to the perspective of the different department heads. The fiscal department views the lowest level of inventory possible as desirable because it permits greater cash flow. The operating or user departments typically insist on having the highest possible level of inventory to meet all departmental needs irrespective of the cost. The purchasing officers take a balanced view of the situation in wishing to maintain low inventory, appropriate safety, avoidance of stockout loss, minimal orders, low costs, and rapid inventory turnover.

When considering the quantity of inventory to purchase, two opposing factors must be kept in mind, as noted earlier: (1) as reduction in the quantities of inventories purchased occurs, carrying costs fall and ordering costs rise; (2) as the amounts of inventories ordered rise, the situation is reversed. A critical concern in an organization is to find a way to satisfy material needs in the most economical manner.[18] Thus a way must be found to order and reorder inventory at the appropriate points in time.

Many approaches have been used to aid in determining economic order quantity in establishing optimum order volume for inventories, but the most widely used formula is as follows:

$$EOQ = \sqrt{\frac{2 \times \text{annual usage} \times \text{purchase order cost}}{\text{unit cost} \times \text{inventory carrying cost}}}$$

Example: Assume a nursing home uses 2,000 units per year at a cost of $40 per unit.

Order cost = $4
Inventory carrying cost = .28 (28%)
Annual usage = 2,000 units
Cost per unit = $40

$$EOQ = \sqrt{\frac{2 \times 2{,}000 \text{ units} \times 4}{\$40 \times .28}} = \sqrt{\frac{16{,}000}{11.2}} = \sqrt{1428.57}$$

EOQ = 37.74 units or 38 units rounded off.

Figure 4.4
Optimum Ordering Quantity in Relation to Carrying Costs and Ordering Costs

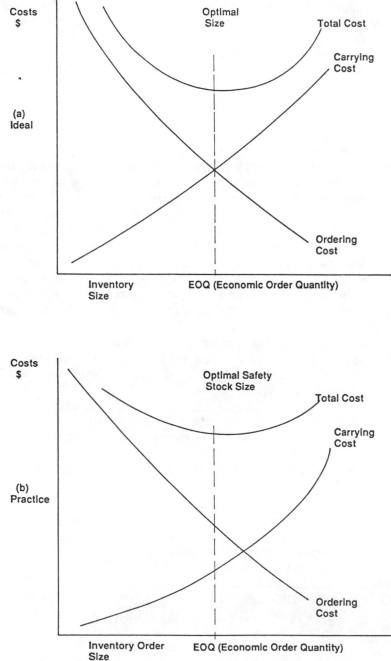

In calculating the EOQ, an accurate identification of all costs involved is required.

1. *Annual usage and unit costs* can be determined by a careful examination of the inventory record. The unit cost may be taken directly from invoice copies either from within the organization or from the supplier.
2. *Purchase order cost* is the total cost per line item. The following additional costs are involved: personnel, fringe benefits, office supplies, utility and maintenance, postage, and telephone.
3. *Inventory carrying costs* are those costs related to holding inventories. There are typically a number of costs that are incurred by government and other not-for-profit organizations: (a) obsolescence, deterioration, and pilferage; (b) storage costs and insurance; and (c) opportunity cost.

CONCLUDING OBSERVATIONS

Because of the large amount of resources allocated to the purchase of goods and services in public and other not-for-profit organizations, the purchasing function attracts significant attention. Obtaining the biggest bang for the purchasing dollar requires expertise and professionalism. While this is possible in large governmental units and organizations, it is often too costly for small governmental units. A variety of means has been devised to aid these small units, such as cooperative and permissive purchasing arrangements.

In large and medium-size organizations, centralized purchasing has become synonymous with effective purchasing practice. That centralized purchasing is indispensable if the best deals and prices are to be achieved is the accepted view.

NOTES

1. Lennox L. Moak and Albert M. Hillhouse, *Local Government Finance* (Chicago: Municipal Finance Officers Association, 1975), p. 209.

2. League of California Cities, "Life Cycle Costing," in *Practical Financial Management*, ed. John Matzer, Jr. (Washington, D.C.: ICMA, 1985), pp. 166-88.

3. Moak and Hillhouse, *Local Government Finance*, p. 210; and Council of State Governments, *State and Local Government Purchasing* (Lexington, Ky.: Council of State Governments, 1983), pp. 18-19.

4. Government Accounting Office (GAO), *Study of Selected Local Procurement Systems Part I* (Washington, D.C.: GAO, 1978). p.1.

5. S. Randolph Hayes, "Total Centralized Purchasing: Can It Ever Be Achieved?" in *Hospital Purchasing*, ed. Charles E. Housley (Rockville, Md.: Aspen Systems Corporation, 1983), p. 29.

6. Ontario, Ministry of Intergovernmental Affairs, *Managing Purchasing* (Toronto: Government Book Store, 1981), pp. 13-14.

7. Ibid., p. 15.

8. Ontario, Ministry of Intergovernmental Affairs, *Managing Purchasing*, pp. 13-14.

9. Council of State Governments, *State and Local Government Purchasing*, pp. 65-67.

10. Ibid., p. 68.

11. Ibid., p. 69.

12. GAO, *Study of Selected Local Procurement Systems Part I*, p. 17.

13. Ibid.

14. Ontario, Ministry of Intergovernmental Affairs, *Managing Purchasing*, p. 55.

15. Council of State Governments, *State and Local Government Purchasing*, p. 104.

16. GAO, *Study of Selected Local Procurement Systems Part I*, pp. 20-21.

17. Bruce G. Haywood, "Understanding Economic Order Quantity," in Housley, *Hospital Purchasing*, p. 161.

18. Ibid., p. 165.

CHAPTER 5

CASH MANAGEMENT

In recent years attention has been focused on cash management at all levels of government and in other not-for-profit organizations. There are a number of reasons for this interest. The 1970s ushered in a period of high inflation, recession, and high interest rates. These factors were compounded by rising citizens' demands for greater amounts of goods and services. All of this occurred at a time when taxpayers were beginning to resist paying more taxes and donors to not-for-profit agencies were finding it more difficult to maintain or increase their contributions. Better management of cash was seen as one means of stretching available dollars to meet the expenditure pressures. The process was facilitated in large part by new computer technology that permitted the use of more sophisticated methods of cash management, changes in federal laws affecting banks and financial institutions, and improved communication among cash managers.[1]

This chapter reviews cash management practices, the development of the role of the cash manager, and techniques for effecting cash management improvements.

DEFINING CASH MANAGEMENT

The bank law changes enacted in recent years have increased the number of bank services and better defined their cost. In some ways, these changes have added to the complexity of the variables, constraints, and alternatives that must be understood in fashioning an effective cash management program.

Cash management may be defined as a process that is concerned with two important objectives: (1) providing and insuring maximum cash availability, and (2) securing maximum yield on short-term investment of idle cash. To achieve these objectives a communication and monitoring system must be in place to identify the point at which revenue is earned and to track the point and time that an expenditure payment clears the bank. Cash management is thus focused on "the conversion of accounts receivable to cash receipts, the conversion of accounts payable to cash disbursements, the rate at which cash disbursements clear a bank account and what is done with the cash balances in the meantime."[2]

THE CASH MANAGEMENT SYSTEM

In the pursuit of maximum cash availability and maximum yield, as noted above, cash management objectives inevitably conflict, since cash that is maintained for use cannot be employed to produce higher yield. This conflict can be avoided only if an ideal or optimum balance can be determined. While methods for estimating these balances do exist, determining the optimum balance is not an easy task, especially among smaller units of government and other not-for-profit organizations. Patitucci and Lichtenstein have suggested that the availability objective be pursued first, and then the yield goal.[3]

The effective operation of a cash management system requires the consideration and understanding of a number of elements, including the following:

- policies and constraints
- cash budget
- cash collection and disbursement
- borrowing
- bank/institution relations
- investment of securities
- investment strategy

POLICIES AND CONSTRAINTS

Policies set the legal and procedural guidelines for facilitating the execution of the day-to-day activities of the cash management program. Guidelines typically identify the objectives and criteria for evaluating the progress and achievements of the cash management program. There are many constraining factors to which the cash manager must give due cognizance, such as local, state, and federal laws which directly impact upon cash management practices, "determining when monies can be collected, when obligations must be paid, where deposits can be placed and what securities can and cannot be purchased."[4] Other not-for-profit organizations must conform to the funding agencies' stipulations. For example, the United Way requires agencies that have free cash or surplus to return amounts in excess of $5,000 at the end of a fiscal period. Though the policy is not rigidly enforced, it does create some degree of uncertainty.

Risk related to investment in securities is another constraint factor which public agencies must control. Unlike in private enterprise, government laws and regulations help to minimize this problem. For example, most governments are permitted to invest in relatively safe instruments such as Treasury notes and bills. Thus most governmental units are not likely to lose large amounts of their investments.

THE CASH BUDGET

Cash budgeting requires a keen understanding of the major and minor sources of cash receipts and disbursements in order to estimate cash availability. Unlike revenue and expenditure budgets that are based on obligations and commitments, cash budgeting requires the identification of specific receipts and disbursements as well as the relevant dates. Due to the length of time (from one to sixty days) between commitment or obligation indicative of the regular/traditional budget, this is not a useful predictor of cash levels.

To achieve a realistic cash budget, historical experience of past and prospective developments must be studied carefully. The cash budget projection may be made weekly, monthly, quarterly, or semiannually. Whatever the projection period is, the cash budget must be updated when information and conditions require. When estimates are made for quarterly or longer periods, the need for updating becomes more urgent. For larger governmental units and other not-for-profit agencies, prudence and accuracy may require weekly or perhaps daily cash budgets.

The cash budget is not used as an allocating instrument, nor is it concerned with programs or operating functions. The cash budget merely identifies projected expenditures and revenue aggregates for the year. These projections will enable the cash manager to determine how much cash will be available or idle at various times during the year and for how long. An analysis of information will permit the cash manager to develop an effective basis for making investment decisions.

CASH COLLECTION AND DISBURSEMENT

This element is critical to success in achieving the maximum cash availability objective and to meeting cash and investment needs. If cash collection can be speeded up, the twin aim of increasing cash inflow and enhancing the potential for greater earnings on investment is achieved. There are a number of impeding or constraining factors. For example, (1) various tax due bills cannot be mailed out before a given date; (2) hospitals may not be able to influence third party payers to speed up scheduled payments; and (3) cash inflows at universities are limited by registration dates.

There is always a lag between the time checks are mailed and the time the funds are credited to an organization's checking account. The period involved in mailing, recording, processing, and clearing is known as the float time. The length of the float time directly affects the availability of cash. The objective is to find a means to shorten or minimize the float time.

A number of methods have been used to minimize the float time, such as the *lock-box system*, which allows clients of public and other not-for-profit agencies to send their checks to a post office box. The bank collects the checks daily from the lock-box and deposits them daily directly to the client's account, reducing the float time and making the money more quickly available, typically two to four days sooner.[5]

While the lock-box system is a useful innovation, it may not fit the needs of every organization. Before adopting this approach, cost versus benefits should be assessed. The positive side includes the returns that result from the added cash, speeding up inflow of funds and/or reductions in costs associated with internal processing. The negative side consists of a fixed monthly charge assessed by the bank plus a per-item processing charge.

The following formula aids in assessing the costs and benefits of the lock-box system:[6]

$$BAL = (NUM) \times (AVG) \times (TIM) \qquad \text{[Equation 5.1]}$$

When BAL = usable balances generated due to the lock-box system
    NUM = number of checks per day
    AVG = average value per check
    TIM = reduced number of transit days

Based on the increase in the usable balances (BAL) and the annual interest rate (INT), the annual dollar returns related to the additional funds (ADR) generated from the lock-box system can be determined. They are represented by the following:

$$ADR = (BAL) \times (INT) \qquad \text{[Equation 5.2]}$$

To find the total annual cost (ATC) of the lock-box system, we need to identify the bank processing cost per check (UC) and the number of checks processed during the year (ANU), generating the following:

$$ATC = UC \times ANU \qquad \text{[Equation 5.3]}$$

Finally, the determination of the break-even point, where the benefit generated is equal to the system's costs incurred, is shown as follows:

$$ADR = ATC \qquad \text{[Equation 5.4]}$$

Whenever the benefits of the lock-box system exceed the cost, the system should be implemented (i.e., ADR > ATC). If the reverse is true, it should be rejected. An application of the lock-box approach may be analyzed from the following example.

The city of Bradmore is examining lock-box systems for possible implementation in the collection of its water bills. It has been estimated that a lock-box system will reduce float time by four days. The 10,000 participants have an average $200 monthly tax bill. Bradmore earns 10 percent on its short-term investments. The bank charges $.20 for each check it processes. Should Bradmore adopt the lock-box system?

Assuming the number of working days each month is twenty and that checks flow at this rate, the number of checks processed per day (NUM) is:

$$NUM = \frac{10,000}{20} = 500 \text{ checks per day}$$

Using Equation 5.1 to calculate usable balances:

$$
\begin{aligned}
BAL &= (NUM) \times (AVG) \times (TIM) \\
&= 500 \times \$200 \times 4 \\
&= \$400,000
\end{aligned}
$$

Note that the implementation of the lock-box system will provide an additional $400,000 for investing. This amount can be invested at 10 percent to produce an annual dollar return (ADR) as follows (using Equation 5.2):

$$
\begin{aligned}
ADR &= (BAL) \times (INT) \\
&= \$400,000 \times .10 \\
&= \$40,000
\end{aligned}
$$

The $40,000 equals the annual benefit which is generated as a result of the implementation of the lock-box system.

The annual number of checks processed per year (ANU), assuming customers are billed on a monthly basis, is determined as follows:

$$ANU = 10,000 \times 12 = 120,000$$

The cost for implementing the lock-box system is calculated by using Equation 5.3:

$$
\begin{aligned}
ATC &= UC \times ANU \\
&= \$.20 \times 120,000 \\
&= \$24,000
\end{aligned}
$$

Since the ADR is $40,000, and the ATC is $24,000, the benefits are greater than the cost by $16,000.

Electronic transfer and *branch deposits* are other means for speeding up cash collection. By means of the Federal Reserve Wire System, banks may electronically move balances from one bank to another. Like the lock-box system, it is used to reduce transit time and to speed up check collection. Since the cost of transferring funds ranges between $1 and $6 per transaction, it should ideally be used for larger transfers. In those states and jurisdictions where branch banking is permitted, deposits can be made in outlying branches to be immediately credited to the individual agency account.

Pre-authorized checks are signatureless checks that can be used to accelerate the collection of fixed payments. Under this arrangement the client or customer signs an agreement with the public or not-for-profit agency to allow it or its bank to write a check, for a given amount, on his/her account. By means of computer file, the agency sends the bank the necessary information to carry out the function. By similar means, the bank informs the agency of the deposit and the availability of funds. The process has the advantage of reducing the float time while creating greater certainty of cash inflows.[7] Smaller agencies may wish to explore it.

COLLECTION PROCEDURES

Complexity of collection procedures increases with the size of the government or other not-for-profit organization. Small organizations typically have one bank account to which all the checks and monies are deposited. Larger organizations may have many bank accounts and many sources from which cash inflows originate. As noted earlier, the objective is to get the dollar into the organization's account as soon as possible and to keep it for as long as permitted in order to increase its earnings on investments. Collection can often be facilitated by a number of simple commonsense actions, such as billing outside agencies for services as soon as performance is completed; facilitating for citizens and clients the payment of taxes and fees; and establishing and maintaining good relations with funding agencies. Coordinating and making more likely the achievement of cash management goals involve the following:

- Establishment of revenue collection policies and procedures for each major revenue source.
- Provision for special deposit procedures to deal with major revenue processing problems. Such problems may result from the quarterly or annual collection of property taxes.
- Establishment of deposit procedures for each type of revenue base or location.[8]

To aid the collection procedure, a detailed checklist of each revenue source should be developed, identifying the specific activities to which close attention should be given. Rosenberg, Stallings, and Coe suggest a good example, as shown in Table 5.1.

DISBURSEMENT PROCEDURES

Ideally, cash should be disbursed only when absolutely required and at the last possible moment. While this practice should be carried out in a manner that avoids fines for late payment and minimizes poor vendor and community relations, efforts should be made to hold or delay payments to clients.

Effective disbursement requires that accounts payable be well managed. Invoices should be analyzed and filed according to their dates for payment to permit discounts to be taken and to facilitate timely payment. Factors such as the following should be considered: "the discounts available, the standard policies for handling different types of invoices, the past history of the vendor for requiring rapid payment and the method by which the payment will be made (e.g., mail or pick-up)."[9]

A means that is sometimes used to improve the availability of cash is the use of the warrant. A warrant is like a non–interest-bearing note payable which the issuer promises to pay upon presentation at some specified future date. The warrant is typically presented to a clearing bank for payment. Subsequent to payment, the clearing bank presents the warrant to the governmental unit and receives payment. The warrant is unlike a check in that there need not be money in the bank when it is written. Money does not have to be made available until the warrant is presented for payment. The ability to use the warrant allows the governmental unit to retain the cash for a longer period than might otherwise be the case. Some opponents say that it denies vendors the opportunity to use their money. Normally, a higher fee is charged for the extra processing required.[10]

CONSOLIDATING OR POOLING CASH

Governmental units and most other not-for-profit agencies use the fund accounting system, which tends to have a negative impact on cost management. The fund accounting practice requires that restricted funds be segregated and that receipts and disposition of resources be accounted and reported separately. It is not uncommon to find government and other not-for-profit agencies maintaining separate bank accounts for each fund. The maintenance of separate bank accounts, useful perhaps for control, is an impediment to effective cash management because it requires that the cash manager keep track of the individual balances with their separate cash flow patterns.

Table 5.1
Checklist of Detailed Procedures in Collection of Revenue
Sources for Municipalities

Licenses and permits

- Deposit all monies intact.

- Maintain a list of all delinquent licenses or permits and strictly enforce collection of delinquencies uniformly.

- Require all licensees or permit holders to display their licenses and/or permits. Instruct government offices to look for such licenses and/or permits and notify the collection agency when violators are suspected.

- Utilize reports submitted to other government agencies, such as taxes paid the state treasury, to verify gross receipts, if fees are based on gross receipts.

Parking lots, golf courses, swimming pools

- Indicate in plain sight at all locations a schedule showing the full range of fees.

- Design a standard format for use at all locations if tickets are used.

- Check all cash register receipts to ensure that cash and ticket counts reflect recorded frequency and monetary totals.

- Rotate attendants through different facilities and work schedules at frequent intervals.

- Practice close supervision and surveillance.

- Have all keys to lock boxes, cash registers, etc., under control of authorized supervision and not available to attendants.

- Schedule frequent unannounced visits by internal auditors who will review inventory of tickets, count cash, require authorization for all exemptions, etc.

Source: Adapted from Philip Rosenberg, C. Wayne Stallings, and Charles K. Coe, *A Treasury Management Handbook for Small Cities and Other Governmental Units* (Chicago: Municipal Finance Officers Association, 1978), pp. 54-55.

Parking meter collections

- Establish, number and describe meter routes.

- Select coin collection equipment that will be secure against theft.

- Consider maintaining weight records by route.

- Rotate the schedule of route collection periodically.

- Collect coins at hours which coincide with heavy traffic.

- Safeguard keys to coin meter receptacles; issue daily to coin collectors.

- Mutilate and destroy worn keys.

- Order new keys only on authorization of responsible persons.

- Require meter collectors to wear distinctive uniforms.

- Supervise the coin counting process.

- Ensure the security of the coin counting area.

- Have meter collectors report the location of all broken, stuck, or pilfered meters as they are discovered.

- Maintain dollar and/or weight records to provide for periodic comparisons of collections for each weight.

- Issue receipts daily to collectors.

- Establish procedures to make reconciliations of cash deposits. If coin counting machines which register total values are used, such values can be reconciled to deposits.

- Schedule periodic unannounced reviews of all phases of operation. Spot-check collection and counting procedures, personnel rotation, revenue comparisons, etc.

Property taxes, parking and vehicle code fines, sales taxes, gasoline taxes, cigarette taxes, liquor license fees, and motor vehicle fees

- Establish written contracts with other agencies as provided by law.

Table 5.1 (continued)

- Test receipts to treasury record periodically to verify that all receipts are deposited properly and in a timely fashion.

- Request confirmation from agencies doing the collecting and distributing, and compare information received from them with the municipal records.

Federal and state grants

- Prepare status reports for each grant. These reports show such data as:

  - grant description;

  - granting agency;

  - total amount of grant;

  - terms and restrictions concerning the use of the grant; and,

  - anticipated payment terms of the grant.

- Bill granting agency as soon as permitted by grant guidelines

---

The proliferation of bank accounts leads to a number of unacceptable results: (1) administrative costs rise, (2) the cash manager's ability to make accurate projections of each separate cash flow decreases, and (3) uncoordinated and fragmented investments are produced. Review shows that consolidation and pooling of cash can minimize most of these problems.[11]

A number of methods have been developed to facilitate pooling of cash while permitting separate fund bank accounts to operate. The single-concentration account has been gaining acceptance among municipalities because it permits the pooling of all cash receipts while allowing a separate zero-balance account for cash disbursement.[12] The operation of a concentration account allows local banks to automatically transfer funds to the concentration account. Several advantages are gained by this method: (1) it permits separate checking accounts to be used for disbursements; (2) it permits cash consolidation; (3) it makes it easier and less expensive to invest idle cash in short-term market instruments; (4) it reduces the problem of maintaining minimum balance in each account; and (5) it minimizes disbursement float time (the time between writing a check and having it charged against the bank account).[13]

BORROWING

Since debt management affects the flow of receipts and disbursements, it should be given due consideration. Long-term borrowing in public and other not-for-profit organizations is intended mainly to finance capital projects which are expected to have several years of useful life. Usually the money is received in large amounts and is held for specific time periods. During these periods care must be given to the way the money is handled. In governmental units, for example, federal arbitrage regulations should be observed (borrowing at lower tax exempt rates and reinvesting at higher rates is also forbidden by most state governments).

Short-term borrowing should be used only during those periods when the paucity of cash inflow causes temporary gaps. Identifying the gaps before they occur and taking appropriate actions to deal with them is one of the principal objectives of effective cash management.

Among the most common types of short-term borrowing are the following: (1) tax anticipation notes (TANs), which are issued for a specific period of time to be repaid upon the collection of a specific tax; (2) bond anticipation notes (BANs), which are short-term notes in anticipation of a bond issue and are retired from the proceeds of the particular bond issue; and (3) revenue anticipation notes (RANs), which are issued to obtain cash in anticipation of revenue that is not a tax source.

BANK RELATIONS

Banks occupy important roles in communities by providing access to primary and secondary markets and by providing essential services. In most communities the local governmental units are large depositors whom the bank usually attempts to attract. Many elements contribute significantly toward achieving the goal of effective cash management. They include:

* keen knowledge of available bank services
* information about the cost of each bank service provided
* competition among banks for the deposits of the governmental unit
* continual evaluation of the banking relationship
* maintenance of day-to-day competition among banks in order to obtain the best values when making investment decisions[14]

It is especially important that banks give attention to *community involvement*. Policies such as providing loans to individuals and businesses in the local community and participating in local government bond issues provide both tangible and intangible benefits to the community that cannot easily be expressed in quantitative dollar terms.[15] When a bank community involvement policy is positively oriented toward the community, the bank may occasionally justify sacrificing a higher potential yield to encourage such relationships.

The *cost of bank services* is normally determined in two ways. The first is based on the cost accounting system of a bank. The information provides the bank with a basis for imposing a monthly service charge according to the number and kinds of services provided (for example, the number of checks processed, the number of coupon redemptions for a local jurisdiction's bonds, and disbursement account reconciliations).

The use of compensating balances in non-interest-bearing accounts such as demand deposits is the second approach. These deposits represent "free money" to the bank, which invests them to generate earnings for itself. In those cases where banks pay interest on amounts in checking accounts, such interest is significantly lower than what the deposits actually earn. Banks sometimes use the float time (the period between depositing and paying funds) to earn money that helps to defray their costs.

Compensating balance may be calculated using the following formula:

$$\text{Required Compensating Balance} = \frac{\text{Annual charges for services}}{\text{Earnings factor (return bank expects to earn on deposits)}} \div (1 - \text{reserve requirement})$$

Example: for the city of Bright, assume annual charges of $4,500, earnings factor for bank 5%, and reserve requirement 15% of deposits.

$$\text{Required Compensating Balance} = \frac{\frac{4500}{.05}}{1 - .15}$$

$$= \frac{90,000}{.85} = \$105,882.35$$

When the banks cannot or do not furnish an analysis of their compensating balance costs and minimum requirements, a third approach for paying banking services may be considered:

Many business firms and governmental entities avoid the problem of computing an amount as a compensating balance by the simple expedient of agreeing with the bank that the account will return a profit. To this end banks are asked to provide monthly analysis of the account. The bank analyzes and records earnings from account balances, less the cost of all transactions, and subtracts costs from earnings, indicating either profit or loss.[16]

INVESTING IN SHORT-TERM SECURITIES

Engaging in short-term investment is necessary because of the uncertainty about how much cash is needed to fully meet operating needs. The instruments used most for government investments are bank certificates, money market funds, U.S. Treasury obligations, time deposits, repurchase agreements, and U.S. agency securities. Collectively, these investments are known as marketable securities. They are relatively risk-free interest-bearing paper assets, having a high degree of liquidity in that they are easily sold. To make maximum contribution toward the achievement of cash management goals requires that the cash manager be knowledgeable about the characteristics of different investment securities, including their yield and their primary and secondary market status.

TREASURY BILLS

Treasury bills (commonly known as T-bills) and Treasury certificates are U.S. government short-term instruments. Treasury bills are initially issued in $10,000 denominations having 91 to 182 day maturities, while certificates are issued having 9 and 12 month maturities. Since T-bills bear no interest, they are sold at a discount. The interest return or yield is the difference between the purchasing and selling or maturity price of the notes.

A testimony to the liquidity of the T-bill is the very active secondary market that exists. T-bills may be bought and sold at any time between the issuance and the maturity date. This is a major reason why they are so attractive as an option for idle cash investment. For the same reason T-bills carry the lowest yield of all money market instruments.

GOVERNMENT AGENCY SECURITIES

A number of U.S. government agencies, such as the Farmers Home Administration, the Federal National Mortgage Association and the Export-Import Bank, issue securities that are fully guaranteed, while organizations such as Banks for Cooperatives, Federal Home Loan Bank, TVA Federal Land Bank, and Federal Intermediate Credit Bank issue securities that are not fully guaranteed. There is a large secondary market for these securities, but their liquidity is not as great as that of Treasury bills. This accounts in large part for the yield spread between Treasury bills and government agency securities.

CERTIFICATES OF DEPOSIT

These consist of negotiable and non-negotiable receipts for monies normally deposited in large commerical banks for a specified period of time with a specified rate of interest. Certificates of deposit (or CDs, as they are commonly called) are, in essence, time deposits. CDs issued by larger banks usually have greater liquidity than those of smaller institutions. Like Treasury bills, they are traded on the secondary markets, though not as actively. Typically, CDs trade in secondary markets in $1 million amounts or multiples of $1 million, though odd lots can be obtained in multiples of $100,000 and $250,000.

COMMERCIAL PAPER

These are business promissory notes specifying a future payment date. They are usually sold at a discount and are supported by the general credit of the agency or company. Maturity dates range from thirty days to nine months, carrying a yield that is one-quarter to one-half greater than that of Treasury bills. Laws in many states prohibit local governments from participating in this type of investment.

REPURCHASE AGREEMENTS

A repurchase agreement is a type of short-term investment that permits governments to invest cash for short periods of time, typically between one and seven days. The governmental unit or agency enters into an agreement to purchase Treasury bills from banks which agree to repurchase the securities at some specified date for a specified higher amount. The investment is virtually risk-free.

MONEY MARKET FUNDS

Money market funds are mutual funds that invest in marketable securities. This involves the pooling of cash from a number of investors to purchase different types of market securities such as CDs and Treasury bills. The return from the investment is shared proportionately. While no commission is normally charged, a small management fee is permitted. Money market funds have grown over the past fifteen years due in large part to their returns, which have been significantly higher than the rates on passbook savings accounts.

For public and other not-for-profit organizations, money market funds offer a number of attractive features.

1. They permit small organizations to obtain expert management of their idle funds.
2. They provide yields that are much higher than those obtainable from savings banks.
3. They provide virtually risk-free investments since most instruments are Treasury securities, CDs, and commercial paper.
4. They provide flexibility for entering and/or withdrawing funds.
5. They require small numbers of participants.

INVESTMENT STRATEGY

The investment strategy is an important element in the cash management program in that it provides guidelines for determining "what will be purchased, when, and for how long, and what the target investment mix should be on specific dates."[17] An investment strategy should ideally be written and aimed at assisting the cash manager to best invest available funds for the time period covered by the strategy. In preparing the investment strategy, consideration should be given to the following:[18]

• Explicit assumptions about prospective market conditions, cash availability, and the desired mix of securities.
• Guidelines and timetables for purchasing specific types and amounts of securities.
• A clearly delineated system for selling or pruning securities if unstabilizing conditions so demand.
• Clearly defined procedures for accelerating investment when excess cash is available to expand purchases.
• Development of specific performance indicators to assess the cash manager's achievement.

DETERMINING OPTIMUM CASH BALANCE

In order to collect, process, and disburse cash in the most efficient manner, it is most useful to know the minimum cash balance that is necessary. Because of the uncertainties related to cash inflows and outflows, it is difficult to determine the optimum cash balance. A rule-of-thumb approach has been suggested. The rule is that the governmental unit or not-for-profit organization may hold cash sufficient to cover the expected average expenditure that is likely to be incurred for a specific period, such as a week. This amount would be held as security against running out of cash. Amounts above this imposed level will be invested, while amounts below this target will trigger the selling of securities. When this rule of thumb is used jointly with an accurately projected cash budget, it provides a reasonable basis for meeting cash needs, especially those of smaller public and other not-for-profit organizations.

CONCLUDING OBSERVATIONS

Attention to cash management is a recent phenomenon, developing in response to high interest rates and inflation, coupled with taxpayers' resistance toward paying more taxes and decreases in donations to not-for-profit organizations. Improved cash management is seen as one way to increase available resources. Effective cash management requires the coordination of many factors, among them a well-thought-out investment strategy, an efficient and timely collection and disbursement system, an effective short-term securities investment progam, and timely and strategic monitoring.

A successful cash management program requires that a way be found to speed up the collection of cash while slowing down its disbursement as much as possible. The objective must be perceived within the context of the organization's policies and implemented in a way that limits the impairment of client services and vendor relations. A number of improved procedures have been introduced to speed the availability of cash, such as the lock-box system, the electronic transfer of cash, the concentration account, and the zero-balance account. Finally, the pursuit of greater earnings on idle cash should be carried out with prudence to avoid unnecessary risk.

NOTES

1. Michael Dotsey, "An Investigation of Cash Management Practices and Their Effects on the Demand for Money," *Economic Review* 70, no. 5 (September/October 1984): 3; see also Raymond L. McCabe, "Electronic Funds Transfer as a Cash Management Tool," *Governmental Finance* 10, no. 4 (December 1981): 9-14.

2. Frank M. Patitucci and Michael H. Lichtenstein, *Improving Cash Management in Local Government: A Comprehensive Approach* (Chicago: Municipal Finance Officers Association, 1977), p. 4.

3. Ibid.

4. Ibid.

5. Dotsey, "Investigation," p. 11.

6. Ronald Braswell et al., *Financial Management for Not-for-Profit Organizations* (New York: Wiley and Sons, 1984), pp. 150-52.

7. Dotsey, "Investigation," p. 4.

8. Patitucci and Lichtenstein, *Improving Cash Management*, p. 27.

9. Ibid., p. 29.

10. Ibid.

11. See Walter P. Berg, "Selecting a Municipal Depository," *Municipal Finance* (November 1969): 94.

12. Dotsey, "Investigation," pp. 4-5.

13. Ibid., p. 4.

14. Patitucci and Lichtenstein, *Improving Cash Management*, p. 32.

15. Ibid., p. 33.

16. Berg, "Selecting a Municipal Depository," p. 94.

17. Patitucci and Lichtenstein, *Improving Cash Management*, p. 40.

18. Ibid., pp. 40-41. *See also* Nathaniel B. Guild et al. *The Public Money Manager's Handbook* (Chicago: Crain Books, 1981), Chapter 3-4.

CHAPTER 6

RISK MANAGEMENT

Until 1978, risk management aroused little interest in the public sector and not-for-profit organizations. This changed radically due in great part to the erosion of sovereign immunity of governmental units as a municipal defense following the *Monell v. City of New York* decision (1978), in which the U.S. Supreme Court extended the right of citizens to sue the government for negligent acts of its employees. Because of this ruling, governmental entities became vulnerable to a number of suits.

During the period of the mid-1970s and through 1982, the insurance industry was able to obtain extraordinary earnings on its cash investments, due to the prevailing high interest rates. Simultaneously, the industry was experiencing low demand for its services, inhibiting it from pursuing aggressive pricing policies. However, as interest rates fell and as the market demand firmed in 1984, the insurance industry, mindful of its huge losses in 1983, instituted major increases in premiums. Increases of 100 percent or more have become widespread. It is significant that these sizeable increases are taking place while deductibles are rising and the amount of liability coverage is falling.[1]

The repercussions of the New York City case made increases in insurance premiums inevitable. The number of suits and magnitude of awards could not be sustained by the old premium structure. Suits and awards such as the following have been occurring since 1978:

- In Newport Beach, California, the Orange County Superior Court (1985) awarded a $6 million payment to a man who became a paraplegic after diving into the water and hitting himself on a sandbar.

- Merrill, Michigan, with a population of 1,710 and a budget of $250,000, was ordered to pay its former police chief $250,000 for wrongful discharge.
- An award of $2.6 million was granted to a woman in Torrington, Connecticut, "because the police failed to protect her from her estranged husband."[2]

The city of Dallas, Texas, reports that when it solicited bids in January for insurance coverage it expected its insurance to rise perhaps 100 to 200 percent and that a number of insurers would bid. The city received a single bid asking for $1.5 million in premiums compared to $154,000 only the year before.[3]

The risk management crisis is especially difficult for governmental units because, unlike businesses, they are newcomers to the insurance field. Few public entities have developed expertise in risk management. A large number of governmental units operate fragmented risk management programs. The risk management crisis has brought about rapid change, forcing government and other not-for-profit agencies to recognize the desirability of a systematic, centralized approach to protect themselves against loss.

DEFINING RISK MANAGEMENT

Until recently risk management in the public sector has been oriented around insurance management. The manual on risk management by Charles K. Coe, *Understanding Risk Management*, is indicative of this approach. Although the author indicates that risk management is not insurance management, the manual reads that way.

Risk management is a comprehensive and systematic approach aimed at identifying, measuring, and controlling an entity's exposure to accidental loss, theft, and liability involving human, financial, physical, and natural resources. Examples of these types of loss include: (1) damage or loss of property; (2) income loss due to destruction of records; (3) expense incurred in replacing or repairing damaged or obsolete property or equipment; (4) liability due to wrongful acts by an entity's employees or officials; (5) personal liability due to job-related injuries resulting in loss of productivity.[4]

This chapter attempts to provide an understanding of risk management and the options that are being used to achieve maximum safety at a reasonable cost.

RISK MANAGEMENT PROCESS

Though there are slight differences regarding the sequence of steps in the risk management process, there is general agreement that there are five basic elements: (1) discovery and identification of risk, (2) measurement and evaluation of risk, (3) risk control, (4) risk financing, and (5) risk administration.

Discovery and Identification of Risk. An important first step in risk determination is the identification and inventory of the resources of an organization that are exposed to potential loss. This involves: (1) an examination and analysis of items such as liquid assets (cash, checks), capital assets, budgets, contracts, leases, organizational charts, policy and procedure manuals, annual reports, capital projects, and other financial records; (2) regular or periodic inspection of premises owned or leased by the government or not-for-profit agency; (3) use of well-conceived risk discovery questionnaires identifying major types of possible losses; and (4) use of reputable insurance brokers to aid in exposure analysis.[5]

Measurement and Evaluation. Once the exposure has been identified, measurement and evaluation comprise the next logical step. Measurement requires quantification, which relies heavily on the current records of insurance carriers. In measuring the risk, a thorough review of an agency's past loss experience, frequency, and the severity of each exposure must be carried out. This is not an easy task; "measurement of identified risk exposures is the most difficult and least precise step in the art of risk management."[6]

Data should be organized for each identified exposure and coverage as follows: (1) the frequency of a particular incident over a specified time period, perhaps four to six years; (2) the amount of claims resulting from the incident over that time period; and (3) the type of incident involved (e.g., foot, leg, back) for the same time period.[7] Attention should be focused on those items or situations that have the greatest potential for financial loss.

Risk Control. This step is essentially an analysis of the relevant alternatives that might be selected to reduce or eliminate the identified exposure. This is perhaps the most critical step in risk management. A decision must be made to determine if the risk can be eliminated entirely, reduced significantly, assumed partially or totally by the governmental unit, or transferred to the insurers.[8]

Risk reduction in many local governmental organizations is complicated due to fragmentation among different departments with responsibility for risk management. This is a major factor operating against efficient management of risk control. The National Safety Council statistics for 1975 demonstrate this point, showing that the national average loss of time due to personal injury was 13.1 hours per million hours worked. For industries such as chemical, automotive and aerospace, the average was less than 4 hours, and for the federal civilian work force the rate was 6.5 hours. For the same period, however, municipalities averaged 41.3 hours. For police, refuse, and fire, they were extremely high—54.8, 98.7, and 149 hours, respectively, due to time lost because of accidents in 1975. Eight years later, in 1983, the ratio remained high.[9]

If improvements are to be realized, governmental units must reduce the frequency and severity of loss by eliminating hazards and unsafe conditions. This necessitates greater coordination than has been usual in local government to date. To achieve the risk reduction objective requires that actions such as the following be pursued:

- Identify risk control areas, policies, and procedures relating thereto.
- Assist each department in interpreting and applying the rules.
- Monitor compliance of the policies and procedures on a periodic basis.[10]
- Establish safety and training programs (both in-house and external courses).
- Develop effective recordkeeping systems.
- Centralize responsibility for risk management.
- Involve all levels of employees in helping to identify unsafe conditions.

Risk evaluation should ideally be viewed as a preventive measure in that the potential for exposure to loss is recognized and dealt with before it materializes. The main means of eliminating risk are to change the way the things are being done or to terminate the activity or service.

Risk Assumption/Retention/Funding. This may occur in two ways—by unexpected assumption and by planned assumption. Unexpected assumption occurs most often because of ignorance and neglect, because the risk manager failed to thoroughly understand the following implications of the actions taken:

- Failure to realize that unless specifically stated *actual value* (ACV) means current replacement less accumulated depreciation
- Failure to carry the required amount of insurance or percentage of coverage to meet the co-insurance clause stipulation
- Failure to properly state or identify risks
- Failure to take timely action to insure against risk exposure[11]

Because of the difficulty experienced by public and other not-for-profit agencies in obtaining insurance coverage, risk retention has been pursued as a viable option. Before a final decision is made, a thorough evaluation of the governmental unit or agency's ability for risk retention should be undertaken.

Three basic ingredients have been viewed as essential for an effective loss financing program:

- The governmental unit or organization should have the financial capacity to meet its anticipated losses while accommodating its ordinary operating and capital needs.

- There should be exposure distribution across the entire organization sufficient to have economy of scale that provides a relatively stable loss exposure.
- The entity should insure against losses. "Layers of insurance above the self-retained levels must be purchased so that the risk of loss greater than the entity is capable of absorbing is transferred to a commercial insurance carrier."[12]

The size of the governmental unit or organization is an important consideration; the larger the organization is, the greater will be its ability to absorb claims against it. Small and predictably recurring claims can be more economically handled by the entity, thus avoiding the extremely high cost of insurance carriers.

Once the conditions and basic criteria for evaluating the organization's capability for retarding risks are known, a decision can be made regarding the assumption of risks. To aid in this endeavor, a frequency severity matrix or protective pyramid may be used.

An examination of Figure 6.1 suggests that the left side of the matrix, that containing the high frequency/low severity and low frequency/low severity loss, can be assumed by the organization because one is predictable and the other has a low risk factor.

Figure 6.1
The Frequency Severity Matrix

High Frequency Low Severity	High Frequency High Severity
Low Frequency Low Severity	Low Frequency High Severity

On the right side of the matrix, low frequency/high severity provides a situation in which risks are such that the organization should obtain commercial catastrophic insurance. For the high frequency/high severity case, the situation is more problematic. Because of the high risk in terms of both occurrence and severity, the price for such insurance may be too high to pay. Thus, an evaluation of the situation will heavily influence what risks might have to be retained or transferred.

The protective pyramid is analogous to the matrix approach in that the large number of exposure cases of high frequency/low severity is found at the base of the pyramid; such cases are capable of being handled by individual self-insurance. The smaller number of cases of low frequency/ high severity is viewed as being at the top of the pyramid, requiring catastrophic insurance. In the middle of the pyramid there are myriad possibilities, such as pooling and other arrangements.

Several types of risk insurance coverage are typically available to municipalities and other not-for-profit organizations, including the following:

- damage to property, including fire, automobile, machinery, water, earthquake, flood, and radiation
- business interruption and data processing equipment
- loss of property due to dishonest acts or crimes by employees or private citizens
- liability coverage for actions such as automobile-related accidents, workman's compensation, professional errors and omissions, and medical malpractices and public official liability
- loss of income-producing properties or increased cost due to fire to property, bridges, tunnels, boiler, and machinery

When the governmental unit employs the partial or total self-insurance option, there are two options, involving large deductibles or co-insurance. Under the partial or total self-insurance approach, an insurance fund is set up and managed to provide payment for unexpected losses. If the fund is professionally managed, it has the potential of replenishing itself, and perhaps in time it may be a source of income.

Under the co-insurance approach, amounts are budgeted and appropriated each year. Co-insurance is essentially a pay-as-you-go concept. While the co-insurance approach is widely used, it has some potential drawbacks. If the amount of liability fluctuates widely, it can present a problem for governmental units and organizations that have inflexible budgets. This may also occasion steep rises in insurance premiums.

The steep rise in insurance premiums for government and other not-for-profit agencies has generated pressure to find better ways to induce the insurance industry to cover risk at more reasonable costs. Self-insurance and pooling are becoming the only options for some governmental units if they wish to maintain risk coverage and avoid termination of private insurance policies. "There are 15,000 public entities being covered in these [munici-pally sponsored self-insurance pools] and other intergovernmental pools."[13]

In an effort to limit awards for damages, the state of Colorado has attempted to specifically define its Governmental Immunity Act by listing the areas for which it will be liable, including the following:

• Operation of state motor vehicles

• Operation of public hospitals, parks, and correctional facilities

• Dangerous conditions which interfere with movement of pedestrian or vehicular traffic

• Operation and maintenance of any public facility, including water supply plant, electrical, gas and other power facilities, sanitation plants, and swimming facilities[14]

Risk Administration. In large units of government, risk management is likely to be a separate and distinct function headed by a risk manager. In small units of government this function is performed by the financial officer. As noted earlier, clearly written policies and procedures should be an indispensable requirement. The main responsibilities are to oversee the implementation of the risk management process, which involve identifying exposure; evaluating, controlling, and funding risks; and other duties and activities related to the risk management function. These include evaluating and reviewing important leases and contracts, maintaining a risk manage-ment information system, and allocating costs, losses, and premiums. Finally, the risk manager acts as a communication channel for disseminat-ing risk-related information and reports throughout the organization on a timely basis.[15]

RISK MANAGEMENT AND QUALITY ASSURANCE: THE CASE OF THE MEDICAL INDUSTRY

The skyrocketing liability insurance costs experienced by doctors, hospitals, and other medically related functions has forced the industry to take a closer look at its risk management activities. Hospitals have long practiced quality assurance as a way of attempting to maintain quality in the delivery of medical services. When the need arose to streamline the risk management function, it was found that many of the activities required for quality assurance parallel those for risk management. The Joint Commis-sion of Accreditation of Hospitals (JCAH) felt that "the integration of risk management and quality assurance made good business sense as a means to improve patient care, reduce liability and maintain harmony in the labor force."[16]

In the 1974-1976 period, when the crisis in malpractice insurance costs became a major concern, commercial insurance carriers indicated that if hospitals developed acceptable in-house risk management programs, they would be given favored treatment. The "promise of reduced premium based on in-house risk identification, evaluation, reduction or elimination and consequential favorable claims history . . . provided the initial motivation of boards of trustees and administrators."[17]

Incident Reporting. In 1978 a total of 3,293 incidents in a psychiatric center were reviewed. It was found that accidental injuries generated one-third of the incidents; the major categories included "leave without consent, patient fights and assaults."[18] This initial count led to the analysis of the incidents and the identification of possible trends, convincing the hospital officials that such reports had considerable potential, especially if more detailed information (for example, type of incident, nature, frequency, witnesses, sex and age of patient, day and hour of occurrence) was available. It was felt that obtaining these data would aid in achieving two important objectives: (1) improving patient care while minimizing risks to patients and staff; and (2) realizing insurance savings due to claims reduction because the hospital would have its factual investigation report available to shield it from unfounded and unsubstantiated claims.

Judgmental factors still play a part in determining when a specific event should or should not be considered an incident. The following criteria are used to identify incidents:

* actions contrary to plans for the best quality patient care
* actions that place patients or staff at risk
* actions that put a program or facility in a tenuous legal or political position[19]

Following the 1978 test year, a computerized incident reporting system, containing over thirty types of incidents (ranging from biting and assault to incorrect medication), was instituted in 1979, permitting the answers to be obtained to a variety of questions. So far the system appears to be producing the intended results: reducing liability and producing better utilization of resources in delivering cost-effective patient care. Expansion of the program to other areas of the hospital is under way.[20]

CONCLUDING OBSERVATIONS

Emphasis on risk management is a recent development. The erosion of the governmental unit's sovereign immunity has occurred at a time when insurance premiums have skyrocketed for liability coverage in the medical profession. In both areas better risk management has been seen as one way to minimize the high cost of risk exposure.

The risk management problem among governmental units has reached crisis proportions. The insurance industry, which has sustained losses during the past few years, sees two converging trends: demands for improved insurance, and an increase in the number and size of awards. To recoup some of its losses, the industry has increased insurance premiums steeply. This has forced governmental units to seek and develop alternatives such as pooling and self-insurance. Additionally, it has generated an urgent need to find better ways to manage risks.

NOTES

1. Natalie Wasserman and Dean G. Phelus, eds., *Risk Management Today* (Washington, D.C.: ICMA, 1985), p. 1; Eric Wiesenthal, "Public Liability Woes Threaten Localities," *Public Administration Times*, November 1, 1985, pp. 1, 12.

2. Wiesenthal, "Public Liability Woes," p. 12.

3. Ibid.

4. Phyllis Sherman, *Basic Risk Management Handbook for Local Government* (Darien, Conn.: Public Risk Management Association, 1983), pp. 5-10.

5. Charles K. Coe, *Understanding Risk Management* (Athens, Ga.: Institute of Local Government, 1980), pp. 13-14.

6. Institute for Local Self-Government, *Public Agency Liability: The Law and the Risks; Management, Avoidance and Transfer* (Berkeley, Calif.: Institute for Local Government, 1978), p. 58.

7. Jesus J. Pena et al., "Combining Risk Management and Quality Assurance," in *Hospital Quality Assurance*, ed. Jesus J. Pena et al. (Rockville, Md.: Aspen Corporation, 1984), pp. 256-68.

8. Coe, *Understanding Risk Management*, p. 21.

9. Laurence C. Cragg and H. Felix Kloman, "Risk Management: A Developed Discipline," in Wasserman and Phelus, *Risk Management Today*, p. 13.

10. Ibid.

11. Coe, *Understanding Risk Management*.

12. Institute for Local Self-Government, *Public Agency Liability*, p. 96.

13. Wiesenthal, "Public Liability Woes," p. 12.

14. Ibid.

15. Cragg and Kloman, "Risk Management," p. 21.

16. Pena et al., "Combining Risk Management and Quality Assurance," p. 253.

17. Ibid., p. 254.

18. Ibid.

19. Ibid., p. 255.

20. Ibid., p. 269.

CHAPTER 7

BORROWING AND DEBT MANAGEMENT

The responsibility for long-term borrowing and debt management is critical in public and other not-for-profit agencies. Particularly in smaller agencies, imprudent decisions can lead to serious financial problems. Because of this, it is very important for the officials that oversee borrowing and debt management to have a general understanding of and a degree of familiarity with the different types of debt, the structure of debt, debt instruments, and the process by which bonds are bid and sold.

This chapter examines the critical role of the management process for the sale of long-term debt mainly as it takes place in governmental units. Attention is focused on the types of debt instruments and their proper use, the functions and responsibilities in the debt management process, and the many potential problems that can be avoided in the debt issuance process.

Debt financing takes place at all levels of government. Despite this reality misunderstanding about the scope and nature of public debt is common, due perhaps to the minimal amount of information that is exchanged about public financial undertakings. Another contributing factor is the unwise attempt to equate public and private debt. Additionally, there has long been an antipathy against borrowing, suggested by the following comment: "It [borrowing] is a system which tends to make us less thrifty—to blind us to our real situation."[1]

Borrowing is a substitute for taxing citizens immediately, replacing present taxes with future taxes and thus necessitating the payment of interest on the debt. In essence, "public borrowing is a means by which people with relatively low preference for present consumption lend to those with relatively high preference for present consumption."[2] Until the late 1930s government borrowing was considered a very abnormal event. It was referred to as "extraordinary finance," suggesting that "it was a method that was used only during extraordinary times such as war and depression."[3]

Government borrowing can be classified as either current or capital, depending on the purposes for which it is being used. Goods and services to be consumed in a period of a year or less are viewed as current, while those that will be consumed over longer periods (a year or more) are capital expenditures, typically for long-lived physical assets such as schools, utility plants, and highways. Because of the long time span for capital projects, benefits generated and outlays made cannot be easily synchronized.

While the federal government and a few states may run deficits as a permissible policy to fund current spending, this option is closed to local government and to most other not-for-profit agencies. Borrowing for current operations is not permitted for periods longer than a year. Such borrowing typically coincides with tax revenue inflow for the period or with grants from other governmental units. Short-term debts so created are known as *tax or revenue anticipation loans.*

Besides the restrictions on current borrowing, most states have constitutional provisions limiting their debt-creating capacity. More than half require a constitutional amendment beyond a specified debt limit. Most state constitutions require that a special tax be levied to cover debt service and stipulate that the state may not lend its credit to individuals or corporations.[4]

State restrictions on local government debt are quite specific and stringent. Usually there are stipulations regarding the following: (1) the purposes of the borrowing, (2) methods indicating how the debt should be incurred, (3) the amount of local debt, (4) the interest rate, (5) the term of the debt, (6) the retirement provisions, and (7) the form of the debt. The most common stipulation relates to the amount of allowable debt versus the assessed value of the local jurisdiction. In most cases, different assessment-ratio debt limits are applied to the various types of debt. The greatest restrictions are placed on the smallest communities; less stringent provisions apply to school districts.

Debt limitation requirements have not been without detractors. Property tax, which constitutes the major source of local revenue and on which the tax limitation is predominantly based, varies significantly among communities, permitting differing degrees of limitation. To compensate for this disparity local governments have manipulated the assessed valuation of property in order to raise their debt limitation ratio. The assessed valuation of the property is raised, while the tax rate or millage is reduced. Particularly significant is that the use of the property tax as the determining factor ignores the fact that an increasing source of local spending is grants from other governments.[5]

TYPES OF DEBT FINANCING

A number of avenues are open to public and other not-for-profit organizations to finance borrowing needs, typically for long-lived assets or capital projects. The financing option pursued will be influenced by a number of factors, among them the financial strength of the governmental unit or organization, the nature and scope of the project being financed, and the predictability of the cash financing flow. Among the general options that may be available are (1) pay cash, (2) set aside cash reserve for the prospective acquisition, and (3) borrow.

Before selecting a financing option, a thorough analysis of the costs and benefits of each should be made. Generally, a sound approach will involve a combination of the three approaches.

The payment of cash or the pay-as-you-go approach is essentially self-financing but allows interest payments to be avoided; it enhances the borrowing capacity of the organizational unit or other not-for-profit agency. Though very popular, it has distinct shortcomings. This approach assumes that a community or organization will have sufficient revenues to meet current operations plus an excess to meet capital facilities requirements. "Pay as you use" is a related concept, suggesting that the payment of the borrowed funds will be returned as people pay user charges for the services rendered.

Short-Term Debt. This comprises obligations that will mature within a year. Most often short-term debt is assumed to provide temporary or interim funding. Short-term debt may be used for the following purposes:

- cash to initiate or begin a project
- provision of cash as an interim financing means to await improved market conditions before issuing long-term debt
- start-up cash for initial construction
- provision of cash as a stopgap measure while resolving financial problems
- provision of cash to accommodate underbudgeted expenditures
- minimizing cash flow fluctuations[6]

There are a number of short-term *instruments* used to generate cash to meet expected spending needs. The following are three important instruments with which financial managers should familiarize themselves:

- *Tax anticipation notes (TANs)* are used to meet shortfalls occasioned by lags in tax collection; the anticipated revenue is used as security or pledged for the bank's advancing the loan (see discussion in Chapter 5).

- *Revenue anticipation notes (RANs)* are used to provide cash to overcome lags involved in receipt of intergovernmental revenue. The anticipated revenues are pledged as security for the cash advance. Upon receipt of the revenues the loan is repaid (see Chapter 5).

- *Bond anticipation notes (BANs)* are used to generate funds to initiate a capital project, especially in cases in which interest rates are volatile. In such situations, it may be necessary to wait until interest rates stabilize for long-term debt issues.

Long-Term Debt. This is typically used to provide permanent financing for major capital improvements, construction, and acquisition of capital facilities. As a general rule, long-term debt should not be used to fund current expenditures. It is important that the term of the bond issued be at least equal to the life of the asset being financed. There are several categories of long-term bonds.

- *General obligation bond (GO)* indicates that the security standing behind the bond is the total credibility and unrestricted resource of the government unit or other not-for-profit agency. The bond is said to be issued with the full faith and credit of the issuer. In a governmental unit, the general tax revenue provides the ultimate source of funds. Though at one time general obligation bonds were the only tax exempt debt that was issued, this has changed significantly. Now a large amount of tax exempt debt is represented by revenue bonds—approximately 56 percent in 1982.

- *Revenue bonds* are obligations issued to finance a revenue-generating project or enterprise. Both the principal and interest of revenue bonds are required to be paid exclusively from the generated earnings. The massive growth in revenue bonds has come about as a way of reducing dependence on general obligation bonds. It has had the effect of shifting the burden away from taxpayers to users, avoiding referendums and imposed debt ceilings. Typical uses of the revenue bond include financing of sewer and water systems, airports, toll roads, hospitals, parking facilities, and industrial developments.

- *Industrial bonds* are issued by governments to construct facilities for a private corporation that makes lease payments to the government to service those bonds. Such bonds may be general obligation bonds, combination bonds, or revenue bonds. The state legislature enacts enabling legislation to permit local governments, typically municipalities, to finance the acquisition or construction of industrial facilities. The major purpose of these bonds is to encourage local economic development efforts. Originally industrial bonds were used almost entirely to attract, expand, or retain industrial facilities in a community. The uses of industrial bonds have expanded in recent years to include financing of sports facilities/stadiums, hospitals, transportation, pollution control, and industrial parks.[7]

Unique borrowing vehicles have been developed in recent years "to take advantage of the expanded public role in the delivery of goods and services, [and] the desire of the private sector to capture the benefits of tax exempt financing."[8] Among the activities that have been undertaken are (1) resource recovery involving a privately owned waste disposal plant; (2) mortgage finance permitting tax exempt bonds to be sold by a governmental unit or authority, which uses the proceeds to make low interest mortgage loans; (3) joint action allowing governmental units to cooperatively own a power plant; and (4) municipal assistance corporations, permitting a city to issue tax exempt obligations supported by special revenue sources; this approval may be used especially in those situations where the city's credit does not make the debt issuance possible. The receipts obtained from the bond issue may be used for governmental purposes, as during the New York City fiscal crisis in 1975.

DEBT CARRYING CAPACITY

It is important to know the precise debt capacity of a governmental unit because it indicates how much that unit may reasonably borrow. In a governmental unit, debt capacity is dependent upon the quantity and quality of available resources that can be legally and practically drawn upon to meet the articulated needs.

Before debt capacity can be determined, the debt burden—the legitimate obligations that a governmental unit or agency is responsible for liquidating at some time in the future—must be calculated. The debt burden can therefore be compared to the amount of taxes or monetary resources that taxpayers are required to provide in order to finance outstanding debt service. When overlapping governmental units (e.g., school districts, public authorities, or special purpose districts) extract taxes from the same taxpayers, those analyzing debt capacity must be cognizant not only of debt obligations in an individual unit but also of the composite debt responsibility in all the units concerned.

Among the main components that may be evaluated in determining relative tax capacity are the following:

- property value per capita
- human resources in terms of age, employment, education, and type of occupation
- per capita personal income
- per capita disposable income
- productivity of the tax system (indicators include per capita tax collections and per capita taxes as a percentage of per capita income)
- political, legal, and administrative constraints against expanding or broadening the tax base
- property tax base
- stability of tax system
- tax base growth rate[9]

An underlying premise for evaluating fiscal capacity is that, given ordinary conditions, the debt of a governmental unit or agency parallels the size and growth of the governmental unit's tax base. It is important that schedules of debt repayment be prudently arranged to avoid excessive pressures on operating expenditures, minimizing the possibility of impairing the governmental unit or agency's credit rating. To aid in monitoring changes in debt structure, the Financial Trend Monitoring System (FTMS) discussed in Chapter 18 is most useful. The FTMS follows the change in debt, the scope, and the cost of capital items that will be purchased or overlapping debt.[10]

PLANNING A BOND ISSUE

An initial activity involves the determination of the purpose for incurring debt, the scope, and the cost of capital items that will be purchased or contracted. Ideally, bonds should be issued as part of a governmental unit's capital improvement program (CIP), physical improvements required to meet community service needs (see discussion in Chapter 11). It is in the CIP that the definition of quantity and quality of services to be delivered is indicated.

Carefully determining the cost of the project to be financed is critical. If the costs are overestimated, unnecessary interest and associated costs will be incurred. Underestimating the cost of the project is likely to be even more expensive because it may necessitate a supplemental bond issue. This requires that a bond be issued for an optimal amount.[11] To aid in selecting means to obtain necessary financial resources for funding the project decided upon, the governmental unit or agency should seek expert assistance from consulting agencies, financial advisors, and bond counsel to minimize costs and legal problems and to facilitate document preparation.

Once a decision has been made about the amount of resources needed, the available options other than incurring debt must be explored, such as existing revenue sources, federal and state grants, and bond funds from prior issues. It should be determined how advantageous it would be to sell bonds through public bid versus private negotiations where this option is legal. The bond debt option should include consideration of selling general obligation versus revenue bonds. A choice between the two options would require an assessment of the following:

- prospective beneficiaries (direct and indirect) over the expected life of the project
- potential alternative revenues obtainable from user charges
- legal authority to issue general obligation bonds
- potential for bond being approved by voters
- political and legal authority to raise or increase taxes
- implications and impact of the bond issue, especially demands on general obligation versus other financing priorities
- comparative costs of general obligation and revenue bonds[12]

GENERAL OBLIGATION AND REVENUE BONDS: PARTICULAR CONSIDERATIONS

In cases in which revenue bonds do not require voter approval, fewer problems are encountered than with general obligation bonds. But revenue bonds typically carry higher rates because they are not secured by the full faith and credit of the issuer. The structure of the bond issue depends on whether it consists of general obligation (GO) or revenue bonds. A critical consideration by a prospective purchaser relates to the degree of coverage for the debt service from revenue pledged in support of the debt. As a general rule, the purchaser/investor is more comfortable with a high coverage ratio than a low one. If possible, a comparative check of similar projects in other jurisdictions should be made. Another concern is the patrimony (undepreciated value of the facility or the net asset value), which may have been negotiated in earlier years but is not likely to provide enough security for interest payments in later years. This position accords with the view that the maturity of a debt should not be allowed to extend beyond the useful life of the facility financed.[13]

Unlike the revenue bond, which depends on revenue generated from a specific project, the GO bond relies upon the revenue or total estimated annual revenue of the governmental unit. Since the same pool of revenue must be used to service all GO bonds, it is important that current expenditure in any given year not exceed the projected revenue.

DEBT MANAGEMENT TERMINOLOGY

Consulting engineer. This is one who provides technical advice and conducts feasibility studies in areas such as designing and constructing roads, water and sewer facilities, and public buildings, making revenue and operation cost estimates.

Financial advisor. This is an individual who provides a wide spectrum of services to a debt issuer, including assessing the borrowing capacity; assembling an array of financial statistics and economic data such as tax rates and overlapping debt; making user charge estimates; projecting revenue flow estimates; advising on marketing methods; writing call provision features; assisting in preparing and distributing notice of sale and bid form; determining the need for rating services; arranging analysis of creditworthiness; coordinating delivery of bonds; and ruling on acceptability of bids.

Bond counsel. The bond counsel's main objective is determining if there are conflicts with constitutional and other constraints such as monitoring/limitations, arranging required elections, reviewing bond-related statements for conformity with the law, ensuring that competitive sales are advertised and that an underwriter is secured for negotiated sale, rendering opinion on the status of tax exempt bonds, and answering questions posed by prospective purchasers and public officials.

Negotiated sale. This is a method that is used for selling securities in which the terms of the sale are arrived at through negotiation between issuer and purchasers without formal competitive bidding. This may include sales of securities directly to commercial banks or consortiums of commercial banks, investment banking firms or syndicates, and private placements by issuers.[14]

Callable bond. This is a type of bond which permits the issuer to call in and pay the obligation before the stated maturity date by notifying the purchaser of the redemption in the manner specified in a bond contract.

Maturity date. This is the date on which the principal amount of security becomes due and payable.

Debt service. This is the required amount of money necessary to pay interest and principal for a given year or years. When the term *debt service payment* is used it refers to the service of all bond payments that mature at some specified time.

Series bond. This is a bond whose principal is repaid in periodic installments over the life of the issue.

Call Provision. When a bond has a call provision, the investor may be required to redeem the bonds at some time other than the specified maturity date. The call may apply to a portion or to all of the outstanding bond. If the optional payment of principal is not specified in the bond contract, the call option can be used only with the consent of the investor. The call provision is usually included to permit the issuer to achieve a number of objectives, including the following:

- voluntarily reduce outstanding debt
- reduce debt in accordance with bond agreement (indenture)
- reduce interest cost by refunding
- reorganize debt voluntarily[15]

The call provision provides flexibility in unstable markets. It also provides the issuer with the option to reduce the bond's interest rate when interest rates decline, allowing the issuer to reduce costs but reducing the earnings potential for the investor. To compensate for this, the investor usually requires higher interest return on callable bonds than on non-callable bonds. Investors may also require a period of time by which the bond may not be called after issuance. This is known as the *deferment period*. When the bond is called, the difference between the call price and its par value is referred to as the *call premium*.

Advance Refunding. In those cases where a deferment call provision exists but interest rates decline significantly before the deferment period, the issuer may issue bonds prior to the callable date when the outstanding bonds become due or callable. The proceeds from the advance funding are deposited in an escrow account and invested in securities, typically U.S. Treasury bonds or other authorized securities to be used to redeem the underlying bonds at the maturity or call date and to pay interest on the bonds refunded. It is important to note that refunding is normally desirable only when interest rates are high enough to generate a benefit.

Credit Rating Agencies and Investors. One of the most crucial factors influencing the success or failure of a debt offering are the governmental unit or agency's credit rating, whether or not the sale of a major bond issue rating is obligatory. Credit rating is used to designate the quality of governmental bonds and directly affects the interest rate that is required to be paid. Standard and Poor's Corporation, Moody's Investor Service, and Fitch Investors Services are the three main rating firms in the United States providing professional judgments or opinions concerning the quality and security or creditworthiness of debt issuers. Moody's and Standard and Poor's are by far the two dominant giants in the rating business. Moody's has been in operation since 1918 and rates approximately 15,000 municipal bonds and 4,500 new issues per year. Standard and Poor's began its municipal bond rating in 1940 and presently has 7,000 ratings outstanding. Each year it rates approximately 1,500 new issues.[16]

Each rating service charges a fee for its services based on rate schedules which vary according to the size and extent of the analysis desired. A host of factors is considered by investors and rating agencies, as shown in Figure 7.1.

As can be seen from Table 7.1, Standard and Poor's rates bonds from AAA (highest quality and extremely strong capacity to pay principal and interest) to CC (highest degree of speculation) and D (indicating bond in default). Moody's Investor Service ratings range from Aaa to C, with Baa having the lowest investment grade.

Bond Insurance. This is a relatively recent development, arising to insure government-related bonds against the possibility of default by the issuer. In such an event, the insuring company assumes the obligation to make all necessary payments for coupons and maturity amounts required for investors. The initiating insurer in 1971 was the American Municipal Bond Assurance Corporation (AMBAC), whose objective was to reduce the interest cost to the issuer. For a one-time premium ranging between 0.3 percent and 3 percent of the total interest and principal amount of the bond, the issuer can receive insurance protection for the principal and interest.

In 1974 Municipal Bond Insurance Association (MBIA) was created as a competitor to AMBAC. Unlike AMBAC, whose ultimate backing consists only of its net worth, MBIA is made up of five underwriters: Aetna Insurance Company, Fireman's Insurance Fund, Aetna Casualty and Security Company, Travelers Indemnity Company, and Continental Insurance Company. As with AMBAC, premiums are determined on the basis of the

Figure 7.1
Factors Considered by Investors and Rating Agencies in Determining Rates

The Amount and Nature of the Debt and Debt Service Requirements:
- Total amount of debt and per capita debt levels
- Purposes for which debt has been created
- Rate at which debt has increased
- Debt repayment schedules and overlapping debt
- Degree of reliance on-short-term debt

Economy of the Community and the Region of Which It Is a Part:
- Geographical area and past history of growth
- Educational and income characteristics of the population
- Location of area served and general character of future potential
- Sources of economic activity—employers,diversification, and dependence
- Maintenance of the economic plant
- Leadership
- Wealth of the community—taxable property, resources, transportation

Social Factors:
- Educational opportunities
- Cultural opportunities
- Recreational facilities
- Community record for handling social unrest
- Housing stock
- Characteristics of the population

Management of Local Government:
- Overall governmental structure—professionalism vs. balkanization
- Degree to which the government is well-administered
- Organization of financial administration
- Effectiveness of capital planning and programming
- Quality of revenue administration—passive collector of taxes vs. active
- Revenue base—new reliances
- Revenue calender out of sync
- Reputation for prudent financial management
- Conditions of the physical plant
- Contingent liabilities
- Sinking fund management

Other Considerations:
- Debt limitations—higher regulatory controls
- Capacity of government to deal with local problems
- Security of deposits—guarantees of banks
- Bondholder's remedies—explicit or implied
- Subdivision controls—poorly planned expansions
- General regulatory codes

Table 7.1
The Major Rating Systems: Moody's and Standard and Poor's

Standard and Poor's Corporate and Municipal Rating	Moody's Municipal Rating	Description
AAA	Aaa	Highest quality, unquestionable ability to pay interest and principal.
AA	Aa	High quality and very strong capacity to pay interest and principal.
A	A	Upper medium quality, strong capacity to pay principal and interest.
BBB	Baa	Medium quality with adequate capacity to pay interest and principal, though subject to adverse economic conditions over extended periods.
BB	Ba	Predominantly speculative quality with low issuer's capacity to pay principal and interest.
BB,B,CCC,CC		BB is the lowest degree of speculation, CC the highest degree of speculation, and B medium speculation regarding issuer's capacity to pay principal and interest.
C		Income bond on which no interest is being paid.
D		Default on interest and principal.
	B,Caa, C,Ca	Speculative with low capacity to pay principal and interest.
	Con (...)	Conditional, requiring some act or fulfillment of some condition secured by a future project earning.

size of the total interest payment and principal and may be paid by either the issuer or the bond underwriter. While "Standard and Poor's rates both AMBAC-insured and MBIA insured bonds as triple 'A'," Moody's assigns no rating to insured bonds.[17]

Disclosure. Typically about a month before a bond sale the issuer publishes a preliminary official statement or prospectus, describing the contents of the bond issue to enable potential investors to effectively price the bond. Subsequent to the sale of the bonds, the final official statement is developed, providing details relating to the issue and coupon rates. Governmental units are not required to comply with regulations of the Securities and Exchange Commission and other federal agencies.

The events of 1974-1975 relating to the financial crisis of New York City and the problems of a number of other cities, including Cleveland, raised the concern that the problems created were due in part to faulty reporting systems or manipulated reporting. Because of these developments, agencies, states, and a number of professional associations began calling for better disclosure guidelines. In some cases, legislation was introduced at the state and federal level stipulating minimum disclosure guidelines.

The Municipal Finance Officers Association (MFOA) published perhaps the most influential document, *Disclosure Guidelines for Offering of Securities by State and Local Governments*. Two years later, in 1978, MFOA issued *Guidelines for Use by State and Local Governments in the Preparation of Yearly Information Statements and Other Current Information*. MFOA also offers a Certificate of Conformance based on how well a governmental unit's financial statement conforms to generally accepted accounting principles (GAAP).

Negotiated versus Competitive Sale. The issuer has the option to sell competitively or by negotiated sale in revenue bond, while most states require general obligations to be competitively bid. The competitive sale permits underwriters to bid against each other to buy an issuer's bond. Acceptance of the competitive approach is widespread because there is a general feeling that it removes the possibility of favoritism, resulting in lower interest rates to the issuer.

In a negotiated sale there is no formal bidding; the underwriter is chosen beforehand. Typically the issuer contacts a number of underwriters to solicit information regarding the expected interest rate or underwriter's *spread* (profit). The usual practice is that issuers exchange information on their proposed sale with underwriters with whom they have had satisfactory dealings in the past. The underwriter selected usually assists the issuer in a number of activities, including putting the issue together in terms of maturity date, maturity amount, and call provisions; preparation of the official statement; credit rating assistance; the pinpointing of market timing for the issue; the cultivation of potential investors; and compliance with legal requirements. Once the selection is made, the issuer and the underwriter work together to determine the structure, timing, and price of the bond for the underwriter. The negotiated bond approach is considered suitable when interest rates are high and volatile and the issue is complex. Since 1978 the number of revenue negotiated bond sales has increased sharply—from 25 percent in 1973 to 50 percent of the dollar value of municipal revenue bonds.

In both the negotiated and the competitive method, the underwriter is a focal participant in that the issuer sells the bond to the underwriter, who in turn sells to investors. For smaller issues, the underwriter buys the entire issue; larger issues are sold later by a syndicate for resale. Whether the sale method is competitive or negotiated, the underwriter assumes complete risk and responsibility for selling the bonds. Because of the negotiated underwriter's ability to time the sale of the bond and investigate the demand for the bond beforehand, the risk is more limited.

When the underwriter decides to make a bid, he/she needs to determine the yield that will be necessary to attract investors, gain the winning bid and enable the bond to be offered to investors, and permit a profit. It is important that the underwriter make an accurate assessment of the market for the bond because miscalculations would result in the offering price of the bond being lowered, minimizing or eliminating the underwriter's profit. An important point is that the underwriter's costs for searching and preparing the bid are recovered only if he/she is successful in winning the bid. Thus the potential risk for not recovering out-of-pocket costs restricts the underwriter's search and preparation effort.

There are a number of options available to the negotiated sale underwriter which are not available to the competitive underwriter. If the negotiated sale underwriter recognizes that he/she can sell the offering at a lower interest rate or that investors want different amounts of bonds than were planned, the underwriter can modify the terms of the issue to reflect the changed circumstances.

Precisely what type of bond sale is desirable for a given issue depends on a host of variables. Among the factors that might affect the choice are the following: the stability of the market, the experience of the issuer in the bond market, the size of the issue, the complexity of the issue, and administrative regulations in the state and/or local governmental unit.

Notice of Sale. When an issue is to be sold, advertisements are placed, usually in national and local media, announcing the proposed sale. Thus the traditional advertising document is known as the Official Notice of Sale. Active issuers will normally send copies of the Notice of Sale to prospective bidders and to legal publications. Because of its stature in bond underwriting, advertisement in the *Daily Bond Buyer* is typically required or recommended. The information in the Notice of Sale includes the following:

1. Amount of issue, including maturity and call features
2. Authorization for the bond sale

3. Type of bond (e.g., revenue, GO)
4. Name(s) of the bond counsel
5. Bid form and basis of award
6. Amount of good faith check if required
7. Denomination and registration privileges of investors
8. Time, place, and date where bids can be accepted
9. Maximum interest cost permitted
10. Statement of purpose of bond and security

Basis of Award. When the issue is to be bid competitively, it is important that the issuer determine the basis on which the decision to sell debt will be made. The best known bases for award are the true interest cost (TIC) and the net interest cost (NIC).

The NIC is derived by determining the total interest payment for a debt issue and dividing it by the amount of the bonds outstanding by the number of years they are outstanding. When bonds are issued at a discount, the latter is added to the interest payments. Conversely, when the bond is issued at a premium, the latter amount is subtracted from the interest payments. The formula for calculating NIC is as follows:

$$\text{NIC} = \frac{\text{Total Interest payments} + \text{discount (or} - \text{premium)}}{\text{Number of bond year dollars}}$$

Example: Interest payment = $500. An amount of $50 is paid out for final maturity, due in one year and each year thereafter for the life of the bond.

Years to Maturity	Par Value	Coupon	Coupon Payment per Maturity	Bond Year Dollars
1	$1,000	5%	$ 50	$1,000
2	1,000	5%	100	2,000
3	1,000	5%	150	3,000
4	1,000	5%	200	4,000
Total	$4,000		$500	$10,000

There are no premiums or discounts. The bond year dollars equal $10,000. The NIC is 5%.

$$\text{NIC} = \frac{\text{Total coupon payments}}{\text{Bond year dollars}} = \frac{\$500}{\$10,000} = .05 = 5\%$$

A more involved example will help to clarify the NIC calculation. An issuer sells $20,000 of bonds with five separate maturities and no discount or premium. The serial maturities and coupons are as follows:

Years to Maturity	Par Value	Coupon	Coupon Payment per Maturity	Bond Year Dollars
1	$2,000	5.25	$105	2,000
2	2,000	5.30	212	4,000
3	4,000	5.50	440	8,000
4	6,000	5.70	798	14,000
5	6,000	5.80	1,160	20,000
Total	$20,000		$2,715	$48,000

$$\text{NIC} = \frac{\text{Total Interest}}{\text{Bond year dollars}} = \frac{\$2,715}{\$48,000} = 5\%$$

If the issue had been sold at a discount, the interest rate would be higher. For example, if the issue had been sold for an average price of $96, the issuer would have received $400 less. The NIC with the $400 discount added to the total interest payment is as follows:

$$\text{NIC} = \frac{\$2,715 + \$400}{\$48,000} = \frac{\$3,115}{\$48,000} = 6\%$$

The TIC method is considered a superior alternative to the NIC. A major criticism of the NIC approach is that it ignores the present value or the timing of interest rate payments. Thus it misleads the issuer to choose a higher bid than he/she otherwise would. The TIC accounts for the time value of money.[18] It recognizes the interest rate that must be paid on the actual purchase price, which is the face amount minus the premium or plus the discount, in order to yield the bond coupon, giving a more accurate picture of the costs involved.

CONCLUDING OBSERVATIONS

Debt management, which was once relegated to relative obscurity, became a front-burner issue during the early 1970s due to financial crises in a number of cities such as New York and Cleveland. To be effective as a financial manager, and to some extent as a chief executive, in a governmental unit or agency requires a degree of understanding that will improve the chances of recognizing potential problems and the ability to seek advice to avert them. Because debt represents a significant portion of spending in many governmental units it requires close attention.

NOTES

1. David Ricardo, *Principles of Political Economy and Taxation* (1817; repr. Homewood, Ill.: Richard D. Irwin, 1963), p. 140.

2. Richard E. Wagner, *Public Finance* (Boston, Mass.: Little, Brown and Co., 1982), p. 308.

3. Ibid., p. 303.

4. Alan Walter Steiss, *Local Government Finance* (Lexington, Mass.: Lexington Books, 1975).

5. Ibid., p. 75.

6. U.S. Conference of Mayors, *A Mayor's Financial Management Handbook* (Washington, D.C.: U.S. Conference of Mayors, February 1980), pp. 111-19; and Lennox L. Moak and Albert M. Hillhouse, *Local Government Finance* (Chicago: Municipal Finance Officers Association, 1975), p. 250.

7. See Congressional Budget Office, *Small Issue Industrial Revenue Bonds* (Washington, D.C.: CBO, 1985).

8. Ibid.

9. Moak and Hillhouse, *Local Government Finance*, pp. 391-96.

10. See *Evaluating Financial Conditions Handbook 2* (Washington, D.C.: Internal City Managers Association, 1980).

11. A useful approach has been identified by Philip M. Low, Jr., "How to Calculate the Size of Your Bond Issue," *Special Bulletin 1976B* (Chicago: Municipal Finance Officers Association, June 1, 1976).

12. George Kaufman, "Debt Management," in J. Richard Aronson and Eli Schwartz, *Management Policies in Local Government Finance* (Washington, D.C.: ICMA, 1981), p. 308.

13. Lennox L. Moak, *Municipal Bonds* (Chicago: Municipal Finance Officers Association, 1982), p. 232.

14. See Center for Capital Research, *Planning, Designing and Selling General Obligation Bonds in Oregon: A Guide to Local Issues* (Eugene, Ore.: University of Oregon, 1978); see also Philip Rosenberg et al., *A Debt Management Handbook for Small Cities* (Chicago: Municipal Finance Officers Association, 1979).

15. Ibid., p. 214.

16. Public Securities Association, *Fundamentals of Municipal Bonds*, rev. ed. (New York: Public Security Association, 1982), p. 40.

17. Ibid., p. 64.

18. See Chapter 11 for the method for computing present value.

CHAPTER 8

THE BUDGETING FUNCTION

Public budgeting grew out of the political and social necessity to share power. It was through the budget that the English aristocracy, in Article 12 of the Magna Carta (1215), obtained both symbolic and substantive control over the king's absolute power of the purse. The barons obtained the power to say "no" to the king's revenue-raising objectives. Prior to engaging in domestic or foreign activities, the king was required to consult the barons and follow a recognized procedure before resources could be raised. The budget is thus "the product of the institutionalization of the rules and processes wrested from a sovereign, excessively jealous of his prerogatives."[1] Over time, the budget evolved as a formal instrument guaranteeing accountability and as an important instrument of control in the modern democratic state.

Whatever our political ideologies, the scope and significance of the budget cannot be ignored. Budgets are essential to every type of organization. Their impact on the fortunes of governments and agencies has long been recognized. The British statesman William Gladstone remarked, "Budgets are not merely affairs of arithmetic but in a thousand ways go to the root of prosperity of individuals, the relations of classes and the strength of kingdoms."[2]

This chapter provides the reader with a brief overview of the components and issues essential to the understanding of modern budgeting techniques and philosophy. It also provides an introduction to Chapters 9 through 14, which examine the uses and types of budgets found in practice.

PERSPECTIVES ON BUDGETING

The budgeting function represents the third step in the financial system shown previously in Figure 1.1. The budget makes the potential implementation of the planned programs specific and concrete.

Budget and Planning. All budget making involves some planning. The articulation of goals, objectives, strategies, and priorities is indispensable to the development of a sound budget. It is the planning function that sets the stage for all subsequent activities in budget preparation. Figure 8.1 presents a conceptual view of the linkage of planning and budgeting. Note that the budget amounts of the prior period become a major input of the new planning cycle. Existing programs are evaluated; desired programs are identified; environmental or external factors are assessed; changes in the government/agency are determined; strategic plans are formulated; the policy directive necessary to guide program development (program planning) and the detailed work plan (budgeting) are put together.[3]

Figure 8.1
Planning and Budgeting

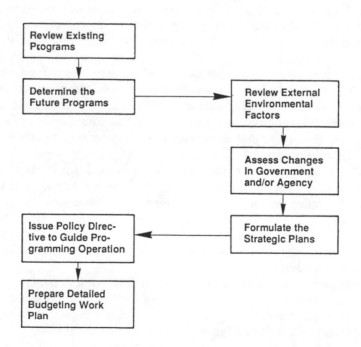

WHAT IS A BUDGET?

A budget is an economic, planning, political, and social document. It is a comprehensive financial work plan covering a specific period of time. The plan outlines the services and activities or projects to be provided and indicates the necessary expenditures and available resources in quantitative terms. The plan takes into account community preferences as competing claims and indicates how the resources will be allocated to satisfy these claims. All those whose preferences count are represented in the budget in dollar amounts, that is to say, the groups or individuals receiving benefits—subsidies in the form of welfare, tax relief, day care, and the like—will be indicated.

The budget links the financial resources and human behavior necessary to accomplish policy objectives. Because the budget allocates scarce resources, it is an economic instrument (Table 8.1). It is a political instrument because it settles conflicts in determining who will get how much of the available scarce resources and when. It is a social instrument because it is a device for distributing benefits and costs according to community preferences.[4]

Contrasting Public and Private Budgeting. The pricing and market system acts as the strategic resource allocation mechanism in the private sector, while the budget performs this function in the public sector. In the private sector, expected revenues are directly tied to the quantity and quality of goods and services produced and sold. Revenues are a good indicator as to whether planned levels of activity have been realized. Unlike the private sector, public and non-profit agencies must determine in advance the amounts that must be raised to achieve projected levels of activity and the means to raise them. Failure to collect expected fees does not mean that the expenditure plans can be changed to match revenue intake. The public agency can resort to supplemental appropriations, which are often viewed with hostility. Similarly, the non-profit agency must rely on reserve funds or on its funding sources. The latter usually do not like to provide additional funds. Agencies that are under budgeded learn to live with their mistakes.

In both public and non-profit agencies, yearly budgets are fixed and all funds provided are expected to be spent. Not spending the funds results in expenditure reductions according to the amount unspent. This approach is counterproductive and "weakens the sensitivity of the budget as a measure of performance."[5]

The control aspect of the budget is far more critical to public and non-profit organizations than it is to private ones. Several reasons may be advanced to account for this phenomenon. Particularly in private manufacturing companies, most costs are engineered costs. Thus, in these companies most costs can be identified with the products produced. In non-profit agencies most costs are discretionary because the amounts to be spent typically vary widely depending on management decisions.[6]

Table 8.1
The Budget as an Instrument

Planning Instrument--sets goals, priorities, and strategies and coordinates the community/agency resources into an expenditure plan identifying what programs or activities will take place and at what levels.

Political Instrument--involves competing interests attempting to influence a government/agency to form policy favorable to them.

Social Instrument--provides a vehicle to grant and deny privileges and disburse burdens and benefits to individuals and businesses.

Economic Instrument--offers powerful potential for affecting the growth and productive capacity of the community and its citizens.

Legal Instrument--grants authoritatively the rights, responsibilities, power, and guidelines that regulate the budget format, timing, and process.

Adapted from Jerome B. McKinney and Lawrence C. Howard, Public Administration: Balancing Power and Accountability (Oak Park, Ill.: Moore Publishing Co., 1979).

Unlike the fixed budgets of non-profit organizations, the budgets of profit-oriented companies tend to be tentative. Management is expected to adjust to the changing conditions that affect sales. Managers are expected to revise plans so that the profit objective can be maximally achieved. But conditions in government and non-profit agencies are viewed as essentially stable and predictable. For example, the number of miles of road to be built, the number of hospital beds, or the number of students enrolled at a university are not likely to change significantly from one period to the next during a year.[7]

PURPOSES OF BUDGETING

One unarticulated objective[8] of a budget is to minimize uncertainty and to make the future more predictable by identifying what is wanted, how much of it is available, and when it is available. The budget quantitatively articulates planned intentions and priorities. Ideally, every proposed dollar of expenditure is specifically identified with an organizational unit known as a responsibility center, the manager of which has control over the use of that dollar.

Of all the components of the financial management system, budgeting is perhaps the most important. The continuing pursuit of the balanced budget enhances stability in financial management because it fosters a matching of revenue (intake/inflow of resources or money) with expenditure (outflow/outgo of resources or money). As a detailed work plan, the budget gives direction to the implementation of articulated policies and significantly facilitates the achievement of organizational objectives.

Policy Direction. As a plan, the budget indicates a specific policy direction for a specific period of time. It contains a set of coordinated choices aimed at achieving articulated or implied goals and objectives.

Mutual Contract. The budget may be considered as a mutual contract between the provider of resources and the deliverer of goods and/or services. This makes it especially important to involve those who will implement the budget. In spite of this desired norm, a number of non-profit agencies exclude service deliverers from the budget process when crucial decisions are made. There have been cases when the budget submitted to the resource providers has been sharply reduced but the service provisions have been left intact.[9]

In the public sector the legislature and chief executives agree to provide the executing agencies with funds, with the understanding that the agencies expend the funds according to objectives previously agreed upon. In like manner, the governmental budget can be viewed as a contract between the legislature and the citizens of the governmental unit. The citizen implicitly agrees to pay taxes on condition that the government provide certain general and specific services.

Communication. A budget should communicate the objectives and standards of performance expected of all decision makers. Externally, the budget can detail the costs and expenditures of operations by identifying the inputs, such as materials and equipment, and the outputs of specific goods and services, such as miles of road built or repaired, number of patients treated, or number of manuscripts submitted for publication. When management is concerned not only with inputs and outputs but also with results or effectiveness, such as the percentage of patients successfully treated (health care and/or welfare organizations), the number of degrees and diplomas awarded (universities), and the reduction in crime rate (police departments), the budget can be a useful instrument in providing such information.

Motivational Control. The budget can be used to motivate employees by dispensing or withholding rewards. The use of the budget as a means of control over departmental and functional expenditures has dominated much of the history of budgeting. Traditional line-item and incremental budgets (discussed in Chapter 12) were designed to control administrative discretion in the spending of agency funds. In fact, the line-item budget is so directed at limiting specific expenditures (e.g., personnel and materials) that it has been referred to as the dollar accountability budget. Furthermore, each spending organizational unit is treated as a cost center to which responsibility can be specifically assigned and from which accountability can be obtained.

Monitoring of Service. The budget can be used to monitor and assess the performance of various constituent units and programs by providing continuing feedback on their progress. Variance analysis of performance at timely intervals permits corrective action to be taken. For example, analysis of wages may show variance because of an increase in pay rate subsequent to the preparation of the budget, poor deployment of staff (for example, the use of more highly paid workers than planned), or both (see Figure 8.2). The information equation needed to analyze a budget is as follows:

	Budgeted	Actual
Hours	5	3
Wages	$6	$8
Labor	30	24
Variance		6

- (Budgeted Hours: 5) − (Actual Hours: 3) × (Budgeted Rate: $6) = (Labor Use Variance: $12)

- (Budgeted Wage Rate: $6) − (Actual Wage Rate: $8) × (Actual Hours: 3) = (Wage Rate Variance: $6)

- (Budgeted Labor Cost: $30) − (Actual Wage Cost: $24) = (Net Wage Variance: $6)

Figure 8.2
Graphic View of Labor Cost Variance

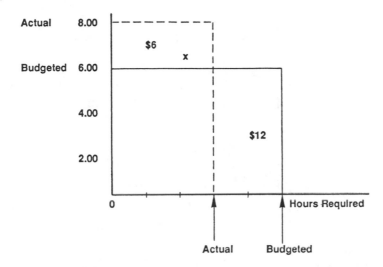

Like labor, materials may be analyzed for variance because of price increases, excessive use of materials, or both (see Table 8.2). The same conceptual approach employed for labor can be used to calculate materials variance.

- (Budgeted Quantity) − (Actual Quantity) × (Budgeted Rate per Unit of Output) = (Materials Variance)
- (Budgeted Rate per Unit Quantity) − (Actual Rate per Unit Quantity) × (Actual Quantity Used) = (Variance Because of Price of Materials Input)
- (Budgeted Cost of Materials) − (Actual Cost of Materials) = (Net Materials Price Variance)

In government and most non-profit agencies, budgeted cost is a surrogate or substitute for standard cost. The latter represents the amount that a procedure or service should cost. Though development and use of standard cost are infrequent in the public sector, they are widely used in private industries and some non-profit organizations such as hospitals. Standard costs have very important potential. They are a valuable aid in budget preparation for several reasons. (1) They are objectively predetermined. (2) They can assist management in measuring performance by comparing actual cost with planned standard cost. They therefore provide information that permits management to isolate and explain variations from plans. (3) They provide a useful means of valuing or costing inventory that is transferred out or carried from one period to the next. (4) They provide a dependable basis for pricing goods and services.

Table 8.2
Variance Report: Police Department

Activity	Item	Budgeted Costs	Actual Costs	Variance	Allowable Variance	Remarks
Field Inspections	Personnel	$100,000	$130,000	$30,000 (UF)	10%	Due to Overtime
Community Services	Materials	45,000	35,000	10,000 (F)	15%	Due to Reduced Price
Downtown Patrol	Supplies	5,000	7,000	2,000 (UF)		Due to Increased Price
	Totals	$150,000	$172,000	$42,000		

Note: F = Favorable
        UF = Unfavorable

Whether the objective standard (determined by rigorous engineering requirements) or the budgeted standard (amount appropriated by the authorizing body) is used, the responsibility center may regularly conduct variance analyses. A threshold point is established to permit top management to focus its attention only on those variances that exceed the threshold limits (see Table 8.2). This approach is similar to the management practice known as *management by exception* (only a deviation from a given threshold level [for example, an item that exceeds budgeted cost by 20 percent] is reported to management).

Resource Allocation. The allocation of resources to the most worthy alternative is a major goal of budgeting. The allocation criteria determine how limited resources are to be divided among alternative uses. If these criteria are defective it is likely that a maldistribution of government resources will result. Resources will go to some centers that should not receive them, while units that do need them may not get enough. This outcome denies the organization or governmental unit the best potential use of its scarce resources.

Accountability Instrument. The budget sets forth, in dollars, an agreement or compromise between the legislative and executive branches, and the administrative officials and relevant members of the community. In the non-profit sector a budget sets forth an agreement between the governing board and the officials of the agency. The programs provided for in the budget are targeted implicitly or explicitly to clientele and constituents over a specified time period. By means of the performance indicators included in the budget, an assessment can be made to determine whether the promised services and goods have been delivered at the time and place specified and in the manner, quality, and quantity desired.

By means of performance indicators (see Chapter 10 on performance measures), the budget permits managers to know whether they are using the same amount of resources to achieve more and better benefits for their clients and constituents or whether they are using a reduced level of funding to realize the same or better results.

In the final analysis, accountability can be most effectively accomplished only when the controlling instruments (the performance measurement system, i.e., the accounting, auditing, efficiency and economy, reporting, and evaluation systems) are directly linked to responsibility centers that are then pinpointed to key personnel responsible for delivering specific goods and services to the target population. Take, for example, the manager of the dietary service in a hospital. He/she oversees the performances of subordinates responsible for patient food service, the kitchen, the cafeteria, and so on. The manager of the dietary service is in turn accountable for his/her performance to the head of administrative services.

It may be useful at this point to briefly summarize the attributes of a good budget. A budget is a device to:

1. Indicate policy direction for a specified period of time

2. Explain the effects of budget requests on tax rate or charges

3. Explain the effects of intergovernmental relationships

4. Explain proposed expenditures of estimated revenues

5. Identify the level of services to be produced based on the projected revenue

6. Show the short-range and long-range consequences of reducing or eliminating goods and/or services

7. Facilitate control over expenditures

8. Communicate the objectives and expected standards of performance which will be compared with results

9. Motivate employees to achieve articulated objectives in their individual units

10. Aid in maintaining a monitoring system to assess performance of the various units and to provide timely feedback information on their progress

11. Assess the impact of goods and services on the target population

DEVELOPING THE BUDGET

Budgeting is an ongoing and dynamic process that is typically marked by regular phases: (1) planning, needs assessment, and priority setting; (2) preparation, including expenditure forecasting and development of performance measures; (3) legislative reviews of agency reports and appropriations; (4) execution of proposed programs; and (5) audit and evaluation of agency expenditures. Budgeting takes place in a context that is characterized by "deadlines, reports, hearings, policy reviews, and work experience and is deeply immersed in politics."[10] Figure 8.3 provides a schematic view of the dynamic context of budget making. Five phases in budgeting resource allocation are indicated. Each of the budget phases will be discussed here.

1. The community (the general public, clients, constituents, and other relevant groups) expresses what it wishes the government or agency to do or not do.

2. The gatekeepers receive the reports and compare them with available resources. Basing their conclusions on perceptions and on consultations with policy makers (executive and/or legislative officials), the gatekeepers accept, modify, or reject the requests.

3. The policy makers review the existing resources and evaluate the power and influence of the participating interest groups. Through a process of bargaining and mutual compromise, policy makers determine the distribution of available resources as a balance between the vote that they are likely to obtain at the next election and what they feel is in the best interest of the public. Non-profit agencies attempt to obtain the largest amount of resources the funding agencies can provide and the largest amount of fees that can reasonably be collected from users. The objective is to expand or at least to survive.

Figure 8.3
Budgeting Resource Allocation

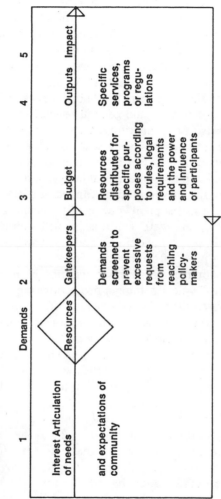

1	Demands	2	3	4	5
	Resources	Gatekeepers	Budget	Outputs	Impact

Interest Articulation of needs

and expectations of community

Demands screened to prevent excessive requests from reaching policy-makers

Resources distributed for specific purposes according to rules, legal requirements and the power and influence of participants

Specific services, programs or regulations

4. The compromises become the basis for the allocation of resources, resulting in a policy that specifies services, programs, and regulations.

5. The impact, i.e., the benefits and costs, on the target population is assessed and fed back into the system.

Despite the dynamics taking place in the allocation of resources, the emphasis is on maintaining the status quo. Few significant changes or innovations ever occur in budget making.[11] At the national level, neither the chief executive nor Congress has significant discretionary control over yearly expenditure because most of the budget is determined by previous commitments that are made at the federal level. These include programs such as Social Security and veterans' benefits. Additionally, there are required payments on outstanding contracts for public works and defense, interest payments on the national debt, and general revenue sharing.

Since in the budgets of non-profit agencies there tends to be no ironclad agreement that the funding agencies will continue to support recipient agencies, the budgets of those agencies are controllable. Once relationships have been established and the incremental budget system has been adopted, however, non-profit agencies tend to be funded as a matter of policy. Like public sector agencies, recipient non-profit agencies, especially those funded by United Way, cultivate relationships with volunteers, review committees, clientele, and corporate opinion makers in an effort to gain support for their claim for a piece of the budget pie.

The approach to budget preparation has not been marked by a high degree of uniformity. Typically, budget projections tend to represent historical priorities. Resource allocation is based less on planning than on control, as noted earlier. If non-profit and public sector agencies hope to improve their budget decisions they must find answers to questions like these: What amount of service is needed? What level of service can be produced? What is the desired level of service? How can the available resources be used efficiently to achieve the stated objectives? Can the service be better provided by in-house staff or by contractors? To better answer these questions, the planning process should precede the budgeting phase.[12]

In initiating budget development, factors such as the following should be considered: (1) the analysis of elements that affect public demand; (2) the constraints and limits on fiscal resources; (3) the extent to which federal, state, and other resources are available; (4) the adequacy of the current level of service; (5) the implications of population changes; (6) the political sensitivity of contemplated programs; and (7) the minimum standards of goods and services to be delivered to clientele and constituency.[13]

To aid rational decison making in the budget-making process, needs assessment, cost projection of services, and priority setting should be considered.

NEEDS ASSESSMENT

Needs assessment is the examination of the aggregation of observed and articulated desires, needs, and expectations of individuals, groups, and the community. Needs may be reflected in each community. Data may be obtained by observing conditions such as poverty, deterioration of bridges, and crime, and by evaluating direct feedback from clientele and constituents.[14]

To obtain reliable information on current needs, the following procedures should be followed: (1) The quality of available data at all levels of government—federal, state, and local—should be examined and the criteria for identifying the need should be established. (2) The policy statements of legislative and executive officials, position papers, the census, demographic information available from various planning agencies, departmental files, special studies on the target population, records of public hearings, and surveys conducted by other agencies (public, private) that may provide information regarding similar services should be analyzed.[15] These data should then be converted into specific demands for goods and services, suggesting the level and quality of services to be provided.

PRIORITY SETTING

Priority setting is a process by which an agency or entity articulates the functions or programs that are considered most important to the attainment of service objectives to be pursued during a coming fiscal period.[16] Priority setting is critical because of the scarcity of resources and the desire to optimize benefits. The director/manager of each responsibility center is responsible for identifying those programs that have the highest priority. This identification process may result in the shifting of resources among programs to improve an agency's ability to meet its objectives. For example, a district police station that experiences a sharp drop in crime or a hospital trauma center that has a significant decline in patients cannot continue to justify the same level of staffing; personnel should be shifted to other areas where they can be better utilized.

Priority setting is deeply immersed in values, especially in the public and non-profit sectors, where resource allocation is not based on the profit criterion. Priority setting may be an exceedingly difficult process. The outcome of such a process is greatly influenced by the ability to mobilize power and to exercise influence. The allocators determine what individuals, groups, or organizations will benefit, when they will benefit, and to what extent. Priority setting is easier when there are generally agreed upon norms and perceptions of the clients' and constituents' needs.

If economic rationality is a desired objective, the priority-setting process can be facilitated when participants in organizations or communities agree in advance to abide by allocations made on the basis of cost-effectiveness and/or a ranking process similar to the one employed in zero-base budgeting (ZBB) or a predetermined, objective rating scale. Such a scale could rate the functions of the agency in order of importance (the numbers 1 to 6 representing descending order). Next, each function may be rated numerically in order of importance, as shown in Table 8.3. If equity is the main objective to be maximized in Table 8.3, it is given the highest rating: 1. Similarly, the importance of community development permits it to be rated 1. Maximizing the equity objective while pursuing community development gives a matrix score of 1 (#1 equity rating × #1 community development rating), the highest priority rating possible. The rating of the neighborhood improvement objective as 6 and the rating of the transportation function as 5 provide a total matrix score of 30. When priorities are articulated in public and non-profit agencies, they can be most useful in executive budget making.

THE EXECUTIVE ROLE

The executive role in budget making in the public sector has been influenced by a cultural fear of executive power and a concern for accountability. These influences caused the establishment of a system of checks and balances which led to fragmentation in financial management until the reform movement of the late 1800s. The movement culminated in the introduction of state and local executive budgets (which make the chief executives of these governments directly responsible for preparing budgets, submitting them for approval, and administering the approved budgets). With the passage of the Budget and Accounting Act of 1921, Congress instituted the executive budget at the national level. The act created the Bureau of the Budget (now known as the Office of Management and Budget [OMB]) as an arm of the executive branch to assist in preparing the budget. The act gives the chief executive significant coordinating powers.

To further expand the powers of the chief executive, Congress passed the Employment Act of 1946, creating the Council of Economic Advisers as a direct counselor to the president. The main aim of the council is to assist the president in forecasting and controlling fiscal policies. Under the Employment Act of 1946, the Joint Economic Committee was also established to provide Congress with additional means for examining the premises on which the annual budget was prepared.

Over the past two decades many efforts have been made to improve the quality of the information used by the chief executive to make decisions. The introduction of the planning, programming, and budgeting system (PPBS) was the first major attempt in all levels of government to introduce analysis as an aid to decision making in the executive branch. This was followed by the introduction of the concept of management by objectives and

Table 8.3
Priority Setting Matrix

Maximizing Outcome or Objective	Rating	Government Functions					
		Community Development	Human Resources	Environmental Resources	Health and Safety	Transpor-tation	Legislative and Citizen Participation
Equity	1	1	2	3	4	5	6
Economy	2	2	4	6	8	10	12
Standard of Service	3	3	6	9	12	15	18
Service Improvement	4	4	8	12	16	20	24
Service Coordination	5	5	10	15	20	25	30
Neighborhood Improvement	6	6	12	18	24	30	36

Source: Adapted from Barry M. Mundt et al., *Managing Public Resources* (Stamford, Conn.: Peat Marwick International, 1982), p. 33.

zero-base budgeting (ZBB). Like PPBS, ZBB is aimed at assisting central management to better allocate scarce resources and control their use.

An examination of the attributes and functions of the executive budgets of chief executives at the federal, state, and local levels, as shown in Table 8.4, reveals few divergences. Thus it would be logical to conclude that the structure and operations of the executive budget at all levels of government are marked more by similarities than by differences.

Though seldom discussed, the physical location of the budget office holds particular symbolic and substantive implications for the allocation and control of available resources. At the federal level, the OMB is located in the Executive Office Building. In some states the executive budget office is located in departments of administration directly responsible to the governor. The state constitution of Missouri places the budget office in the Department of Revenue, but relatively early in this state's history the budget office was moved to the governor's office, where it remains to this day.

Local governments have experimented with a number of budget office locations. In some cities it is directly under the authority of the chief executive officer or of a comptroller, department of finance, or division of a department of management. In all cases, however, the responsibility for control and decision making resides with the chief executive or, as in metropolitan Toronto, Canada, with an executive committee.

In the non-profit sector, the executive budget is the norm, although it is not easy to make broad statements about this practice because of the variety of models found. Most often the executive director of the agency is given executive powers similar to those found in governmental units. He/she exercises those powers under the scrutiny of a finance committee. The interest, expertise, and activism of the committee members and/or the board determine the degree of vigilance.

Where an executive budget is the norm, executive influence over the budget process is pervasive. The chief executive's authority to recommend expenditure and revenues provides a powerful means for establishing the agenda and focusing attention on his/her preferred use for budget resources. Because of the dominance of the chief executive and his/her budget staff over budget matters, the chief executive exercises a monopoly over the information that is released to relevant publics and various participants in the budget-making process. As noted earlier, the budget is the primary tool with which to effect coordination and integration of agency or governmental activities. By means of the central administrative budget establishment as well as planning and management studies, the accounting control and personnel systems become closely integrated.

Functions performed by the administrative budget establishment include: (1) establishing policy direction guidelines and service levels; (2) overseeing the preparation of the budget; (3) reviewing, critiquing, adjusting, and approving expenditure reports; (4) developing revenue estimates; (5) con-

Table 8.4
Chief Executive Comparative Executive Budget Functions and Responsibilities

Attributes/Functions	Federal	State	Local	Non-profit
Balance budget requirements	no	yes	yes	yes
Staff is required to provide information/intelligence for better budget decision making	yes	mostly yes	mostly no	mostly no
Budget is effective coordinating instrument/extension of executive personality	yes	yes	yes	mostly yes
Executive is most visible political official	yes	yes	yes	no
Executive has exclusive power to prepare budget	yes	yes	yes	mostly yes
Executive authority to exercise item veto over approved budget or appropriation including:	no	yes	yes	no
- Allotment powers	yes	mostly yes	no	no
- Executive has problem with career bureaucrats	some	some	minimal	minimal
- Power over program execution	yes	yes	yes	yes
- Budget staff exercise strong management efficiency role	no	yes	yes	no

ducting economic research studies and salary surveys; (6) presenting proposals before legislative or review committees or boards (the latter in non-profit agencies only); (7) overseeing the administration of the budget; and (8) designing and implementing financial performance reports.[17]

Phase 1 above provides the chief executive with an opportunity, via the "call for estimates" and the transmittal letter, to put forth budget policy as specifically as possible. He/she will include at least the following: (1) a general budget outlook that reviews economic, social, and other critical factors likely to impact on the agency or governmental unit; (2) assumptions about revenue from general and other funds, indicating tax rates, and about projections, indicating budget targets; (3) projections of expenditures (especially those from the general fund), indicating "the likely increment and opportunities for program substitution and displacements";[18] (4) suggested changes and/or modifications in budget procedures; (5) contemplated changes in debt service policy and requirements; and (6) projected capital programs and special programs.

The budget timetable and specific procedures of budget making may differ significantly among units of governmental and non-profit agencies. All these agencies perform essentially the same functions in developing the budget document.[19]

Hospital-Generalized Budget Process Steps. The following are the steps in making a hospital budget:

1. The authorizing board of trustees sets the goals and objectives that will guide the institution during the coming period.

2. The hospital budget committee identifies budget guidelines, which are then approved by the hospital administration. Within this context, a number of internal and external factors, such as the following, are considered relevant to planned activities: how economic factors such as inflation may affect the budget; statistical assumptions regarding patient days; changes in building requirements; the introduction of new services; the number of procedures that must be followed by the laboratory and major departments such as radiology; outpatient visits; and proposed government legislation and regulations.

3. Budget packages are distributed to department heads or responsibility centers, who are also given technical assistance in preparing their individual budgets.

4. Departmental hearings are conducted. The budgets of responsibility centers are coordinated and reviewed; the hearings and promises agreed upon are summarized to assist controllers in future monitoring.

5. The budgets are approved and distributed to all department heads and responsibility centers.

The Executive Budget Cycle. Timetables for the completion of particular activities are especially important in public budgeting because designated times are typically established by statute and thus are legally binding. In addition, actions to be completed can have significant implications for resource allocation. For example, economic forecasts and revenue estimates may determine the level of spending within a program or whether the program can be undertaken at all.

The executive budget cycle timetable at the federal level is shown in Table 8.5.

THE LEGISLATIVE ROLE

As noted earlier, by identifying policy direction and preparing and formally presenting the budget to the legislature or authorizing body, the executive limits and determines the legislative fiscal policy agenda. The budget-making process is essentially the same at the legislative and executive levels of government and in non-profit organizations.

Typically, the presentation of the budget contains a budget overview, i.e., major economic and social assumptions and a summary of major issues. The budget document is presented in a clear and understandable manner. (1) Revenue estimates are broken down and identified by source. (2) Statements of proposed expenditures are detailed. Budget format is designed to set forth the purpose, cost, and expenditure source of each service. (3) Amounts requested by each department or responsibility center and recommended by the chief executive are identified. (4) Narrative statements justifying supporting requests are included.

At the federal and state levels, and to some extent in local governments, department heads are usually present during budget discussions to respond to legislative questions. However, department heads, especially of local government units, as a matter of strategy may be asked to stay out of sight unless requested to attend. The apparent operating premise is out of sight, out of mind.

The participation of citizen and interest groups in public hearings is an operating norm at all levels of government. Indeed, most states require local units to hold open hearings on the budget. But while some local governments encourage citizen participation in budget discussions, many make little effort to build a well-designed system that encourages such participation, despite the opportunities to promote better policies that such a system would offer. If due care is taken in designing and implementing a system of citizen participation, disruptions and delays in proceedings can be minimized.

Until recently, legislatures at all levels of government were unable to influence and to participate in budget making and fiscal matters to the same extent as elected chief executives (especially in those systems operating on the executive budget model). Because of minimal intelligence-gathering and lack of expert staff, members of these bodies have been limited to routine review and oversight. With the exception of a few states like California, there is no single head to coordinate and lead the legislative staff. Except in a few states and in most local governments, there is no systematic coordi-

Table 8.5
The Executive Budget Cycle

Actions to Be Completed	Dates
Develop economic assumptions (by Council of Economic Advisers); review forecasts of international and domestic situations; issue policy guidelines regarding the preparation of materials for review.	March-May
Determine initial planning figures and cost projections for the coming year; compare total proposed outlay estimates with revenue estimates; present fiscal policy, program issues and budget levels of the president.	
Establish general guidelines and agency targets for annual budget; issue internal annual budget estimates. President (through OMB) provides agencies with policy assumptions and budget planning target for each agency.	June
Assist agencies in developing detailed estimates.	July-September
OMB holds hearings to review agency budget requests. Economic assumptions and fiscal policies are reexamined in cooperation with the Council of Economic Advisers and the Treasury Department. Assumptions are discussed with the president, and recommendations to the president are made. Agencies are notified and recommendations are revised to reflect the president's decisions.	September-November
Again, review economic and fiscal outlook with the president in cooperation with the Council of Economic Advisers and the Treasury Department. Draft president's budget and transmit recommendations to Congress within 15 days after Congress reconvenes in January.	December-February
With the approved appropriations, the Treasury Department and the General Accounting Office sign appropriation warrants and forward them to agencies.	August-September

nation of revenue and spending bills. Typically, revenue and spending measures are parcelled out to a number of different subcommittees. The vacuum created by the legislature's fragmented management of fiscal policies has given the chief executive a dominant role in fiscal policy making. In most units of government, as many as 75 to 85 percent of all budget proposals are initiated by the chief executive or by the executive branch, over which the chief executive exercises control.

At the national level, the Congressional Budget and Impoundment Control Act of 1974 attempted to address the unequal influence exercised by the president vis-a-vis Congress. Until the passage of the act, uncertainty and virtual chaos characterized the congressional budget process. A major feature of the act was the creation of the Congressional Budget Office (CBO), which attempts to add greater rationality to the legislative policy-making process (see Table 8.6).

Prior to this act there was no coordinating committee in the House of Representatives or the Senate that was capable of considering the president's budget as a whole. When the executive budget reached Congress it was broken up and sent to a number of committees, as indicated earlier. Budgeting decisions were made without regard to their impact on the general economy. "No systematic procedure existed for resolving conflicts among authorizing, appropriation and tax committees on the basis of conscious congressional decisions related to the national goals and priorities."[20] As can be seen in the congressional budget cycle, the act created budget committees in both the House and the Senate that are responsible for developing priorities.

The CBO is headed by a nonpartisan official who coordinates the congressional budget staff in its functions as a research arm and as an aid to Congress in evaluating the president's executive budget. Congress is thus provided with the means for examining the premises on which the president's budget is based and for making independent projections regarding the deficit, employment, and the general state of the economy.

CONCLUDING OBSERVATIONS

This chapter has presented an overview of the functions, structures, and purposes of modern budgeting. It has stressed that budgets are multipurpose in that they can be used to achieve accountability/control, political, social, planning, and economic ends. The interplay among the executive, legislative, and other relevant groups in the budget process has been examined, with emphasis on how theory and practice are interrelated.

Table 8.6
The Congressional Budget Calendar

Actions to Be Completed	Dates
CBO submits first-year projection of current spending.	October 1 or soon thereafter
President submits current services budget, indicating projected spending for existing programs.	November 10
Joint Economic Committee provides budget committee with analysis of current services budget.	December 31
President submits his budget.	15th day after Congress meets In January.
Budget Committees conduct hearings and commence work on first budget resolution.	Late January-March
All legislative committees submit estimates/reports to the budget committees.	March 15
CBO submits report to budget committees.	April 1
Budget committees report first concurrent resolution.	April 15
Congress completes action on first resolution, providing new budget authority and new spending authority. (Until the resolution is adopted, neither the House nor the Senate may consider new budget or spending authority bills, revenue changes, or changes in the debt limit.)	May 15
Congress completes action on first appropriation and concurrent resolution on the budget.	May 15
Congress completes action on bills and resolutions providing for new budget authority and new spending authority.	7th day after Labor Day
Congress completes second concurrent resolution. Neither the House nor the Senate may thereafter consider any bill, amendment, or conference report that increases budgeting authority amounts or decreases revenues beyond amounts agreed to in the second resolution.	September 15
Congress completes action on reconciliation bill or resolution. Adjournment of Congress takes place only after it completes action on second resolution and reconciliation measure.	September 15
Fiscal year begins.	October 1

NOTES

1. Jerome B. McKinney and Lawrence C. Howard, *Public Administration: Balancing Power and Accountability* (Oak Park, Ill.: Moore Publishing Co., 1979), p. 319.

2. Mark Mills and George Starr, eds., *Readings in Public Finance and Taxation* (New York: Macmillan, 1972), p. 763.

3. Aaron Wildavsky, "Budgets as Compromise Among Social Orders" in Michael J. Boskin and Aaron Wildavsky, eds., *Federal Budget: Economics and Politics* (New Brunswick, N.J.: Transaction Books, 1982), p. 22. See also Marcus G. Raskin, ed., *The Federal Budget and Social Reconstruction* (Washington, D.C.: Institute of Policy Studies, 1978), p. XV.

4. Jerome B. McKinney, *Understanding ZBB: Promise and Reality* (Chicago: Public Policy Press, 1979), p. 2.

5. Charles L. Harper et al., *Financial Systems for Community Health Organizations* (Belmont, Calif.: Lifetime Learning Press, 1982), p. 122.

6. Robert Anthony and Regina Herzlinger, *Management Control in Nonprofit Agencies*, rev. ed. (Homewood, Ill.: Richard D. Irwin and Co., 1980), p. 328.

7. Ibid.

8. In many public and non-profit agencies, goals are not articulated but are implied based on the allocation of the budgeting resources.

9. Harper et al., *Financial Systems*, p. 130.

10. McKinney and Howard, *Public Administration*, p. 322.

11. Ibid.

12. Philip Rosenberg and C. Wayne Stallings, *An Operating Budget Handbook for Small Cities and Other Governmental Units* (Chicago: Municipal Finance Officers Association, 1978), p. 40.

13. Lennox L. Moak and Kathryn W. Killian, *A Manual of Techniques for the Preparation, Consideration, Adoption, and Administration of Operating Budgets* (Chicago: Municipal Finance Officers Association, 1962), p. 131.

14. Keith A. Neuber et al., *Needs Assessment: A Model for Community Planning* (Beverly Hills, Calif.: Sage Publications, 1975), p. 10.

15. Barry M. Mundt et al., *Managing Public Resources* (Stamford, Conn.: Peat Marwick International, 1982), pp. 24-25.

16. United Way, *APPBS Approach to Budgeting Human Service Programs for United Ways* (Alexandria, Va.: United Way of America, 1974), p. 18.

17. Moak and Killian, *Manual of Techniques*, p. 29.

18. Edward A. Lehan, *Simplified Governmental Budgeting* (Chicago: Municipal Finance Officers Association, 1981), p. 62. See also State of Massachusetts, *Approaches to Budget Preparation and Presentation* (Boston: division of Community Services, 1980), p. 23.

19. Hospitals may often break down their budgets differently, developing revenue, expense, operating, and cash budgets.

20. Committee on Economic Development, *The New Congressional Budget Process and the Economy* (New York: CED, 1975), p. 2.

CHAPTER 9

EXPENDITURE FORECASTING

Because of the many types of expenditures that must be projected in both the public and private sectors, there is no single, all-encompassing approach to the forecast of expenditures. No exotic mathematical model can be used to project expenditure with a high degree of accuracy. There is considerable evidence to support the view that simple approaches to projecting expenditures are as effective as the more sophisticated methods.[1]

This chapter examines a number of approaches that are employed in forecasting expenditures. First, traditional approaches used in budget development are examined. Then expenditure components, standard costs, the least squares method, multiple regression analysis, and controllable and uncontrollable costs are considered.

PROJECTING COST OF CURRENT SERVICES

Projecting the cost of existing activities is based on factors typically outside the agency's control, such as population changes; inflation rates as they affect items such as salaries, wages, benefits, materials, supplies, and contractual services; government mandates; existing staffing levels; discretionary and nondiscretionary expenditures emanating from policy commitments, such as the funding of pension benefits and subsidies; equipment replacement and repair schedules; capital costs, i.e., expenses associated with construction, operation, and maintenance; debt amortization; and lastly, volatile cost centers subject to unpredictable cost changes, such as municipal convention centers, which are typically affected by the cycle of the economy. The projections are guided by assumptions and constraints set down by top management (the president, mayor, or manager in the public sector; the board of governors or trustees in the non-profit sector).

The cost projection of current services serves several useful purposes. It provides continuity between present and future costs. It promotes the development of a dependable data base from which projections in each responsibility center can easily be made. Finally, it provides a dependable basis upon which to evaluate whether future services should be improved, expanded, or reduced.

APPROACHES TO BUDGET DEVELOPMENT: SOME GENERAL GUIDELINES

Moak and Killian have suggested several orientations that may be used as general guidelines in budget development.[2] The methods may be used singly or in combination with each other.

Open-Ended Budget. Managers who are given no explicit guidelines regarding budget amounts are allowed to submit whatever amounts they consider necessary to run the optimum program for the agency.

Fixed-Ceiling Budget. Unlike the open-ended budget, the fixed-ceiling budget is constrained by a dollar amount that is specifically stated for each department prior to the preparation of the budget. Thus, the budget may fall below the fixed ceiling, but it may not exceed it.

Work Measurement and Unit Costing. This approach requires that a measuring criterion be established to determine the number of products or service units to be generated. Based on the number of products or service units desired, the cost per unit can be determined and the budget projected.

Increase versus Decrease Analysis. This method is closely related to the popular incremental approach to budgeting. Cost projections are made by identifying the costs to be increased and decreased in comparison with the previous year's costs. The items so determined are analyzed and projected.

Priority Listings. This approach, especially the ranking phase, is akin to the zero-base budgeting (ZBB) approach discussed in Chapter 14, requesting projects in order of priority.

Shared Management Method.[3] This approach encourages top and bottom managers (middle- and lower-level managers) to share information and perceptions about the factors that are likely to affect expenditure projections. The shared approach allows top management to contribute its overall perception of the organization, while middle- and lower-level managers, for example in a health-care institution, contribute insight acquired through their greater sensitivity toward physicians' needs, desires, and priorities relating to such activities as laboratory tests, changes in radiological procedures, and physical condition of facilities. Additionally, middle- and lower-level managers will typically have knowledge about top management's short-range and long-range plans and strategies, especially if the management style in the organization encourages some degree of management involvement in the shared decision-making system. Shared decision making requires that both top and operating managers study and exchange their knowledge of the following key resources:

1. Historical data and trends relating to in-patient and out-patient days
2. Departmental goals and strategies
3. Governmental and third-party decisions; for example, changes in federal law that alter the age requirement for medicare eligibility, impacting on the number of in-patient days and causing changes in the reimbursement method
4. Outside competition; for example, the establishment of neighboring health care facilities (hospitals, health maintenance organizations, and clinics)
5. Other known facts or rumors[4]

Item-by-Item Control. Like the priority-setting method, this approach contains some of the attributes of ZBB, particularly as it relates to the emphasis on questioning and justifying the necessity and desirability of each item. But the item-by-item control method is more in line with the line item/object budget focus.

Alternative Proposals. Attributes of the ZBB system are very evident in this approach. Emphasis is put on the basic budget (indicative of the ZBB minimum-level practice as discussed in Chapter 14) and on the analysis of the consequences of pursuing each alternative (ZBB consequences of not undertaking a level of service).

Historical Analysis. Requests for nonpersonal service items are evaluated in terms of past experience and current trends.

Factorial Estimating. Making budget projections by this method involves virtually no discretion or judgment. Program units are clearly defined. Tables of organization and equipment are made up, providing a basis from which future requirements can be estimated.

Marginal Productivity Analysis. This approach emphasizes optimal use of scarce resources. Application of this method shows that successive resource increments yield increasing benefits only up to a point. Beyond this point each increment produces successively smaller (marginal) benefits or satisfactions, demonstrating that unlimited income is an inadequate reason for allowing unlimited expenditure on a large number of programs. The greatest total utility or satisfaction is realized when the application of resources is limited to a smaller number of uses (programs). Allocation of resources to alternative uses should be continued until the last additional increment of expenditure yields the same amount of additional satisfaction. The principle of marginal rule yields the following conclusions: (1) Given available resources, the magnitude or scale of an activity should be expanded as long as its net marginal yield is positive, and up to the point where its net marginal yield is zero. (2) When resource constraint does not permit an activity to be expanded to the zero-yield point, the activity should be expanded to the point where its marginal yield is equal to the marginal yield of the alternative.

An application of the marginal rule principle may be demonstrated in the case of police assignments. Assume that a study of the records of a police department reveals the data shown in Tables 9.1A and 9.1B. Assume additionally that a citation represents a reasonable output benefit (surrogate). A total of nine officers is to be assigned to Districts X and Y. Applying the marginal rule principle, District X would receive four officers and District Y five officers. Note that the five officers of District Y would yield a marginal benefit of eight, while District X would yield a marginal benefit of six. Therefore we assign five officers to District Y and four to District X, basing our decision on the marginal rule principle.

Applying Cost-Benefit Criteria. This approach, though not widely used, has potential. In the typical social service agency it is very difficult to identify any single factor that may be used as the criterion for making program selection. Since selection decisions must be made, a basis for making them while maintaining a degree of uniformity among decision makers is required.

The establishment of decision rules or selection criteria can be most helpful. Before the selection basis can be determined, the costs and benefits relevant to the programs must be estimated. Identification of the costs and benefits permits the display of data relating to each program, as shown in Table 9.2.

In Table 9.2, program alternatives, estimated costs, estimated benefits, benefit-cost ratio, decision rationale, and selection constraints for each decision are identified. Given the constraints, Alternative A is eliminated because it does not meet the minimum benefit constraint. Alternative C is accepted because it meets all the constraint factors.

The development and application of a particular criterion must depend on each individual situation. But once a decision rule system has been established, as shown in Table 9.2, it provides a useful method that permits a degree of decentralized budget making/decision making while maintaining a measure of central control.

EXPENDITURE: ANALYSIS OF MAJOR COMPONENTS

Personnel Services. These are the most important costs in public and not-for-profit organizations, amounting to more than 90 percent in some agencies. Close consideration must therefore be given to this input. Estimates of personnel services typically are based on one or more of the following: (1) experience in prior years; (2) workload trends; (3) staffing patterns as shown on the current organizational chart; and (4) guesstimates.[5]

Additional factors to be considered in estimating the cost of personnel services include:[6] (1) departmental manning tables (an assessment of the tasks/functions/duties of the personnel in each unit/subunit or responsi-

Table 9.1A
Marginal Cost Analysis—Police District X

Number of Officers Assigned	Total Citations	Average Citations	Marginal Citations
0	0	--	--
1	15	15	15
2	40	20	25
3	54	18	14
4	60	15	6
5	60	12	0
6	54	12	-6
7	49	9	-5

Table 9.1B
Marginal Cost Analysis—Police District Y

Number of Officers Assigned	Total Citations	Average Citations	Marginal Citations
0	0	--	--
1	12	12	12
2	26	13	14
3	39	13	13
4	48	12	9
5	56	11.2	8
6	60	10	2

Source: Adapted from James Snyder, *Fiscal Management and Planning in Local Government* (Lexington, Mass.: Lexington Books, 1977), p. 245.

Table 9.2
Program: Benefit-Cost Estimates

Alternative	Estimated Cost	Estimated Benefits	Benefit-Cost Ratio	Decision Rationale
A	$100,000	$150,000	1.50	eliminated due to minimum benefit constraint
B	$250,000	$225,000	.90	does not meet minimum efficiency constraint
C	$295,000	$475,000	1.61	meets benefit and efficiency constraints
D	$295,000	$310,000	1.05	does not meet efficiency constraint
E	$125,000	$190,000	1.52	meets minimum cost constraint and benefits constraints
F	$340,000	$510,000	1.50	exceeds maximum cost
G	$125,000	$175,000	1.40	does not meet benefit or efficiency constraints
H	$299,000	$511,000	1.70	provides maximum benefit and meets efficiency constraints
I	$280,000	$490,000	1.75	provides maximum efficiency and meets other constraints

Constraints: (a) Maximum budget $300,000
                     (b) Minimum benefit must be at least as great as program (E)
                     (c) Minimum efficiency must be greater than program (A)

Source: Adapted from James Snyder, *Fiscal Management and Planning in Local Government* (Lexington, Mass.: Lexington Books, 1977), p. 245.

bility center); (2) workload trends; (3) classification plans (defining position duties with the aim of reclassifying and/or allocating the duties to existing or new positions in the classification plan in cooperation with the central personnel unit and with the appropriate operating line official); (4) estimates of salary savings; (5) use of overtime and premium time; (6) management studies (conducted to coincide with the budget hearings to provide information that will assist in evaluating personnel requests); (7) sick leave and annual leave; (8) quality of the workforce; and (9) impact of new capital facilities.

While manning tables are confined to larger organizations, workload data are quite useful in smaller organizations because of the close relationship between the workload and the personnel needed for a particular job. Other factors that impact upon workload trends are: (1) new policies, or changes in existing ones; (2) commitments to program changes; (3) workload consolidation; and (4) changes in systems and/or procedures.

Salary Savings. For several reasons the budgeted salary figure and the actual salary figure seldom coincide. Examples of reasons are vacations, vacant positions, and time lags in hiring for approved positions. This lack of coincidence has led to the common practice of adjusting the salary amounts downward at periodic intervals. The experience of prior years is the major determining factor in calculating the current percentage of gross and unused personnel services adjusted for any known changes.

Overtime and Premium Time. A hallmark of effective management is the efficient use of human resource components. "Few operations move in such measured cadence that management can avoid some non-productive time or can avoid the necessity for overtime to help meet peaks in workload."[7]

Many view overtime as an evil to be avoided. However, overtime has long been associated with well-managed operations. The problem is to keep it in proper proportion and under control.

Contractual Services. The purchase of personnel services has become increasingly important in public and not-for-profit agencies. Some of the reasons services are purchased are summarized by the following objectives: (1) to minimize costs; (2) to obtain task specialization; (3) to control the growth of permanent staff; and (4) to lessen the pressures brought on by seasonal and unplanned increases in workload.

Materials, Supplies, and Equipment. Efficient management of an agency's materials, supplies, and equipment requires that acquisition, maintenance, and control systems be instituted that facilitate achievement of the purpose of the organization. Several key factors should be considered in assessing an agency's materials and supply needs: (1) existing inventory and agency policies in relationship to current conditions; (2) price levels; and (3) changing patterns in the use of materials and material requirements in the light of changing rules and methods aimed at producing the best results.

Budgeting for equipment from operating funds is concerned primarily with equipment replacement; however, some portion of the annual equipment budget for many departments represents a net increase in inventory of equipment. These two aspects should be considered separately at all stages of the budget process. Of course, the line of demarcation becomes obscure when the replacement item is a substantial improvement over the item replaced.[8]

The following should be established when the type, quantity, and quality of equipment necessary to achieve an agency's objectives need to be determined: (1) equipment replacement schedules; and (2) a dependable inventory system that includes the following information: (a) description and quantity of equipment on hand, (b) purchase data, (c) location of equipment, (d) condition in terms of number of operating hours and maintenance costs, (e) life expectancy, and (f) classification and code number.

Finally, the most efficient equipment replacement practices can be best achieved by clear policy development. Such policies should consider: (1) definition of the work to be performed, i.e., planned maintenance schedules; (2) permanent inventory and service records; and (3) inspection procedures to ensure and validate that an item definitely needs to be replaced.

EXPENDITURE FORECASTING USING STANDARD COSTS

It is generally agreed that the critical category in expenditure forecasting is personnel service costs because this category is the largest and most frequently affected by changes in such items as salary, fringe benefits, and authorized versus actual levels of staffing.[9] Since each personnel position is assigned an identification number, all cost data can be used to control personnel service costs, to determine seniority pay, and to permit the development of a longevity profile. The latter can be used to "tailor seniority pay as an incentive to minimize turnover to reduce salary costs by granting increases to groups that are projected to turnover frequently."[10]

Position can be used as the centerpiece for accountability information on all related personnel costs, providing a high degree of versatility. Data can be organized to serve a number of objectives. Unlike the traditional line-item categories (travel, material, and personnel costs), which conceal information about specific kinds of costs important to management decision making, the position technique permits any costs that are of interest to be identified. Examples of such costs are: costs that vary directly in proportion to the volume of products or services produced, such as tons of concrete needed to build a street; semi-variable costs; costs that vary, but not directly, in proportion to the volume or level of activity, such as the cost of maintaining equipment that requires varying amounts of periodic upkeep but not in proportion to the volume or number of service units produced by the equipment; and fixed costs—costs that stay the same regardless of the volume or activity level, such as depreciation expenditures. Once cost is captured and separated out, a standard cost system (one that determines the most desirable cost of completing an activity, given normal conditions) can be developed from which a budget projection can be made.

Standard costs projections may be developed as shown in Table 9.3.

Assume that a police department wishes to create three or more new beats. One police cruiser is required for every three officers or any portion thereof, at a cost of $10,500 plus $2,000 a year for maintenance. Additionally, the instruction fee per officer is $19,610. Up to forty new officers can be trained for the fixed cost of $36,000. A beat consists of twenty-four hours a day for seven days a week. Six officers are required. The component costs projection is shown in Table 9.3.

Table 9.3
Calculating Variable Costs

Personal Services:

Salary	$12,010	
Cost of Living	2,200	
Hospitalization	1,800	
Pension Contribution	2,300	18,310

Other Expenses:

Supplies	400	
Uniforms	350	
Physical Examination	250	
Administration	300	1,300

Total		$19,610

Type of Cost	Units		Standard Costs Per Unit	
Variable	6 officers	x	19,610	= $117,660
Semi-variable	2 cruisers	x	12,500	= 25,000
Fixed	Classroom Instruction		36,000	= 36,000
				$178,660

Three Beats Required:

Type of Cost	Units		Standard Costs Per Unit	
Variable	12 officers	x	19,610	= $235,320
Semi-variable	4 cruisers	x	12,500	= 50,000
Fixed	Classroom Instruction		36,000	= 36,000
		Total		$321,320

The standard costs approach offers much potential. It can be used to effect service reduction or expansion. If care is taken in projecting individual items, it provides reliable projections with greater ease than other methods. "Additionally, if elements of budget preparation are decentralized,"[11] this approach allows the central budget staff to quickly check the expense estimates developed by the operating units. Perhaps the greatest asset of this standard approach is that it enables management to change plans quickly to meet altered situations that often occur, especially in local government.[12]

Calculating the Standard Costs Requirement for a Laundry. The objective of creating any standard is to make it useful to those for whom it is intended. It is important that the standard be accepted by the users. The participation of the potential users in the design and development of a standard is therefore a crucial factor that should not be ignored. By participating in the design and development process, the future users are unconsciously selling themselves on the acceptability of the standard.

In determining staffing requirements, managers must contend with both full-time and part-time employees. Additionally, employees never work at 100 percent capacity. Part-time and full-time employees can be converted into full-time equivalent (FTE) employees (one FTE equals 2,080 work hours per year). Since employees cannot be cut in pieces, the employee staffing patterns must be determined in a step-variable or a production range, as shown in Figure 9.1.

Figure 9.1
Weekly Staffing: Laundry Department

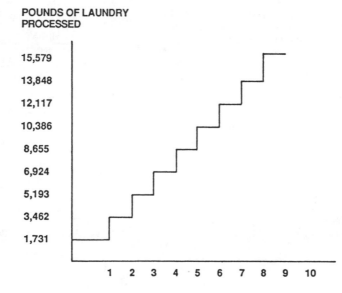

The calculation of the normal annual hours of the step-variable range, assuming that a laundry worker averages 90,000 pounds of laundry a year, is as follows:[13]

a.	Paid hours per week		40
b.	Weeks per year		52
c.	Annual paid hours (a × b)		2080
d.	Less benefit hours:		
	10 holidays × 8 hours	80	
	20 vacation days × 8 hours	160	
	7 sick days × 8 hours	56	
	Total benefit hours		296
e.	Normal annual work hours		1784

The hourly production standard for the average employee can be determined in the following manner:

$$\frac{\text{Total annual units per employee}}{\text{Total normal work hours per employee}}$$

$$= \text{standard per work hour} = \frac{90,000}{1,784} = 50.45 \text{ pounds per work hour}$$

The above may be summarized as follows:

Description	Yearly Standards	Weekly Standards
Pounds of laundry	90,000	1,731
Total weeks	52	1
Actual hours worked	1,784	34.31
Benefits allowed	296	5.69
Paid hours	2,080	40.00

Applying the data indicated above, we can convert paid hours into FTEs, as shown in Table 9.4

Once standard rates are determined, calculation of the budget becomes a simple matter, as shown in Table 9.5

Least Squares Method (Simple Regression). This is the most commonly used mathematical method for forecasting expenditure level or volume. The method is based on the assumption that if a straight line is fitted to time series data or to a graph, it produces a trend line that can be used to project future years' volume.

Table 9.4
Weekly Laundry Staffing Workload

Pounds of Laundry Processed	Actual Work Requirement	Paid Hours Requirement	FTE Requirement
1,731	34.31	40	1
3,462	68.62	80	2
5,193	102.93	120	3
6,924	137.24	160	4
8,655	171.55	200	5
10,386	205.86	240	6
12,117	240.17	280	7
13,848	274.48	320	8
15,579	308.79	360	9

Table 9.5
Projecting Dietary Budget Using Patient Days and Standard Rates, Bright Memorial Hospital

Cost Component	Standardized Rates	Computation	Budget*
In-patient days	NA	NA	95,000
Patient meals served	3.25 patient meals served per patient day	Patient days x standard = meals served 95,000 x 3.25	308,750
Person-hours paid	1.65 patient meals served per person-hour paid	Patient meals served / standard = person-hours paid 308,750 / 1.65	187,121
Salary expense	$3.15 average hourly rate	Person-hours paid x standard = salary expense 187,121 x $3.15	$ 589,431
Food expense	$1.15 per patient meal served	Patient meals served x standard paid expense 308,750 x $1.15	$ 355,063
Other non-salary expense	$ .30 per patient meal served	Patient meals served x standard = other non-salary expenses 308,750 x $ .30	$ 92,625
Total expense	$3.35 per patient	Patient meals served x standard = total expenses 308,750 x $3.35	$1,034,313

*Numbers are rounded to the nearest dollar

Hamburg indicates that the least squares method permits a line to be drawn through a series of plotted points in such a way that the sum of the squares of the deviations from the observed actual points above and below the trend line is at a minimum.[14] Thus, when the straight line is fitted to a set of data, the least squares method provides the "best fit" because the squared deviation is less than it would be for any other possible straight line (see Table 9.6).

Figure 9.2 uses a solid line to show the actual tons of garbage collected and a broken line to show the least squares trend. Examination of the graph reveals that the further the forecast extends beyond the middle year, the less accurate the trend becomes. Figure 9.2 and Table 9.6 illustrate the least squares fit to a progressive or advancing trend.

As already noted, the least squares method is based on historical data and simply projects the trend line according to the information available. Attention is not given to other factors and variables, such as holidays, weather conditions, and vacations. Weaknesses such as these must be compensated for in each individual situation by the manager's experience and judgment. Finally, the annual forecasts must be broken down to reflect monthly variations and seasonal trends as needed by each organization.

MULTIPLE REGRESSION ANALYSIS

Many of the problems associated with the least squares method, most of which are caused by the use of only one variable, may be overcome by the more sophisticated method of multiple regression analysis. Many variables that are likely to have an impact on future volume can be included in this method. Projection of the tons of garbage, for example, might include time series data such as the number of garbage trucks, the condition and age of each truck, the number of garbage collectors, the weather conditions during collections, the population density served, and the economic and educational background of the population served.

The multiple regression analysis method holds much potential for sophisticated analysis, but a thorough examination of it is beyond the scope of this book. Also, it cannot be overstressed that the objective of forecasting is not sophistication but rather the ability to make accurate projections given costs, benefits, political factors, and other constraints.

CONTROLLABLE AND NONCONTROLLABLE COSTS

For both program management and budget forecasting there must be a clear understanding of the specific costs that can be controlled and the specific times for controlling them. A controllable cost is one that can be restrained or changed by a responsibility center head. Ultimately, all costs are controllable in a relative sense at some level of the organization where

Table 9.6
Least Squares Formula

Let X = time deviation of each year from middle year

    Y = historical level or volume (e.g., tons of garbage)

Time series data are as follows:

Year	Tons of Garbage
1978	250,000
1979	255,000
1980	258,000
1981	261,000
1982	237,000

Year	Actual tons of Garbage	Time Deviation of Each Year From Middle Year	Square of X Deviation		Trend Ordinates (Expected Y Value)
X	Y	X	X^2	XY	Y
1978	250,000	-2	4	-500,000	251,000
1979	255,000	-1	1	-255,000	254,000
1980	258,000	0	0	-0-	257,400
1981	261,000	+1	1	261,000	260,000
1982	263,000	+2	4	526,000	263,800
Total	1,287,000	0	10	32,000	
Average	257,400				

Sum of XY divided by sum of X^2

    Let XY = + 32,000

        X = 10

$$= \frac{32,000}{10} = 3,200 \text{ annual increment}$$

The midpoint year, 1980, equals Q, with the average of 257,400 and annual increments of 3,200. Thus, to determine the trend ordinates, use the following method.

Year

1978   257,400 + (3,200 x -2) = 251,000

1979   257,400 + (3,200 x -1) = 254,200

1980   257,400 + (-0-   ) = 257,400

1981   257,400 + (3,200 x +1) = 260,600

1982   257,400 + (3,200 x +2) = 263,800

1983   257,400 + (3,200 x +3) = 267,000

1984   257,400 + (3,200 x +4) = 270,200

Figure 9.2
Fitting a Trend Line to a Progressive Trend Using Least Squares Method

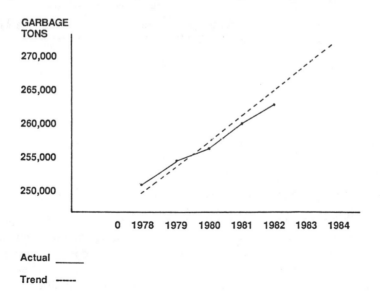

the specific authority to do so resides. Since we cannot directly affect uncontrollable costs, our discussion will be focused only on the controllable components.

Controllable and uncontrollable costs provide varying degrees of restraints and freedom of choice. Uncontrollable cost typically defines what the organization must do and cannot do.[15] These restraints and degrees of freedom emanate from statutes, regulations, federal, state, and local laws, funders' requirements, union contracts, and professional ethics.

Usually controllable costs provide greater leeway to exercise discretionary decision making. Among the factors that constrain controllable cost decisions are:

- agency goals and policies
- program objectives
- accountability and evaluation requirements
- sound fiscal procedures
- local situations: similar agencies and competition
- professional practices[16]

Controllable costs also offer opportunities to ameliorate restrictive factors. Discretionary decisions may be used to enhance program objectives and improve efficiency, working conditions, and staff and community relations.

Before cost projections are made, it may be helpful to identify all line-item costs in terms of three categories:

- fully controllable
- partially controllable
- fully uncontrollable

Once these identifications have been made a strategy for influencing the cost may be devised.[17]

CONCLUDING OBSERVATIONS

There is no one best way to project public and other not-for-profit organizations' expenditures. The sophisticated quantitative methods that have been devised to project expenditures have not been, to date, notably more successful than the manual, incremental, and piecemeal approaches which are still in wide use. A major reason for this concerns the political realities to which budget decision makers must give due cognizance.

If politics could be excluded from the expenditure equation, the calculation for each service unit would be a simple matter: service unit output measure × unit variable costs + service fixed costs = forecasted dollar amounts.

Finally, in public and other not-for-profit agencies understanding of controllable costs is an important input in making cost projections.

NOTES

1. Charles Harper et al., *Financial Systems for Community Health Organizations* (Belmont, Calif.: Life Learning Publications, 1981), p. 131.

2. Lennox L. Moak and Kathryn W. Killian, *A Manual of Techniques for the Preparation, Consideration, Adoption and Administration of Operating Budgets* (Chicago: Municipal Finance Officers Association, 1963), pp. 128-29.

3. Allen G. Herkimer, Jr., *Understanding Hospital Management* (Germantown, Md.: Aspen Systems Corp., 1978), p. 112.

4. Frank Maple, *Shared Decision Making* (Beverly Hills, Calif.: Sage Publications, 1982), chap. 4.

5. Lennox and Moak, p. 134.

6. Ibid.

7. Ibid., p. 135.

8. Ibid., p. 142.

9. Robert M. Cramer, "Local Government Expenditure Forecasting," *Governmental Finance* (November 1978): 4.

10. Ibid.

11. Ibid., p. 7.

12. Ibid.

13. Herkimer, p. 100.

14. Morris Hamburg, *Statistical Analysis for Decision Making*, 2nd ed. (New York: Harcourt Brace Jovanovich, 1977), p. 368.

15. Robert D. Vinter and Rhea K. Kish, *Budgeting for Not-for-Profit Organizations* (New York: The Free Press, 1984), p. 173.

16. Ibid., p. 175.

17. Ibid.

CHAPTER **10**

BUDGETING AS A
MANAGEMENT TOOL

The history of modern budgeting has been marked by a keen desire on the part of management to tightly control the expenditure of resources. In the private sector the control orientation was once marked by emphasis on financial accounting (concerned primarily with preparing and reporting financial information to various groups, including investors/stockholders and creditors, outside the agency). This contrasts with the more recent emphasis on management accounting, which is aimed at providing information useful for internal management decision making.

In public and other not-for-profit agencies, the control orientation emphasizes compliance with legislative and administrative mandates and with the mandates and regulations of other oversight bodies. The widely used line-item budget was developed to meet the control need. The emphasis in this type of budget is commonly on accountability in the narrow sense. Attention is focused on items such as travel, supplies, and personnel expenditure. The major objective is to prevent allocated funds from being stolen or expended for unauthorized purposes. Though the control orientation is still important in public and other not-for-profit agencies, the demand for better use of scarce resources has forced these agencies to seek more innovative approaches to the conservation of available resources.

This chapter emphasizes ways that the management decision-making role can be enhanced in allocating and managing scarce resources in public and other not-for-profit agencies.

DEVELOPING PERFORMANCE MEASURES

The development of performance measures (see Figure 10.1) is essential before monitoring can be established as a basis for effective evaluation of program execution.

Figure 10.1
Linkage Among Performance Measures

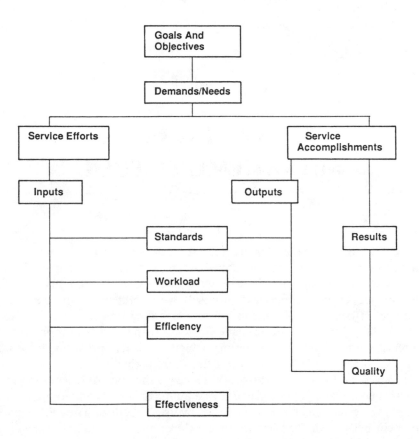

The development of performance measures is dependent upon what the controllers (those in authority, whether individuals or groups) view as important or useful in assessing the implied or articulated objectives of the budget. For example, in most budgets, goals and objectives are seldom articulated, and even when they are articulated they often remain unclear. When a budget identifies funds for a particular organization or responsibility center and allots so many dollars for supplies, travel, repairs, and utilities, the implied objective is to control the amount of money to be spent on each. As noted earlier, this control orientation is known as dollar accountability.

Once the goals and objectives have been established, the development of performance measures is the next logical step in determining how well the goals and objectives have been articulated. This facilitates the formulation and design of performance measures.

Performance measurement implies an evaluation of the possible consequences of directing resources to one use rather than another. It promotes effective resource allocation because it allows decision makers to see what different uses of resources are likely to achieve. For example, the achievement of a welfare agency's goal to remove unemployed fathers from welfare dependency and the achievement of a health care agency's goal to reduce the incidence of lead poisoning among children can be measured using information showing the welfare agency's costs and its success rate in removing fathers from welfare dependency versus the health care agency's costs and success rate in reducing the number of children hospitalized and/or the mortality rate from lead poisoning. Policy makers are thus provided with a rational basis upon which to make decisions. Performance measurement can be used to promote the improvement of operations and output, to develop and control budgets, and to effect individual and organizational accountability. There are several general types of performance measures. The most common include need or demand measures, workload measures, efficiency/productivity measures, and effectiveness measures. The attributes of these performance measures are shown in Figure 10.2.

Demand measures highlight the need for a given public service. The measure indicates the scope and magnitude of a problem. Examples of demand measures include number of restaurant inspections required, number of citations and arrests to be made, number of patient days, number of people to be served, number of manuscripts to be submitted for publication, number of school children in need of inoculation against childhood communicable diseases, and number of burglaries in residential districts. Demand measures provide responsible officials with an important aid in understanding why particular services are needed.

Workload measures can easily be developed from demand measures. While demand measures identify what needs to be done, workload measures indicate the amount of work to be performed on a given activity for a specific period of time. Based on the required workload, resources needed to realize the activity can be determined.

Workload measures are the most widely used performance indicators in public and other not-for-profit agencies because they are easily quantifiable and readily understood by the public and by service recipients.

In normal operations planning, workload measures are used to project staffing requirements, to develop plans, to prepare budgets, and to "establish work schedules and measure and evaluate operational output and efficiency."[1] Workload measures can assist management by showing trends in work performance from one time period to the next. For example, take the night patrol activity of a police department. Knowing the number of hours spent on patrol from period to period provides a basis for ascertaining and

Figure 10.2
Attributes of Performance Measurement

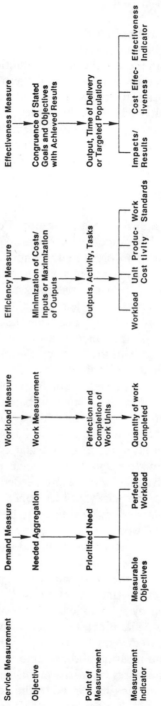

Source: Some ideas are drawn from Alan Walter Steiss, *Management Control in Government* (Lexington: Mass.: Lexington Books, 1982), p. 221.

monitoring the amount of work being done by particular patrol teams. Moreover, the work performed can be compared with standard hours to determine what unit amount of time each officer or team needs to prepare standard budgets and work schedules.

Workload measures are operation indicators that typically provide little qualitative information.[2] They are often nonfinancial expressions of products or services produced. Examples include miles of street built in a given period, number of automobile licenses issued, number of welfare recipients visited, number of garbage pickups made, and number of examinations administered. An operations indicator may be expressed in financial terms, such as the amount of federal assistance to minority business programs, including grants, loans, and gratuities, from $X in 1980 to $X in 1982. Workload measures are not very useful in determining to what extent stated needs are being met. As noted earlier, they are often used because they are simple and easy to understand.

Efficiency measures define the relationship between resources (money, personnel, materials, and capital) and outputs. The concept suggests the organization of resources for the purpose of carrying out a program, activity, or function at minimal cost.

Efficiency measures indicate the amount of service output in comparison to the input required to produce it. They provide managers with insight on how allocated resources are being used. For example, the number of inspection hours per health inspector, the number of nursing staff hours (inputs) per patient, and the number of patrol hours per patrol officer indicate how much time these personnel are spending on administrative assignments or duties other than their main tasks.

A major problem in the use of efficiency measures is that they are often considered interchangeable with workload measures. Thus it is not uncommon to find that workload measures are used to justify budget requests. The brief descriptions of types of efficiency measures that follow may aid in understanding how they are applied.[3] (1) The efficiency measure most widely used in public and other not-for-profit agencies is the *input-output ratio*, which permits the use of workload as a unit of output—for example, the number of tons of garbage collected per employee. (2) The *output-input ratio* (emphasizing effectiveness), though helpful, is seldom used. This indicator not only reports the cost of producing a product or delivering a service but also tells whether the product or service is acceptable or satisfactory. For example, it is not enough to arrest suspected burglars; it is also important to know the percentage of burglars that are convicted. (3) The *equipment and personnel utilization ratio* shows the extent to which an important resource is in service. Typically, this ratio shows a resource's available hours versus the hours it is actually in use or the percentage of time it is utilized. (4) The *relative change measure* permits the tracking of the percentage of increase or decrease in productivity from one period to another or from a selected base period (usually given a value of 100), providing a measurement of relative rather than absolute change. For example, suppose 3,000 potholes were patched in the base year and 3,500 in the succeeding year. This gives a productivity index of 3500 ÷ 3000, or 116.67. Assuming that there was no change in resource inputs during the base period and the succeeding years, the change reflects a 16.67 percent increase in productivity. (5) Input efficiency (one input, such as cost of labor, is compared to total staff hours) is used widely, especially in public and other not-for-profit agencies that have large personnel service costs. For example, the input efficiency ratio for the mental health/mental retardation program would be total costs divided by total staff hours.

Effectiveness measures show the degree to which program objectives have been achieved in terms of quality. Effectiveness indicates the congruence between legislative intent or policy objectives and the actual achievement of the program or function designed to achieve them. The measurement of effectiveness includes the concepts of adequacy (how well the identified needs are met) and responsiveness (how the services are provided and whether they are convenient or timely). Effectiveness measures are the most critical factors in program evaluation and cost-benefit analysis. Their objective is to measure directly the benefits or service delivery to the target population. Examples are the percentage of reduction in air pollution following a new enforcement program; the degree to which the rate of arrest of individuals enrolled in a criminal justice rehabilitation program has decreased; the average amount of time and the minimum number of errors involved in operating a computer system; and the average police response time to emergency calls.

Effectiveness measures have a number of functional uses: (1) program planning, i.e., defining the intended results of a given use of resources; (2) defining management operation, i.e., showing to what degree services are achieving their objectives; (3) evaluating, analyzing, and developing program standards with which performance audits can be compared; (4) establishing targets that enable the monitoring of employees, organizational units, responsibility centers, and contractors.[4]

Ideally, all four performance indicators should be used to evaluate each activity. Since this will not always be possible, especially in human service activities, it is highly desirable that performance measures be related directly to needs as much as possible. It is clear from the foregoing discussion that all performance measures are logically linked, as shown in Figure 10.3.

BUDGETING AND PRODUCTIVITY

Defining Productivity. The most generally agreed upon definition of productivity views it as a ratio of outputs (goods and services produced) to inputs (money, materials, and labor). Productivity measures show how well resources are expended in accomplishing stated objectives. According to Mali, "Productivity is a measure of how well resources are brought together in organizations and utilized for accomplishing a set of results. Productivity is reaching for the highest level of performance with the least expenditure of resources."[5] Because productivity focuses on ways or means of delivering goods and services at the least possible cost, process (precisely how resources are transformed into outputs) is a major concern in pursuing it. For example, a Rolls Royce may be used to deliver meals-on-wheels to elderly residents over a four-block area. While this use of a resource achieves the mission effectively, it results in the misallocation of resources because of the unnecessarily high unit cost of delivering the meals.

Productivity may be viewed as a combination of effectiveness and efficiency when there is equal concern for the quality and the quantity of services/goods to be produced. In this situation, productivity, efficiency, and effectiveness are inextricably linked. In determining how well resources are being utilized, a comparison can be made between the volume of the results produced (output effectiveness) and the volume of resources consumed (efficiency). The following is a formula for determining the productivity index.

$$\text{Productivity Index} = \frac{\text{Output Obtained}}{\text{Input Expended}} = \frac{\text{Achieved Performance}}{\text{Resources Consumed}} = \frac{\text{Effectiveness}}{\text{Efficiency}}$$

To enhance productivity, it is necessary to develop measurable indicators for output (performance achievement) and input (resources consumed). Where measures cannot be developed for outputs and inputs, the organizational process should be reorganized to facilitate measurement.[6] Calculating the productivity ratio requires the identification of the output and input measures. When these two measures are lacking, productivity cannot be analyzed and the productivity index cannot be developed. To calculate the productivity index, assume the following:

Assume the *goal* is cost reduction and the *performance objective* is to reduce costs from $30,000 to $15,000 by December 31. The *performance standard* is satisfactory only if costs are not greater than $15,000 per year. To achieve the performance standard, enhanced techniques will cost $1500. Applying the productivity formula, we find that:

$$\text{index} = \frac{\text{output}}{\text{input}} = \frac{\$15,000}{\$1,500} = 10$$

Setting priorities and establishing a performance measurement system provides a solid basis on which to effect productivity improvement.

Demand/need, workload, efficiency, and effectiveness are used to determine productivity. While Figure 10.3 shows a general schematic representation of input/output linkage, Figure 10.4 shows a more specific measurement linkage of social services, fire protection and police patrol functions.

Figure 10.3
Schematic Input/Output Linkage of Performance Measures

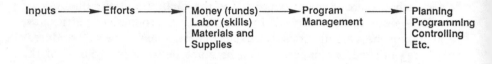

Figure 10.4
Examples of Performance Measure Linkages

Function	Demand/Need	Workload	Output
Social Services	No. of cases requiring services	No. of cases to be served	No. of cases served
Fire Protection	No. of places requiring inspection	No. of inspections to be made	No. of inspections made
Police Protection	Emergency call and no. of burglaries	No. of patrol hours- beat -drive No. of arrests made (clearance)	No. of patrol hours; No. of arrests

Examination of Figure 10.4 reveals the following: (1) Demand/need indicates quantitatively how much work clients and constituents require to meet their articulated needs and desires. (2) Workload indicates quantitatively the amount of work necessary to carry out a given activity. (3) Output represents the amount of goods produced or services provided in the day-to-

Efficiency	Effectiveness	Goal
Cost per case served	Percentage of eligible cases served	Ability to provide for individual needs
Cost per Inspection made	Dollar amount lost due to fire	Fire Prevention
Cost per patrol hour; Cost per citation issued	Dollar lost due to crime; Cost per degree of security experienced by resident	Crime Prevention

Table 10.1
The Goal/Objective Performance Measure Linkages

Department: Traffic Safety

Program: School Guards

Goals:

1. To provide for the safety and welfare of all school children walking or riding buses or bicycles to school.

2. To maintain order at school bus stops and to file written reports on motor vehicle violations that threaten the safety of school children.

Objectives:

1. To provide each school guard trainee with at least 20 class sessions.

2. To provide for the safety and control of children entering and leaving school buses.

3. To provide bicycle safety talks at local schools.

4. To reduce reported motor vehicle violations involving school children by 10 percent.

| | Objectives | | |
Demand Measures	Prior Year	Current Year	Projected Budget
Number of complaints from concerned parents about the lack of school guards at unattended school crossings	100	90	140
Number of accidents involving school children entering and leaving school buses	115	192	200
Number of dangerous street crossings at new school location	475	510	580

Number of safety prevention classes to be conducted for school children	40	75	120

Workload Measures

Number of school guard training classes conducted	150	165	192
Number of school guards attending the training classes	NA	NA	NA
Number of hours spent watching children entering and leaving school buses	105	110	90
Number of hours in hearings	250	375	420

Efficiency/Productivity Measures

Number of school guard training sessions conducted per officer	10	11	12
Average cost per training class	$205	$200	$195
Number of bicycle talks presented per officer	29	25	28
Average cost per bicycle talk	$48	$50	$43
Average number of accidents involving children entering and leaving buses	14	15	10
Average number of motor vehicle violations reported per school guard	85	98	50
Average cost per report filed	$53	$75	$45

Impact/Effectiveness

Degree of satisfaction with school guard training classes	NA	NA	NA
Number of accidents involving school children entering and leaving school buses reported	5	6	1

181

Table 10.1 (continued)

| Percentage of increase or decrease in bicycle accidents reported | 15% | 20% | 5% |
| Percentage of decrease in motor vehicle violations involving school children reported | 75% | 85% | 95% |

Budget Costs*

Prior Year	Current Year	Projected Budget	Over/Under Current Year	Explanation
$189,000	$225,520	$251,520	$36,000, mainly for new officers' training and for overtime report writing.	

*All of these amounts can be broken down by objects of expenditures.

day activities of an agency without considering the quality of the work performed. (4) Efficiency is the ratio of inputs to outputs. It identifies the cost required to achieve identified objectives. In an examination of efficiency, attention is directed to such questions as the following: What is the cost per fire inspection? What is the cost per patient examined by the outpatient department? What is the cost per ton of garbage collected? Emphasis is directed to the process of converting inputs into outputs. (5) Effectiveness attempts to match the stated goals with the achieved or actual results. The greater the match (congruence), the more effective is the result.

In Figure 10.4 if all the social service clients are satisfactorily served, the match between stated and actual results is perfect and effectiveness is maximized. In the case of fire protection, no losses from fire means that maximum effectiveness has been reached.

To be most useful as a productivity instrument, the budget must be closely linked to the management decision-making process. The development of a performance measurements system as shown in Figure 10.4 and Table 10.1 produces an important framework that can be used to enhance productivity. The management decision-making process involves the following: (1) articulation of the community's needs and goals and the specification of policies to meet those needs; (2) specification of service objectives designed to meet the service level; (3) determination of the desired organizational and procedural changes; (4) provision for a performance monitoring system; (5) evaluation of results and initiation of the action necessary to bring about the improvement (see Figure 10.5).

Figure 10.5
Management Process Activity Flow

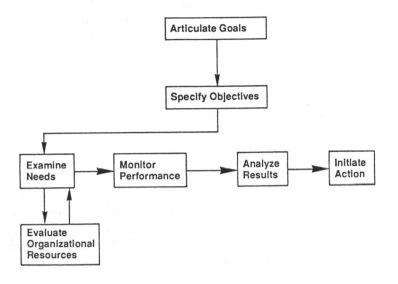

Once management decides that it will use the budget to actively promote productivity, the process must be institutionalized. The management information system must be designed to generate the kind of performance measures that will be emphasized in the controlling, monitoring, planning, and management decision-making processes. The performance measures developed can be used to aid budget justification and to facilitate variance analysis.[7]

Instituting Performance Measures: Some Practical Concerns. Because the use of performance measures in government and non-profit agencies typically means giving up old habits and modes of decision making, the time frame for the implementation of productivity measures should be based on each organization's situation. Some agencies may take several months to implement productivity measures, while others may require five years or more.

The introduction of a productivity system may take place as follows: (1) The agency or unit that appears most receptive and capable is singled out; (2) line managers are involved in the development of appropriate productivity measures; (3) the central staff is allowed time to assist managers in formulating performance measures; and (4) performance measures are linked to specific services identified in the budget.

Besides the benefits that performance measures offer, they can also produce other unintended consequences. They tend to make managers concentrate their energies more on those programs that are easy to measure. Because final results-effectiveness or quantitative factors are harder to measure, much emphasis in public and other not-for-profit agencies is put on intermediate output, such as the number of food inspections made by a health department inspector, the number of inoculations given, or the number of grant proposals completed. Performance measures are often resisted by managers who fear being evaluated on the basis of results over which they have little or no control. Often managers fail to understand the linkages between the different kinds of measures. For example, a fire department that inspects buildings with the aim of minimizing or eliminating fires may fail to accept responsibility for inspected buildings that are subsequently destroyed by fire. If the linkage cannot be made in a case such as this, then no more resources should be provided for carrying out the inspection activity.[8]

CONCLUDING OBSERVATIONS

The steps involved in the development and use of performance measures in the budgetary context have been emphasized. Throughout the chapter, attention has been focused on how budget performance measures are linked to each other and how these performance measures provide useful insight in assessing program results and accountability in public and other not-for-profit organizations.

NOTES

1. Barry M. Mundt et al., *Managing Public Resources* (Stamford, Conn.: Peat Marwick International, 1982), p. 14.

2. Robert G. May et al., *A Brief Introduction to Managerial and Social Uses of Accounting* (Englewood Cliffs, N.J.: Prentice-Hall, 1975), p. 72.

3. Mundt et al., *Managing Public Resources*, p. 16.

4. Ibid., p. 21.

5. Paul Mali, *Improving Total Productivity* (New York: John Wiley and Sons, 1978), p. 6.

6. Ibid., p. 7.

7. John R. Hall, *Factors Related to Local Government Use of Performance Measurement* (Washington, D.C.: Urban Institute, April 1978).

8. Allan R. Drekin, "Criteria for Performance Measurement in State and Local Government," *Governmental Finance* 10 (December 1980): 4.

CHAPTER 11

CAPITAL BUDGETING

The need for capital budgeting arises in public and other not-for-profit organizations because it is not always possible to find sufficient revenues to accommodate capital needs. Factors which have contributed to this condition include increased demands for service, upward pressures on costs due to inflation, the cutback/retrenchment movement in the public sector, revenue-raising limitations (e.g., Proposition 13 in California), and resources for not-for-profit agencies. The heavy expenditures that are usually needed for capital outlays cannot always be met by the popular pay-as-you-go method, which encourages a governmental unit or agency to spend no more than the revenues available for a specific fiscal period. This principle minimizes unwise or premature commitments of resources and avoids the interest payments and other related costs associated with debt financing, thus enhancing the entity's credit rating.[1]

Despite the public's acceptance of the pay-as-you-go approach, there are a number of problems associated with it. Current taxpayers pay for projects or investments from which they will only partially benefit. On the other hand, the argument can be made that in the interests of equity people should pay for capital facilities during their life span only as they benefit from them. When public agencies engage in long-term borrowing, current taxpayers are relieved from paying portions of their immediate tax burden, deferring it to future generations.

Unlike the business world or other levels of government, the federal government does not manage its capital facilities. There is no effective national capital improvement plan. In fact, the federal government maintains no capital budgeting system or procedure. Most federally owned facilities "are deteriorating and the Government is faced with the prospect of either repairing or rehabilitating them, or risking a staggering replacement burden in the future."[2]

This chapter examines the capital budgeting processes, financing approaches, and techniques for ranking and selecting capital projects. Throughout, stress is put on successful as well as unsuccessful practices.

DEFINING CAPITAL BUDGETING

A number of terms are used interchangeably to refer to capital budgeting, such as public works planning, capital improvements planning, capital facilities planning, and capital outlay planning. The use of so many terms creates confusion about the definition of capital budgeting. Most often the term refers to the legislative plan for proposed capital outlays and the means of financing them for the coming fiscal period. The capital budget is often a part of the regular budget. When a capital facilities or program improvement is in operation, the capital budget will be the first-year component.

Capital Facilities/Program Improvement. This is a plan made up of capital expenditures (the purchase of assets to provide service for many years) to be incurred over a specified number of years in order to accommodate capital improvements set forth in a long-term work program. Each project or planned expenditure is sequentially and specifically identified according to a schedule of priorities which sets forth the full estimated resources available to finance the projected expenditures. Typically the projects are large, permanent, or fixed, with a life range of fifteen to twenty years, and involve nonrecurring expenditures aimed at providing new or additional services. The construction of a public health clinic or a swimming pool is an example of a capital expenditure. Salaries, supplies, or minor equipment replacement are operational expenditures includable in the yearly budget.

All recurring expenditures should be excluded from the capital improvement program (CIP). The following are suggestions to guide financial managers in developing the CIP: (1) that capital items have a life span of three years or more; (2) that acquisition cost be $5,000 or greater; and (3) that all capital items "paid for from the proceeds of long-term debt [be] included."[3]

Unlike the public sector, the business world tends to favor putting as many items in the capital area as possible to take advantage of the tax break.

CAPITAL BUDGET PROCESS

The capital planning and programming role of the chief executive varies according to statutory requirements and the size and type of government.

Typically the chief executive guides the capital planning and programming process and makes recommendations to the legislature. The guidelines for preparing and submitting the capital plan are determined by the legislature, which establishes the time frame for the program, project, or activity, extent of citizen participation, and administrative responsibilities for the capital planning process.[4] In recent years, outside experts have been used to advise agencies on financing options. Additionally, interdepartmental committees have been used to review and rank projects, while citizen advisory committees and citizen surveys, such as the type that is conducted in Dayton, Ohio, are used to facilitate community input into the capital planning process.

Implementation of the capital planning process traditionally has been carried out by the planning departments or the central budget staff. These departments normally play the lead role due to their access to data (e.g., population, land use, transportation, and economic base statistics). This provides the basis upon which to relate community plans. Infrequently, the public works department may be given the capital planning coordination responsibility. The authority to analyze the financial implications and impact of the capital program on the operating budget and to make recommendations on financing approaches is assigned to the finance department. Where a planning commission exists, its main responsibility is to review capital project requests and make recommendations regarding them.

Benefits of CIP. A number of important results flow from an effectively planned and executed CIP. They include the following:

1. It forces communities to examine their goals and needs capabilities.

2. It promotes greater efficiency in the use of tax resources.

3. It provides an important guide to aid the growth and development of the community.

4. It encourages governments or organizations to improve their administrative systems.

5. It is an important means for promoting regional cooperation.

6. It facilitates and promotes sound financial management.

7. It offers an effective way to replace or repair capital facilities.

8. It enhances the governmental unit or organization's opportunity for participation because of the many programs that federal and state governments maintain to aid in the planning and construction of the infrastructure.

There are many differences among governmental units, as the General Accounting Office (GAO) found in its assessment of capital budgeting in public and private organizations throughout the country. The GAO stated that it could not find a comprehensive, precise discussion of the critical elements of a capital budgeting process anywhere in the literature. Thus the process described here is a compression of a number of suggested processes. Among the basic steps that should be followed in the formulation of the capital budget are the following:

1. Inventory and assess the existing condition of the infrastructure, establishing short- and long-term physical needs.
2. Develop alternative projects to meet short- and long-term needs.
3. Select alternatives and establish priority classification for short- and long-term needs.
4. Estimate the required resources and short-term funding allocation.
5. Assess the impact on the governmental organization's financial policies.
6. Establish a monitoring system; control work schedules and financing.
7. Initiate a replacement and maintenance strategy.

Though procedures vary among governmental jurisdictions, the chief executive traditionally oversees the capital budgeting and planning process and makes recommendations to the legislative body.

The capital budget process begins with the development of the capital improvement program. This involves the identification of projects that will meet the entity's needs for a specified number of years. The vast majority of projects are identified by government agencies, though private organizations may make suggestions. Each project submitted is accompanied by a supporting rationale setting forth cost data and a justifying narrative.

Planning departments or central budget offices typically direct the capital budget planning process. While these departments sometimes review the initial submissions, planning commissions usually perform these functions and make recommendations. In carrying out the review of the proposals, interrelationships are determined, costs are evaluated, and priorities are identified. As part of the review of the screening process, schedules for the proposed implementation of the projects are synchronized to minimize foul-ups and wasteful use of resources (e.g., surfacing streets before laying sewage and drainage systems). In addition, projects that can be reasonably postponed are identified.[5]

The Capital Improvement Plan (CIP). This may be viewed as an instrument through which a community lays out its short- and long-term physical growth and development plan. Ideally, the CIP is linked to the community's master and fiscal long-term (ten-twenty year) plans,[6] identifying public improvement needs. The CIP is essentially "a schedule listing capital improvements, in order of priority together with cost estimates and the proposed method of financing them."[7] CIPs are subject to constant changes. Each year, the CIP is reviewed and updated with regard to the changing needs and priorities of the community or organization. By means of the CIP the following activities are undertaken:

1. Projects (e.g., library, community center) are scheduled over a five to six year period.
2. A budget is developed for high-priority projects.
3. A revenue policy is developed for projected improvements.
4. Departmental activities are coordinated to meet project schedules.
5. A system is developed to monitor, evaluate, and inform the public about the proposed capital improvements.

Three documents emanate from or are closely related to the CIP. The first is the capital improvement budget, representing the first year of the CIP as approved by the appropriate legislative body or board, which authorizes required funding to defray the cost of the improvements. The second is the annual operating budget, whose relationship to the CIP is significantly influenced by the way in which projects are implemented. The CIP is usually adopted prior to the completion of the annual operating budget to allow the capital improvement budget to be incorporated into the annual operating budget. This facilitates the linkage "between the CIP and the annual budget and appropriation process used by the community,"[8] as shown in Figure 11.1. Note that the CIP programming approach is not a mandated process in most communities. Thus, though it is highly undesirable to ignore the CIP programming approach, most communities may institute a capital projects plan as long as they meet the legal requirements.

Priority Setting. Priority setting is a necessary activity because the scarcity of resources does not permit a community or an organization to undertake all of the projects that it would like to implement. The agency charged with developing the capital budget can provide invaluable assistance to operating department heads in pinpointing cost projections.

The agency staff can stress the importance of long-range needs, interpret instructions, and complete the forms required to promote uniform application of policies and procedures. In addition, a number of officials (e.g., budget director, city engineer, and city attorney) may be needed to answer questions such as the following:[9]

1. In what ways and to what extent will the proposed project impact on general city or government development?
2. Who will be benefited or hurt by this project?
3. Is this project a replacement of an existing structure or a new, added responsibility to government?
4. Will the project expand the taxable property and economic base of the community? That is, what will be the impact on existing revenue (increase, decrease, or neutral)?

5. What effect will the project have on the efficiency and cost-effectiveness of service performance?
6. Can the city or governmental unit afford the proposed capital improvement?
7. Will the project be a revenue producer?
8. What is likely to be the extent of citizen and/or political opposition?

Figure 11.1
CIP Linkage with Capital and Operating Budgets: Conceptual View

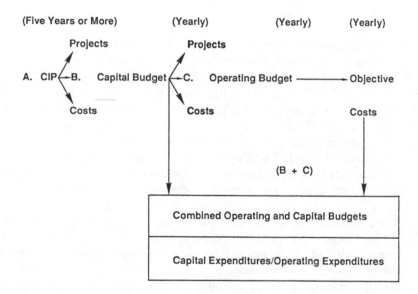

In the priority-setting process, an initial review should be conducted to eliminate proposals that appear obviously impractical to implement during the ensuing period. Once this is done, simple and precisely defined selection criteria should be established to enhance the community or organization's present and future financial viability. Perhaps general criteria such as the following for a CIP priority system may be employed:

Rank	Category	Applicable Criteria
1	Urgently needed a year or less	Immediate implementation to relieve danger to public health, welfare and/or safety.
2	Necessary or essential 2 to 3 years	Complete projects to bring about major improvements, to remove existing deficiencies and or impediments.

| 3 | Desirable improvements | Project identified to meet anticipated or projected future needs. |
| 4 | Deferable improvements | Foreseeable needs for projects cannot be effectively supported as part of the present CIP. |

In recent years a numerical rating system has gained popularity. For example, a specific number of points (e.g., 0-50) is given to a project as it conforms to such factors as economic development, environmental quality, revenue generation, potential for revitalizing neighborhoods, citizen neighborhood participation, and useful life expectancy. Locations where the rating system is in use include Dade County, Florida; Dayton, Ohio; Montgomery County, Maryland; and St. Paul, Minnesota.

In summary, five specific activities should be considered sequentially when officials attempt to establish project priority:

1. Development of clearly defined criteria
2. Development of a point system to permit the assignment of points to each criterion
3. Comparison of each project with the identified criteria
4. Assignment of an appropriate score and ranking to each project
5. Preparation of a priority listing of the projects

Capital Budgeting: Elements Contributing to Success and Failure. In its extensive study of both public and private organizations' capital budgeting practices, the GAO identified elements that either contribute to or jeopardize success. The elements found in a successful organization range from critical to helpful attributes (see Figure 11.2). Similarly, the elements found in an unsuccessful organization range from harmful to destructive attributes.

The successful organization is able to minimize the impact on its service delivery system when operating conditions change its environment. The GAO states: "A successful organization is one that, can even under adverse conditions, acquire[s] and/or maintain[s] physical capital without jeopardizing its mission or its clientele. By adverse conditions, we mean declining resources, political instability, or severe conflict among interest groups."[10]

FINANCIAL ANALYSIS

While the pay-as-you-go approach (discussed earlier in this chapter) has been exceedingly popular in government and other not-for-profit agencies,

Figure 11.2

Elements Contributing to Success and Failure in Capital Budgeting

Elements Found In Successful Organizations	Elements Found In Unsuccessful Organizations
Critical	**Destructive**
Extensively links planning to budgeting.	Does not link planning to budgeting when planning takes place.
Concerned about long-term effects.	Pays little attention to long-term effects.
Incorporates up-to-date information on physical capital into decision-making process.	Does not consistently feed information on the condition of physical capital into the decision-making process.
Important	**Damaging**
Recognizes the effect of deferred maintenance and minimizes it to the extent possible.	Has limited, if any controls; misses many financial and work targets.
Protects capital investment funds from being used for operations.	Defers structural maintenance; focuses on cosmetic repairs.
Considers related operations and maintenance costs when making capital budgeting decisions.	Cuts budget with "closed" eyes.
	Harmful
Considers alternative methods of meeting the objectives of capital.	Lets funding mechanism drive priorities.
Monitors capital investment and the condition of physical capital.	Sees individual projects as pork barrel.
Does not have internal conflicts that disrupt capital budgeting activities.	Lets special interest groups get out of control.
Sees individual projects as modernization, revitalization, and investment.	
Uses funding mechanism to protect priorities.	
Uses incentives to meet work and financial targets.	

Source: GAO, *Federal Capital Budgeting: A Collection of Haphazard Practices* (Washington, D.C.: GAO, 1980), p. 40.

Helpful

Figures out ways to allocate something
for everyone (keeps things even, moves
on all fronts).

Uses categories for decision making that
are important to the organization, e.g.,
productivity items.

Routinely assesses physical capital and
adherence to a maintenance schedule.

most governments have not been able to adopt this option and still meet the
needs of their citizens. Older communities (especially those with recurrent
expenditure), having most of their infrastructure in place, are in a better
position to adopt the pay-as-you-go approach than newer communities and
those experiencing rapid growth and development. The pay-as-you-go
approach has two particularly appealing features: (1) in the long-run it is
more economical because financing costs are eliminated; and (2) there is a
generally held view among public finance experts that greater efficiency is attained when taxpayers feel the burden/cost of the undertaking immediately.[11]

When the pay-as-you-go approach cannot be followed, a number of
modifications of it may be pursued: (1) Adopt a policy requiring that the
length of all future debt instruments be successively shortened as they are
issued. (2) Make an initial down payment from current revenues and
increase the portion until the capital outlay can be easily accommodated by
current revenues. (3) Declare a moratorium on payment until all outstanding debts are substantially reduced.[12]

A critical part of the CIP process is the development of the financing
plan. The governmental unit or agency must determine how much can be
spent, the sources from which the money will come, and the people and/or
entities that will bear the burden. Satisfying projected capital needs requires
the identification and scheduling of funding sources (known as financial
programming). Action must be taken regarding the following: (1) tax
rates; (2) the desired balance between debt service and expenditures; (3)
available aid from state and federal government; and (4) new revenue
sources.

Analysis of Revenues and Expenditures. A review of the revenue collection and expenditure record for the past five years is an important first step.
It provides a benchmark against which future revenue and expenditure can
be measured. On the revenue side, special attention should be given to
recurring items such as property taxes, user fees, and proposed changes

affecting valuation tax rate, special limitations on property tax, prospects for the local job market, inflation, trends in population, and other important changes that might be discernible.[13]

Using data from the same period as the revenue review, the expenditures should be categorized as follows: recurring operating expenditures, capital expenditures, and debt service payment. Aspects such as changes in the work force (especially new employees), salary and benefit trends, and types and terms of existing bonded indebtedness should also be considered.

Future Revenue and Expenditure Projections. With the completion of the revenue and expenditure review, revenue and expenditure for the duration of the proposed CIP may be forecast. This permits linkage of the CIP with the community's resource capability. Regardless of the methods used in making revenue and expenditure projections, various assumptions must be clearly defined. These assumptions involve changes in variables such as population as well as residential, commerical, and industrial growth. Once the new revenue and expenditure projections have been made, the capital facility plan for each year can be completed. The difference between projected expenditures and projected revenue represents the amount that the governmental unit or agency will need to generate to finance the proposed capital improvements.[14]

A number of options are available to a governmental unit or agency to obtain sufficient funds to carry out its CIP. Among the main options are the following:

- *General obligations bonds* (GO) are legal obligations of the unit issuing the bond. They are used to build public facilities such as jails, sewers, and bridges.

- *Limited or special obligation bonds* are unlike GOs in that they do not carry the same statutory and constitutional security as general obligation bonds. They do not enjoy the "full faith and credit" of the issuing unit, though they have priority over all nonproject creditors. In many states specific sources of taxes are designated to pay limited bond obligations. A few states do not permit bonds to be general obligation unless they are pledged by the property tax; others make a bond a general obligation if any revenue not generated from the project is pledged to pay for its repayment.[15]

- *Revenue bonds* are a type of limited obligation bond which includes those issues on which governmental units "promise to pay debt service . . . exclusively from the revenue derived from user fees and charges from the project constructed."[16] Examples are turnpikes and major public improvements including special assessment bonds.

- *Lease purchase agreement* involves a facility that is built by a private or not-for-profit organization.

- *Joint financing with other governmental units* may be arranged.

- *Private development funds* may be used, such as in cases where new infrastructure is required in new developments.

- *Sources of government revenues* including taxes, special assessments, and user charges may be employed.

The public sector pays for virtually all of the country's infrastructure (roads, bridges, mass transit systems, sewers, water, etc.). The resources to fund most capital facilities have been obtained mainly through federal sources and long-term debt issued by state and local governments. Historically, general obligation bonds have been the chief financing source for state and local governments. (The general obligation bonds are secured by the unit promising to pay the principal and interest from its general revenue resources.)

Because of public resistance, the financing source for capital improvements has been declining in recent years. More popular are revenue bonds that permit the debt service (principal and interest payments) to be paid from the revenue produced by the specific project. While the revenue bond financing approach is likely to enjoy popularity as a means of financing capital improvement, there is a distinct limit as to how many capital improvements can be self-financed. Limitations are caused by resistance to the amounts of user charges that people may want to pay. The demands on state and local governments to provide increased resources to finance improved capital facilities are likely to rise appreciably. But the major financing source (the federal government) already has begun to decrease the funds available in this area.[17]

CAPITAL BUDGET ANALYSIS

Since government and other not-for-profit organizations have limited resources or revenues, the costs of desirable programs and projects always exceed available revenues. If the best possible use is to be made of scarce revenues, only those projects providing the maximum social gain to the community should be undertaken. Capital budget analysis is comprised of those techniques that are used for evaluating the social benefits of alternative uses for available scarce resources. Stated another way, the process consists of an orderly sequence of steps organized to produce relevant information for choosing investments. The following steps are required:

1. Identification of relevant investment alternatives
2. Estimation of the cash flow for each alternative
3. Selection of appropriate choice criteria to apply to the projected cash flow in order to facilitate a measure of comparison
4. Arrangement of data for each alternative (project), interpretation consistent with the specified criteria, and selection of those projects with maximum social gain

Identifying Alternatives. This step demands that the various choices be clearly understood. The benefits to be gained from a project should be compared with the benefits that can be achieved from an alternative application of resources.

Estimating the Cash Flow. Because the accounting system allocates costs on a responsibility or departmental basis, there may be confusion about costs relevant to decision making. Thus a few useful rules have been suggested in deciding which costs should be included or excluded in capital decisions:

- Include only those inflows and outflows that can be directly related to the project; exclude those that would occur irrespective of the project. A capital expenditure is a cash outlay over a number of years intended to produce a flow of future benefits. A capital expenditure may be viewed as consisting of three distinct elements: expected future benefits, time factor, and risk related to the realization of the expected benefits.
- Focus only on future cash flow since all past flow decisions relate to *sunk costs* and cannot be changed.
- Pay close attention to cash flow and not to accounting reports, which may differ because of the accrual accounting system. (The cash system and the cash flow approach will usually be nearly identical.) It is important to keep in mind that the data on costs and benefits are determined at this stage. That is, costs and benefits in dollars must be identified for the entire life of the roject or program.

Applying Capital Budget Criteria: Techniques for Project Analysis. Decision makers in most not-for-profit agencies to find that it is easier to identify cost (the input factor) than to estimate benefits. The situation is even more difficult when the explicit intention of an expansion is to increase service capability or quality. It is critical to select the criteria that will generate information useful for ranking in order to enable the decision maker to accept or reject different investment objectives. Five criteria used from time to time in public and other not-for-profit organizations are:

- simple rate of return/average rate of return
- payback period
- net present value
- excess present value
- internal rate of return

The simple rate of return (SRR) expresses the average net profits generated yearly by an investment as a percentage of the original investment or of the investment over its expected life. The following is one of a number of ways to calculate the simple rate of return:

$$SRR = \frac{Y}{I}$$

Where Y = average annual profits (minus depreciation)
projected for the new investment

I = the initial investment

SRR = the average annual or simple rate of return

Each investment is ranked according to the relative size of its SRR. Its profitability is then judged by comparison with the investor's required rate of return (RRR). After due consideration of the risk, liquidity, and other relevant factors, the following decision rules are applied: When SRR exceeds RRR, accept the investment; when SRR equals RRR, be neutral or indifferent; when SRR is less than RRR, reject the investment.

Table 11.1 shows the projected average annual rates of return for investments X, Y, and Z (see Table 11.2). Applying the simple rate of return criterion, investment X would be the first choice, followed by Y, and lately Z. Since 8 percent is the required rate of return, the three projects are profitable.

Note that the simple rate of return does not consider the time element related to the different cash flows. When each flow pattern has large differences, use of the simple rate of return may lead to erroneous conclusions.

Table 11.1
Simple Rate of Return: Three Hypothetical Investments

Project	Net Costs Plus Depreciation	Depreciation	Average Annual	Simple rate of return
X	$ 31,000	$20,000	$2,000	10%
Y	30,000	20,000	1,800	9%
Z	29,000	20,000	1,600	8%

The Payback Period. This is a very simple quantitative technique widely used for evaluating investment opportunities. It provides an estimate of the time required to recover the cost of an investment. The payback period can be calculated as follows:

$$\text{Payback period} = \frac{\text{original investment}}{\text{annual cash flow}}$$

In not-for-profit organizations, two approaches are used: (1) the annual cash flow may be the actual inflow generated by the investment of a piece of equipment; or (2) the amount of savings produced as a result of the investment may be substituted for the annual cash flow. Either approach is acceptable.

As an illustration, assume that a hospital wants to purchase one of two comparable X-ray machines. Machine X costs $100,800 with an annual cash inflow of $12,000. Machine Y costs $120,000 and generates $16,000 annual cash flow. The application of the payback criterion would require that Machine Y be chosen. The payback for the machines may be computed as follows:

Machine X:

$$\frac{\$100,800}{12,000} = 9 \text{ years}$$

Machine Y:

$$\frac{\$120,000}{16,000} = 7.5 \text{ years}$$

Because of the ease of the payback calculation, it may be conveniently used at lower management levels to approve small expenditure projects. The chief advantage of the payback period approach is its ability to pinpoint the time it takes an investment to pay for itself. In addition, it is easy to calculate and to understand.

Specific investments are ranked according to their relative payback periods. The projects with the shortest payback period are the most favored. The criterion for acceptance or rejection is based on the investor's required payback period (RPP). The decision rule is applied as follows: When the payback period is less than RPP, accept the investment; when the payback period equals RPP, be neutral or indifferent; when the payback period exceeds RPP, reject the investment.

A major disadvantage of the payback period approach is that it ignores all cash flows beyond the payback period. For example, Machine X above continues to generate cash inflows for three years beyond the payback period, while Machine Y generates no revenue beyond the payback period. When all of this information is considered, Machine X would be selected rather than Machine Y.

Time Value of Money. The use of this approach is known as the discounted cash flow method for capital budgeting decisions. Unlike the payback period and simple rate of return approaches, the time value of money recognizes that use of money has a cost. Interest is analogous to the rent one pays for the use of a piece of equipment or building. The discounted cash flow method recognizes the fact that $10 to be received or spent in the future does not have the same value as $10 received or spent today. To use a specific example, if you deposit $100 in a bank at 8 percent interest, at the end of the year you will have $108, assuming the interest is compounded annually. If the individual feels that $100 today is equivalent to $108 one year from now, then the 8 percent interest rate constitutes the *opportunity cost of time*, that is, the one-year wait for the money. The 8 percent rate measures the willingness to exchange $100 today (*present value*) for $108 at the end of the year (*future value*). The present value is computed as follows:

$$\text{Present Value} = \frac{\text{Future Value}}{1 + \text{Interest Rate}}$$

or

$$100 = \frac{108}{1 + .08}$$

Note that the cash flow method is concerned only with *cash* inflows and outflows. This is in sharp contrast with the accounting method (e.g., the simple rate of return), which is affected by depreciation and other noncash transactions.

Net Present Value (NPV). This method indicates the extent to which an investor will be better or worse off when he/she accepts a given project as opposed to investing in other available options. The net present value (assuming a given rate of interest) is equal to the discounted inflow minus the discounted outflows. When the present value is greater than the outflows, the positive net present value is said to be the excess present value return earned on the project.

In evaluating NPV options, the sign and size of an investment's present value influences its ranking and acceptability. When all investments being considered are income-generating, the one that has the largest NPV is given the highest ranking. The following decision rules apply: (1) When NPV exceeds zero, accept the investment; (2) when NPV equals zero, be neutral or indifferent; (3) when NPV is less than zero, reject the investment.

When the investment options are cost-reducing, the projected cash outflows reflect outlays (i.e., expenditures). Cost-reducing comparisons require that the chosen criterion be based on the minimum net present value of each of the outlays.

To calculate the net present value, five types of data are required:

1. INV = the initial capital investment.
2. P_n = the annual net cash flows attributed to the investment that can be withdrawn periodically or yearly.
3. V_N = any salvage or other terminal investment value.
4. N = the time horizon (N) or the summation for n = O to N.
5. i = the interest rate or required rate of return.

The formula is set up for a nonuniform series of payments as follows:

$$NPV = -INV + \frac{P_1}{(1 + i)} + \frac{P_2}{(1+i)^2} + \ldots \frac{P_N}{(1+i)^N} + \frac{V_N}{(1+i)^N}$$

If projected cash flows are a uniform series of payments (an annuity), USPV is designated as a simplified notation for the *uniform series present value* over N periods at interest rate (i). The formula is as follows:

$$NPV = -INV + A[USPV_{i,N}] + \frac{V_N}{(1+i)^N}$$

Assuming that an investor is evaluating investments X, Y, and Z and requires a 10 percent rate of return as shown in Table 11.2, the NPV of investment X can be determined. The NPV of investment X is:

$$NPV = -20,000 = \frac{4,000}{(1.10)} + \frac{4,000}{(1.10)^2} + \frac{6,000}{(1.10)^3} + \frac{8,000}{(1.10)^4} + \frac{10,000}{(1.10)^5}$$

The conversion factors $(1.10)^{-n}$ are found in Appendix II, Table I, $i = .10$ and values of n range from 1 to 5. The NPV is:

$$NPV = -20,000 + 2,000\ (.926) + 4,000\ (.856)$$

$$+ 6,000\ (.794) + 9,000\ (.735) + 10,000\ (.681)$$

$$= -20,000 + 1,852 + 3,424 + 4,764 + 6,615 + 6,810 = \$3,465$$

Table 11.2
Three Investment Cash Flows

Year	Investment X	Investment Y	Investment Z
0 Present	-$20,000	-$20,000	-$20,000
1	2,000	6,000	10,000
2	4,000	6,000	8,000
3	6,000	6,000	6,000
4	9,000	6,000	4,000
5	10,000	6,000	1,000

An alternate way for computing net present value (NPV) requires the following:

1. Determination of estimated annual cash flows directly from each investment
2. Determination of estimated number of years or economic life that the investment will generate cash flows.
3. Determination of net amount of costs associated with the investment.
4. Determination of the required rate of return.

The Net Present Value may be calculated using the following formula:

Net Present Value = (Cash Flow × Present Value Factor) − Investment

$$NPV = (CF \times pvf) - I$$

Using the data in Table 11.2 investment Y above and Appendix II, Table II the net present value is calculated as follows:

1. Annual cash flow $= \$6,000$
2. Economic Life $= 5$ Years
3. Net investment amount $= \$20,000$
4. Rate of return $= 10$ percent

$$NPV = (CF \times pvf) - I$$
$$= (\$6,000 \times 3.791) - \$20,000$$
$$= \$22,746 - \$20,000$$
$$= \$2,746$$

This suggests that the investment is financially feasible.

Following the same procedure, the calculated net present value for investment Y is $2,746 and for Z is $4,443. While all three investment alternatives are acceptable, given the NPV decision rules investment Z is preferred over X and Y.

Internal Rate of Return. Though internal rate of return (IRR) is perhaps the more widely used name, it is also known by a number of other names: the discounted rate of return, the marginal efficiency of capital, or the yield of an investment. IRR refers to that rate of interest which is equal to the net present value of a projected series of cash flow payments at zero.

To find the IRR for an investment apply the NPV formula with the appropriate projected cash flows (INV, P_n, P_N, V_N), set NPV equal to zero, and solve for i:

$$0 = -INV + \frac{P_1}{(1+i)} + \frac{P_2}{(1+i)^2} + \ldots + \frac{P_N}{(1+i)^N} + \frac{V}{(1+i)^N}$$

The interest rate that satisfies the equation is the internal rate of return (IRR).

As an illustration, determine the IRR for an investment requiring an initial payment of $1,000, yielding $1,300 one year from today.

The IRR is calculated as follows:

$$0 = -1,000 + \frac{1,300}{1+i}$$

Transposing the equation, the yield is

$$1 + i = \frac{1,300}{1,000} = 1.30$$

$$\text{and } i = .3$$

$$\text{Thus IRR} = 30 \text{ percent.}$$

Assume that the $1,300 payment was received after two years rather than at the end of one year. The IRR is calculated as follows:

$$0 = -1,000 + \frac{1,300}{(1 + i)^2}$$

Transposing the equation, the yield is

$$(1 + i)^{-2} = \frac{1,000}{1,300} = .7692$$

$$\text{Thus } i = .14$$

Note that the conversion factor is determined by using Appendix II, Table I to find the value of i, given $n = 2$, providing the conversion factor of .769. In using Table I, find the number of periods equated with n. In this case it is 2. Then move along to the right of Table I until you find the conversion factor equal or nearest to .769. For this example, the conversion factor for $n = 2$ and $i = .14$ occurs exactly at .769. Thus the IRR is exactly 14 percent. When the factor for i falls in between two interest rates in the table, the best estimate of IRR may be determined through interpolation.

To find the IRR for a series of payments, consider the IRR for $30,000 with a series of payments of $6,000 per year for five years. Appendix II, Table II is used to find the value of i where $N = 5$, given a conversion factor of 2.941. When $N = 5$, the value for $i = .21$ is 2.991, while the value for $i = .20$ is 2.926. Thus the IRR for the investment falls between 20 and 21 percent. To obtain a more accurate approximation of the interest rate, interpolate as follows:

IRR	Conversion Factor

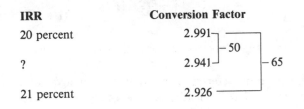

The estimate for the IRR is $\frac{50}{65}$ or 20.77 percent. Like the capital budget evaluation techniques discussed previously, the IRR method can be used to accept or reject investment alternatives. The ranking system is based on the relative sizes of the IRRs. The investments having the largest IRR are the most favored. Each investment acceptability is dependent upon comparison with the investor's required rate of return (RRR). The following decision rules apply: When IRR exceeds RRR, accept the investment; when IRR equals RRR, be indifferent or neutral; when IRR is less than RRR, reject the investment. It is important to remember that these decision rules are subject to considerations of risk and liquidity.

It should be observed that the net present value is closely linked to the IRR; each uses the same discounting approach. While the NPV specifies a given interest rate, the IRR identifies the interest rate that yields a zero NPV.

Excess Present Value. This approach calculates the positive or negative percentage of streams of inflows over outflows of a project. By means of this approach, an index is calculated as follows:

$$\text{Excess present value index} = \frac{\text{Present Value}}{\text{Required Investment}}$$

This index can be used to compare and rank competing projects. Since it shows the present value of a project per dollar of investment, it provides a means of ranking projects of different sizes. This greatly simplifies finding the optimum solutions for competing projects when the budget for capital outlays has been arbitrarily determined. The criteria for selection and rejection are simple. Projects are ranked in order of profitability based on indices above 100 percent. Projects rated below 100 percent are undesirable because the cost of capital would exceed the adjusted rate of return. To illustrate, look at the example of a machine to process mail bought at a cost of $22,000.

Assume that money cost is 16 percent and that the machine generates cash flow of $5,000 per year for 10 years.

PV = $5,000 × 4.833 (using Appendix II, Table II) = $24,165

Excess Present Value = $24,165 − $22,000 = $2,165

$$\text{Excess Present Value Index} = \frac{\text{Present Value}}{\text{Required Investment}}$$

$$\text{or } \frac{214,165}{22,000} = 109.8 \text{ percent.}$$

Determining the Discount Rate. Though seldom discussed, the determination of the discount rate to be used in calculating the net present values and benefit cost ratios is critical. Two general ways have been used: (1) examining the cost of obtaining funds for the project; and (2) examining the return or alternative investments.

At the federal level, the Office of Management and Budget has endorsed 10 percent as a rate that may be used in government programs.

CONCLUDING OBSERVATIONS

Capital budgeting has great potential for public and other not-for-profit organizations. If effectively carried out, capital budgeting can aid a community's economic development and generate confidence in a governmental unit's ability to wisely manage its resources. Similarly, in other not-for-profit agencies, appropriate selection and good management of capital equipment can faciliate better allocation of resources and minimize the possibility of becoming fiscally strained.

Given the magnitude of resources required to fund capital projects, it is difficult for all but a few governmental units to use the popular pay-as-you-go funding approach for capital projects. Thus capital budgeting requires that decision makers give serious thought to optimum methods for selecting the capital progam mix that would yield the greatest payoff for the amount of dollars expended. The method of financing is especially critical since the selection of a particular option can result in significant savings or additional costs.

Unlike in the past, a large number of public and not-for-profit organizations have been applying various techniques for analyzing and choosing among capital projects. Techniques employing internal rate of return, net present value, and excess present value approaches have been successfully applied.

NOTES

1. Alan Walter Steiss, *Local Government Finance* (Lexington, Mass.: Lexington Books, 1975), p. 4.

2. GAO, *Federal Capital Budgeting: A Collection of Haphazard Practices* (Washington, D.C.: GAO, 1981), p. i.

3. ICMA, "Planning for Capital Improvements," *MIS* 16, no. 18 (August 1984): 5.

4. GAO, *Federal Capital Budgeting*, pp. 17-18.

5. ICMA, "Planning for Capital Improvements," pp. 2-3.

6. John L. Mikesell, *Fiscal Administration* (Homewood, Ill.: Dorsey Press, 1982), pp. 100-101.

7. Ibid., p. 3.

8. Ibid.

9. Steiss, *Local Government Finance*, p. 35; see also ICMA, "Planning for Capital Improvements," p. 13.

10. GAO, *Federal Capital Budgeting*, p. 39.

11. Steiss, *Local Government Finance*, pp. 104-5.

12. Ibid.

13. ICMA, "Planning for Capital Improvements," p. 8.

14. Ibid., pp. 8-9.

15. Dillon, Read and Co., "Infrastructure Financing: An Overview" (unpublished) (November 1963), p. 4.

16. Ibid.; ICMA, "Planning for Capital Improvements," p. 10.

17. Dillon, Read and Co., "Infrastructure Financing," pp. 1-2.

CHAPTER 12

LINE-ITEM AND PERFORMANCE BUDGETING

While the last two chapters dealt with concepts and uses of budgets generally, this chapter examines two types of budgets that are found in practice—line-item and performance budgets. Emphasis is focused on how each of these budgeting approaches allocates scarce resources among desirable courses of action. The development of the line-item and performance budgets is examined, as well as how they are used for allocating, maintaining, and controlling financial resources.

LINE-ITEM BUDGETING

The line-item budget (also called the object-of-expenditure budget) was the earliest budget format used in public and not-for-profit institutions. It came hand in hand with the development of modern budgeting. Its introduction was considered an innovative development by reformers at the turn of the century. It replaced the lump sum budgeting approach.

The reformers sought to improve the economy and efficiency of organizations and to ensure the legality of expenditures in an effort to control graft and corruption in government. The line-item budget took prominence with the establishment of the executive budget, which reposed responsibility and accountability for government spending with the chief executive. This gave the chief executive a powerful instrument for controlling agency demands for money.

DEFINING LINE-ITEM BUDGET

The line-item budget is a technique in which line-items (also known as objects of expenditure) are the main focus of analysis, authorization, and control. Typical line-items include supplies, personnel, travel, contractual services, and capital outlays. These are the items upon which major attention is focused and by which financial resources are controlled.

While there is no way of determining what the line-item budget will accomplish, it is easily understood. Table 12.1 clearly indicates the services or commodities to be purchased and the total amount of money that the city of Bright will spend for police services. The budget identifies items that administrators and elected officials can relate to in terms of their own experience. The fact that the line-item budget presents specific items that can be easily increased or reduced without debating the merit or demerit of a program enhances the opportunity for compromise.

A number of control objectives are associated with the line-item budget: (1) the avoidance of scandals by making sure that funds are spent for authorized purposes; (2) the accomplishment of the legislature's programmatic objectives; and (3) the maintenance of a balanced budget. Of the objectives, (3) and most especially (2) are the major concerns of the line-item/object budget.[1]

Table 12.1
City of Bright—Simplified Line-Item/Object-of-Expenditure Budget FY 1986
(Classified by Organizational Unit and Object of Expenditure)

Police Department:

Salaries and Wages:	Rate		
1 - Chief	20,000	20,000	
1 - Assistant Chief	15,000	15,000	
3 - Captains	10,000	30,000	
2 - Sergeants	9,000	9,000	
20 - Patrolmen	8,000	160,000	
4 - Radio Operators	7,000	28,000	262,000

Supplies/Materials:		
Stationery and related supplies	500	
Janitorial and related supplies	200	
Gloves	100	
Gasoline and oil	4,000	
Uniforms	3,000	
Other	800	8,600

Other Service Charges:		
Telephone	1,000	
Out-of-town travel	2,000	
Parking tickets	1,000	
Utilities	3,000	
Other	300	7,300

Capital Outlay:		
2 - Motorcycles	2,500	
4 - Patrol cars	24,000	
Recondition	10,000	36,500

Total Police Department	$314,400

Line-item budgeting is the most widely used budgeting system today. It has wide appeal because of the degree of accountability (narrow, legal control) it emphasizes. Attention is given to means for ensuring fidelity—how to prevent funds from being stolen and expended for unauthorized purposes. Emphasis is put on things or commodities to be bought rather than on the type and quality of services to be produced. For example, in a typical department, as indicated in Table 12.1, there are separate lines for wages and salaries; purchase of automobiles, equipment, and supplies; and expenditures for other services, such as utilities; the list is limited only by the number of items or services requested.

A typical monthly budget report includes: the budget category, the approved budget amount, amount expended this month, amount expended this year, and percentage of budget expended and outstanding encumbrances (see Table 12.2).

Development of the line-item budget involves the following steps:

1. The first step requires that categories of responsibility for expenditures be clearly defined. This action facilitates the development of an effective budget process, establishing clear lines of individual responsibility for each activity.

2. The amount of work and the kinds of skills required for each activity should be determined.

3. The budgetary unit desired to facilitate planning and controlling of expenditures should be defined.

4. A calendar should be prepared specifically identifying individual or group responsibility and the target dates for completion.

5. Review of the object-of-expenditure classification chart should be undertaken to standardize and permit consolidation or summary of like items in departments.

6. Account codes should be examined and revised when necessary to make them consistent with the budgetary classification system.

The line-item process requires that agencies submit requests to the chief executive in terms of types of expenditures to be made according to established line-items. The chief executive modifies these requests and submits them to the legislature or the appropriate board. The latter then reviews, modifies, and appropriates funds on the line-item basis.

Once the budget is appropriated, the executive sets up the accounting system to record the line-item amounts as specified by the legislature or board. Additional controls are instituted for personnel hiring, transferring funds among intra-agency and inter-agency accounts, and regulating amounts permitted to be spent from period to period. To facilitate the latter, an allotment system is set up to accommodate individual agency expenditure needs, based on past practice and the projection of expected expenditures during the fiscal period. Typically, each agency's appropriated funds are allocated on a monthly or quarterly basis, or whatever time period

Table 12.2

City of Bright—Monthly Budget Report, August 31, 1986

Budgetary Category Department: Police Department Activity: Patrol	Approved Budget	Amount Expended This Month	Amount Expended This Year	Amount Unexpended Budget	% Budget Unexpended	Outstanding Encumbrances*
Salaries & Wages	128,000	11,000	88,000	40,000	31.2	-0-
Fringe Benefits	32,000	2,500	20,000	12,000	37.5	-0-
Supplies/Materials	8,600	1,000	3,000	4,600	53.5	2,000
Equipment	36,000	22,000	22,000	14,000	38.9	2,500
Total	204,600	36,500	133,000	70,600		4,500

*Obligation or liability for amount of goods or services ordered but not yet delivered.

is considered acceptable. The allotment system provides a direct control device. Allotment amounts may not be increased without specific permission from the controlling budget official.

Whereas the allotment system tends to be used in larger agencies and governmental units, an expenditure plan (a less formal system) may be used by smaller agencies and governmental units. In this latter system the budget or staff official who has the responsibility for monitoring expenditures on a monthly or quarterly basis works with spending units to develop projections based typically on a five-year quarterly or monthly average corrected for any unusual events of the past and any expected abnormal occurrences in the coming fiscal period. When units or departments report that spending levels are higher than anticipated in the expenditure plan without an acceptable reason, prompt corrective action can be initiated. Among the actions that may be taken are transferring funds among activities, modifying work plans, reducing service levels, or cutting back expenditures on nonessential functions.

ADVANTAGES OF THE LINE-ITEM BUDGET

The line-item budget assigns expenditures on the basis of existing organization rather than on a responsibility center basis. There are a number of advantages associated with this type of budget. Namely, the line-item budget:

1. permits hierarchical authority to control inputs before the expenditure is made or obligated;
2. constrains the exercise of discretionary powers by managers;
3. helps to curtail the number of personnel positions, salary increases, and purchases—the largest costs in public and non-profit agencies;
4. provides for uniform controls throughout an agency;
5. provides for the comprehensive control of all financial transactions and permits easy compilation of financial data, facilitating accounting and auditing systems and minimizing computational costs. (Records are collected in the everyday course of administrative activity. Information is derived directly from vouchers, purchase orders, and other documents in use.);
6. promotes clearcut controls, minimizing the opportunity for circumvention of hierarchical controls, yet controls can be flexible for favored agencies and stringent for others that engage in unacceptable practices;
7. facilitates budget reductions. When agency spending exceeds revenues, cuts can be made without impairing the program objectives;
8. avoids the possibility of making large and costly mistakes;
9. provides continuity between past, present, and future policy;
10. allows managers to operate with a greater degree of certainty;

11. permits legislators to effect easier confirmations on dollar amounts rather than requiring agreement on program outcomes, thereby reducing or minimizing the potential for political conflict and deadlock in the political system.

INCREMENTALISM AND THE LINE-ITEM BUDGET

Incrementalism and line-item budgeting go hand in hand. Incremental budgets focus on limited alternatives that differ slightly from existing policy. Prior levels of expenditure become the major decision criterion for allocating resources. Typically, the budget makers accept amount X from the prior year's budget, and add a small increment, amount A, which is a percentage of X. The budget formula thus becomes $X + AX$.[2]

The incremental budget method has a built-in upward bias. Small changes when added together over successive years can be significant. The incremental approach is accommodative to the advocates of existing programs because it allows recurring programs to continue their growth with minimal scrutiny.

The Incremental Syndrome. The general orientation of budget makers directs them to add or subtract a percentage to last year's budget. When times are good, there is a reasonable expectation that more money will be available. Additions are routinely made "to all line-items or selectively whenever it seems to make the most sense."[3] Likewise, in bad years small increments are added or subtracted, depending on the revenue outlook.

Decision rules (rules of thumb, generally agreed upon benchmarks or criteria for facilitating decision making) typically characterize traditional incremental budget preparation. Once an amount is granted to a program or activity, it becomes the base or part of the basic budget[4] from which "fair share" increases or decreases are added or subtracted. Only amounts proposed above the fair share amount need to be justified. Expenditures for programs already in existence that do not exceed the fair share guideline go unquestioned and unchallenged.

Marginal or incremental changes constrain attempts to redirect social objectives. Policy making tends to be short-range and tactical. Since no comprehensive analysis or weighting of cost and benefits of objectives is undertaken, no effort is made to make the best decision among available alternatives. The present budget is a mirror of the past, and the future is a projection of the present.

DISADVANTAGES OF THE LINE-ITEM BUDGET

The main shortcomings of the line-item budget include the following:

1. There is total preoccupation with material acquisition or inputs.
2. Accountability is focused on a narrow concept of what money can buy and not on output and impact (i.e., changes produced as a result of the program).

3. Little attention is given to organization and/or program goals, making it difficult or virtually impossible to provide information for evaluating the efficiency and effectiveness of an agency's activities.

4. Most budget items require no justification.

5. Once a program has been funded, the program is likely to continue indefinitely, barring major adverse publicity.

6. It provides fragmented historical cost data that are not useful for program execution and evaluation.

7. Reports based on the line-item budget produce very few financial data that can be used in planning, programming, and evaluating an agency's activities.

8. Input planning decisions are made at the lower levels and move upward rather than the reverse.

9. Goals and objectives of the organization are made on the basis of dollar amounts allocated to various activities. Operating procedures become policy. Thus purposes are not consciously considered, and achievement of objectives is due more to chance than to design. (The city of Pittsburgh's Department of Lands and Buildings budget provides a good illustration. The line-item budget has six responsibility areas. However, there are no stated objectives for any activity; yet, performance statistics are included in the budget, providing no basis for effective evaluation.)

10. Neither the executive branch nor the legislature is given information that permits it to allocate available resources wisely.

11. Though it facilitates compromise it promotes poor decision making.

12. It fails to address policy or management issues.

POLITICS AND THE LINE-ITEM BUDGET

Despite the fact that line-item or incremental budgeting is viewed as stable, predictable, and conservative, the politics that surrounds its preparation, particularly in the public sector, may permit small increases to explode into unmanageable programs with huge cost overruns. For example, the Mark 48 torpedo was sold to Congress as an almost invulnerable torpedo at a total cost of $680 million. A combination of participants, including Westinghouse and Pennsylvania State University, were selected to build the torpedo.[5] To minimize the possibility of cost overruns, Congress hired Peat Marwick & Mitchell Company to monitor program costs. Between the time the project got started in 1963 and its completion in 1973, the cost moved from $680 million to $4.5 billion, a sevenfold cost increase. Initially the torpedo system was estimated to appear low in cost but high in terms of effectiveness. The expenditure increments continued for several years before a more accurate cost for completing the project was estimated. If at the outset the real cost was estimated to be $4.5 billion, the project might never have been undertaken. This is a constant problem in public administration, especially in government contracting, where payment to the contractor is based on a cost plus fee arrangement.

The political practice undergirding incremental budgeting has generated several rules that are used in preparing and submitting a budget. They include the following:

1. Avoid asking for sums smaller than the current appropriation.

2. When an implementing agency wishes to avoid close scrutiny and review, increases are put in the basic budget. Since new requests are subject to close scrutiny, it is good strategy to identify them with the basic budget or the high-priority areas whenever possible.

3. Never give the appearance that you are making fundamental changes from existing policies. All necessary increases must be made to look small, appearing to grow out of existing operations.

4. Make it possible to permit budget reviewers to look good. Leave something for them to cut. This allows the budget reviewer to look good while you achieve your objective.[6]

Like the budget preparers, the reviewers or gatekeepers also employ decision rules such as the following:

1. When new personnel are requested, decrease or eliminate the request.

2. Renovate and/or repair facilities rather than replace them.

3. As a general policy, avoid cutting safety or health-related requests, especially those programs that have substantial public support.

4. Decrease requests of department that have poor or bad reputations.

5. Reduce or eliminate all nonoperating requests by some fixed percentage.[7]

PERFORMANCE BUDGETING

At the national level, the Taft Commission of 1912 advocated a functional work-based classification approach to budget expenditures. This became known as performance budgeting (also identified as the cost data budget). It was first implemented in the borough of Richmond, New York City, before World War I. Few units of government gave performance budgeting serious consideration until it was popularized by the Hoover Commission in 1949. The commission report stated: "We recommend that the whole budgeting concept of the federal government should be refashioned by the adoption of a budget based on functions, activities, and projects: This we designate the 'performance budget.'"[8] It was widely talked about and practiced throughout the 1950s.

DEFINING PERFORMANCE BUDGETING

The National Committee on Governmental Accounting defines the performance budget as one that is "based primarily upon measurable performance of activities and work programs."[9] Stated another way, performance budgeting comprises specific techniques directing attention to the services to be provided and the work to be performed. Services are broken down and described in terms of required inputs and projected outputs. The analysis of the efficiency of existing operations is a main objective. Its main tools are cost accounting and work measurement. The budget account is classified by organizational functions, activities, and objects of expenditure, for example.

Public Safety (Function)

Department (Police)

Activity (Patrol)

Object of Expenditure (Personnel Services, Materials, etc.)

Performance budgeting requires that standard unit costs be established which permit budget projections to be determined by multiplying the unit costs by the number of work units in an activity for the coming fiscal period. Each budget has a narrative description of proposed activities that are supported by cost estimates with expected accomplishments identified in quantitative terms. Input and output resources and total cost are clearly identified (see Table 12.3).

Performance budgeting seeks answers to questions such as the following: What are the agency's objectives? What services are being provided to justify the agency's existence? What are the required activities to realize the agency's objectives? What is the volume of work required to achieve each activity? What are the level of expenditure and the unit costs for both inputs and outputs for the items requested? Note that attention is focused on major functions and work activities such as street cleaning, inspecting, and tree trimming. Each activity must be identified in terms of work or output unit, for example, a mile of street cleaned or an inspection completed. All major resource *input units* for items such as materials and supplies used and person hours worked are specifically identified. The cost per unit of input and the cost of output per unit of things produced are determined by dividing the cost of resources by the level or volume of items involved (e.g., 200 person-hours were worked at a cost of $1,000, or a per unit input cost per hour of $5; thirty miles of streets were paved at a cost of $30,000 or at a cost per output mile completed of $1,000).

Successful performance budget development requires a lengthy period of strong leadership. In the initial implementation phase attention should be given to the development of the budget structure, cost centers, performance measures, and the account coding system. Next, the recent past performance history of the agency should be organized. Given the new structure and the information on cost performance, the budget estimates can be developed.[10]

Table 12.3
City of Bright—Sample Performance Budget

```
      FUND:  General
DEPARTMENT:  Police
  ACTIVITY:  Patrolling
```

PROGRAM AND PERFORMANCE

FUNCTION:

      The Patrol Division of the Police Department provides prevention, suppression, and detection of criminal activity, traffic law enforcement, and general public safety to residents of the City of Bright.

PROGRAM COMMENTS:

      The Patrol Division responds directly to calls for service received at its headquarters and through the county-wide emergency number 911. The program proposes twenty full-time patrolmen and two sergeants. This year's budget includes $20,000 in out-of-state funds to expand patrolling downtown. An increase of $24,000 is requested in this FY 1985-86 budget.

PROGRAM MEASUREMENT:

	Actual 1983-84	Estimated 1984-85	Proposed 1985-86
1. Patrolling Residential Areas (hrs.)	9,825	10,927	11,308
2. Patrolling Business Areas (hrs.)	10,570	10,925	12,215
3. Issuing Citations #	6,514	7,528	8,721
4. Issuing Citations (hrs.)	1,500	1,800	2,312
5. Appearing in Traffic Court (hrs.)	1,395	2,189	1,556
6. Patrolling Special Events (hrs.)	2,007	2,500	2,715
7. Patrolling Events #	31	43	59
8. Arresting D.W.I. #	573	841	733
9. Patrolling for Crime Prevention (hrs.)	3,500	2,900	3,182
10. Patrolling School Crossing (hrs.)	2,967	3,100	3,300
11. Patrolling Supervision (hrs.)	2,537	3,528	4,176
12. Vacation Sick Leave (hrs.)	513	795	897

WORK DESCRIPTION:

1. Patrolling Residential Areas			
Unit: Hours	9,825	10,927	11,308
Unit: Cost	3.571	3.651	3.885
Total Cost	35,085	39,894	43,932

2. Patrolling Business Areas
   Unit: Hours   10,570   10,925   12,215
   Unit: Cost   3.726   3.866   3.707
   Total Cost   39,384   42,236   45,281

3. Issuing Citations
   Unit: Hours   1,500   1,800   2,312
   Unit: Cost   3.902   3.991   3.893
   Total Cost   5,853   7,184   9,001

4. Overseeing Traffic Accidents
   Unit: Hours   1,125   2,189   2,531
   Unit: Cost   4.229   3.789   3.774
   Total Cost   4,758   8,294   9,552

5. Appearing in Court
   Unit: Hours   1,395   1,556   2,217
   Unit: Cost   3.887   3.728   3.757
   Total Cost   5,422   5,801   8,329

6. Patrolling Special Events
   Unit: Hours   2,007   2,500   2,715
   Unit: Cost   4.037   3.941   4.120
   Total Cost   8,102   9,853   11,186

7. Patrolling School Crossing
   Unit: Hours   2,967   3,100   3,300
   Unit: Cost   4.037   3.982   3.941
   Total Cost   11,998   12,344   13,005

8. Arresting D.W.I.
   Unit: Hours   380   580   701
   Unit: Cost   3.900   4.100   4.21
   Total Cost   1,482   2,378   2,951

9. Patrolling for Crime Prevention
   Unit: Hours   3,500   29,000   3,182
   Unit: Cost   3.75   3.82   3.91
   Total Cost   13,125   110,780   12,442

10. Patrolling Supervisor
    Unit: Hours   2,537   3,528   4,196
    Unit: Cost   5.25   6.10   6.43
    Total Cost   13,319   21,521   26,980

11. Vacation, Sick Leave
    Unit: Hours   513   795   897
    Unit: Cost   3.52   3.71   3.87
    Total Cost   1,806   2,949   3,471

    Grand Total   140,334   263,234   186,130

The development of a performance budget involves seven steps:[11]

1. Define individual work activities in terms that are measurable and in terms that can be related to resource requirements.

2. Inventory the work units and the kind of work that must be performed on each.

3. Develop quantity standards for each activity to permit estimation of the amount of work required during the year, expressed in terms of annual number of units of work (tons, cubic yards, gallons, acres mowed, etc.). Quantity standards are used to define the workload to be undertaken and the minimum acceptable quality of work necessary to carry out an activity.

4. Determine the number of work units per activity. This task is made easy after the quantity standards and the inventory of the amount of work to be done on each activity have been established.

5. Establish production standards. The efficiency with which work is performed is a function of how the workers are assigned and equipped and the methods used in performing work activities. Responsibility should then be assigned to investigate and evaluate alternative methods for accomplishing each activity.

6. Compute resource requirements by applying production standards to the defined work program. For example, the production standard for premix patching stipulates the following conditions:

Crew size: 3 persons or workers
Equipment: 1 dump truck
Accomplishment/crew day: 3.75 tons premix
Production rate: 6.4 person-hours/ton

Activity	Quantity Standard	Work to be Done		Work Units
Mowing	3 Mowings	x	2,500 mowable acres	= 7,500 acres
Pothole Patching With Gravel	2,500 cu.yds. gravel/mile	x	400 miles	= 1,000,000 cu.yds.
Patching With Premix	7.5 tons premix/mile	x	100 level miles	= 750 ton premix

Assuming that the activity called for 750 tons of premix patching, the resource requirement would be:

crew days   = 750 tons ÷ 3.75 tons/day = 200 days
person-hours   = 3 persons × 8 hours/day × 200 days
               = 4,800 person-hours

or

person hours	= 6.4 person-hours/ton × 750
	= 4,800 person-hours
equipment	= 200 days × 8 hours
	= 1,600 hours for dump truck
materials	= 750 tons of bituminous premix material

7. Collect cost data and convert the performance budget resource requirements into financial terms. The procedures for each work activity would be developed as follows favor premix patching:[12]

Object of Expenditure	Resource Requirements	Average Unit Cost ($)		Annual Cost
Labor	4,800 per hour	x 3.00/hour	=	$ 14,400
Equipment	1,600 dump truck hours	x 1.50/hour	-	2,400
Materials	750 tons of premix	x 6.00/ton	=	4,500
Total				$ 21,300

USES OF THE PERFORMANCE BUDGET

Performance budgeting is intended to help administrators assess and improve the efficiency of an agency. It is management-oriented and is especially useful at the middle management level to aid in monitoring performance and coordinating work activities and in providing useful information for review of operations. Additionally, it promotes accountability to top management and improves work planning and scheduling.

The advantages of performance budgeting are that it (1) allows the relaxation of control over inputs; (2) deemphasizes external control and puts greater stress on internal control; (3) shifts the focus from budgeting control to administrative control; (4) regularizes post audit and post control; (5) promotes better work planning and scheduling; (6) enhances the responsibility and acceptability of management; and (7) facilitates the use of variance analysis and performance reporting as an important management control device.

PERFORMANCE BUDGETS:
SOME IMPORTANT DISADVANTAGES

Perhaps a major reason for the failure to adopt performance budgeting in public and non-profit agencies has been the number of problems inherent in it. These problems include (1) input and output unit costing; (2) accounting and cost data requirements; (3) diffused organizational responsibility; and (4) emphasis on volume of work done rather than on quality and effectiveness.

Input and Output Unit Costing. The unit costing feature, which is an integral part of performance budgeting, has a number of potential problems. Factors such as inflation, strikes, and transportation delays may impact upon unit cost, causing it to change. Thus some opponents of performance budgeting advocate that unit costing be replaced by work measurement (the person-hours or the physical number of units used) in budget development. The use of person-hours makes especially good sense in public and non-profit agencies since it represents about 80 percent of input cost factors.

Accounting and Cost Data Requirements. Most human services organizations present particular problems with regard to output unit cost measurements. In government agencies, and to a lesser extent in non-profit organizations, accounts are maintained on the expenditure basis rather than on the full cost basis. This makes it exceedingly difficult to collect data that can be used to determine unit output costs. To overcome or minimize these problems requires extensive accounting and data gathering facilities which may be too expensive for small municipalities and non-profit agencies.

Diffused Responsibilities. Since the identification of work activities and unit (input and output) measurements is the critical component of performance budgeting, attention is focused on the contribution of each activity. Little attention is paid to how activities relate to specific organizational units. Table 12.4 shows five possible combinations of activities. While the matrix indicates four activities (#2, #3, #4, and #5) contributing to each other, activity #1 provides no input or assistance to the others. This is a typical problem associated with performance budgeting; it does not facilitate integration or coordination of information among activities.

Table 12.4
Activity Grid or Matrix Reporting

Unit	Activity #1	Activity #2	Activity #3	Activity #4	Activity #5	Total
A	$100,000	$ 25,000	$ 16,000	$ 14,000	$ 40,000	$195,000
B	--	80,000	5,000	12,000	35,000	132,000
C	--	10,000	70,000	30,000	5,000	115,000
D	--	6,000	8,000	4,000	25,000	43,000
E	--	13,000	21,000	90,000	20,000	144,000
Total	$100,000	$134,000	$120,000	$150,000	$125,000	$629,000

These problems must be overcome if public and non-profit agencies wish to be effective instruments for the delivery of public goods and services.

Performance budgeting has enjoyed far less success than line-item budgeting because it demands greater investment of time and skill. Performance budgeting demonstrates how government and non-profit agencies could develop techniques to measure performance. Its emphasis on measurement and efficiency is its greatest strength. Performance budgeting efficiency pursuit is a narrow focus emphasizing the quantity and unit cost of things produced but not the impact or results they achieve. Minimal attention is given to budgeting policy decisions, limiting the effectiveness of performance budgeting in decision making.

Lack of Emphasis on Effectiveness. Performance budgeting focuses attention on process rather than on end purposes and results. Output units measure volume or the amount of work performed. Stress is put on countable quantities of things (e.g., miles of streets paved, tons of garbage removed, and number of library books loaned). The measures do not reveal the quality (e.g., the quality of the road paved, the cleanliness rating obtained as a result of the garbage removal, or the number of books requested but not available at the library) of the goods and services produced. Yet in a number of cases the quality attributes can be identified without too much difficulty. By incorporating the quality factor, performance budgeting proponents can blunt the criticism that the budget tends to concentrate on activities that are easily quantifiable while excluding or minimizing those that are not.

CONCLUDING OBSERVATIONS

While line-item budgeting has many admirable points, it also has many weaknesses. Its simplicity, practicability, and understandability are major reasons why it has enjoyed great popularity. On the whole, however, the shortcomings of line-item budgeting outweigh its strengths. Its preoccupation with inputs, narrow control, and dollar accountability and its lack of issue and policy orientation are serious impediments.

NOTES

1. Thomas J. Kane, Jr., "Budget Directors View Budget Control," *Public Budgeting and Finance* 2, no. 2 (Summer 1982): 44.

2. Edward J. Luksus, "Strategic Budgeting: How to Turn Financial Records into Strategic Assets," *Management Review* 70 (March 1981): 44.

3. Robert Leduc, "Financial Management and Budgeting," in *The Nonprofit Organization Handbook*, ed. Tracy Daniel Connors (New York: McGraw-Hill Book Co., 1980), part 6, pp. 61-62.

4. These are the resources designated necessary to minimally carry out the functions of a program to prevent it from falling below an agreed upon acceptable standard.

5. Daniel Guttman and Barry Willner, *The Shadow Government* (New York: Parthenon Books, 1976), pp. 42-44.

6. See Thomas Anton, *The Politics of State Expenditures in Illinois* (Champaign, Ill.: University of Illinois Press), pp. 6-51; and Aaron Wildavsky, *Budgeting* (Boston: Little, Brown and Co., 1975), p. 24.

7. Ibid.

8. Commission on Organization of the Executive Branch of the Government, *Budget and Accounting* (Washington, D.C.: Government Printing Office, 1949), p. 8.

9. Municipal Finance Officers Association, *Governmental Accounting, Auditing and Financial Reporting (GAAFR)* (Chicago: Municipal Finance Officers Association, 1980), Appendix B-70.

10. See Allen Scheck, *Budget Innovation and the States* (Washington, D.C.: Brookings Institution, 1971), pp. 44-52.

11. Highway Research Board, *Performance Budgeting Systems for Highway Maintenance and Management* (Washington, D.C.: Highway Research Board, 1972), pp. 13-19.

12. Ibid., p. 20.

CHAPTER 13

PPBS: A RATIONAL BUDGETING SYSTEM

The planning, programming, and budgeting system (PPBS) was developed in response to dissatisfaction with traditional line-item budgeting and performance budgeting. It was felt that line-item budgeting was overly preoccupied with control and too little concerned with policy and results. Performance budgeting, which was expected to overcome many of the weaknesses of the line-item budget, produced problems of its own. Performance budgeting focused on units of work completed and unit costing, drawing attention away from alternative costing approaches that linked organizational goals and objectives. Emphasis was put mainly on things measurable and countable. Thus, while there was concern for output, little effort was made to link output with policy goals and objectives.

This chapter covers the theory and practice of PPBS. The reader is provided with the basic philosophy and techniques that underlie the PPBS approach to the allocation of scarce resources.

EARLY PROGRAM BUDGETING

The early development of program budgeting represented a bridge between the performance budget and PPBS. Because of the different emphases of program budgeting and PPBS, they are discussed separately.

Like PPBS, the program budget emphasizes results.[1] The approach focuses on information more useful to the administrator than to the accountant. The program budget includes a more comprehensive view of the budget process than either the line-item or performance budget.

Program budgeting has the following attributes: (1) it encourages identification of program purpose, program development, and commitment to planning; (2) it brings considerable order to masses of detail in terms of understandable issues and specific plans; (3) like PPBS, it emphasizes multi-year planning and periodic reevaluation of program results; (4) unlike PPBS, it begins below top management, at the middle and operating level, guarding against overcentralization; (5) it gives less attention than PPBS to the systematic consideration of alternatives; and (6) it stresses input-output linkage, facilitating cost-benefit analysis.

Program budgeting is an extension of performance budgeting in that it defines program objectives and obtains measures (output) to assess these objectives. However, it differs from performance budgeting in its emphasis on program planning and assessment of output results. It is unlike PPBS in that it gives less attention to alternative analyses in making program selection. The definition of program is essentially the same in both systems, referring to a combination of resources, manpower, materials, and facilities (e.g., equipment, capital, and skills) that are put together to achieve a common set of objectives within a specified period of time.

PLANNING, PROGRAMMING AND
BUDGETING SYSTEM (PPBS)

Definition. PPBS is a planning, implementing, and control system. As a comprehensive decision-making instrument, it is designed to accommodate and integrate multiple functions (see Figure 13.1). It provides an important link between strategic planning (long- and medium-range) and operating plans. PPBS is a systematic effort concerned with the integration of planning, programming, and budgeting. It requires the articulation of explicit goals, purposes, and objectives from which strategic output-oriented programs are identified. It generates output budget information from which effective resource allocations can be made. Viewed as such, PPBS is a subsystem of systems analysis as discussed below. Once the program outputs have been specified, expenditures can then be converted into traditional line-item requests.

A major focus of PPBS is on the purpose(s) for which an agency is requesting funds. As a policy-oriented and decision-making system, PPBS seeks to improve resource allocation by assisting agencies in making the best selection among competing alternatives in the pursuit of organizational goals and objectives. PPBS is thus an important analytical tool designed to help decision makers achieve assigned responsibilities with optimal results.

The underlying premises on which PPBS is based are perhaps best revealed in the answers to the following questions: (1) What are the basic goals and objectives being pursued? (2) What are the alternative means for achieving articulated goals and objectives? (3) What are the costs (present, future, and full) of each alternative, in both financial and nonfinancial terms? (4) What are the benefits to be achieved from each alternative and

Figure 13.1
Conceptual View: PPBS as an Integrative Decision-Making Process

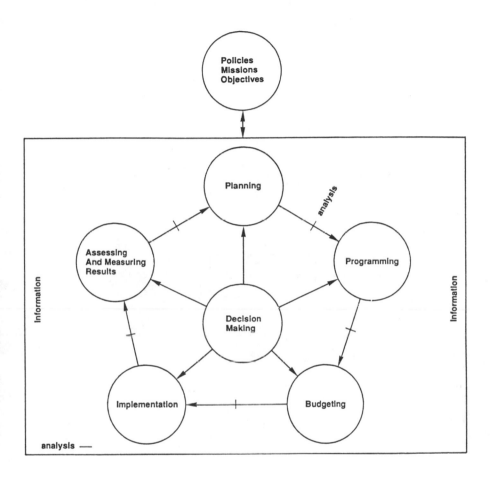

how effective will each be in achieving articulated goals and objectives? (See boxed material on factors in cost-effectiveness studies.)

Before PPBS can be initiated, an agency must develop an analytical capability to examine in depth its objectives and the programs identified to achieve those objectives (see Figure 13.2). There is a need to create an improved budgeting mechanism to facilitate broad program decision making and to translate it into budgeting outcomes to be presented to the chief executive and legislative or board officials for action. Figure 13.2

Figure 13.2
Schema of the PPBS Process

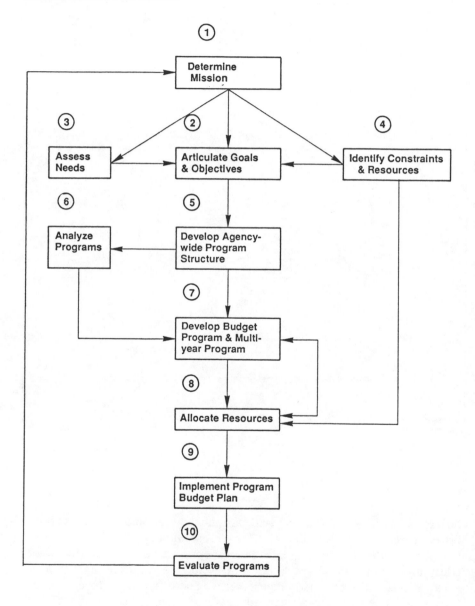

shows the steps that may be involved in developing a PPBS budget. Based on an assessment of needs and an evaluation of resource constraints, goals and objectives are articulated. Next, an agency-wide program structure is developed. Programs are fitted into the structure and analyzed, after which a multi-year program budget and financial plan is constructed.

Figure 13.2 clearly indicates that a budget is an instrument for implementing long-range plans. Unlike traditional line-item budgeting, in which budget decision making is primarily upward, PPBS decision making is mainly a downward aggregative information flow process. In contrast to traditional budgeting systems that take a retrospective view in assessing what was done with resources, PPBS takes a prospective focus about the future impact of resource application. An unarticulated but implied premise of PPBS is that it is better to implement the right decision inefficiently than to implement the wrong decision efficiently.

FACTORS IN
COST-EFFECTIVENESS STUDIES

The cost-effectiveness study should result in a written document which contains all of the basic elements of good analysis:

1. A clear definition of the problem(s).
2. Identification of the basic objectives involved.
3. Selection of "criteria" or "measures of effectiveness" which will permit estimation of progress against the basic objectives. These should not be limited to only those criteria that are believed to be quantifiable. So-called "intangibles," if pertinent to program selection, should be included.
4. Identification and description of the key features, and of the alternative ways of attempting to meet the problem(s). Alternatives may be in the form of different programs, or different levels of a program, or both.
5. Estimates of the full cost implications of each alternative, including future as well as immediate implications.
6. Estimates of the full effects of each alternative (relative to each of the criteria identified as being important) to include future as well as immediate implications.
7. A clear presentation of the "tradeoffs" among the alternatives considering the costs and effects as estimated in (5) and (6). Charts, graphs, and tables are useful presentation devices.
8. Identification of the major uncertainties, and the quantification of the uncertainties, to the extent possible. Uncertainty,

often considerable uncertainty, can be expected to be present in any realistic analysis. The effects of these uncertainties on potential decisions should be estimated.

9. Identification of the major assumptions made in the study with an indication of the degree to which program choices may be sensitive to these assumptions.

10. Documentation of the study in such a manner as to permit others to understand and evaluate what was done in the analysis and to obtain a feeling for how accurate the basic data and the findings can be expected to be.

A cost-effectiveness analysis may use, if applicable, many of the techniques of mathematics, operations research, economics, etc. It may also draw upon various technical and nontechnical studies previously done which are pertinent to the study at hand.

The cost-effectiveness analysis treats such problems as those identified in individual issue papers or perhaps will examine one category of the program structure or a group of interacting categories.

Source: Adapted from George Washington University, "State-Local Finances Project," in Ralph G. Caso, *Management Information Systems* (Nassau County, N.Y.: Fiscal Administration, 1971), part 3, p. 7.

PPBS: ANALYZING THE CONCEPTS

PPBS comprises concepts, systems, processes, techniques, and formats. It is a management decision-making instrument that ties long-range, medium-term, and short-range plans with budgeting. The PPBS approach is designed to accommodate and integrate multiple management functions into an operating plan of action, as noted above. Figure 13.1 schematically depicts the four main concepts (planning, programming, budgeting, and systems) in the PPBS decision-making system. The schema shows policies, missions, and objectives as the major inputs into the PPB system, which is held together by a decision-making network. This network links a dynamic and interactive process that is to be maintained among the major components in the existing information system.

Planning. Planning is the most fundamental activity in program budgeting because it is based on planned programs which give it a unique identity vis-a-vis other types of budgets. Since PPBS is a mission-oriented and management-oriented system, planning (the first "P") is the focal point and ingredient that facilitates the effective clustering of activities around objectives. Thus planning begins by defining objectives or outcomes to be achieved and concludes by suggesting the optimal way to realize those objectives. Planning is the formulation of a future course of action, specifying and classifying long-range and short-range goals. It is an important means for coping with a dynamic environment that generates the uncertainties of changing mission, goals, priorities, and procedures.[2]

Planning does not take place in a vacuum. It is undertaken to achieve some goal or objective. Examples include welfare, health, and education planning. All organizations have goals and objectives. Planning is the means that is used to achieve them. Typically, organizational goals and objectives are identified in a structure which may be broken down into subgoals or a goal-objective structure. Goals may be viewed in a hierarchical structure as indicated in Figure 13.3, in which the goal is subdivided, becoming more specific and quantitative at each descending level of division.

Figure 13.3
A Hierarchical Goal Structure in a Large Organization

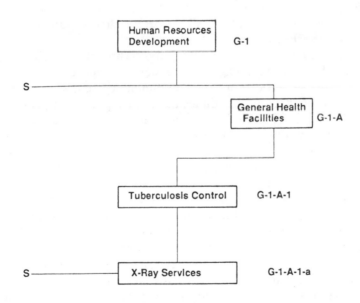

G-1:	Optimal development and enhancement of human resources to permit each individual to expand his/her potential to the fullest.
G-1-A:	Provision of general health facilities to aid in the prevention and treatment of diseases.
G-1-A-1:	Development and maintenance of tuberculosis control services.
G-1-A-1-a:	Maintenance of X-ray services for screening and diagnosing.

Planning Constraints. Figure 13.2 indicated constraints as an important factor to be considered in the analysis and selection of program alternatives. What may appear to be a theoretically sound alternative might not be feasible in the real world due to operating constraints. Thus constraints should be considered early in the planning stage so that they may be used as guidelines in the development of goals and alternative methods of achieving them.

Program analysis is an important factor during the planning stage, when selection must be made among alternative courses of action in the pursuit of articulated organizational goals. Program analysis requires the establishment of selection criteria. The latter permits the elimination of clearly unfeasible alternatives without resorting to detailed analysis. Once these initial eliminations have been made, detailed analysis is undertaken to identify the alternative program that meets the established criteria. The analysis typically focuses on three aspects: (1) monetary and other resources needed for the program; (2) kinds of benefits that will accrue from the program; and (3) comparisons of total program costs with total benefits. Completion of these actions permits the program that is suitable and implementable to be selected.

Implementing Points to Consider (Planning). Three PPBS planning activities should be kept in mind: (1) the development of budgeting guidelines; (2) the identification and definition of goals; and (3) development of needed information. Budgetary guidelines are indispensable if the budget request is to be more than incremental resource allocation. The guidelines should contain three important components: assumptions, constraints, and priorities.

Assumptions identify economic, political, social, and other external factors that are likely to impact the agency. It is important that both assumptions and constraints be dealt with as early as feasible in the planning process because it is vital to know the conditions that will impede or limit the scope and method of an agency. For example, it would be unwise to request an expansion of a program at a time when an influential group with direct access to policy makers feels that the program should be cut back or abolished. Finally, the articulation of priorities shows the importance of the rank ordering that the agency or community attaches to the allocation of resources for the coming year.

Explicit, clear, and precise definition of goals is critical to program budgeting. The goal statement indicates to the public the kinds of problems that government and other not-for-profit agencies are mobilized to solve, the conditions to be ameliorated, and the extent to which articulated desires and expectations will be realized.

PROGRAMMING

Programming enters the process after the mission, purpose, objectives, and broad program outlines have been determined. It identifies program components, tasks, or activities and fits them into a time frame specified in the goal and objective structure. Programming aids in the generation of alternative approaches to the achievement of program goals and objectives. Perhaps the most essential step is the identification of activities around program objectives and the development of operational plans (e.g., the assignment of resources such as personnel, materials, and facilities) to achieve them. Programming occurs during the program analysis stage or after program selection has been made. Programming acts as an important bridge between planning and budgeting, assuring that all strategic decisions and projected expenditures are integrated into the program format for the fiscal and/or planning period. Answers should be sought to the following questions: Given the political, economic, and social reality, is the alternative feasible at this time? What are the legal constraints, if any, to this program? Given the resources available, can this program achieve the most effective and efficient outcome for the resources applied? Considering the life span of the program, what will be the financial requirements to continue the program in future years? Is alternative funding available for this program?

A critical opportunity is present in the programming phase. This is the phase which permits the manager to consider whether changes in the agency's programs are desired. The decision must be made to add new programs, to eliminate existing ones, or to modify them. Obviously the action taken to add, eliminate, or modify programs must be based on comparative analysis of benefits in which the advantages and disadvantages are clearly identified.

Implementing Points to Consider (Programming). Through a process of self-study analysis, programming facilitates making the best choice among alternative programs. Through this process programming is able to determine the extent to which existing or proposed programs complement or overlap other programs. The main activities undertaken to aid the programming process involve examination of current programs, analysis of feasible alternatives, and identification of desired programs. This step requires (1) a brief description of each program; (2) a review of the kinds of personnel employed in executing the programs; (3) a detailed description of the target groups or clients served and the time span over which the services have been operating; (4) materials and equipment required; and (5) total costs and the different kinds of costs (direct and indirect).

BUDGETING

A program budget is much more than a listing of expenditure by program. All dollars are systematically related to goals and objectives in the program structure. Based on the cost or expenditure allocations, a budget indicates where the emphasis and priorities of the agency are being put. The dollar amounts are incorporated into both the current year program budget and the multi-year financial plan (projection of alternative programs for several years, usually five years).

Implementing Points to Consider (Budgeting). The budgeting phase has four steps: specification of financial support, budget request review, budget modifications, and allocation of available funds.

The completion of the programming phase—specification of the financial support or resources needed to implement the program selected—permits the budget implementation phase to begin. The quantity of resources needed is estimated, and required dollar amounts are entered in the agency books according to the standard chart of accounts. (Depending on the system the agency uses, such as object of expenditure, functional, or program, the dollar amounts are expressed in terms that can be accommodated by that system. Depending on the system's requirements, the budget amount may be broken out to show salaries, health and retirement benefits, and other items needed to implement the program.)

The design of the system to review the program budget request requires that participants other than the proposers review the budget requests. Unlike in other budgeting systems, however, the review is conducted in terms of program goals, objectives, and costs. This is done to ensure that the purpose of the program matches budgetary guidelines and that the identified accomplishments match accepted and articulated goals and objectives. Additionally, it must be determined if the proposed size of the program will adequately serve the target population and if the best alternative has been chosen. In those cases where program changes have been requested, it must be determined whether they make sense within the budgetary guidelines. Examination is made to determine if the dollar amounts requested are adequate or exceed required limits; amounts requested are checked for accuracy.

The completed budget requests are compared with projected revenues to determine if and where budget modifications may be necessary. In those situations where modification is required, the following options are available: (1) total or partial elimination of a program; (2) reduction of services in one or more programs; (3) identification of areas where resources could be shifted to effect efficiencies; (4) determination of sources from which to borrow funds or obtain external grants (in the case of government, tax increases; in non-profit organizations, access to foundations, business, or campaign drives).

SYSTEM

The systems concept implies that different parts of an organization act interdependently in achieving a common purpose. In PPBS, planning, programming, and budgeting are interdependent activities that are synchronized to optimally achieve articulated goals and objectives. This requires that mission, goals, and objectives be directly linked to programs and subprograms, objectives, activities, output, and impact, and to their costs (direct and indirect).

In summary, the systems approach suggests that an organization is (1) focused on a set of objectives aimed at satisfying a predetermined plan; (2) used to convert resources (inputs) into outputs; (3) viewed as having elements and components that are interactive and interdependent; and (4) devised to contain a monitoring system to determine deviations from targeted objectives.

PROGRAM MEASURES

Figure 13.4 shows different types of measures that may be developed for the City of Bright for the Department of Housing. From Figure 13.4 we can see the linkage among program mission, activities, and performance measures.

DEVELOPING THE PROGRAM BUDGET FORMAT

High priority should be given to the program budget format. There are two main elements in the program format: the program structure and the cost structure. Each program is broken down into subcategories with the presentation of cost estimates projected over the planning time horizon, typically five years (see Figure 13.5).

Program Structure. The program is the basic framework and building block in program budgeting. Thus great attention must be given to program structure because it plays an important role in the success or failure of program budget. The program structure translates an agency's fundamental mission, goals, and objectives into a program hierarchy, ranging from the largest program to the basic constituent or element. The program components are subdivided as desired by management to facilitate planning, budgeting, controlling, and reporting (Figure 13.6).

The program structure should ideally be a link between an agency's goals and objectives and the financial control system of the traditional object-of-expenditure budget, as shown in Figure 13.6. An agency's output should be directly linked to articulated goals and objectives. The key aim in PPBS is to develop appropriate classifications which will permit measurement and evaluation of performance in relation to assigned responsibilities. The program is the highest level of work performed by an agency that carries out assigned responsibilities. All programs are directed at producing some product that is definable and measurable.

Some programs do not conform to existing organizational structures. For example, a state program (see Figure 13.7) dealing with alcohol-related problems may involve many other agencies, such as the department of

Figure 13.4
Suggested Program Budget, Department of Housing, City of Bright*

Department Mission/Goal: To provide adequate, safe, and sanitary housing conditions for all residents in the City of Bright.

Objectives:
1. To make it easier for private builders to construct new housing and rehabilitate old housing.

2. To present Bright neighborhoods as good places to live.

3. To protect the sound housing in the community through timely and effective repair and maintenance programs.

4. To develop and implement programs to prevent housing abandonment.

5. To rehabilitate or demolish already abandoned units.

6. To develop long-range plans for housing involving the public and private sectors and neighborhood residents.

7. To create a professionally and efficiently run Housing Department, responsive to the changing conditions and circumstances.

Program Area: Housing Development

Goal: To create a healthier development climate in the city, making it easier for private developers to construct new housing and to rehabilitate old housing.

Objectives:
1. To encourage private developers to construct 25 percent more new homes.

2. To encourage private developers to rehabilitate 20 percent of the old homes.

*A five-year budget is normally projected for each program.

232

Workload Measures:

1. Number of housing units rehabilitated.

2. Number of rehabilitated units sold.

3. Number of new home buyers attracted to the city through its program.

4. Number of Community Development Block Grants distributed.

5. Number of man-hours spent implementing each phase of the programs.

Efficiency and Productivity:

1. Cost per unit of homes rehabilitated.

2. Numbers of homes rehabilitated per worker.

3. Number of Community Development Block Grants processed per worker per period.

4. Number of home buyers attracted per marketing staff per period.

Impact/Effectiveness Measures:

1. Percentage of abandoned homes satisfactorily rehabilitated.

2. Percentage of substandard homes satisfactorily rehabilitated.

3. Number and percentage of people actually buying substandard homes.

4. Amount of Community Development Block Grants effectively allocated for rehabilitating homes.

Figure 13.5
Program Budget Format

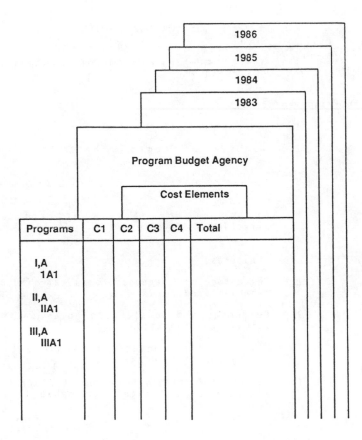

Figure 13.6
Program Classification System

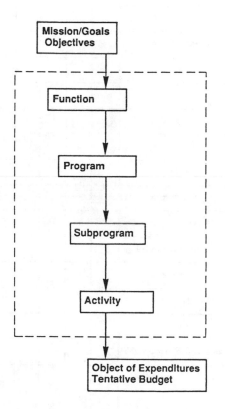

Figure 13.7
Expenditure for Alcohol Treatment Program

ORGANIZATION	PROGRAMS	I. Prevention of Alcoholism				II. Restoration (Early Stages)						III. Care (The Chronic)						
			A. Education	B. Law of Economics	C. Research		A. Detection	B. Diagnosis	C. Treatment	D. Rehabilitation	E. Research		A. Detection	B. Diagnosis, Evaluation, Referral	C. Treatment	D. Rehabilitation	E. Domiciliary Care	F. Research	Etc.
Dept. of Welfare																			
Employment																			
Dept. of Education																			
Police																			
Youth and Adult Correction																			
Atty. Gen. Office																			
Highway																			

Source: Adapted from C. W. Churchman and A. H. Schainblatt, "PPB: How Can It Be Implemented?" *Public Administration Review* 29 (March/April 1969): 1982.

health and welfare, highways, youth and adult correction, employment, and education, as well as the attorney general's office. The question is, How should these overlaps be handled? Two approaches have been suggested. The first is simply to define programs across organizational boundaries. Thus all related activities contributing to the program goal taking place in other departments are grouped. The funding for the program is thus allocated to a number of departments. By means of a matrix or grid, resource allocation and responsibility can be displayed (see Figure 13.7).

Perhaps the most practical approach requires that programs be defined within major organizational units. This approach sometimes results in more programs, but it enhances control and responsibility reporting. In addition, it provides sufficient information that permits program analysis to modify or eliminate duplicating activities.

An important and continuing question is, How detailed should the program and subprogram be made? Though there are no specific criteria, each situation should dictate the precise subdivision of a program budget hierarchy. A few observations may aid our understanding. Beginning with the mission of the organization down to the smallest subdivision of the program, there must be logical linkage throughout the program structure. For example, once the mission, goals, and objectives have been stated for an agency, each functional area must be consistent with them. Additionally, there must be as many functional areas as necessary to achieve the agency's mission/goal. Similarly, there must be as many programs as required to achieve the goal and objective of the function. At the program level, the number of subprograms identified is determined at the point at which the program goal and objective have been recognized. Note that for each objective stated, there should be at least one impact/effectiveness indicator to determine how well the objective was achieved (see Figure 13.4). If there are, for example, five objectives and only two impact indicators that can be identified, it means that the other objectives are not important or that there is confusion about their logical relationships.

It is thus critical early in the program structuring stage to define precisely the legitimate services to be provided and their probable recipients. This gives a rough idea for relating the program goals and objectives with impact indicators and the intended clients and provides answers to the questions "what" and "for whom" the program is intended. As far as possible, each program should be broken down to answer "what" and "to whom" until the point at which the question "how" the activity is to be performed can be answered.

A basic function of PPBS is to relate the cost of government and/or agency to the services provided. All program structures relate operating organizational units to functional areas, programs, subprograms, and activities. The functional areas identify the major purposes of an agency. The size of the functional area increases as one moves from small to large organizations. For example, the state of Wisconsin divided the state's operation into five functional areas: commerce, education, environmental resources, human relations and resources, and general executive functions.

A program is a division of a functional area providing services for an identifiable group or target population in order to achieve a specific purpose. The program combines a homogeneous group of services to meet similar needs, disabilities, or attributes. Stated another way, a program "is a clustering of activities and resources around one or more objectives focused on the production of similar outputs."[3] The Home Repairs Loan Program in the Department of Housing in the city of Bright provides a good example:

What

Program: Home Repairs Loan

Subprogram: Home Insulation

For Whom

Home Owners

(more specifically) Home owners needing insulation

How

Activity 1: Processing applications

Activity 2: Applying cut-off criteria

Activity 3: Approving matching insulation grant

Subprogram B: Emergency Home Repairs Loan

Home owners having code violations

How

Activity 1: Processing applications

Activity 2: Applying cut-off criteria

Activity 3: Granting loans to eligible home owners

As can be noted from this example, a subprogram is a breakdown of a program into more specific services being provided for a specific segment of the target population. Similarly, the activities are specific actions and techniques applied to implement the programs.

ISSUE ANALYSIS

Issue analysis attempts to identify, clarify, and analyze significant problems facing a government agency (see boxed material). Sometimes called special study analysis, issue analysis is an important supplement to PPBS, providing its analytic foundation. It aids decision makers in formulating policy regarding addition, rejection, or confirmation, or it may simply be used to provide vital input for the strategic planning process. Two kinds of issue analysis have been used: one for resolving budget or fiscal year issues, and one with a time frame that extends beyond a budget year that is aimed at aiding future development and resource allocation decisions. It is the issue analysis input that makes planning, programming, and budgeting substantive and dynamic.

OUTLINE OF ISSUE PAPER

The issue paper is a written document that attempts to identify and describe the major features of a major problem facing the government. It essentially attempts to "define the problem."

The issue paper may either stand by itself as a description of the problem area in order to gain an improved perspective on the problem, or, more important, it can be used to set the framework, to act as the first phase, of an in-depth, cost-effectiveness analysis of the issue.

The issue paper should address such questions as:

1. What is the real problem?
2. What are its causes?
3. Who are the population groups affected? (That is, if other than the general public, identify their characteristics, such as age group, race, income class, special handicaps, locations, etc.)
4. What is the magnitude of the problem? How widespread is it now and how large is it likely to be in future years?
5. Toward what objectives should programs for meeting the problem be directed?
6. How can estimates of progress against these objectives be made?
7. What activities are currently being undertaken by this government that are relevant to the problem?
8. What other sectors of the community, or other levels of government, in addition to this government, are involved?
9. Are there major constraints, including political ones, that seem to affect the problem?
10. What are the types of alternatives that should be considered for meeting the problem?

Note that answering questions such as the above does not specifically answer the question of what should be done to meet the problem. Answering the question, "What should be specifically done?" is *not* a function of the issue paper but rather of a cost-effectiveness analysis that ideally should follow the issue paper. The issue paper rather attempts to define the problem and direct attention to the specific information that

---

will need to be obtained and examined before deciding what to do about the problem.

Some quantification might be attempted in the issue paper, such as providing estimates of the number of persons in the target groups that are affected by the problem (question #4 above) and providing estimates of the costs and pertinent outputs of current, relevant government activities (question #7).

A government should not be surprised if the problem identified by the time the issue paper is completed is *not* the same as the problem conceived of at the beginning.

Source: Adapted from George Washington University, "State-Local Financial Project," in Ralph G. Caso, *Management Information System* (Nassau County, N.Y.: Fiscal Administration, 1971), part 3, p. 6.

CROSSWALK AND PPBS

A number of names, such as grid and matrix, have been associated with the term *crosswalk* in program budgeting. Crosswalk has come to mean the design of a program budget system that allows data to be converted from the program system to the traditional line-item budget, providing both a management and a control orientation. Typically the conversion is made only for one budget year at a time.

The need to make the budget conversion or classification occurs when the program budget differs from the existing budget structure. By use of the crosswalk, the program budget is transformed and regrouped from a policy-making format to one concerned with program implementation and control. Through the use of computers, the conversion process has been made less difficult than it otherwise would be. An important requirement is the establishment of a coding method to facilitate ready reclassification of budget items.

By means of the crosswalk system (see Table 13.1) flexibility is increased to enable the provision and use of traditional budget data to meet administrative, operations, and performance requirements. Significantly, it provides for the integration of planning, analysis, and budgeting.

PPBS: CONCLUDING OBSERVATIONS

PPBS is an accountability instrument and a well-organized management information system that compels continuing self-study as a means of generating innovation and self-renewal. It is a means for examining the financial implications of programs over their expected life spans. This typically requires the examination of the consequences of expanding or contracting a program as well as its spillover impact. PPBS provides a

Table 13.1
Expenditure Crosswalk Year 1

Account	Object Categories	Totals	Program I	Program II	Program III	Program IV
X 2	Salaries	75,000	30,000	10,000	15,000	20,000
X 3	Materials	85,000	40,000	5,000	20,000	30,000
X 4	Travel	20,000	8,000	2,000	5,000	5,000
X 5	Utilities	25,000	10,000	2,000	8,000	5,000
X 6	Rent	25,000	15,000	5,000	2,000	3,000
X 7	Consulting	110,000	50,000	1,000	4,000	10,000
X 8	Maintenance	35,000	15,000	2,000	10,000	8,000
	TOTALS	375,000	168,000	36,000	64,000	81,000

framework for planning, facilitating the organization of information that can systematically analyze the fiscal and nonfiscal consequences of proposals, and then selecting the best possible course of action.

PPBS: Advantages. (1) It can help decision makers focus on objectives and overall goals of an agency, indicating how they are linked with intra- and/or inter-agency programs and how they can be reached; (2) it links planning, programming, and budgeting in an integrated system; (3) it makes long-range and multi-year planning routine; (4) it promotes efficient means for allocating resources; (5) it provides understanding that enhances inter-agency coordination and cooperation; and (6) it provides the information and data necessary to permit in-depth analysis of alternative courses of action.

PPBS: Disadvantages. PPBS requires massive amounts of data, expertise, and staff time, making it time-consuming and costly to operate. Its great emphasis on goal clarification and goal setting forces explicit value identification and operating philosophy that may not be compatible with all or most participants in the budget process. The charge has been made that PPBS minimizes politics, on which budgets heavily depend. Additionally, because of its emphasis on rationality, its demand for performance, its requirement for policy impact, and its focus on explicit statement of objectives, PPBS is not likely to be consistent with participants' expectations in the budget-making process. Most participants prefer inexplicit articulation of objectives because they believe that it provides a better means for protecting their resource base.

NOTES

1. Harry P. Hatry and John F. Cotton, *Program Planning for County and City* (Washington, D.C.: George Washington University, January, 1967), p. 16.

2. Jerome B. McKinney and Lawrence C. Howard, *Public Administration: Balancing Power and Accountability* (Oak Park, Ill: Moore Publishing Co., 1979), p. 76.

3. Stephen Knezevich, *Program Budgeting PPBS* (Berkeley, Calif.: McCutchan Publishing Co., 1973), p. 48.

CHAPTER 14

ZERO-BASE BUDGETING

Interest in zero base budgeting was not widespread until the end of the 1960s and 1970s. The sixties were marked by a period of full employment, with inflation virtually unknown. When sufficient resources for programs could not be found at the state level of government and at foundations, the federal government became an eager partner. In the 1960s federal revenue grew so fast that federal policy makers were beginning to fear that people would demand tax reductions. Chief Economic Advisor Walter Heller and others began talking about a fiscal dividend—a scheme (quite similar to the present revenue sharing system) whereby the federal revenues would be returned to local governments and distributed and spent according to federal formulae and criteria. The widespread practice of traditional incremental budgeting, with its built-in bias toward continuity and growth, became ever more entrenched, and efforts at implementing PPBS and management by objectives (MBO) in the 1960s to achieve greater rational allocation of resources failed to make headway in the public budgeting process. This chapter examines ZBB and explores the forces that favor its implementation.

BACKGROUND AND DEVELOPMENT OF THE ZBB APPROACH

The economic, social, and political philosophies that shape priorities have been undergoing radical change. By the early 1970s, the long duration of the Vietnam War, a continuing high level of unemployment, unmanageable inflation, deep recession, and the apparent end of cheap and plentiful energy ushered in a period of conservation. People began asking for a greater degree of certainty, and it seemed irrational to continue to make choices by the traditional incremental muddling-through approach. This was particularly true at a time when demands for government services were rising while available resources were falling, thus necessitating contraction and retrenchment rather than expansion.

As government attempted to cope with these problems, emphasis shifted to control by (1) direct citizen input; (2) reorganization; (3) legislative input (sunset laws); and (4) ZBB. The citizen input approach attempted to limit spending and revenue raising through referendums. For example, in 1978 Proposition 13 cut property taxes nearly 60 percent in California.[1] As McCaffery and Bowman have indicated, however, direct citizen input may have good intentions, but it does not necessarily produce the most desirable outcomes. Unintended results, such as reduced federal aid, shifting of taxes toward home owners, and greater dependence on state government, often occur.

Because of the ineffectual history of reorganization (structural changes that deemphasize substantive social and political problems), it gained few supporters. Sunset laws and ZBB received the greatest attention. The sunset approach (initially adopted by Colorado in 1976 for evaluating its forty-one regulatory agencies) is a legislative instrument employed to control the cost and quality of government programs. Government programs, accordingly, are evaluated before a terminal date and are kept functioning only if the evaluation demonstrates satisfactory performance and continuing need for the service.

The concept and practice of the sunset approach are commendable; however, if inappropriately applied, it engenders opposition rather than support toward legislators for their policy making. For example, in 1977 Alabama state representatives were expected to vote yes or no on 207 agencies in three hours. It has also been said that if this method were widely practiced, highly qualified individuals would be discouraged from entering government service because promises could not be made about the tenure of an agency.[2]

Zero base budgeting is in some ways similar to sunset laws, but ZBB permits a more comprehensive set of continuing controls and is executive-oriented. In addition, it focuses yearly attention quantitatively on allocative, administrative, and economic efficiency, and qualitatively on effectiveness. The emphasis shifts to control not only of dollars expended but of performance and the achievement of the greatest policy outcome for the fewest number of dollars. This requires that social changes be undertaken only as they are understood as trade-offs between benefits to be gained and costs to be incurred. This approach is important to governments, especially in those geographic areas that are experiencing general economic decline. It is in this context that the potential application of ZBB may be viewed.

DEFINING THE ZBB CONCEPT

Unlike traditional budgeting, "with ZBB nothing is assumed. Every function of every department is questioned. Existing programs are scrutinized as much as expanded or new programs. The entire budget is viewed as a series of supplemental requests with a theoretical base of zero and each supplement must be analyzed."[3] ZBB requires that managers defend every activity under their control before funds are allocated. To qualify for any allocation of funds, every programmatic activity or function to be performed must be identified, evaluated, and ranked in terms of costs and benefits.

ZBB is the only budget system that examines a budget request below its base. It aims to cut dollars, not service. Attention is drawn to the harm that cutbacks may entail. Yet greater emphasis is put on the decremental, in contrast to the incremental orientation which is standard practice in the traditional line-item budget.

ZBB is mainly a short-range tool employed in a managerial process to achieve objectives in the most cost-efficient manner. It is a "bottom-up" approach involving all management levels. The approach has built-in flexibility, for managers are given a range of choices to facilitate priority setting and establishment of funding levels. Subordinates do not send their budgets up to higher management on a take-it-or-leave-it basis. Clear choices and options are an integral part of the ZBB approach. In writing about the Garland, Texas, experience, Leininger and Wong observed: "ZBB is a management tool which provides a systematic method for evaluating all operations and programs, current or new, allows for budget reductions and expansions in a natural manner and allows the reallocation of resources from low to high priority programs."[4]

A key consideration in ZBB is the search for alternative ways for achieving articulated objectives. The ZBB manager is expected to start from scratch by assuming that an activity (any that may be considered for implementation) does not exist. The manager can then reconstruct the operation from zero, asking the question: Should things be done the way they are now, or should the manager reorganize, consolidate, centralize, decentralize, subcontract, or implement the activity in an entirely different way? By employing this process it is believed that more goods and services will be delivered at the same or lower cost. Innovative thinking is promoted, thereby enhancing productivity and improving economic performance.

Contrasting ZBB with the traditional line-item budget vividly highlights the differences between the two approaches, emphasizing ZBB's changes from the status quo (see Table 14.1).

WHERE SHOULD ZBB BE IMPLEMENTED?

ZBB should be implemented in any organization or unit where we can develop cost-benefit analysis and which does not presently have a standard cost system. Most governments and non-profit organizations fall into this category. Typically most service and overhead areas, such as personnel, counseling, accounting, legal, management service, and research also fall into this category. ZBB is most suitable for people- and capital-intensive activities where productivity standards are not easily obtainable to apply in making cost projections.

Table 14.1
Contrasting Traditional Line-Item Budgeting with ZBB

Incremental Budgeting	ZBB
1. Operating budget is estimated.	1. Operating budget is developed by evaluating current activities and alternatives.
2. Accepts existing base and estimates cost of new activities (only).	2. Assumes "clean slate" and estimates all costs associated with activities.
3. Estimates costs and benefits for new activities.	3. Identifies and evaluates costs and benefits for all activities including alternatives.
4. Emphasis is put on dollars as the main initiating concern in preparing detailed budgets.	4. Initiating emphasis is put on purposes and activities and on priorities.
5. Little or no effort is made to examine alternative ways of accomplishing activities.	5. New approaches are explicitly examined.
6. Process results in "take it or leave it" budget.	6. Process results in trade-off options/choices for different levels of service and costs.

The ZBB process is used in organizations that have a desire and commitment to achieve speedy, favorable financial results and improve the effectiveness of managers. It is also used in communities and agencies concerned with reallocating resources to meet new and changing priorities, where there is a need to improve productivity and cost-effectiveness in program implementation, and where there is a need to reduce or minimize costs. In communities and agencies where the manager's attention is focused on specific objectives to be pursued related to activities and resources required to realize them, managers are encouraged to develop and reassess factors and constraints impeding performance; these managers are given encouragement to carry out operational planning, to better identify priorities, and to improve organizational communication.[5]

The matrix in Figure 14.1 shows how we may conceptualize the extent of potential change and the degree of impact that ZBB's implementation may have on an organization. The horizontal arrow indicates minimal (very stable conditions) to extensive changes. This suggests that the success of ZBB in an organization depends on the conditions prevailing in the management environment. An examination of the latter will indicate how

Figure 14.1
Evaluating the Impact of ZBB on an Organization

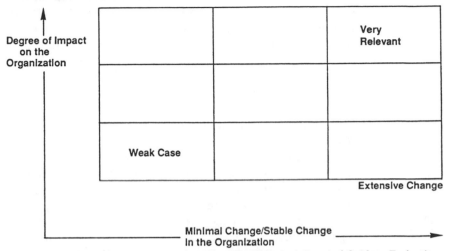

Source: Adapted from Henry C. Knight, *Zero-Base Budget: A Practical Guide to Evaluation,*
Implementation and Use (Hamilton, Ont.: Society of Management Assoc., 1979),
p. 71.

burdensome or how attractive the ZBB process is likely to be for the organization.

As can be readily seen from Figure 14.1, the greater the forecasted change (e.g., the likelihood of large budget cuts, high inflation, large drop in client workload, sharp decline in revenue sources, perceived lack of efficacy with clientele and constituency, and deteriorating public usage), the more likely managers will be to reassess and readjust their operations and programs. When this situation (significant impact and extensive change) obtains, change can easily be imposed from the outside. When minimal change/high stability is the prevailing state, the environment for the implementation of ZBB is less attractive, creating the inclination to more easily revert to the traditional incremental budget. It is not enough to want to install ZBB because it is a good idea. There must be a defensible rationale for its implementation, which requires in-depth study of the organization's environment.

EXAMINING THE ZBB PROCESS

Before the ZBB process can begin, an organization needs to clearly identify (1) its goals and objectives and (2) its structure. There must exist a framework for linking operations planning (identification of short-term objectives) and long-term planning (or what Robert Anthony calls strategic planning). Answers to the following questions with short-term implications should be sought: What outcomes are desired from ZBB? What kinds of technology will be utilized? Who will be the main users of the information for which the ZBB process is being designed? What is the appropriate linkage between the present management information system and the ZBB process? What implementation strategies will be followed? The relevant questions on long-term implications include: Where is the government or agency now? Where should it be headed? Is it moving in the right direction?

An organization should not attempt to apply ZBB without a clear understanding of its own structure and support as suggested in Figure 14.1. For this reason it is essential to know at the outset if the existing organization is acceptable for the installation of ZBB. If the organization is not amenable to ZBB, what programmatic changes are presently being considered and what changes are planned for the future?

The ZBB process may be viewed as having four essential steps, as shown in Figure 14.2. The process begins with the development of planning assumptions and articulation of goals and objectives. The planning assumptions, goals, and objectives are the major inputs to the operating departments to aid them in budget preparation. (As in the case of traditional budget making, managers need to know projected inflation rates, salary increases, and service level requirements.) The next important step is the definition of decision units. (A decision unit is an organizational responsibility center for which a manager can be held accountable.) The decision unit facilitates the grouping of activities and the analysis of inputs/costs and outputs/benefits. Typically a decision unit is a program or organizational entity with common and measurable objectives for which budget requests are prepared and individual or specific accountability can be assigned.

Figure 14.2
The ZBB Process: Overview

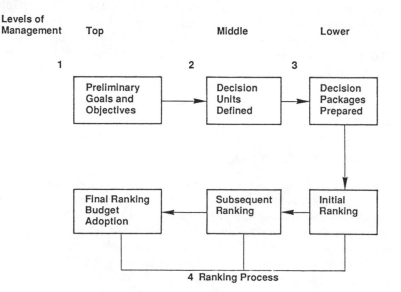

With assumptions specified and planning goals and objectives defined, top management is in a position to identify agency activities/responsibility areas and the person responsible for performing each activity. The middle- and lower-level managers can now sit down with program managers and define decision units. The latter may be projects, training, maintenance, client service, recreational pool, budget units, specific activities, or a grouping of existing or proposed activities (a program) that management views as meaningful for planning and budgeting purposes. (A specific activity might be street paving, while a grouping of closely related activities—a program—would be street maintenance.)

Since each decision unit is viewed as a *responsibility center,* there must be a manager who can make important decisions about spending and the quality of work (as noted above). A decision unit may be a line-item, a project, an activity, a program, or an entire organization, depending on the level of management responsibility for the preparation of the decision package.

In most cases decision units are formed within the existing organizational structure. This is especially true in those cases where PPBS has been operating, for it provides a logical structure that can easily accommodate ZBB. The fit or correspondence with the existing structure has the advantage of maintaining the linkage with the accounting system. Where a new decision unit must be designed, the accounting linkage must be incorporated and continued.[6]

Setting decision unit objectives is a function given to the unit managers in the initial implementation of ZBB. The pyramid of objectives is identified with the concurrence of superiors. As the ZBB system evolves and develops, unit goal setting is more closely integrated with the higher-level planning process that sets the overall organizational goals and objectives. Because of the conditioning role that objectives play in the ZBB system, the organization that practices management-by-objectives (MBO) finds its process readily accommodative with ZBB.

Developing decision packages is the third step in the ZBB process. It is through decision packages that goals and objectives are translated into concrete plans. A decision package is a request document (indicating in monetary terms the amount of resources a manager would like to have) identifying, describing, justifying, and providing information on a specific activity, program, function, or operation to permit managers to make informed judgments about the allocation of scarce resources. The information provided in a decision package should allow management to rank it with competing activities.

Decision packages contain the projected outputs which a manager believes are achievable and the required resources to realize them. A decision unit set should be complete, whole, and discrete. The activities of each decision unit should provide sufficient information to identify results, evaluate options, analyze costs, and assess benefits. It is important to note that a decision package is considered effectively prepared only when management is able to rank it with other packages. A schematic view for developing decision packages is presented in Figure 14.3. It should be recognized that the number of levels of efforts (n) typically equals three (3) while the number of options (m) is independent of the number of levels of efforts and may often exceed three (3).

Decision packages constitute the basic building block in the ZBB subsystem. Every unit has three or more decision packages except in those cases in which the cost of the program or activity is mandated for some specific reason. In such cases only one package is prepared. There are normally three decision packages: (1) *minimal level or base,* (2) *current level,* and (3) *advanced or enhanced level* (see Figure 14.4 and 14.5). Each decision unit package is prepared at the lowest operating level where the best cost-benefit information can be obtained.

Figure 14.3
Schematic View for Developing ZBB Decision Packages

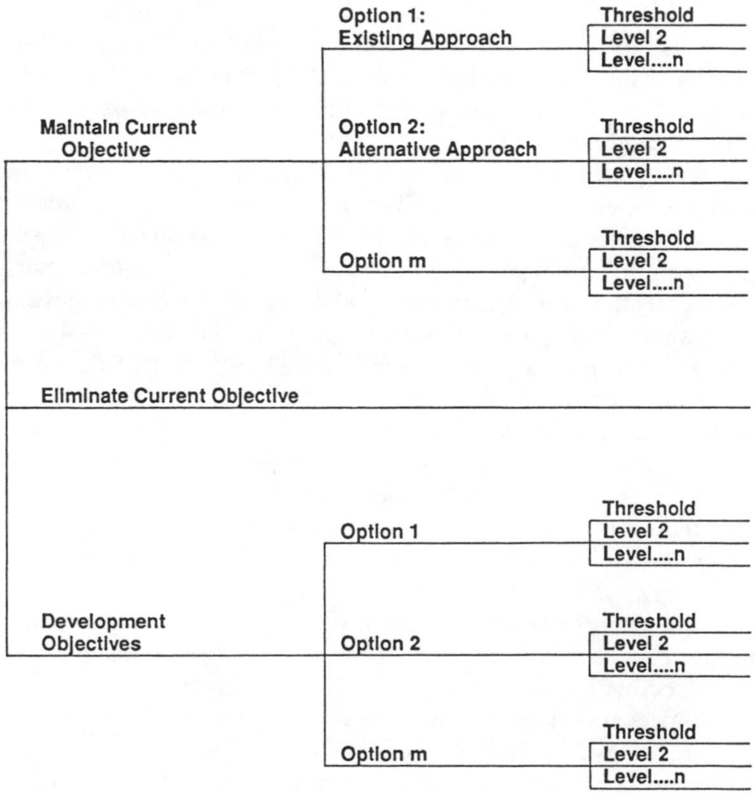

Figure 14.4
Decision Package Preparation Process—Perspective #1

1. Initiating Process

2. Alternatives

3. Levels of Service or Efforts

4. Benefits

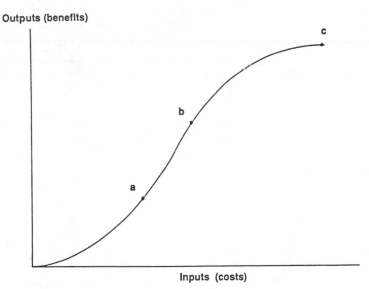

Figure 14.5
Graphic View of Levels of Service/Efforts and the Concept of Diminishing Returns—Perspective #2

Point "a" represents the threshold minimum level of effort. From point "a" to point "b" there is a marked acceleration of the increasing benefits. This point ("b") may be considered the current level of effort or service. After point "b", benefits continue to increase but at a decelerating rate until point "c". The advanced level is reached, producing the maximization of benefits. Most activities should operate at point "c" when possible because from that point onward there is rapid deceleration of benefits.

Several related steps are involved in the formation of the decision package: (1) define the purpose or goal of the particular activity or function; (2) describe and document existing operations and resources, determining what will be done, when, and how; (3) evaluate the alternative ways or means of achieving objectives; (4) identify benefits to be achieved from specific funding levels (also known as levels of effort) and the consequences that are likely to result from nonfunding (if funding for a described activity cannot be obtained, this information should be clearly outlined); and (5) define the performance measures upon which the activities will be evaluated. (See Appendix I—Decision Unit:Crime Prevention.)

Where capital outlays can be specifically identified with particular program improvements, they ideally should be included in the decision package. For example, if the snow removal maintenance crew needs a new truck, it should be assigned a cost and be included in the budget as a separate package. In those cases where direct identification of capital outlays with a program is not possible, individual or consolidated packages are developed. Thus before decision packages are funded, such items as debt service must be examined.

The Ranking Process. Once the decision package has been prepared, the stage is set for the final step in the ZBB process—priority ranking. Properly done, this step allows management to achieve the most productive and cost-effective allocation of its scarce resources. Because of its multiple and hierarchical character, ranking allows managers with budget responsibilities to participate in determining the decision unit and overall agency priorities.

Ideally, the person responsible for subsequent rankings (all ranking above the decision unit) should make a concerted effort to be familiar with lower-level managers' submissions. It may be necessary for ranking managers to meet individually with unit managers to obtain a clear idea of submissions. Additionally, all cost-benefit information, program measures, and evaluative materials that can sharpen the critical and analytical focus of the ranking manager should be provided. The ranking process permits the separate decision packages, representing the various levels of service for a given alternative, to be ordered to determine which proposed work item will be funded in the next budget year. The process then places a program function or activity in descending order of priority based on the benefits to be gained from each undertaking at the various spending levels.

Decision unit managers rank decision packages for which they are responsible. These rankings are then placed in competition with other decision units. Rankings within one division or between divisions or departments of an organization are shown in Figure 14.6. The consolidated decision packages are reviewed at different management levels until a final ranking is made. At some point in the process top management will generally know (based on the best revenue projection) the budget cut-off

Figure 14.6
The Ranking Process: A Consolidation of Decision Packages (with Budget Cut-offs)

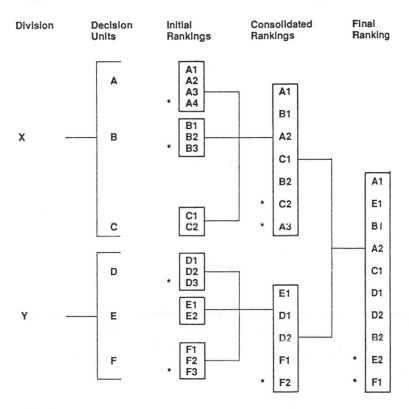

| Division | Decision Units | Initial Rankings | Consolidated Rankings | Final Ranking |

* Budget cut-off points represent relevant packages not sent upwards.

point—that is, the total funds that will be included in the budget—and can determine which decision packages will be funded and which will not. For each level of service the resulting benefits must be specified as they relate to profit margins in the private sector and to particular target populations in the public sector.

Ranking systems and criteria vary widely among governmental units and non-profit organizations. Mt. Lebanon, Pennsylvania, provides a good example (see Table 14.2). Decision managers are typically given a number of votes equal to the number of packages prepared and having a ranking value between 1 and 6, with the highest priority decision packages given a value of 6.

Using the same voting system, Mt. Lebanon used a municipality-wide ranking committee "composed of all department heads, the finance officer, the personnel and purchasing officer and a student intern who ranks the

Table 14.2
Criteria for Vote Casting

1.	Importance of service levels In terms of perceived health, welfare, safety, and satisfaction of the township's residents;
2.	Statutory, charter and contractual commitments met by the service level;
3.	Potential consequences (Including political) If the service level Is not provided;
4.	Federal and/or state funds received dependent on a particular expenditure or match of funds;
5.	Informal assessment of the quality of the service provided;
6.	Cost-effectiveness of the service level.

Source: Mt. Lebanon, Pennsylvania, 1979 Budgeting Manual (Finance Office, May 1, 1978), p. A-8.

decision packages, prepared and initially ranked by decision unit managers.'''[7] Mt. Lebanon's manager participates but does not vote. He reserves the right to make changes in the decision packages' ranking before they are submitted to Mt. Lebanon's Township Commission. The department heads are given an opportunity to discuss their concerns with the commission, which determines the final funding priorities.

In ranking we cannot take a myopic view that seeks to maximize the short-run gain and ignore long-term applications. Lowering taxes by one or two mills (because of the insignificant material gain to most taxpayers a symbolic gesture at best) to win an election but failing to plan to replace crumbling bridges is a dramatic example of such shortsightedness (an example of being penny wise and dollar foolish).

Monitoring Performance. Once the ZBB budget has been approved,the development and implementation of a clearly defined and understood monitoring system is indispensable. Typically, the monitoring system is established and integrated with the normal management review cycle.

ZBB AS A MEANS FOR DEALING WITH RECOGNIZED PROBLEMS

Once serious thought is given to the potential implementation of ZBB, there needs to be an evaluation of the extent of, and the need for, ZBB. Simultaneously with the examination of the ZBB system, the benefits and the costs of other methods that are capable of achieving the organization's identified needs should be explored. This is especially important when one realizes the changes in forms, relationships, procedures, and attitudes that may be necessary with the installation of the ZBB approach.

Among the factors that may indicate the need for the ZBB system is a desire to improve the effectiveness of managers. This may require a reallocation of resources involving reduction in both costs and expenditures. There may be a recognized need to improve operations due to unclear lines of authority, unclear policies and procedures, and poor channels of communication.

CONCLUDING OBSERVATIONS: THEORY AND PRACTICE CONCERNS

Although ZBB is expected to be innovative and rational in practice, it tends to be status quo oriented and highly political. Although decisions are expected to be made based on a cost-benefit analysis, in practice this is seldom the reality. The general view of ZBB as an integrative planning tool seldom obtains. The requirement that ZBB be initiated through goal clarification and goal setting by top management is not achieved. Most agencies permit goal articulation to be done at the department level.

The ranking process requires the greatest amount of trust and commitment to the ZBB objectives because it permits the exercise of a high degree of discretion; but, most critically, it is a focal point for determining the allocation of scarce resources. The discretionary element, the lack of quality information, and the significant influence exercised by the decision unit manager, has permitted the ranking system to be used as a means for political manipulation. The reasons for this outcome include the following: (1) the haphazard ways in which decision units tend to be defined within individual departments, making comparability difficult; (2) unspecific ranking criteria; (3) inadequate trust and lack of continuous feedback between upper and lower levels of management (decision unit managers fear that explicit identification of alternatives may transfer control over their programs to other potentially unsympathetic persons); (4) lack of monitoring devices to check on ranking practices; (5) lack of an incentive system to encourage managers to minimize the manipulation of information and priorities; (6) lack of emphasis on productivity in the ZBB system; (7) lack of coordination between legislative sunset laws and the executive-oriented ZBB approach; and (8) loss of vitality to initiate change due to easy adaptation to traditional budget routines. (For a contrast between theory and practice problems in ZBB, see Table 14.3.)

When implementing ZBB, it is useful to view it not as a set of specific techniques to be mastered and religiously implemented in every specific detail. Instead, it should be viewed as a philosophy—a way of thinking that gives life and substance to a technique that may be usefully employed in effecting resource allocation. Goals and objectives must be clearly

Table 14.3
ZBB: Theory and Practice

Category	Theory	Practice
Planning		
1. Budget base	None, minimum base	All programs have a base; true zero not considered; arbitrary service levels.
2. Overall	Explicit; expenditure-related	Not explicit; seldom considered
3. Decision-package objectives	Explict; output; and productivity measures	Not always explicit; seldom have links to productivty or output
4. Policy determination	Exhaustive consideration	Minimal; little consideration
5. Preparation of alternatives	Short range and comprehensive; cost-benefit	Little or no cost-benefit analysis; no systematic criteria
6. Levels of effort (Service Levels)	Cost-benefit for each level; zero base identified	No explicit cost-benefit analysis; no superficial consideration, irrelevant levels in some cases
7. Programming	Not explicit	Nonexistent
8. Integrated	Not explicit	Nonexistent
9. Depth of analysis	In-depth	Minimal; superficial at best
10. Time span	Short-range; tactical	Short-range; tactical

Organization Theory and Management

1. Organizational structure	Decision unit oriented; responsibility unit	Decision units generally conform to existing organizational structure
2. Programmatic	Well developed	Well developed
3. Ideology	Innovative; dynamic; and neutral	Conservative; status quo; highly political process
4. Value agreement	Managerial efficiency	Minimal or totally lacking in practice
5. Management level involvement	Middle and lower	Minimum at top; maximum at bottom; inadequte feedback between levels

Decision-Making

1. Focus of decision-making	Participation at all levels	Focus on lower-level managers
2. Decision-making flow between management levels	Bottom up	Bottom up, with high degree of reduction of information upward
3. Ranking identified effort	Comprehensive, explicit, rational	Unsystematic, political rationality and expediency; minimal information
4. Administrative documents	Moderate	Many more than PPB

257

Table 14.3 (continued)

Productivity,Monitoring, and Evaluation

1. Emphasis for measuring objectives	Measures output	Heavy reliance on workload measures; unsystematic
2. Evaluating results	Required, pre, continuing, post analysis	Haphazard, unsystematic
3. Evaluating on-going programs	Continuous	Seldom or not done at all; very unsystem-atic
4. Staff and time requirements	Minimal to moderate	High

understood and collectively agreed upon. The information system must be designed to meet user needs and be closely integrated into the accounting system. From the outset it should have the wholehearted support of top management.

Finally, it should be borne in mind that ZBB is not installed in a vacuum. It must compete with entrenched ways of doing things. Whenever a new system is installed, participants want to know what it means to them individually. Placing emphasis solely on efficiency and productivity measures produces anxiety. This may exacerbate latent fears. Perhaps decision making in ZBB should be tempered by the view implied in Figure 14.7 that the most acceptable and best decision outcomes perhaps lie in a compromise between the political rationality and economic rationality producing the "mixed satisficing [sic] decision."

Figure 14.7
ZBB and Decision Making

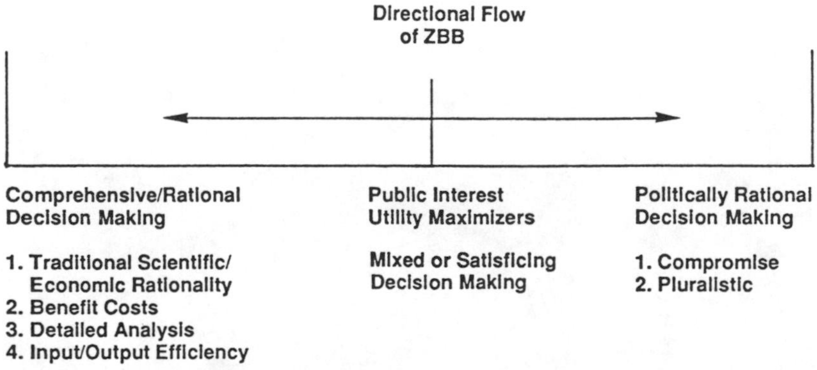

Directional Flow
of ZBB

Comprehensive/Rational Decision Making	Public Interest Utility Maximizers	Politically Rational Decision Making
1. Traditional Scientific/ Economic Rationality	Mixed or Satisficing Decision Making	1. Compromise
2. Benefit Costs		2. Pluralistic
3. Detailed Analysis		
4. Input/Output Efficiency		

NOTES

1. Jerry McCaffery and John H. Bowman, "Participatory Democracy and Budgeting: The Effects of Proposition 13," *Public Administration Review* (November/December 1978): 533-36.

2. Jerome B. McKinney, *Understanding ZBB: Promise and Reality* (Chicago: Public Policy Press, 1979), p. 54.

3. Mt. Lebanon, Pennsylvania, *1979 Budgeting Manual* (Finance Office, May 1, 1978).

4. David Leininger and Ronald C. Wong, "Zero-Base Budgeting in Garland Texas," *Information Report* #8/4a (Washington, D.C.: International City Managers' Association, April 1976).

5. Henry C. Knight, *Zero-Based Budgeting Process: A Practical Guide to Evaluation, Implementation and Use* (Hamilton, Ont.: Management Society of Management Accounts of Canada, 1979), pp. 25-33.

6. For more discussion, see Executive Office of the President, Office of Management and Budget, *Zero-Base Budgeting 77-79* (April 1979).

7. Mt. Lebanon, Pennsylvania, *1979 Budgeting Manual* (Mt. Lebanon, Pa.: Finance Office, May 1, 1979), p. A-8.

CHAPTER 15

INFORMATION NEEDS AND FINANCIAL MANAGEMENT

There is a growing need for information management in government and not-for-profit agencies. In the delivery of social services, the demand for greater efficiency and effectiveness of programs, the internal reporting requirements, and the availability of new information technology have made the management of information a critical as well as a difficult undertaking. These circumstances also point to the compelling need for the development of a coherent *management information system* (MIS). Despite this reality, a large number of government and other not-for-profit organizations have not given the problem the attention it deserves. This situation, however, has been changing for the reasons stated above but especially because of citizens' and clients' demands for greater stewardship and accountability. This chapter focuses attention on the continuing changes taking place in the narrow, traditional financial management information system, and the new, more integrated user-oriented approach to financial management.

Government and not-for-profit organizations' responses to their information management problems have been hindered by the excessive attention to the "physical" aspects of their problems, such as computers, forms, and files, and by the minimal emphasis on qualitative factors and results. This has led to neglect of the ultimate goal for which all agencies have been created—the effective delivery of goods and services to clients and constituents. The design of effective information management systems, consequently, should be concerned primarily with the information produced, and secondarily with the physical makeup of the system.

While many management information systems have been developed around computers, others are not computer-based. Effectively operating

MIS dependency on sophisticated data-processing hardware varies according to the particular needs of each organization. In fact, there are some qualitative types of management inputs that are not readily susceptible to computerization. When excessive attention is given to the computer hardware and how data is processed, it may have negative impact on the design of the MIS. Typical is this observation by Litechy and Wilson: "All too often, hardware vendors short-circuit the preferred approach by selling their own immediate solution to data processing problems."[1] The hardware aspects of the MIS should follow the initial determination of the user's information needs. Though certainly not unimportant, computer hardware needs should be relegated to a secondary position.

DEFINING MANAGEMENT INFORMATION SYSTEM (MIS)

While many tend to define MIS as an electronic data processing or computer system in which information flow is automated, this is not a complete definition. In fact, MIS is much more than a computer system. Essentially, it is a process for ordering information and communicating it on a timely basis to aid management in solving specific problems as they arise. What a management information system is may be better understood by considering each element in its name.

Management comprises activities that are concerned with resource use. These management activities or functions involve planning, programming, organizing, budgeting, accounting, implementing, controlling, and evaluating the use of resources in accordance with stipulated guidelines and practices. A characteristic of effective managers is their ability to enhance the capacity and flexibility of an organization to respond to changing demands and conditions. The efficacy of the MIS can be evaluated in terms of its ability to facilitate management to effectively achieve its objectives—the communication of information for decision making.

Information and *data* are used interchangeably, but they are not the same thing. Data are facts and figures that have not been organized for specific use. Examples include accounting transactions, files, and reports. Data do not become information until they are organized to permit comparisons to be made and to identify relationships that can aid management to make decisions. Information, therefore, is data that are purposefully compiled and interpreted for management's use. The continual storage of information provides the MIS with valuable resources for potential use by management in the future.

A *system* consists of two or more elements which come together to collectively achieve a common purpose. Systems typically possess a set of subsystems arranged in a hierarchy from large to small. For example, the judicial system in the United States extends from the federal Supreme Court (the apex of the hierarchy) to the justice of the peace in a given locality.

Effective operation of the judicial system requires that all courts consistently apply the procedures and rulings of the higher courts. This drive toward unison and the pursuit of the common goal of justice may be described as synergy, meaning that the elements of the system work better together than independently. Thus the MIS generates information that helps management to make improved decisions because of the synergistic context in which the information is derived and used.

THE FINANCIAL MANAGEMENT INFORMATION SYSTEM

Most financial management activities, especially in local governments, tend to be highly fragmented. A historical examination of the development of the financial information system reveals that it typically has had an independent beginning, arising almost entirely from within each independent financial function. Accounting personnel created systems to satisfy particular reporting requirements while budget personnel developed systems to meet their needs, such as expenditure estimating and budget control. Over time such diverse systems with their own terminologies and procedures, unconstrained by imposed or agreed upon criteria and/or guidelines, were duplicative, inconsistent, and counterproductive.[2]

In Chapter 1, we defined the fiscal management system as consisting of three core financial processes: (1) financing—raising required financial resources; (2) budgeting—a work plan stated in both financial and nonfinancial terms; and (3) controlling—concerned with assuring adherence to the articulated budget plan. The operation of these financial components requires three basic, substantive management processes: (1) planning—defining the goals and objectives to be pursued; (2) programming—selecting the appropriate activities to achieve the goals and objectives that have been stated and planned; and (3) evaluating—assessing the quality and usefulness of the articulated goals, objectives, and activities that have been implemented.

The six different processes, ideally, should be incorporated and built into each organization as standard operating procedures. Transactions relating to such activities as payroll, purchasing, inventory, receiving, and disbursing should be guided by uniform procedures. To be effective, these processes must be serviced by an information and reporting system under the continuing surveillance of designated responsibility center officials.

Because the fiscal management system (FMS) that we have just articulated follows essentially a rational approach, the question may be asked: Doesn't every organization use such a system? In varying degrees the answer is definitely yes, despite the fact that management may not always be aware of the fact. The point is that each organization requires an FMS for its operations regardless of whether the need for one is clearly understood.

The financial process has both financial and nonfinancial impacts. Thus information generated from the financial system relating to both financial and nonfinanical activities must be stored and maintained. This is the job of the financial management information system (FMIS). The FMIS organizes and converts the financial data into information which enables management to monitor, control, and effectively direct the operation of the organization. This is what is traditionally referred to as the integrated financial management system. It is essentially a system that is coordinated to bring relevant financial information together to aid in developing policies and practices for raising, storing, applying, and evaluating the use of monetary resources.

More recently the view and meaning of what constitutes the integrated financial management system has been changing. The new emphasis is no longer on planning, programming, and financing.[3] Instead, stress is put on three aspects of controlling—budgeting, accounting, and auditing—and on performance management. Performance management is a by-product of these components. Note that unless the budget process incorporates planning and programming these aspects are likely to be minimized. This leaves accounting (a recordkeeping and expenditure control instrument) as the key information provider to managers and oversight legislative officials.

An integrated financial management information system should include information that will facilitate executive, legislative, and staff decision making about the allocation, administration, control, and evaluation of resource application (see Figure 15.1). The kinds of information useful to decision makers include:[4]

1. Budget
    *   comprehensive listing of all the funds expended by programs, functions, activities, and organizational units, including the objectives, functions, and activities
    *   description of and qualitative data on service outputs of program functions and activities
    *   benefits increased or decreased at each service level
    *   cost-benefit analysis of existing and alternative methods for delivery of services
    *   cost data by organization unit, programs, functions, activities, object-of-expenditure, and percent of service or workload cost
    *   established procedure for updating revenue estimates
    *   future expenditure of proposed programs
    *   a breakdown or listing of financial data for capital budget improvements and the projection of future program impacts on the operating budget
    *   a multi-year financial plan

Figure 15.1
Financial Information and Resources Management (FIRM) System: City of San Francisco

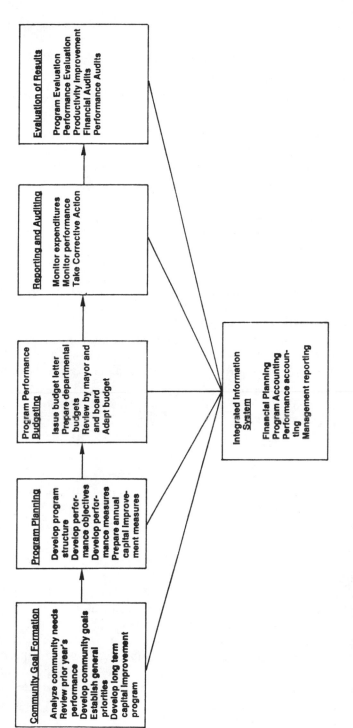

Community Goal Formation

Analyze community needs
Review prior year's performance
Develop community goals
Establish general priorities
Develop long term capital improvement program

Program Planning

Develop program structure
Develop performance objectives
Develop performance measures
Prepare annual capital improvement measures

Program Performance Budgeting

Issue budget letter
Prepare departmental budgets
Review by mayor and and board
Adapt budget

Reporting and Auditing

Monitor expenditures
Monitor performance
Take Corrective Action

Evaluation of Results

Program Evaluation
Performance Evaluation
Productivity Improvement
Financial Audits
Performance Audits

Integrated Information System

Financial Planning
Program Accounting
Performance accounting
Management reporting

Source: Adapted from *Program Measurement Handbook* (San Francisco, Calif.: Resources Management Program, Office of the Mayor, City and County of San Francisco, February 1980), Figure 5, p. 33.

2. Budget/Accounting Implementation
    *   definition of periodic allotments (e.g., monthly, quarterly)
    *   appropriated funds allocated to organizational units/responsibility centers
    *   budget modification criteria
    *   comparison reports of actual expenditures, encumbrances, and revenues versus approved budget
    *   maintenance of accrual accounting data for enterprise activities
    *   a flexible accounting structure permitting the recognition of encumbrance for any given program or activity
    *   a common data system to permit the recognition of expenditure and revenue programs, activities, etc., to permit performance data to be collected
    *   ability to determine full costing of all undertakings

3. Performance Management
    *   system for assessing performance of activities, programs, projects, and/or responsibility centers for measuring indicators, such as workloads, output, effectiveness, or quality of performance
    *   periodic system for setting and reporting on planned performance targets with annual performance plan to the chief executive, clientele, or public
    *   indicators showing performance measurement linkages to the budget
    *   reporting of performance analysis with budget expenditure data and comparison of performance targets with recommended appropriations

4. Auditing
    *   maintaining results data on important problems and recommendations emanating from independent audits and others deemed necessary
    *   maintaining important findings and recommendations of performance audits
    *   identifying systems for showing response and corrective actions taken due to audit recommendations
    *   identifying systems, plans, and guidelines to be followed before each audit is undertaken
    *   process for selecting activities and/or programs to be audited

Advantages of the Integrated Financial Management Information System. Unlike fragmented financial management systems, the integrated financial management information system is able to respond effectively to citizens' demands. It generates performance data to enable decision makers to better evaluate agency and/or responsibility center accomplishments. It facilitates the conduct of performance and effectiveness audits. The integrated system enhances policy makers' ability to organize data around significant issues instead of the expenditure or object classification which is the norm under the existing fragmented systems.

In summary, the following benefits are associated with the integrated system model:

1. Information can be presented in a relevant framework.
2. Data can be better analyzed and categorized before they are reported and/or disseminated.
3. Information has greater opportunity for reaching decision makers on a timely basis.
4. The opportunity to design the system to produce data to meet users' needs is facilitated.
5. The opportunities for data analysis and for conducting cost-benefit analysis are enhanced.
6. There is greater opportunity to standardize, centralize, and increase the consistency of information.
7. Greater computerization can be justified.
8. It forces the agency or governmental unit to train and upgrade staff. Typically local governments and other not-for-profit agencies tend to hire consultants rather than develop in-house capability.
9. The integrated system minimizes duplication and jurisdictional problems in exchanging information and facilitates efficient information sharing.

Disadvantages of the Integrated Financial Management Information System. Despite the many benefits to be gained from the integrated system, there are disadvantages as well. They include the following:

1. It tends to be expensive and difficult to design and build.
2. When a system is large, the problems associated with the system tend to be bigger and more involved.
3. Since these systems are highly coordinated and operate to produce synergistic results, subsystem failures may disrupt the entire system.
4. Maintaining accessibility, privacy, and security of information becomes more difficult.

DESIGNING AN INFORMATION MANAGEMENT NEEDS SYSTEM

In developing an information system, two critical points should be observed at the outset in determining information needs: (1) existing processing problems should be identified, and (2) the new types of information need should be developed to enhance management decision making.[5] Also it cannot be overemphasized that early in the design of the financial information system, key players (all major operating officials with financial responsibilities, e.g., mayor, city manager, chief executive, legislative officials, relevant financial officials) should be substantively involved.

A three-phase approach to designing the financial information system has been suggested. Phase one, acquisition, requires three activities: (1) needs determination, (2) assessment of the government or organization's capacity, and (3) system selection. Phase two, implementation, requires that management be alert and sensitive to personnel and other organizational problems attendant on potential changes. Documentation and testing are important in this phase. Phase three, operation, involves ongoing training, determining and delegating operating responsibilities, and planning for system enhancement. Since our focus here is on needs determination, our discussion will be limited to this aspect.

The Acquisition Phase.[6] The most important first step in system development is the definition of financial information needs, which typically fall into four basic management responsibility areas: planning, organizing, controlling and external reporting/recordkeeping requirements necessary to aid management decision making. The needs determination may be carried out by any method deemed appropriate, though the small committee approach seems to be the most often preferred. When this approach is used a consultant may be employed in an advisory capacity.[7]

A review of the existing information should be undertaken to determine what needs are being met as well as those that should be given more urgent attention and those that are not being adequately met. For example, if the payroll component is operating well, while the expenditure control component is performing below minimal expectations, attention should be given to expenditure control problems before any attempt is made to upgrade the payroll system. It is particularly important that both current and future needs be projected when the needs assessment is being made. Planned improvements will help to prevent problems from arising in the future.

During the needs assessment determination, decision flow analysis may be used to reveal the interrelationships among decisions, identifying decisions that are required to be made and those that have no applicability to current problems. Decision flow analysis can be used to aid in showing "interdependent decisions that are being made independently,"[8] as well as responsibilities, organizational structures, and performance measures that should be modified.

As will be pointed out in Chapter 17 (Reporting), there are differing information needs for different management levels and users. Needs of different kinds of users must be given due recognition if the best quality decisions are to be made. Thus the design of the information system must provide flexibility to generate the appropriate information for each management level in the organizational hierarchy. In a given organization let us assume four levels. At level one the information is routine and standardized. The processing involves mainly collection, recordkeeping, and storage of data. Level two is characterized by low-level decision making. The decision criteria and rules are specific and clearly definable, for example, notifying deliquent taxpayers and determining eligibility for a tax exemption. At level three, information is needed to exercise greater discretion in decision making, such as revenue estimating and applying the tax laws and administrative rules. Finally, level four requires information to plan broad strategy and forecast needs, such as the analysis of the budget's impact on the poor and on unemployment.

There are fiscal users, both internal and external, for whom the information system must be designed to respond on a continuing basis. Drebin et al. suggest five information categories that the potential users may need to aid them in making informed decisions, especially as they relate to accounting statements:[9]

1. *Current financial conditions and flows of short-term financial resources.* This relates to information about liquidity and the ability to convert assets into cash in a reasonably short period of time. It is also concerned with solvency, or the ability to meet current and maturing obligations as they come due. Cash and equivalent items and other resources available for specific uses are identified.

2. *Economic condition and changes in economic condition.* Information about the health, the taxing base, and the economic stability of the entity or community is identified. The purpose is to indicate the entity's ability to deliver regular services, meet future maturing obligations, and maintain acceptable levels of capital improvements.

3. *Legal, fiduciary, and contractual assurance.* Information is included to permit "interested parties to monitor the execution of contractual and legal requirements."[10] It permits public officials to discharge their accountability by reporting on the resources entrusted to them.

4. *Planning and budgeting.* The planning and budgeting system provides information to permit those responsible for it to make alternative analyses to effectively allocate resources to those options offering the best impact or results.

5. *Management and organizational performance.* This information relates to the efficiency and effectiveness with which management achieves articulated and implied organizational goals and objectives.

The information categories discussed above are directed toward two types of internal users and eight types of external users:

Internal information users:
- management
- employees

External information users:
- voters
- taxpayers
- executives

- legislative bodies
- service recipients
- oversight bodies
- vendors
- grantors

THE INTEGRATED SYSTEM: THE DATA BASE MANAGEMENT SYSTEM VERSUS THE DATA MANAGEMENT SYSTEM

An important question to be asked sometime during the needs determination phase concerns the type of software to be installed to aid in retrieving information from the system. The debate centers around the choice between the data base management system (DBMS) and the data management systems (DMS).

The data base management system contains data and procedures which permit a process to be added or subtracted. Such processes can be manipulated to modify or change/convert the raw data to produce desired information. The internal management operation of DBMS minimizes users' efforts to make the system responsive to their needs. The data base approach minimizes data redundancy by maintaining centrally stored data that can be collectively shared by a number of users and utilized for applications.

The data management system (DMS) has a broader or more comprehensive scope than DBMS. It consists of a combination of software programs that automatically generate and update files. In addition, it selects, sorts, and retrieves data. From these data it has the capability to generate different kinds of reports. Perhaps the main differences between DBMS and DMS are the organization of DMS files, users' access to the system, and the language utilized.[11] DBMS permits users greater freedom "to search, probe and query file contents in order to extract answers to nonrecurring and unplanned questions that are not available in regular reports . . . [and] to 'browse' through the data until they have the needed information."[12] DMS permits less user interaction and is guided by structured programs and process information capable of satisfying user demands.

BUDGET AND ACCOUNTING INFORMATION

The budget and accounting systems are normally required to act in concert with each other. To do otherwise would raise the possibility of losing control over the raising and spending of resources. Thus the code of accounts used to identify accounting transactions typically parallels the codes that keep track of budgeting expenditures. The budget amounts serve as the standards that the accounting system uses to track deviations from actual expenditures and allowed expenditures. When the accounting system recognizes deviations from standard, it sends signals to appropriate officials to take corrective action. Viewed in this context, accounting is a powerful subsystem in not-for-profit organizations. In many local governments and other not-for-profit organizations, the accounting system is the only information system.

In the past, when recommendations were made to revamp and improve the effectiveness of the total information system in the public sector, the accounting system was usually ignored. Consequently, accounting, rather than being designed as an effective and integral subset of the total information system, has generally been designed to meet operating, legal, and other budgeting control constraints. As was shown in the chapter on accounting, it focuses on aspects such as the liquidity of assets and their availability to meet maturing obligations.

Conceptually, in an information system accounting must be viewed as a strategic part of the total system which has impact on all other areas. It must be recognized, however, that the conventional accounting system is not sufficient in itself to assess program performance. To assess more than narrow financial or dollar accountability, which conventional financial accounting permits, a variety of information is needed. It is important that the system be user-oriented and designed to produce both financial and nonfinancial information. This requires that each entity organize its information system to capture information that will have multiple and comparative capability and applicability to the governmental entity.

Ideally, the accounting, budgeting, and management information system should be integrated as shown in Figure 15.2. It shows the interconnection of all the processes of management which are tied into the accounting system. The planning, programming, financing, and budgeting phases represent future orientation, while the controlling, evaluating, and accounting phases represent the past and present state of things.

CONCLUDING OBSERVATIONS

Fragmented and traditionally oriented information systems, while tolerable in small not-for-profit organizations, have limited usefulness in larger organizations. Due to the many demands to which these organizations must respond, essential information can no longer be collected, maintained, and compartmentalized in individual units. Public demands for efficiency and effectiveness in the delivery of public goods and services require that a whole range of substantive and financial information needs be coordinated and integrated into one system. Narrow object-of-expenditure or dollar accountability control data are still useful, but there is greater need for data that are organized around issues that facilitate better decision making.

Figure 15.2
Financial Information System

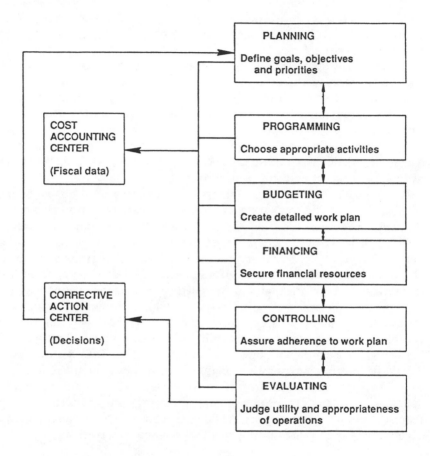

Too often managers in not-for-profit organizations equate an information processing system with computer hardware, leading many organizations to acquire expensive computer equipment which has produced unacceptable payoffs. This need not be so. The computer is only one important element in the development of an information system. The computer should be considered only after the information needs and the context of the organization, including the support staff, have been carefully considered. It should be kept in mind that computer magic does not happen by chance but through well-conceived and -designed plans developed to achieve specific objectives.

NOTES

1. Charles R. Litechy and Earl R. Wilson, "Systems Development for Small Governments," *Governmental Finance* 10, no. 3 (September 1981): 11.

2. Frederick O'R. Hayes et al., *Linkages: Improving Financial Management in Local Government* (Washington, D.C.: Urban Institute Press, 1982), p. 182.

3. David A. Grossman and Frederick O' R. Hayes, "Moving Toward Integrated Fiscal Management," *Public Budgeting and Finance* 1, no. 2 (Summer 1981): 41-42; see also Hayes et al., *Linkages,* pp. 12-20, 131-37.

4. Hayes et al., pp. 12-20.

5. Litechy and Wilson, "Systems Development for Small Governments," p. 11.

6. Rhett D. Harrell, *Developing a Financial Management Information System for Local Government: The Key Issues* (Washington, D.C.: Government Finance Research, MFOA, 1980), p. 2.

7. William J. Kettinger, *Information Resource Management and the Use of Information in Local Government: A Policy Guide* (Columbia, S.C.: University of South Carolina, 1980), pp. 31.

8. Alan Walter Steiss, *Management Control in Government* (Lexington, Mass.: Lexington Books, 1981), p. 123.

9. Allan R. Debin et al., *Objectives of Accounting and Financial Reporting for ⟩vernmental Units: A Research Study, Vol. 1* (Chicago: National Council on ⟨⟨ ernmental Accounting, 1981), pp. 101-4.

Richard A. Bassler, "Data Bases, MIS and Data Base Management Systems," in ⟩ ⟩ard A. Bassler and Norman L. Enger, *Computer Systems and Public Admi⟩ tration* (Alexandria, Va.: College Readings, 1976), p. 203; Jeffrey D. Ullma⟩ *Principles of Data Base System* (Rockville, MD.: Computer Science Press, 1982)⟩ ⟩. 1-5.

11 ⟩hard F. Schubert, "Basic Concepts in Data Base Management," *Dat⟩ ption* (July 1972): 42-47; and James Martin, *Computer Data-Base Or⟩ ⟩zation,* 2nd ed. (Englewood Cliffs, N.J.: Prentice-Hall, 1975), pp. 4-7.

Norman L. Enger, "Data Management System," in Bassler and Enger, ⟩ ⟩uter Systems and Public Administration, p. 205.

CHAPTER 16

AUDITING

Auditing has been with us since antiquity. Records show that the Egyptians employed it as far back as 2000 B.C. to carefully control shipments in and out of the royal treasury (government storehouses). For example, containers of grain destined for the storehouse were accepted only if filled in the presence of overseers and a scribe who duly recorded them. Effective delivery of the grain was made only after receipt was recorded by a scribe stationed at the storehouse. Note that the activities performed by an individual were independently checked and confirmed (in a sense, audited) by another. Brown has observed that: "whenever the advance of civilization brought about the necessity of one man being entrusted to some extent with the property of another, the advisability of some kind of check upon the fidelity of the former would become apparent."[1]

The main purpose of government and not-for-profit auditing throughout history has been detecting fraud and, to a lesser degree, attesting to the fair presentation of an agency's financial condition, detecting technical errors, and detecting errors of principle.[2] Most individuals, due to lack of time or expertise, are unable to assess the credibility of financial statements or management's representation and assertions made therein. The auditor's report fills this gap by providing an expert's independent evaluation of financial reports.

Like the preceding chapter, this chapter is also about information. Auditing tests and validates the information generated by the financial management system. This chapter examines the processes, scope, and contrasting features and nature of the different types of audits found in public and other not-for-profit organizations.

Audits provide feedback information (see Figure 16.1) to those in

Figure 16.1
Actors in the Audit Process

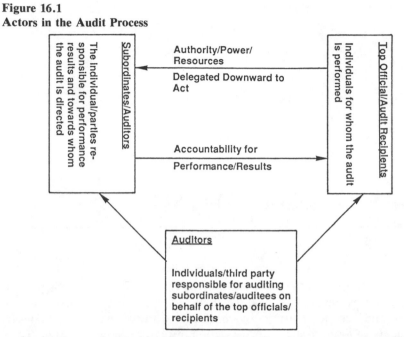

authority (executive and legislative officials) for the purpose of reinforcing and strengthening control systems. Those reviewing audit reports will find three categories of information useful: (1) Audits may be used to assess the reliability of subordinate officials' reports developed to meet stipulated accountability requirements aimed at providing verification of information. Such audits may focus on financial, program, or other performance indicators. (2) When officials need to be informed about existing conditions or results not included in submitted reports, the audits are concerned with information acquisition. (3) When the assurance need emphasizes adequate and appropriate controls for safeguarding and protecting resources and ensuring faithful, efficient, and effective performance, the audit may be referred to as independent assurance.[3]

Auditing suggests a basic responsibility and accountability relationship between top officials (recipients of audit reports), on the one hand, and subordinates (auditees), on the other. This principle directs subordinates to report all relevant information required to review and assess their performance.[4] This view was articulated by the former United States Comptroller General Elmer Staats when he indicated:

A fundamental tenet of a democratic society holds that government and agencies entrusted with public resources and authority for applying them have the responsibility to render a full accounting of their activities. This accountability is inherent in the governmental process and is not always specifically identified by legislative provision.[5]

AUDITING: DEFINING ITS NATURE AND PURPOSES

There is no uniform meaning for the term *auditing*. Agreement on a single definition has been made more difficult by the changing nature, forms, and scope of auditing during the past thirty-five years. An examination of Figure 16.1 shows that an audit is comprised of four parts: (1) the actors-auditors, the auditees (subordinates), and higher officials (audit recipients); (2) the accountability relationship between subordinate and higher officials (audit recipients); (3) the maintenance of independence between the auditors and the subordinates (auditees); and (4) the auditors' review and examination of subordinates' execution of the higher officials' delegated duties and responsibilities.

Participants in the audit process seek answers to several basic questions. *Why* is the audit being conducted? The typical objective is to achieve accountability and management control. *What* is the scope of the audit? It may be financial, compliance, performance, and so on. *Who* are the parties (auditor, auditee, higher officials) involved? *How* is the process to be applied? The audit process consists of preparation, conduct (examination and evaluation), reporting (communicating), and settlement. Auditing, in general terms, may be defined as a process concerned with the collection and thorough analysis of the underlying information or evidence designed to render an independent, informed, and professional opinion about the representation and assertions made in management reports and supporting documents. Auditing is thus a means for independent verification and assurance about the completeness and creditability of financial and related records attesting to "the correctness of a calculation, the existence of an object, the accuracy of a statement, the reliability of a report, or the occurrence of an event."[6]

THE AUDITING AND ACCOUNTING LINKAGE

While there may be qualitative or effective audits without accounting records, there can be no financial or expenditure-related audits without supporting accounting data.[7] In fact, most audits conducted today in state and local governments and not-for-profit organizations are based on accountants' prepared records and financial statements of funds and account groups (records of nonfund accounts, such as land, buildings, and equipment) for the purpose of determining if the financial statements fairly present the financial position and results of an organization in conformity with generally accepted accounting principles (GAAP). Agencies are required to conform not only to GAAP but also to applicable local, state, federal, and other governing authorities' mandated accounting rules and regulations.

In the typical non-governmental, not-for-profit agency, the accounting and budget systems are linked by conforming the budget account exactly to the code of accounts and vice versa. For example, expenditure, appropriation, and revenue are used for both budgeting and accounting purposes. These accounting transactions usually provide the basis for audit reviews in determining whether obligations and expenditures have been accurately recorded. It is important to note that the auditor evaluates the internal control systems that agencies use for authorizing and recording financial commitments.

Finally, the test of an auditable accounting system is that it leaves audit trails to permit transactions to be easily traced through accompanying supporting documentation. Auditable accounting systems have clearly drawn procedures and guidelines indicating the lines of accountability to aid auditors in ascertaining how the accounting system is intended to operate. Accounting systems that lack these basic components provide an insufficient base upon which to perform informed and complete audit reviews.

TYPES OF AUDITS

Audits in Terms of Time. Pre-audit is used to determine the propriety of proposed financial transactions and to control the accuracy of collecting and accounting for revenues and accounting for expenditures and disbursements. Post-audits occur at the end of the accounting period— after events have taken place and transactions have been recorded or approved for recording by appropriate officials. While pre-audits are conducted by individuals internal to the organization and accountable to higher-level management, post-audits are conducted by individuals (usually certified public accountants [CPAs]) external to the organization. The independent post-audit is what is usually meant when people talk about audits. The post-audit will be the focus of attention in this chapter.

Internal and External Audits. Internal audits have all of the characteristics and attributes of pre-audits but are much broader in scope and focus. They are independent appraisals (free of organizational constraints and pressures to avoid compromising objectivity) of the activities or operations performed within an organization to facilitate management and other controls. Indeed, the persons conducting the internal audits (internal auditors) have been referred to as the "eyes and ears" of management and as impartial providers of information to management. Additionally, internal audits may be conducted during or at the end of an accounting period. They may be used to assess employee compliance with managerial policies, to evaluate the effectiveness of various control systems, and to assist members of an organization to better discharge their responsibilities. Internal audits furnish management with analyses, appraisals, recommendations, counsel, and information relating to the activities reviewed. In summary, internal audits appraise the soundness, adequacy, and application of accounting, financial, and operating internal controls.

The external audit is synonymous with the post-audit. As noted earlier, the individuals conducting these audits are independent and owe their allegiance to officials outside of the agency. In government they report to the legislative body, the public, or some authorized statutory official. In non-governmental, not-for-profit agencies, the auditors report to a governing board or an individual designated by the board. External post-audits may be divided according to scope—general and specific. General audits include a review of all financial operations pertaining to an agency at the close of an accounting period. Special audits are restricted in scope or time in that they include only a portion of an agency's financial transactions and records or cover all the transactions and records for a period shorter than a year. It is important to note that internal audits and independent external audits are not substitutes for each other; they are complementary.

Three kinds of groups perform independent external audits: (1) elected audit officials of the governmental unit being examined; (2) officials appointed or elected by a governmental agency other than the one being audited; and (3) independent public accountants providing service for a negotiated fee. Most states and a small number of municipalities elect an independent auditor or have one appointed by the legislative body. If appointed, the auditor reports directly to the legislative body. Elected auditors report directly to the people and are typically the chief accounting officers in their jurisdiction. The effectiveness of these officials has been mixed. This is especially true when auditors are elected as a result of political connections with elected executives or where only minimal qualifications are required for them to hold office.

In some states, elected or appointed state audit officials may audit selected state agencies, local governmental units, and not-for-profit agencies receiving government funds either at or without request. Though most local audits are executed by independent certified public accountants, state agencies have increasingly participated in prescribing standard minimal audit procedures, reviewing independent audit reports to assure compliance with statutes, and conducting spot checks or tests where audit systems and procedures appear weak.

Audits According to Purposes. As an overriding objective, each auditor's opinion assesses whether statements fairly and consistently present (in relation to prior years) the financial position and results of an agency's operations in conformity with generally accepted accounting principles. These objectives may be combined with others to achieve particular audit purposes. Figure 16.2 shows a schematic view of the four basic types of audits. Though economy and efficiency are shown separately, they are bridged by the connecting arrow. The economy component tracks the countable inputs, while the efficiency component oversees the system required to convert the inputs.

Figure 16.2
Schema Showing Different Types of Audits

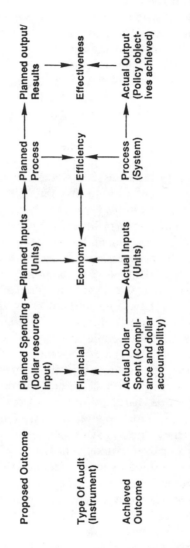

Source: Adapted from Henry A. Butt, "Values of Money Auditing Local Administration," *Public Budgeting and Finance* 5 (Summer, 1985): 68.

Financial and compliance audits or fiscal audits assess whether financial operations are properly conducted. They evaluate whether an entity's financial statements are presented fairly and in compliance with applicable laws, policies, procedures, and regulations. A determination is made about the adequacy of accounting records and procedures and the financial stewardship of the agency. Recommendations for improvement are usually made. This type of audit serves as an accountability and control device which aids in preventing misuses of public funds through inefficiency, inadequate security, and fraudulent practices.

Program results or effectiveness audits assess whether articulated or implied results and benefits as established by the legislature or other authorizing body are being attained and whether an agency is giving ample consideration to alternatives that might be employed to produce acceptable results at lower cost. This may require an analysis of the activities suggested in the statutes to determine if they have been properly developed or designed to achieve the legislative intent.

Program results audits are essentially a form of program evaluation. The implementation of program evaluation, like the audit, is designed to assure a high degree of independence for the auditors or evaluators vis-a-vis management. This type of evaluation, while very appealing conceptually, often has difficulty assessing congruence between expected and achieved results. A major reason for this problem is that "programs are conceived, justified and operated under assumptions that are never verified."[8]

Economy and efficiency audits determine whether an agency is managing or utilizing its resources, such as personnel, property, and space, in an economic manner toward achieving its legislative and/or administrative objectives. Explicit examination is made of the causes of any inefficiencies in agency practices, including inadequacies in management information systems; inefficiencies in administrative methods; defective work procedures; and ineffectiveness in the development, application, and use of automation and organization structure. Stress is put on economical acquisition and efficient use of materials and human resources. The economy aspect suggests minimizing expenditures, while the efficiency aspect implies maximizing benefits produced for the resources expended.

Responsibility and accountability on the part of public officials are at the heart of each type of audit discussed above. Few government or other not-for-profit agencies use all types of audits at any given point in time. Instead, audits are typically designed to achieve the specific articulated needs of an agency, its investors, the regulatory agencies which oversee it, or public interest groups. Usually attention is focused on one type of audit, while the others, if considered at all, are considered to a much lesser degree. The greatest number of audits conducted are of the financial and compliance (fiscal) variety, although an increasing number of audits emphasize economy, efficiency, and program effectiveness. The financial and compliance audit opinions, moreover, are retrospective in orientation, while economy, efficiency, and program results audits render judgments, conclusions, and recommendations that are present- and future-oriented.

AUDIT AND INTERNAL CONTROLS

One of the important objectives of an audit is the examination of an agency's internal control system (1) to determine the reliability and accuracy of the accounting data and the information system in general; (2) to assess compliance with laws and regulations; (3) to promote efficient and effective operating procedures and policy implementation; (4) to evaluate methods designed to safeguard assets; and (5) to encourage adherence to managerial policies.

In determining the adequacy of internal control systems, several critical characteristics must be examined. These include (1) segregation of duties sufficient to safeguard an agency's resources, involving a prescribed system of authorization and record maintenance to obtain effective accounting control over assets, liabilities, revenue, and expenses; (2) a system to guide the execution of duties and functions in each unit or responsibility center of an agency; (3) staff capable of effectively implementing the responsibilities with which they have been charged; and (4) a defined system of internal review. These basic characteristics are so mutually interdependent that the absence or impairment of any one would impede the effectiveness of the internal control system. It should be noted, however, that detailed and minute specification of the internal controls can be prohibitive in terms of cost compared to available resources. Thus each audit should emphasize only those controls which are relevant to the items being audited.

The reliability of the internal control system provides an important input in determining the extent and scope of an audit. Thus, an internal review auditor should give due attention to the process of the internal control system before commencing the audit. It is important to bear in mind that there is no one particular pattern of internal control that can be specified for all governmental units.[9]

SELECTING THE AUDITOR

The requirement to audit and the precise procedures for auditing an agency are different among state governments, local governments, and not-for-profit agencies. Typically, the responsibility for selection of the independent auditor rests with the legislative body or the governing board of a non-governmental, not-for-profit agency. While many governments attempt to select an auditor on the basis of competitive bidding, this approach is not generally accepted as a sound practice. Accountants have expressed the view that the competitive bidding method exerts unprofessional pressures upon the auditor. This selection process may not permit the best auditor to emerge. The view is that qualitative factors required in an audit cannot be easily bought like commodities for which prices can be specified and allowable profits easily determined.

When the profit criterion becomes the major determining factor for the selection of an auditor, it is likely to impact on the professional independence of the auditor. Since judgment and situational factors (e.g., funding needs, internal controls, or other problems) may influence the scope and depth of the audit, this is a reason why the independent auditor should be given considerable latitude to explore important leads when necessary to determine if records are in order and if the agency's system is functioning effectively.

If competitive bidding is chosen over the negotiated approach, requests for proposals (RFPs) should be sent to potential independent auditors, clearly setting forth the scope of the audit and the kinds of services to be performed. Prior to the actual RFP some governments may issue preliminary requests asking independent auditors to submit statements showing their qualifications. Actual RFPs should go only to independent auditors determined to be well qualified. A thorough review should be given to the submitted proposals and due recognition should be given both to price and quality as far as these can be determined.

Included among the information that should be obtained before selection is made are answers to the following questions:

1. What are the experience and qualifications of the independent auditor?
2. What is the time frame for conducting the audit? When the lead time is great, it gives both parties (management and auditor) an opportunity to review and resolve problems that may exist before the audit gets under way.
3. Will management or the auditor close the books? If the auditor closes the books, more time is necessary.
4. What kinds of clerical assistance will be provided to the auditor?
5. If an internal staff exists, will it be made available to the auditor?
6. What recent accounting changes have been made?
7. What is the scope of the audit?

In those cases where the audit price is determined by joint negotiation, both parties need the answers to these questions. In negotiated contracts, the independent auditor's cost estimate should be binding unless unforeseen problems arise, necessitating that the estimates be exceeded. Once all of the details of the audit have been determined, the agenda should be specifically identified in a contract.[10] Such aspects as the departments, programs, activities, and funds to be audited; the period to be covered; and the means of handling unexpected problems should be spelled out.

AUDITING STANDARDS

Auditing performance standards are set forth by a wide variety of private organizations such as the American Institute of Certified Public Accountants (AICPA), and government agencies, such as the General Accounting Office (GAO). The "Standards and Guidelines" enunciated by the GAO basically incorporate and expand the AICPA standards to achieve the specific auditing objectives that are being pursued.

The AICPA has three groups of performance standards: general standards, standards of field work, and standards of reporting.

General Standards. Individuals conducting an audit are required to have appropriate and adequate technical training to effectively conduct an audit. The auditor is expected to have internalized values of independence so that they become an operating norm that influences the auditor's way of thinking and acting. The execution of the audit and the preparation of the audit must be carried out with due professional care.

Standards of Field Work. There must be preplanning and effective supervision of all participants. A review and evaluation of an agency's internal control system is a precondition to all audits to determine the degree of reliance that can be put on the agency's system and the extent of auditing tests that will be necessary. The authority of the auditor's opinion is based on competent evidence obtained by means of inspection, observation, inquiries, and confirmation.

Standards of Reporting. The report is required to state whether the presentation of the financial statements is in accordance with generally accepted accounting principles (GAAP). The report states whether GAAP have been consistently followed in the current report and the preceding one. Where disclosures are necessary to provide material information of the financial statements, the auditor must so indicate. Finally, the report is required to indicate an opinion regarding the financial statement as a whole or an assertion stating that an opinion cannot be expressed. In the latter case, the reasons for the lack of opinion should be clearly articulated. Whenever an auditor signs his/her name to an auditing report, the character of the auditor's examination must be clearly set forth along with the extent of responsibility that he/she is assuming.

GOVERNMENTAL AUDITING STANDARDS

Earlier we examined the various kinds of audits, but we did not discuss the auditing standards that are used in conducting public sector audits. Until 1972, when the U.S. Comptroller General issued *Standards for Audit of Governmental Organizations, Programs, Activities & Functions,*[11] there was no comprehensive statement on governmental auditing standards. The GAO audit guidelines were a response in the early 1970s to the explosion of interest in and demand for better assessment of both financial and nonfinancial activities at all levels of government. The guidelines are used by auditors in and outside of government and by both internal and external independent post-auditors. The GAO standards were adopted by the federal agencies under OMB Circular A-73, which adopted the GAO audit criteria, and OMB Circular A-102, which was revised in 1979 to include the "single" audit. Each kind of audit (e.g., financial, compliance, economy and efficiency, and program results) required that specific standards be used in conducting the audit. Many governmental units have incorporated the GAO audit guidelines as law for the conduct of audits in their jurisdiction.

SINGLE AUDIT

The pressure to move to the single audit resulted from a number of developments during the 1960s and 1970s. Federal grants-in-aid grew from just over $2 billion in 1950 to nearly $95 billion in 1981. Though reduced to around $85 billion in 1985, they still represent a significant funding source for state and local governments. Hundreds and, in some cases, thousands (1,100 in the Department of Health and Human Services) of federal programs were administered by different federal agencies. In many instances, each program established its own accounting requirements. A state or local agency that received aid for forty different programs could have been required to have forty or more accounting systems. Compounding the problem was the fact that each federal agency administering a program which awarded funds to a state or local agency had a right to have on-site audits. Thus, keeping track of the accounting, reporting, and auditing demands was a heavy burden to the state and local governments receiving federal assistance.

Efforts to bring about standardization in the 1960s met with minor success. It was not until 1979, with the issuance of Attachment P (audit requirements to OMB Circular A-102, uniform administrative requirements for *Grants-in-Aid to State and Local Governments*) that the single audit got formal authoritative support. Attachment P requires that audits be done on an agency-wide basis instead of a grant-by-grant basis.

The review of the results obtained with the implementation of Attachment P led to passage of the Single Audit Act of 1984, which includes the following objectives:

1. The improvement of financial management systems of federally assisted programs
2. The establishment of uniform audit requirements for federal assistance programs to state and local governments
3. Promotion of the efficient or effective use of audit resources, with the stipulation that all programs with revenues of $100,000 or more will be subject to the act as of January 1, 1985

The law covers both direct and indirect federal assistance programs, including pass-through funds from another unit of government. Direct cash payments to individuals are the only item excluded. Only smaller units of government will not be audited annually. These programs may elect to have the single audit or be audited as required under the federal financial assistance requirement of the grantor agency or as prescribed by the federal comptroller general.

The audit conducted under the Single Audit Act of 1984 must be done in conformity with generally accepted government auditing and standards applicable to financial and compliance audits. The Single Audit Act does not require economy and efficiency and program results audits or program evaluation unless these approaches are required by plans, regulations, or contracts. Only independent auditors may perform the audits required under the act. All audits conducted pursuant to the act must be made available to appropriate federal officials thirty days after their completion and be made available for public inspection. When material internal control weakness or non-compliance with applicable laws and regulations are found, the audited agency must submit a plan to the appropriate federal officials for corrective action or indicate the reasons why corrective action is not necessary.

The Single Audit Act requires that OMB designate a "cognizant agency" (a specific federal agency) to oversee the implementation of the audit requirement in a given state. The cognizant agency has three main responsibilities: (1) to see that agencies conduct timely audits and conform to stipulations of the act; (2) to make certain that audit reports or corrective actions are transmitted to appropriate federal officials; and (3) where possible to coordinate audits done by contract with those required under the act to aid in developing audit continuity and integration.

OPERATIONAL AUDIT

There is some confusion about precisely what an operational audit is because it is also a type of performance audit. An operational audit is different from a performance audit in that it is more inclusive. An operational audit comprises not only economy and efficiency audits and effectiveness audits but also financial audits. The performance audit, it is important to note, refers only to the economy and efficiency audits and the effectiveness audits as clearly set forth in the International City Management Association (ICMA)[12] special reports on performance audit and *Governmental Accounting, Auditing and Financial Reporting* (GAAFR).[13]

Operational auditing facilitates decentralized management in that it is designed to keep agency management, top executives, and, especially, legislative officials informed about whether an agency is using its resources both legally and effectively. Additionally, the operational audit is employed to review and appraise the soundness, adequacy, and application of all accounting, financial, and operating controls. This audit is not focused solely or mainly on accounting, but it considers how an agency's total resources are being applied. The operational audit attempts to determine the congruence between executive or legislatively articulated or implied objectives of administrative activities, functions, and programs that have been assigned for implementation with achieved results. The auditor is basically concerned with how well an agency is managed and the extent to which it realizes its objectives. Much that is presently done as performance auditing was formerly carried out by management advisory services or consulting concerns.

Operational audits are more difficult to conduct because the standards and criteria to be applied are inexplicit. Many are derived from various sources, though legislative statements tend to be an important source, along with professional organizations which set standards of performance levels for specific fields. Typically, there are no explicit management indicators for accomplishments, economy, efficiency, and effectiveness. Additionally, legislative intent is not always clear. A number of general commonsense standards or guides may be used in carrying out operational audits, covering such areas as: (1) the use of government property for personal benefit; (2) lack of coordination of agencies and/or units implementing related activities and programs; (3) lack of automation and up-to-date techniques; (4) excessive client complaints, unresolved disputes, and unsuitable policies, standards, and regulations; (5) non-adherence to policies, regulations, and procedures; and (6) unreliable reports.

The performance audit procedures parallel those of the financial audit. Financial and operating reports, administrative regulations, laws and contracts, agency policies, financial and operational information, and documentary evidence are examined. The auditor seeks answers to questions such as (1) What are the specific goals and objectives of the audited programs and activities? (2) What is the basis of authority (legal or administrative) under which the program is being operated? (3) How well are the audited objectives being achieved? (4) How well do the established procedures and practices aid in achieving the agency's goals and objectives? (5) What are the specific causes or reasons why existing procedures and practices are positively or negatively affecting the agency's goals and objectives?

Findings are categorized in terms of (1) those favorable to management and (2) those unfavorable to management. For unfavorable findings, the auditor is required to state how widespread or material they are and to indicate the direct and indirect impact on cost. It is not enough to simply identify the problems. Alternative ways for eliminating them must be identified.

Reporting for performance audits is divided into three sections. In section one the scope and objectives of the audit are stated. Section two contains an explanation of the findings of fact, indicating the causes and effects that management is having on the work environment in achieving the agency's objectives. Section three recommends ways to meet the identified problems, indicating the agency's enthusiasm and willingness in contributing to alternative solutions and stating previous recommendations that have not been implemented and current recommendations with which management disagrees.

AUDITS OF NON-PROFIT ENTITIES

Generally accepted accounting principles have particular applicability to colleges and universities, hospitals, and other non-profit organizations. Each of these specialized areas has audit guides peculiar to itself. For example, colleges and universities have Audits of Colleges and Universities;[14] hospitals have American Hospital Association guidelines and the AICPA's *Hospital Audit Guide*.[15] The voluntary health and welfare organizations (also known as human service organizations), which derive most of their resources from contributions, have the AICPA's *Audit of Voluntary Health and Welfare Organizations*.[16]

THE AUDIT REPORT

The various types of audits typically follow the same audit report format, though the operational audit tends to be more extensive. The general standards to be observed in writing the audit report have been summarized by the U.S. Comptroller General as follows:[17]

1. Be concise yet complete to facilitate ready user understanding.
2. Present accurately, completely, and fairly all material and factual information.
3. Present findings and conclusions clearly and as simply as the subject matter permits.
4. Include only factual information that can be adequately supported by evidence included in the working papers. Include supporting information only to the extent that it is necessary to make a convincing presentation.
5. Where possible include recommended actions for operations improvement, providing information on the problems and recommended courses of action to assist management in taking corrective action.
6. Put primary emphasis on improvement, minimize past criticisms, and point out unusual difficulties faced by operating officials.
7. Explain issues and questions requiring study and consideration.
8. Direct attention to noteworthy accomplishments, particularly when the improvements may be applicable elsewhere.

9. Give recognition to the views of responsible officials on the auditor's findings, conclusions, and recommendations.

10. Explain the scope and objectives of the audit.

11. Direct attention to significant and pertinent information that has been omitted because it is deemed privileged or confidential, giving the legal basis for such action.

Audits containing financial reports are required to state the auditor's opinion as to whether the information contained in such a report is presented fairly. When the auditor is unable to express an opinion, the reasons should be indicated in the audit report. Additionally, the auditor states whether the audit is prepared in accordance with generally accepted accounting or prescribed principles applicable to the organization, programs, and functions or activities audited. Appropriate supplementary explanation about the financial reports is included as deemed necessary for full disclosure, including violations of legal or regulatory requirements and other instances of noncompliance.

CONCLUDING OBSERVATIONS

Auditing serves a strategic role in financial management in that it validates and attests to the accuracy of financial statements. In the public sector, it can cost a governmental unit thousands or perhaps millions of dollars if a negative opinion about its financial statement leads to a downgrading of the unit's credit rating.

Auditing can be used as an important management tool. The pre-audit is employed to ensure that policies and activities take place in accordance with management policies and administrative procedures. The post-audit acts typically as a legislative or board oversight and accountability instrument when it evaluates the fairness and compliance of financial statements with statutory requirements and generally accepted accounting principles.

Of the different types of audits found in practice, the financial audit is the most widely used. In recent years, management decision-making requirements and public demand have made it necessary to go beyond the narrow dollar accountability approach that typifies the financial audit. Thus economy and efficiency, effectiveness/results, and operational audits are gaining support.

NOTES

1. Richard Brown, *A History of Accounting and Accountants* (Edinburgh: T. C. and E. C. Jack, 1905), p. 74.

2. Robert H. Montgomery, *Auditing* (Chicago: American School of Correspondence, 1909), p. 12.

3. Lennis M. Knighton, "Four Keys to Effectiveness Auditing," *Government Finance* 8, no. 2 (September 1979): 3-4.

4. Ibid.

5. Comptroller General of the United States, *Standards for Audit of Governmental Organizations, Programs, Activities and Functions* (Washington, D.C.: U.S. General Accounting Office, 1972), p. 1.

6. Ibid., p. 4.

7. Note that the term *expenditure* is used in the not-for-profit sector, while *expenses* is used in the private sector. *Expenditure* emphasizes things bought or acquired, and *expense* refers to actual consumption or expired costs.

8. Frederick O'R. Hayes et al., *Linkages: Improving Financial Managment in Local Government* (Washington, D.C.: Urban Institute Press, 1982), p. 154; for extensive discussion of effectiveness auditing see Richard E. Brown et al., *Auditing Performance in Government* (New York: John Wiley and Sons, 1982), pp. 73-101.

9. See Price Waterhouse, *Enhancing Governmental Accountability* (New York: Price Waterhouse, 1983), chap. 3.

10. Municipal Finance Officers Association, *Governmental Accounting, Auditing and Financial Reporting* (Chicago: Municipal Finance Officers Association, 1980), p. 90.

11. Comtroller General of the United States. This has been revised in 1981.

12. International City Management Association, "Performance Audits in Local Governments: Benefits, Problems, and Challenges," *Management Information Report* 8 (Special Report, April 1975).

13. See Municipal Finance Officers Association.

14. American Institute of Certified Public Accountants, *Audits of Colleges and Universities,* 2nd ed. (New York: AICPA, 1975).

15. See American Institute of Certified Public Accountants, *Hospital Audit Guide,* 4th ed. (New York: AICPA, 1982).

16. American Institute of Certified Public Accountants, *Audit of Voluntary Health and Welfare Organizations* (New York: AICPA, 1981).

17. Comptroller General of the United States, pp. 7-9.

CHAPTER 17

REPORTING

Whenever resources are obtained from sources other than the individuals using and/or spending those resources, reporting to some external group or individual to render stewardship and accountability is a normal expectation. Such accountability may be based on law, contract, policy, or moral obligation. Stewardship refers to the execution of efficient administration. "Reporting on management's stewardship . . . is a principal purpose of financial statements."[1]

Basically, financial statements in not-for-profit organizations must provide information that can be used to assess management's ability to effectively utilize resources to achieve implied or articulated organizational goals. Certain questions immediately arise, such as; To whom should fund users report? What kinds of information should be reported? What should be the format of the reports, and what are the authoritative guidelines and criteria to be followed? Though the answers to these questions appear obvious on the surface, in practice they tend to be difficult to find.

This chapter contains an overview of various types of reports and suggested general guidelines typically followed in preparing reports on the achievements and financial status of public and other not-for-profit organizations.

Historically, the financial reports of public and other not-for-profit organizations present funds flow information. Data are organized to show the sources from which funds are derived and the applications to which they are put within the legal restrictions placed upon each fund, with the aim of promoting budget and fiscal compliance. Financial reporting is a useful aid, helping public officials to indicate how they are faithfully discharging their fiscal responsibility to the electorate. The National Council on

Governmental Accounting (NCGA) views the goal of financial reporting for governmental units as providing financial information that is useful for making economic, political, and social decisions; demonstrating accountability and stewardship; and providing information that is useful for evaluating managerial and organizational performance.[2]

Financial reports have been directed predominantly at meeting the needs of administrators, legislators, service recipients, resource providers, accountants, investors, public employees, and observers interested in public finance and administration. Although the general public's interest in financial statements has increased during recent years due to taxpayers' revolts and the cutback management movement of the 1970s, the average citizen shows little interest in the principal operating funds that generate deficits or surpluses.

An effectively presented financial statement of a governmental unit should describe the principal facilities and the capital improvement program for a period of at least five years, identifying the proposed yearly expenditure application by specific type of asset, planned use, and source of funding. Aggregated original and replacement costs for fully depreciated assets over a five-year period and replacement policy regarding those assets should be presented. Comparative data showing planned versus actual operating and debt service expenditure, including the presentation of the past four years' actual results, should be given, and any recognizable trends should be explained. The report should discuss the past year's accomplishments and the proposed objectives for the ensuing year. Citizens should be told where to obtain available reports, especially those analyzing the efficiency and effectiveness of operations. While this is an inexpensive and relatively effective way to promote good relations, it is often handled poorly by public and other not-for-profit organizations.

To be eligible for consideration for fair presentation and to be in conformity with generally accepted accounting principles (GAAP), three general types of financial statements have been suggested: (1) a combined balance sheet; (2) a combined statement of revenues, expenditures, and changes in fund balances; and (3) a combined statement of revenues and expenditures—budget and actual. While the five types of governmental funds (general, special revenue, debt service, capital projects, and special assessment) are required to be shown separately, a memorandum column indicating totals is permitted.

INTERIM AND INTERNAL REPORTING LINKAGES IN THE FINANCIAL MANAGEMENT SYSTEM

Internal control and public accountability require that timely reports be issued throughout the fiscal year. Depending on administrative needs, daily, monthly, weekly, and quarterly reports may be developed. These interim reports assess ongoing programmatic activities and potential problems that may be developing.

Most governmental units do not publish interim reports; they are produced to assist administrative officials and budget examiners at all levels of the organization or governmental unit. Occasionally legislators may find them useful, especially when they provide data showing how budget plans are being followed. Interim reports help management to evaluate the extent to which administrative agencies are complying with budgetary, financial, legal, and administrative procedures. Such reports are important aids in disclosing deviations or variations from operating plans and thus permit corrective action to be taken. In expressing the need for interim statements, NCGA noted that (1) they reflect monthly and quarterly current financial positions, comparing financial results with estimates, indicating limitations for the month and/or the year to date; (2) they are mostly for internal use; (3) they exclude general fixed assets; and (4) they provide information on budgetary and cash flow projections aimed at facilitating management control.[3]

Annual Reporting. Every governmental unit, in the view of NCGA, is expected to publish a comprehensive annual financial report (CAFR) consisting of all funds.[4] This activity represents the final step in the financial management reporting system, indicating how well executive officials have discharged their responsibilities. The purpose of the report is to indicate the extent to which there has been compliance with appropriations, contractual, legal, and other requirements.

All reporting systems are normally expected to have at least two types of reports: (1) internal reports required for agency use; and (2) external reports for administrative, legislative, and other interested parties. Reports should be prepared to meet specific guidelines. Accountability for the achievement of assigned responsibilities must be clearly identified. A measurement system that is capable of comparing preplanned objectives or standards with actual achievements must be maintained. To be useful, the results must be reported with sufficient promptness to permit corrective action to be taken. If maximum utility of the results is to be obtained, presentation must be consistent for all levels of management from one reporting period to another. Simplicity should be a guiding objective. Clear and concise presentation will enhance the use and understanding of the report.

Ideally, reports intended for internal use should provide information to management that will be useful in effectively overseeing the agency's operations. These reports should assist management in controlling operations (for example, the use of workload analysis) by monitoring how approved plans are being implemented. The reports will facilitate the management of funds, pinpointing the need for supplementary estimates or adjustments of allocations. The product of each report should provide the basis for the development of next year's budget and aid in the review of plans and priorities.

External reports satisfy a number of requirements, among them legal, contractual, and fiduciary ones. Such reports provide information to assist interested parties in monitoring the performance of the agency or governmental unit to determine if its resources have been utilized in accordance with requirements. External reports help taxpayers, grantors, and service recipients to determine whether resources have been applied effectively.

Frequency of Reports. While comparative expenditure reports should be provided to management on at least a monthly basis showing both actual and budgeted expenditures for a given period and for the year to date, some programs or activities may require weekly or even daily reports.

The introductory section of the annual report should contain a letter of transmittal to the mayor and council or legislative body; in recent years, a second letter from the mayor or chief executive to the council and/or the general public, briefly describing changes in financial policies and the important areas of financial management, has become customary; other materials, such as a description of the reporting governmental entity, an organization chart, and a listing of elected officials, may also be submitted. Recently, additional reports have been appended to annual reports. The opinion of the independent auditor or other required post-audit reports are appended. Where the unit of government has qualified for the Certificate of Conformance from the Government Finance Officers Association, it is included.

Each governmental unit is expected to prepare an official annual report, also known as the comprehensive annual financial report (CAFR), containing all funds and account groups. Two major components of the CAFR are (1) the general purpose financial statement (GPFS), showing the fund type and account group (e.g., fixed assets); and (2) combined statement by fund type and individual fund statements.

The Annual Report: A Pyramid Perspective. In Figure 17.1, the pyramid concept shows various levels of fund data groupings which offer different options for annual reporting. The apex (highest level) of the pyramid suggests a financial statement that is greatly aggregated and consolidated, while the reverse is true at the base of the pyramid. The lowest level is made up predominantly of detailed transactions. Neither of these levels of reporting is recommended; rather, a report falling between the two extremes is recommended.

The NCGA has recommended the comprehensive annual financial report (CAFR) as the primary report (also known as the official governmental unit annual report). The general purpose financial statement (GPFS), which is

Figure 17.1
The Financial Reporting Pyramid

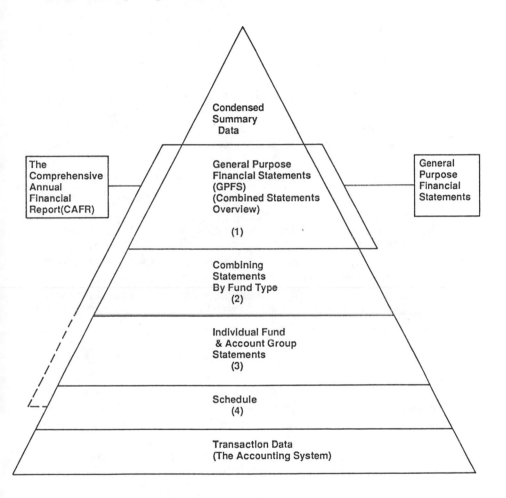

Notes:
_____ Required
-------May be Necessary

included in and accompanies the CAFR, is attached to bond offering materials and is distributed to general users who are less interested in specific financial details.

It is important to keep in mind that the governmental unit or agency should go to that level of the pyramid where the details are sufficient to show the financial position and operating results of individual funds and account groups, to show compliance with legal and contractual requirements, and to provide adequate disclosure of the individual fund entity level.

The Financial Section. This section contains the NCGA recommendations for the auditor's report and the general purpose financial statement, which is made up of the combined statements, as shown in Figure 17.1. The following statements are found in this section:

1. Combined balance sheet, including all fund types and account groups
2. Combined statement of revenues and expenditure and changes in fund balance, including all governmental fund types
3. Combined statement of revenues, expenditures, and changes in fund balances, including budget and actual and general and special revenue fund types
4. Combined statements of revenue and expenses and changes in retained earnings or fund equity, including all proprietary fund types
5. Combined statements of changes in financial position, including all proprietary fund types
6. Notes to financial statements

Statements of Other Not-For-Profit Organizations. The American Institute of Certified Public Accountants' *Audit Guide* lists several types of financial statements that comprise the annual report of an organization.

The statement of support, revenue, and expenses and changes in fund balance is essentially a summary of the financial activities, indicating all sources of support and revenues and all expenditures. The AICPA recommends that the statement of changes in fund balances be made part of this statement, showing balances at the beginning and at the close of the year. Important interfund transactions are included and summarized.

The statement of financial expenses contains a summary presenting an analysis of the entity's object-of-expenditure by program, function, and support. This statement, in essence, indicates how the resources (i.e., money) were spent in carrying out the agency's *program* services and *support* services.

The balance sheet presents assets, such as cash investment, payables, and encumbrances toward which the assets will be applied. The difference between assets and liabilities gives a balance—deficit or surplus.

INTEGRATED ANNUAL REPORTING

The American federal system is made up of many layers of governments often serving the same political community. Not infrequently, a number of governmental units, comprising the county, the city, special districts (e.g., schools), corporations, and authorities, can be benefited if the service delivery performance can be rationally integrated through a single annual report document.

Presentation of a clear, comprehensive, and concise overview of local government finance is the principal objective in putting the integrated annual report together. Thus all changes taking place during the fiscal year should be set forth in a section devoted to operating and/or capital budgets during the fiscal year.

The Introductory Section. A number of general guidelines may be suggested for integrating such a report. Each of the independent participating entities, structures, and frameworks may be briefly described, pointing out the formal and informal linkages with the dominant local government. Common features include accounting structure (such as titles and terminology), accounting basis or bases, fiscal year of the dominant local government, and deviations therefrom. It is important to direct attention to "overlapping and underlying local governmental units and authorities."[5]

The Dominant Local Government: Budgeting Processes. The annual financial report of the major unit of a local government describes the basic preparation and review process, as well as the adoption and administrative process of the annual operating budget. A comparison of operating budget funds with those of several preceding years should be included. As far as possible, the linkages between the operating budget and the capital budget and capital program should be reviewed, indicating the support flowing from the operating funds. The authorization and application made on behalf of the capital budget over several years should be indicated.

Cooperative capital facilities planning is the most useful outcome that is likely to result from these undertakings, though integrated planning need not be the only vehicle by which this is brought about. Finally, the integrated budget system may be an important vehicle to provide statistical information on the following:

1. Assessed and taxable property valuation
2. Exempt properties
3. Revenue sources
4. State aid
5. Federal aid

6. Operating expenditures

7. Capital expenditure[6]

POPULAR REPORTING

Though the most prominent organization presently promoting effective government reporting is the Government Finance Officers Association through its Certificate of Conformance, the Michigan Municipal League in 1944 and the University of Connecticut Institute of Public Service in 1946 initiated programs to promote better understanding of public financial reports. The objective of both organizations was to promote greater public recognition, acceptance, and comparison of reports with other jurisdictions.

The efforts of the University of Connecticut Institute of Public Service continue, but the Michigan Municipal League was terminated in 1966. The following criteria have been used in judging the quality of reports:

1. *Attractiveness*. This indicator is measured by citizen willingness to examine the report due to the appeal of the external appearance and design of the report and the organization and presentation of the materials inside the document. Appeal features include "practical use of type for text and headings, legibility, and effective use of pictures."[7]

2. *Reader understanding*. This indicator attempts to assess the average citizen's ability to better understand local government undertakings. This is determined by an evaluation of the logic, organization of materials, and clarity of the written text. High marks also go to conciseness, brevity, and creative and informative use of appropriate charts and photographs.

3. *Content*. An attempt is made to determine how well the report summarizes the governmental undertakings and the perceived contributions toward the public's understanding of the kinds of services being delivered. This section presents data on the financial status of the community's budget, income, and expenditures, providing comparative analysis of costs, volume, and other statistics on fiscal trends.

4. *Utility*. This attribute is assessed by determining if the size of the report permits easy filing and ready carrying and handling. Facilitative "directory type" information items include table of contents, lists of government officials and organizations, important phone numbers, and calendar of important dates.

Though not specifically identified, the audience must be kept in mind at all times. After all, it is the audience that the publication is attempting "to inform, influence or entertain."[7]

Like commercial enterprises, not-for-profit organizations seek to predict, compare, and evaluate benefits and sacrifices in terms of dollars, time, and risks, despite the fact that results sought are non-monetary. Not-for-profit organizations cannot use the commercially oriented profit yardstick. They seek to achieve goals whose performance involves indicators such as reduction in delinquency, improved health care, or reduction in crime. Ideally, financial statements must permit users to assess past attainments of organizational goals, ongoing efforts to realize present goals, and the probability of future goal attainment.

The AICPA has identified seven qualitative characteristics as useful guidelines in preparing financial reports:

1. *Relevance and materiality.* To meet this test the following question should be asked: Is the information germane, and would its inclusion or exclusion influence or make a difference in a reasonable person's reading of the financial statement? A positive answer indicates that the information in question should be included.

2. *Form and substance.* Substantive economic and program characteristics should govern informative reporting, not the form of the report. Legal and/or technical criteria should establish the guidelines for accounting transactions and other events.

3. *Reliability.* Facts should be presented separately from interpretation. Uncertainties and assumptions related to the information presented should be disclosed. The main point is that users of financial information should be informed about the limitations of the data presented.

4. *Freedom from bias.* This test does not imply absence of judgment, but rather that neutrality, objectivity, and fairness should be guiding aims. The financial statement should not be slanted to benefit any particular reader or group.

5 *Demographic data.* Analysis of population characteristics provides the kind of information that is especially complementary to the financial data. The following are examples of useful demographic data: (1) changes in the population; (2) per capita income and per capita tax burden and changes therein; (3) description and stability of industries; (4) comparative growth rate of main local revenue sources, expenditure, and per capita income; (5) taxable and non-taxable property value; (6) average change in long-term per capita debt; (7) discussion of population and age changes, education levels, school age children, ethnic characteristics, income levels, and unemployment rates; (8) number of government employees funded from own source; (9) percent of employees participating in collective bargaining; and (10) types of clientele.

6. *Comparability.* This guideline suggests that like things be reported alike and unlike things be reported differently. This task is made more difficult in not-for-profit agencies because of the variations that characterize the different kinds of services that are provided. If the guideline is followed, these problems will be minimized.

7. *Consistency.* The operating norm is that comparable events should be treated in a similar manner from period to period. For example, once an accrual system is adopted, to change to a cash system during the period would be considered a violation of this guideline and GAAP.

REPORTING: SOME INADEQUACIES

There are a number of continuing concerns about financial reporting in the public sector and in some not-for-profit organizations. The expenditure reporting system used in the public sector emphasizes the acquisition of goods and services rather than the application (how much is consumed or used up) approach employed in business. Expenditure accounting assumes immediate expiration of resources. The incurrence of debt (e.g., a loan, especially the floating of a bond) is viewed as a source of revenue, and the purchase of fixed assets is recorded as the application of resources irrespective of the useful life of the asset. In order to maintain some degree of control over fixed assets, a separate general fixed asset group of accounts (GFAG) must be developed. It is generally believed that use of the expenditure reporting system is responsible for the poor recordkeeping of fixed assets in many not-for-profit organizations. Because of the expenditure practice, public sector funds require five governmental funds (general, special revenue, capital projects, debt service, and special assessment), two proprietary funds (enterprise and internal service), two fiduciary fund types (trust and agency), and two groups of accounts (fixed assets and long-term liabilities).

Many close observers of the public sector financial scene express the view that the present financial reporting system is plagued by many shortcomings. They contend that (1) it is not possible to determine the cost of services; (2) government financial reports are distorted; (3) there is no system for measuring capital maintenance; (4) there is commingling of sources and uses of funds with interfund transfers; and (5) the heavy emphasis on budgetary compliance does not facilitate meaningful information reporting.[9]

Disclosure Issues. There is no total consensus by accountants and agency managers on precisely what should be included in financial statements. This is a continuing problem—whether government should develop combined balance sheets including all funds while excluding interfund balances. The same could be said about consolidated balance sheets which factor out interfund balances in presenting the balance sheet with one "superfund." The demand for a consolidated balance sheet is based on a number of concerns, including the following: (1) there are too many interfund balances, which tends to obscure or distort the financial position of a governmental unit; and (2) the balance sheet does not present the true net worth of the governmental unit.

Rentals, leases, pensions, fringe benefits, depreciation, and other expenditure items are not always uniformly treated, though a convergence of views on this point is occurring. The biggest area of concern relates to accrued pension liabilities. The method that accounts for pension expenditures only as they are paid to reserve funds ignores significant benefits that have been earned but not paid. Such benefits are commitments and debt that must be paid out at some future date to current employees. Failure by governmental units to reserve funds at the time they become due can bring about major financial crises, as has been the case in several local governments during the last several years.

CONCLUDING OBSERVATIONS

Examination of not-for-profit financial statements clearly shows the basic differences between the for-profit and not-for-profit sectors. Not-for-profit organizations require a set of financial statements unlike those of their commercial counterparts.

To whom accountability and/or stewardship must be rendered is a basic principle underlying all reporting. To be acceptable, not only must reports conform to legal, professional, and regulatory standards, they must also be readily understandable to specific or general audiences. Such financial statements are expected to assess for such groups the efficacy with which management is discharging its responsibilities.

Despite the socially oriented objectives of not-for-profit organizations, most reporting is still based on financial accounting. It is a legal "spend for" concept that emphasizes dollar accountability. Though this approach is changing, it still has some way to go. Finally, the kind of financial statement needed is situational in that each organization must find the level of aggregation that fits its needs, as shown in Figure 17. 1.

NOTES

1. American Institute of Certified Public Accountants, *Objectives of Financial Statements* (New York: AICPA, 1973), p. 25.

2. National Council on Governmental Accounting, *Concept Statements: Objectives of Accounting and Financial Reporting on Governmental Units* (Chicago: Municipal Finance Officers Association, 1982), p. 2.

3. Ibid., pp. 18-19.

4. Ibid., p. 19.

5. Lennox L. Moak and Albert M. Hillhouse, *Local Government Finance* (Chicago: Municipal Finance Officers Association, 1975), pp. 428-30.

6. Ibid., p. 432.

7. Hal Peyer and Gerald Lonergan, "Popular Financial Reporting in the Public Section(?)" *Governmental Finance* 5 (May 1976): 33.

8. Ibid., p. 36.

9. See Coopers and Lybrand and the University of Michigan, *Financial Disclosure Practices of American Cities: A Public Report* (New York: Cooper & Lybrant, 1976), pp. 9-11.

CHAPTER 18

EVALUATING FISCAL HEALTH

Interest and concern for the fiscal health of governmental units and other not-for-profit organizations, especially colleges, heightened in the early 1970s with the financial crises in New York City and Cleveland. Numerous cutbacks were necessary due to the reduction in revenues at all levels of government. The fiscal problems of the cities followed more than a decade of continuous growth in expenditure. Beginning in the early 1970s, the era of endless growth throughout the economy was replaced by increasing inflation, a stagnant national economy, rising costs, and declining productivity. Many larger cities that had expanded social and other types of services found them difficult to maintain as the stagnation and the malaise in the economy continued.

A number of cities, among them Pittsburgh, Pennsylvania, and Chicago, Illinois, slowed expenditures significantly, adapting to the changing economic environment. Cities such as New York and Cleveland continued their incremental budgeting habits, making no adaptation to the decline in revenues; this led to fiscal strain and, ultimately, fiscal crisis.[1] This chapter explores the theories and practices relating to the fiscal health of governmental units and agencies. Particular emphasis is placed on the analysis of fiscal strain and the ways in which it can be identified, monitored, and prevented.

FISCAL STRAIN: REVIEW AND ANALYSIS

As an area of study, fiscal strain was barren of theories and the analysis of such concepts as fiscal stability, economic viability, decremental budgeting, fiscal monitoring, and fiscal strain. Not until the mid-1970s was serious attention focused on the problem of fiscal strain following a number of financial crises experienced by local governments. Though theoretical underpinnings of concepts are beginning to emerge, as evidenced by Clark and Ferguson's *City Money*, most of the literature still tends to be descriptive. Despite this reality, many theoretical and practical insights can be obtained from these sources.

A paradox during periods of fiscal strain and retrenchment management is that the greatest opportunity to develop effective management systems (e.g., management planning, internal control systems, fiscal health monitoring systems, and information systems) occurs during periods when resources are plentiful. But these are precisely the times when these systems appear superfluous or irrelevant.[2] Under conditions of abundance, habit, intuition, snap judgments, and other forms of informal analysis and decision making often suffice because the costs of making mistakes can be easily absorbed without threatening an organization's survival.[3] However, during austerity periods, because resources are restricted, the innovative management systems that were not previously found necessary cannot be implemented despite the critical need. Additional problems abound when retrenchment comes; among them are the following:[4]

- lack of resources to motivate managers, to seek consensus-building solutions, to provide incentive payments, and to minimize resistance to change
- lack of resources to provide promotion incentives necessary to motivate and keep successful managers
- lack of resources necessary to expand (especially in the public sector) due to merit and tenure practice which leads to organizational entropy because new and creative talent cannot be attracted
- lack of resources leading to adoption of inclusionary practices to ensure that participants do not avoid paying their share of increased burden (the exclusionary practice is used during periods of growth to exclude people from enjoying benefits unless they share in the burden)

Defining Fiscal Strain. Most writers fail to give a definition of fiscal strain. One prominent writer in the field, Charles H. Levine, observed that fiscal solvency means the provision of services at a level and with the amount of "benefits that are adequate, equitable and stable."[5] He went on to further define these terms:

- *adequacy*—suggesting sufficiency of goods and services to maintain individual well-being
- *equity*—guaranteeing equal access and opportunity to benefits from goods and services
- *stability*—referring "to the maintenance of goods and services commensurate with the needs and expectation of the citizens."[6]

While intuitively appealing, this definition cannot easily be operationalized because it is too vague. Thus attempts at measurement would be exceedingly difficult. A more useful and operational definition would permit measurement so that we can determine when we are moving toward an acceptable state and when we are increasing fiscal strain. Perhaps the most acceptable definition is one that permits the matching of private sector resources (e.g., employment, population) to government spending and debt. In this way fiscal strain could be determined by the degree to which the expenditures of an organization or government are matched against private sector resources. Once an acceptable match is decided upon, expenditures may be adapted or manipulated to maintain the desired fiscal balance. This could be done by developing fiscal strain indicators or ratios using an equation such as the following:[7]

$$\text{Urban Fiscal Strain} = \frac{\text{Government Spending and Debt}}{\text{Private Sector Resources}}$$

Note that unless approximate or proportionate changes occur in both the numerator and denominator at the same time the system will become unbalanced. Thus, when a change occurred in Pittsburgh's denominator (a decline in the tax base) in the early 1970s, it reduced spending (the numerator), averting a fiscal strain crisis. Similarly, Cincinnati coped with its fiscal pressure by increasing user fees for a number of functions (e.g., water, parking, and the airport), by reducing demand on the general funds, by reducing the municipal work force, by regionalizing services (e.g., transferring the University of Cincinnati to the state, and municipal court to Hamilton County), and by reducing planned capital expansion.[8] When the same events occurred in New York City, it made no effort to reduce spending, which caused a financial strain crisis.[9] The point suggested here is that fiscal strain is determined by two major factors: the governmental fiscal policy output (government spending and debt) and private sector resources (employment, jobs, etc.) of the governmental entity. If the city leaders or organizational officials are able to adapt to changes that occur in the determinants, the governmental units need not reach fiscal strain.[10]

The Making of Fiscal Policy Outputs. As noted above, fiscal policy output is the response to the demand by important relevant groups and individuals for a particular program, project, or benefit. The resultant policy is affected by the philosophy of the participants, who advocate that government spending take a specific direction. Four examples have been suggested: (1) The mid-1960s saw the New Deal Democrats such as Lyndon Johnson in Washington and his imitators in many cities. They were fiscally liberal and saw government social programs as important instruments for disadvantaged blacks and the poor. (2) The ethnic politicians, such as the blacks, resemble the Democrats in that they strove to increase social services and to expand job opportunities for the unemployed members of their constituencies. (3) The New Deal Republicans viewed taxpayers as having more legitimacy than labor unions and organized interest groups. They believed in keeping taxes low and minimizing social programs. (4) The new fiscal populism was exemplified by Jimmy Carter and former Mayor Peter Flaherty of Pittsburgh. Though they were fiscal conservatives, they attempted to respond to the needs of the disadvantaged while attempting to minimize the burden of the average taxpayer.[11]

The making of each policy output typically involves a complex of dynamic, interacting forces. Of the many factors (e.g., citizens' preferences, interest groups, leaders' preferences, and residential choice)[12] impacting on the policy makers, it is important for us to know which has the greatest influence. This knowledge can provide us with insights about the decisions that produce fiscal strain.

Fiscal Strain: New York City. New York experienced windfall increases in revenue from 1966 to 1970. During this period revenues increased about 14 percent per year. This increase was generated by growing local revenues and supplemented with state and federal increases, the latter averaging a 39.7 percent yearly rise between 1966 and 1970. However, in the period 1971-1975, New York's operating revenues experienced a declining rate of increase.[13] The various periods of revenue decline were characterized by distinct administrative responses:[14]

1. During the initial decline, officials engaged in denial and delay, hoping that the increased revenue would mitigate the problem. The denial was complemented by budget manipulation, such as raising operating funds via the capital budget and postponing required maintenance.

2. The second decline was marked by the resistance of agencies and clients to cutbacks and vigorous efforts by agencies to stretch resources. Cutbacks were evenly distributed across departmental programs. Because of an attrition agreement with the labor union, few layoffs were necessary. At the same time, management instituted a number of improvements, such as the automation of the budget to enhance the city's credibility with the financial community.

3. Between 1975 and 1978, across the board cuts continued while few targeted cuts were made.

4. The 1978-1980 period saw the city making deeper, "more targeted cuts," and significant organizational changes.[15]

It is also worthy of note that maintenance postponement and user fee increases took place during each of the periods.

Change in the level of resources was the most crucial factor (variable) in New York's fiscal strain. Each of the five identified levels of resource changes (moderate continuous growth, windfall revenue growth, no revenue growth, moderate decline, and severe decline) affected the political structure and administrative strategies in specific ways. For example, no revenue growth generated weak central control and fragmented interest groups in the political structure, thereby negatively influencing demand and delaying administrative strategies. The fiscal pressure was not great enough to force decisive reductive action.[16]

Each level of service produced different types of outcomes at the departmental, program, and client level ultimately determining who received and who was denied the benefits of scarce public resources. The macro consequence manifested itself in areas such as the quality of the physical infrastructure (buildings, sewers, roads, etc.), the city's capacity to deliver services, and the quality of the city's living conditions.

Cause of Fiscal Strain. In the early analysis of fiscal strain (sometimes also referred to as fiscal distress), the causes were descriptively and loosely identified. The following are some of the principal symptoms or causes:[17]

1. extended and severe economic decline, including unabated population and employment losses
2. long periods of excessive reliance on federal aid and inelastic revenue growth of fixed costs
3. decline in public productivity compared to the overall local work force, perhaps due to unionization
4. deferment of current costs, including maintenance on fixed facilities and incurred pension liabilities
5. financial management practices, including manipulation of accounting and reporting systems

There is wide disagreement on the specific causes of fiscal strain. A grouping of the causes into three categories has been suggested:[18]

1. The *migration and tax base erosion explanation* holds that population migration has been a dominant factor in creating fiscal strain. Migration into the cities was marked by the influx of poor blacks and Hispanics, which overloaded the capacity of cities, especially in the areas of education, welfare, job training, and health. The migration of upper- and middle-class residents out of the city to the suburbs left the cities with a disproportionate number of poor and unemployed, eroding the revenue base. The residents moving in required considerably more services than those moving out. Additionally, the residents moving out caused a significant shift in the base upon which taxes were being levied, creating a revenue gap. Finally, the outmigration movement saw the population moving to the Sunbelt, taking with them industries and technology and creating job loss and population and tax base erosion not only in the city, but also in the region.
2. The *bureaucratic growth perspective* relates to the Public Choice Model, which relies on non-market economics. Proponents of this model posit that the rapid growth of government has negative implications. The growth of government leads to increases in services. People are willing to pay for some services but not for those they believe are unnecessary. This model suggests that the services tend to grow larger than required because requests for services are not regulated or

restrained by the cost factor. That is, all residents enjoy the benefits of the services produced, while only a few may be required to pay for them. The greater the number of residents enjoying these benefits without the tax burden, the greater the number of individuals supporting these services. Likewise, bureaucrats find it in their interest to expand the bureaucracy, enhancing their own career opportunities. Thus they help to use their voting power to expand the bureaucracy when the opportunity arises.

3. The *political vulnerability approach* suggests that cities are more likely to reach fiscal strain as political officials (policy makers) are subjected to demands which compel a positive response. Three conditions occur which increase exposure to political vulnerabilities: (a) voter coalition breakdown, in which important political figures, such as the mayor, are unable to muster a working majority of groups, making it necessary to spend in order to maintain and attract support, and leading to fiscal strain; (b) weaknesses in the formal authority structure, in which a strong mayor and machine government are seen as incapable of resisting demands, while city managers' reforms, which permit the delivery of efficient services at lower cost, could minimize the potential for fiscal strain; and (c) shifting power among interest groups, in which the strongest groups impose their demands on a vulnerable political leadership, having a negative impact on fiscal policy.

FISCAL STRATEGIES THAT FAILED

Intergovernmental revenue and legal reform play important roles in local fiscal policy. The impact of intergovernmental revenues may be significantly affected by the terms of the grant to the local government. Two models that guide grant distribution have been suggested. Under Model I, the local governments are passive actors executing the policies determined at a higher level of government (state or federal). In Model II, local units play a more active role, using intergovernmental revenues to implement local preferences. The Model II approach parallels the traditional decentralized role that most local governments desire. The national government typically favors Model I because it permits greater influence for the implementation of national policies and permits better accounting of the intergovernmental fiscal flows.[19]

Clark and Ferguson disagree with the widely held belief that intergovernmental aid is a significant determinant on local policy: Nonlocal revenues typically reinforce local influences.[20] The evidence (1960 to the late 1970s) in both Europe and the United States shows that intergovernmental assistance does not seem to help local governments avoid the problems associated with fiscal strain. In Europe the cities receiving the greatest assistance experienced the most severe fiscal strain.[21]

The widely accepted view that transfer of functions mitigates fiscal strain has not been borne out in studies.[22] In fact, transfer of functions may have the reverse effect. Also, the plea made by cities such as San Francisco and New York to federalize welfare programs involves many thorny issues. Does New York, with its higher welfare payments, move down to the level paid in Mississippi, or vice versa? Since it is more realistic to expect the average welfare payment to move up to New York's level, more federal resources would be required to finance welfare.

It is generally agreed that the state debt limit on local government does not work unless the debt limit reflects local preferences, because government typically finds ways to get around the limitations.[23] Most communities never reach the debt limit for general obligation (GO) bonds, for which they must use their "full faith and credit," because they want to avoid scrutiny by the state legislature. Thus revenue bonds are floated for facilities such as water; revenues generated from the activity are earmarked to pay the debt.

STRATEGIES THAT WORK

Policies that are adopted reflect the political ideology of the governing officials (e.g., Democrats, ethnic politicians, New Deal Republicans, and new fiscal populists). The general policies of these four groups may be summarized as follows:[24]

Democrats. Typically, the Democrats are disposed toward identifying new revenue sources and increasing taxes. On the expenditure side, tough cutback decisions are delayed and capital expenditures are reduced only when difficult situations demand it. Reduction of employee compensation is viewed as an option to be followed when other alternatives have been exhausted. The most influential inputs in the decision-making process come from the mayor, city council members, employees, party leaders, relevant neighborhood groups, and service recipients.

Ethnic Politicians. While their orientation is similar to that of the Democrats, they emphasize the skill enhancement/job training of ethnic employees on the city payroll. Additionally, they advocate the provision of symbolic services or what is sometimes called "good will gestures" for members of the dominant ethnic group. While similar to the Democrats in their decision-making mode, they tend to defer to elected officials and employees and representatives of influential ethnic groups.

Republicans. Reduction of taxes and services, when the situation demands, is the initiating course of action for Republicans. When implementing policies, neither employees nor interest groups are given mitigating attention or special exemptions. The deepest cuts are made in programs targeted for the poor. If the situation is propitious, a policy for productivity improvement will be pursued. The decision-making process favors the individual taxpaying citizen. Unlike the Democrats and the ethnic politicians, Republicans typically allow programmatic decisions to be determined by professional staff people with inputs made, in varying degrees, by relevant leaders in the community.

New Fiscal Populists. Though their tactics may appear different, their actions and results parallel those of the Republicans. They give the general appearance of responsiveness to the disadvantaged, but programs targeted toward these groups are usually cut. One of the overriding objectives of the new fiscal populists is an emphasis on productivity improvement. The populists stress input from citizens as do the Republicans. But unlike the Republicans, the fiscal populists give precedence to citizen input over that of the professional staff. Leaders use information such as town or open meetings or polls to assess the preferences of citizens. Finally, knowledgeable experts are consulted and ideas about improving productivity are sought.

ASSESSING FISCAL CONDITION

In a narrow accounting sense, the acceptable financial condition (known also as cash solvency) shown in Figure 18.1 may refer to a government or agency's ability to generate sufficient cash to meet obligations maturing in thirty to sixty days. It may also refer to an agency or governmental unit's ability to meet all important expenditures accruing in a budgeting period without incurring a deficit.[25] A broader perspective of financial condition views it as a government or agency's ability to meet long-term and short-term costs as they come due, such as pension payments, accrued leaves, capital replacements, and deferred maintenance. This is referred to as long-run solvency. Ultimately, financial condition provides a reading of how well a governmental unit is capable of providing "the level and quality of services required for general health and welfare of a community as desired by its citizens."[26]

In assessing the fiscal health environment and context, each community or organization must be carefully studied. Key features that should be considered in evaluating a government or agency's fiscal condition include the following:

- fiscal condition of local infrastructure, such as roads, bridges, and sewer system
- dependence on federal financial assistance, particularly support of regularly recurring operating expenses
- pension liabilities, especially unfunded obligations
- employee union demands, especially those that require contractual pay increases without offsetting productivity increases
- militancy of local taxpayers as evidenced by tax expenditure limitations
- inflation and its impact on fixed costs of government
- bond defaults and the ability to finance long-term debt repayment[27]

The traditional approach in using bond rating as the main or sole indicator of a governmental unit's fiscal health is unwise and can be misleading, as the New York financial crisis demonstrated. The city's continued use of short-term debt to meet its chronic budget imbalance was "easily overlooked because of the city's poor accounting and reporting system and its use of long-term debt to finance current operating

Figure 18.1
The Components of Financial Solvency Analysis

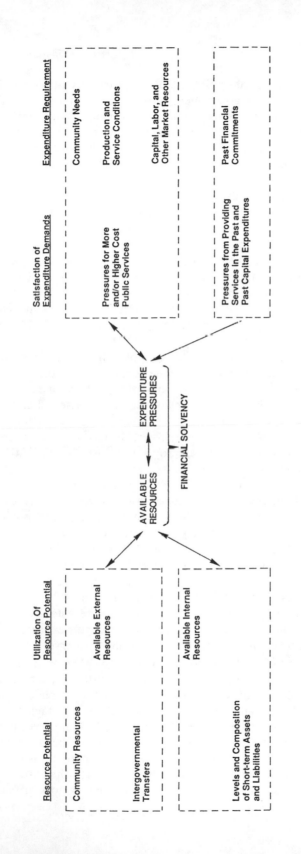

Source: Robert Berne and Richard Schramm, "The Financial Solvency of Local Governments," in *Working Papers in Planning* (Ithaca, New York: Cornell University, January 1979), p. 18.

expenses.''[28] An important point is that the possibility of a bond default is typically equated with a government's ability to pay maturing obligations. This does not say anything about the broader fiscal health of the community. Other important factors include not only an evaluation of the likelihood of default but an analysis of the government's ability to maintain current and/or acceptable levels of service. Sufficient financial resources must be available to weather economic difficulty, to achieve acceptable growth in the local economy, to maintain revenue stability, and to generate the capacity to respond to increased demand for local services.[29]

Traditional financial statements are insufficient as a basis for evaluating the fiscal health of communities. They do provide information on how financial data conform to generally accepted accounting principles (GAAP) and other regulatory and mandated requirements. Typically, information relating to data such as reliance on outside revenue sources, or uncontrollable revenues, industrial growth trends, per capita income trends, capital improvement requirements, and physical plant replacement are not found in financial statements.

Monitoring Fiscal Condition. The field of public financial management has been preoccupied with such short-term concerns as the availability of cash to meet immediate financial obligations while giving little or no attention to the long-term issues that ensure the fiscal stability of the community. Though the investment community has been concerned with debt carrying capacity, as noted earlier, it has not developed broad indicators that could be usefully employed to assess the financial condition of particular governmental units.

Many problems militate against the development of an effective monitoring system. Before the financial crises of the early 1970s, such as New York City's, there was little interest in developing such systems. Data relating to economic and demographic activities could not be easily obtained. Data that were obtainable on governmental functions, revenue structure, and financial reports could not be reliably compared for a host of reasons. Thus it was very difficult to analyze the impact of a decline in employment or a change in the form of a major business (e.g., wholesale to retail) on revenue. No benchmark indicators were established to guide decision makers on, for example, desirable per capita expenditures, long-term and short-term amounts of debt, or levels of reserves.

Financial Trend in Monitoring System (FTMS) is not a simple straightforward task. Many elements must be considered, such as the state of the national economy, local business and economic conditions, population makeup, and employment trends. Many factors must be isolated, quantified, and evaluated. The most critical and specific pieces of data cannot always be determined until they have all been systematically brought together and meticulously evaluated. Such a process is fraught with problems, but the potential yield is likely to be worth the costs.[30]

FTMS identifies, analyzes, and measures the factors affecting the financial condition of a given community. It is a means for organizing internal data (budgeting and financial reports) and other relevant external data (demographic and economic) to produce financial indicators that may be used to monitor financial changes in a given community. FTMS does not provide a single index number to identify fiscal health, but it draws attention to potentially serious problems, suggest hints or clues to the likely causes, and gives time to take preventive action. By means of FTMS, the governmental unit is able to maintain an information system to indicate its relative financial strength and weakness. It can be used as a basis to reorder internal staff priorities, to chart or modify long-term policies, and to institutionalize strategic planning perspectives in the annual budgeting cycle routines.[31] Twelve factors (the primary impacting forces on financial condition) constitute FTMS. The financial condition factors act in concert with thirty-six financial indicators "to measure different aspects of seven"[32] financial factors (see Figure 18.2). The factors have been perfected and can be used to monitor the community's financial condition.

Financial condition factors are classified in terms of environmental, financial, and organizational factors and are generated from the existence of the financial problems of the given community. Taken as a whole, the factors provide a basis on which the financial condition issues are evaluated. The environmental factors are both a source of demand (e.g., increase in population brings increase in service) and a provider of resources (e.g., more population increases wealth and the tax base). Organizational factors indicate the ways governments respond to changing environmental factors. (A rational assumption is that if government officials are given adequate advance warning they will act to avert a financial crisis.) Financial factors provide a reading of the status of internal finances which are determined by the interaction of the environmental and organizational forces (see Figure 18.2).[33]

The external or exogenous factors (community needs and resources, external economic conditions, intergovernmental constraints, natural disasters and emergencies, and political culture) are filtered through the organizational factors (legislative policies and management practices), producing the financial factors (revenues, expenditures, operating positions, debt structure, unfunded liabilities, and capital plant) which describe "the internal financial structure of the governmental unit."[34] The revenue factor informs us about the growth, flexibility, elasticity, diversity, and dependability of the government. The expenditure factor provides insight about the growth, mandated cost, productivity, and effectiveness of government programs. Operating position reveals the liquidity condition.[35]

Indicators. When properly used, the indicators can be one of the strategic means for alerting government about actions that may be taken to minimize or prevent a financial situation from becoming a problem. They are quantified changes about the environmental, organizational, and financial factors. Thirty-six indicators are identified in Figure 18.3

Figure 18.2
Financial Trend Monitoring System

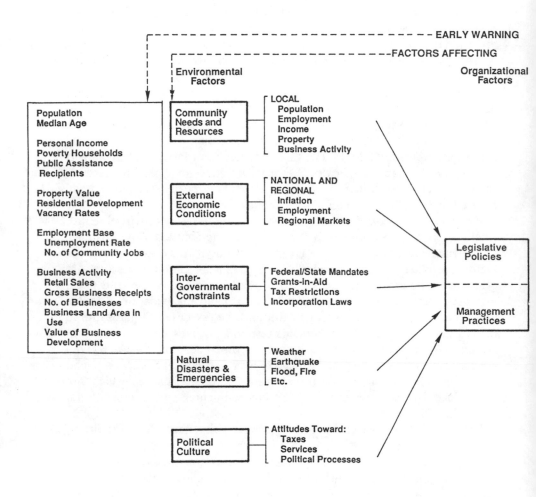

Source: Sanford M. Groves, *Evaluating Local Government Financial Condition, Handbook 2,*
   Financial Trend Monitoring System: A Practitioner's Guide, (Washington, D.C.:
   International City Management Association, 1980), p. 2. Reprinted with permission.

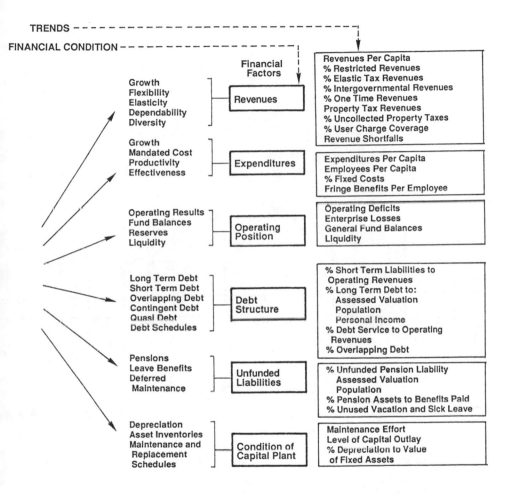

TRENDS

FINANCIAL CONDITION

Financial
Factors

Growth
Flexibility
Elasticity
Dependability
Diversity

Revenues

Revenues Per Capita
% Restricted Revenues
% Elastic Tax Revenues
% Intergovernmental Revenues
% One Time Revenues
Property Tax Revenues
% Uncollected Property Taxes
% User Charge Coverage
Revenue Shortfalls

Growth
Mandated Cost
Productivity
Effectiveness

Expenditures

Expenditures Per Capita
Employees Per Capita
% Fixed Costs
Fringe Benefits Per Employee

Operating Results
Fund Balances
Reserves
Liquidity

Operating
Position

Operating Deficits
Enterprise Losses
General Fund Balances
Liquidity

Long Term Debt
Short Term Debt
Overlapping Debt
Contingent Debt
Quasi Debt
Debt Schedules

Debt
Structure

% Short Term Liabilities to
  Operating Revenues
% Long Term Debt to:
  Assessed Valuation
  Population
  Personal Income
% Debt Service to Operating
  Revenues
% Overlapping Debt

Pensions
Leave Benefits
Deferred
  Maintenance

Unfunded
Liabilities

% Unfunded Pension Liability
  Assessed Valuation
  Population
% Pension Assets to Benefits Paid
% Unused Vacation and Sick Leave

Depreciation
Asset Inventories
Maintenance and
  Replacement
Schedules

Condition of
Capital Plant

Maintenance Effort
Level of Capital Outlay
% Depreciation to Value
  of Fixed Assets

315

Figure 18.3
Financial Trend Monitoring System: Financial Factors, Indicators, Formulas

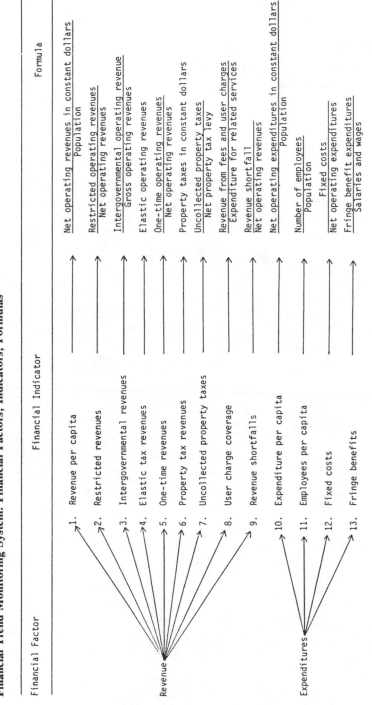

Financial Factor | Financial Indicator | Formula

Revenue
1. Revenue per capita → Net operating revenues in constant dollars / Population
2. Restricted revenues → Restricted operating revenues / Net operating revenues
3. Intergovernmental revenues → Intergovernmental operating revenue / Gross operating revenues
4. Elastic tax revenues → Elastic operating revenues
5. One-time revenues → One-time operating revenues / Net operating revenues
6. Property tax revenues → Property taxes in constant dollars
7. Uncollected property taxes → Uncollected property taxes / Net property tax levy
8. User charge coverage → Revenue from fees and user charges / Expenditure for related services
9. Revenue shortfalls → Revenue shortfall / Net operating revenues

Expenditures
10. Expenditure per capita → Net operating expenditures in constant dollars / Population
11. Employees per capita → Number of employees / Population
12. Fixed costs → Fixed costs / Net operating expenditures
13. Fringe benefits → Fringe benefit expenditures / Salaries and wages

Sources: Adapted from Sanford M. Groves *Evaluating Local Government Financial Condition, Handbook 2, Financial Trend Monitoring System: A Practitioner's Guide* (Washington, D.C.: International City Management Association, 1980), p. 2. Reprinted with permission. See Sanford M. Groves, ''An Introduction to Evaluating Financial Condition,'' in *Practical Financial Management*, ed. John Metzer, Jr. (Washington, D.C.: International City Management Association, 1984), pp. 24-25.

Financial Factor	Financial Indicator	Formula
Operating Position	14. Operating deficits	$\dfrac{\text{General fund operating deficit}}{\text{Net operating revenues}}$
	15. Enterprise losses	Enterprise profits or losses in constant dollars
	16. General fund balances	$\dfrac{\text{Unrestricted fund balance of general fund}}{\text{Net operating revenues}}$
	17. Liquidity	$\dfrac{\text{Cash and short-term investments}}{\text{Current liabilities}}$
Debt Structure	18. Current liabilities	$\dfrac{\text{Current liabilities}}{\text{Net operating revenues}}$
	19. Long-term debt	$\dfrac{\text{Net direct long-term debt}}{\text{Access and valuation}}$
	20. Debt service	$\dfrac{\text{Net direct debt service}}{\text{Net operating revenues}}$
	21. Overlapping debt	$\dfrac{\text{Overlapping long-term debt}}{\text{Assessed valuation}}$
Unfunded Debt	22. Unfunded pension	$\dfrac{\text{Unfunded pension plan vested benefit}}{\text{Assessed valuation}}$
	23. Pension assets	$\dfrac{\text{Pension plan assets}}{\text{Pension benefits paid}}$
	24. Accumulated employee leave liability	$\dfrac{\text{Total days of unused vacation}}{\text{Number of employees}}$
Condition of Capital Plant	25. Maintenance effort	$\dfrac{\text{Expenditure for repair and maintenance of general fixed assets}}{\text{Amount of Assets}}$
	26. Level of capital outlay	$\dfrac{\text{Capital outlays from operating funds}}{\text{Net operating expenditures}}$
	27. Depreciation	$\dfrac{\text{Depreciation expense}}{\text{Cost of depreciable fixed assets}}$

317

Figure 18.3 (continued)

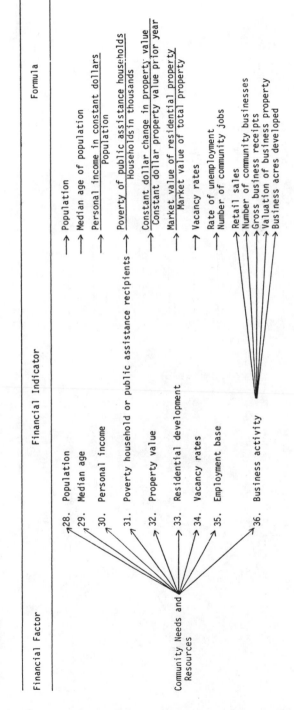

Financial Factor	Financial Indicator	Formula
	28. Population	→ Population
	29. Median age	→ Median age of population
	30. Personal income	→ Personal income in constant dollars / Population
	31. Poverty household or public assistance recipients	→ Poverty of public assistance households / Households in thousands
	32. Property value	→ Constant dollar change in property value / Constant dollar property value prior year
	33. Residential development	→ Market value of residential property / Market value of total property
Community Needs and Resources	34. Vacancy rates	→ Vacancy rates
	35. Employment base	→ Rate of unemployment / Number of community jobs
	36. Business activity	→ Retail sales
		→ Number of community businesses
		→ Gross business receipts
		→ Valuation of business property
		→ Business acres developed

CONCLUDING OBSERVATIONS

The fiscal crises of New York, Cleveland, and many other cities focused attention on the inadequacy of traditional financial statements to effectively manage a community or agency's fiscal resources. The bond rating system, while useful as a means of analyzing a governmental unit or agency's creditworthiness, is too crude to serve as an indicator of the fiscal health or strain of a community.

Early attempts to find a single fiscal health indicator, while not successful, provided insights about the development of a series of indicators and ratios that can give early warning, permitting action to be taken before a potential problem arises.

Analysis of fiscal strain throughout the nation reveals that fiscal strain is not inevitable among older communities, especially those in the Northeast and the Midwest. It can appear in any community that fails to properly manage expenditure and debt (the numerator) and private sector resources (the denominator). If a watchful eye is kept on the changes in these two critical factors, a balance can be maintained and a governmental financial crisis can be minimized or avoided. Pittsburgh and Cincinnati reduced expenditures at the appropriate time, while New York and Cleveland did not, resulting in severe fiscal stress.

NOTES

1. Terry Nichols Clark and Lorna Crowely Ferguson, *City Money* (New York: Columbia University Press, 1983), pp. 5-6.

2. Charles H. Levine, "Organizational Decline and Cutback Management," in *Managing Fiscal Stress,* ed. Charles H. Levine (Chatham, N.J.: Chatham House Publishers, Inc., 1981), p. 15.

3. Ibid., pp. 15-16.

4. Ibid.

5. Charles H. Levine, "The New Crisis in the Public Sector," in Levine, *Managing Fiscal Stress,* p. 12.

6. Ibid.

7. Clark and Ferguson, *City Money,* p. 6; see also J. Richard Aronson, *Municipal Fiscal Indicators* (Washington, D.C.: U.S. Department of Housing and Urban Development, Office of Policy Development, 1980); Sanford M. Groves et al., "Financial Indicators for Local Government," *Public Budgeting and Finance* 1, no. 2 (Summer 1981) pp. 5-19; Lyman A. Glenny and Frank Bower, "Warning Signals of Distress," in *Challenges of Retrenchment,* ed. James R. Mingle et al. (San Francisco: Jossey-Bass, 1981).

8. Nancy Humphrey et al., *The Future of Cincinnati's Capital Plant* (Washington, D.C.: Urban Institute Press, 1979), pp. 7-13.

9. Roy Bahl, *Financing State and Local Governments in the 1980s* (New York: Oxford University Press, 1984), chap. 3.

10. Ibid., pp. 4-6.

11. Clark and Ferguson, *City Money,* pp. 4-5.

12. A resident will move from a locality if the local policies diverge from his/her preferences.

13. Charles H. Levine et al., *The Politics of Retrenchment* (Beverly Hills, Calif.: Sage Publications, 1981), p. 31.

14. Ibid., pp. 31-32.

15. Ibid.

16. Ibid., pp. 43-44.

17. U.S. Department of Housing and Urban Development (HUD), *Local Financial Management in the 1980s: Techniques for Responding to New Fiscal Realities* (Washington, D.C.: Government Printing Office, 1979); and Bahl, *Financing State and Local Governments,* pp. 71-79.

18. See Irene S. Rubin, *Running in the Red State* (Albany, N.Y.: University of New York Press, 1982), chap. 1; Clark and Ferguson, *City Money*, chap. 1; and Levine, *Managing Fiscal Stress,* pp. 16-19.

19. Clark and Ferguson, *City Money*, p. 224; see also Jeffrey L. Pressman, *Federal Programs and City Politics* (Berkeley and Los Angeles: University of California Press, 1975).

20. Clark and Ferguson, *City Money*, p. 227.

21. Ibid.; see also Ken Newton, *Balancing the Books* (Beverly Hills, Calif.: Sage Publications, 1980).

22. See Roy Bahl, "Estimating Equity and Budgeting Effects of Financial Assumptions," *National Tax Journal* 29 (March 1976): 54-72; Edward K. Hamilton and Francine Rabinovitz, *Whose Ox Would be Healed? Financial Effects of Federalization of Welfare* (Durham, N.C.: Institute of Policy Sciences and Public Affairs and the Ford Foundation, 1977); Bernard R. Gilford, "New York City: The Political Economy of Cosmopolitan Liberalism," *Annual Report* (New York: Russell Sage Foundation, 1977).

23. See Dale Hickman et al., "Taxing over Debt Limits," *Public Administration Review* 41 (July/August 1981): 445-53.

24. Clark and Ferguson, *City Money*, pp. 243-55.

25. Robert Berne and Richard Schramm, "Financial Solvency of Local Governments," in *Working Papers in Planning* (Ithaca, N.Y.: Cornell University, January 1979), pp. 3-7.

26. Sanford M. Groves, "An Introduction to Evaluating Financial Condition," in *Practical Financial Management,* ed. John Matzer Jr., (Washington, D.C.: International City Management Association, 1984), p. 14.

27. HUD, *Local Financial Management in the 1980s,* p. 27.

28. Ibid., p. 26.

29. Ibid., pp. 26-27.

30. Groves, "Introduction to Evaluating Financial Condition," p. 17; see also Roy W. Bahl et al., *Taxes, Expenditures and the Economic Base: Case Study of New York City* (New York: Praeger Publishers, 1974).

31. Groves, "Introduction to Evaluating Financial Condition," p. 19.

32. Ibid.

33. Ibid., p. 21.

34. Ibid., pp. 220-21.

35. Ibid.

CHAPTER 19

FRAUD, WASTE, AND ABUSE (FWA)

Though the problem of fraud, waste and abuse (FWA) has always existed in varying degrees in public and other not-for-profit agencies, public attention and concern was not focused on it until the latter part of the 1970s. A number of developments helped to raise the consciousness and concern about FWA: (1) inflation kept spiraling upwards; (2) the cost of conducting the business of government kept rising, causing an increase in complaints about the quality and quantity of goods and services delivered; (3) there were widespread reports of kickbacks, collusion, and corruption among public officials; (4) massive amounts of resources were being directed to the military, yet its readiness and fighting efficiency was being questioned and daily reports were uncovering the outrageous prices that the government was paying for materials from non-bid private contractors.

The public's concern about FWA was a major factor in creating a crisis of confidence in both public and private institutions. A Daniel Yankelovich poll in 1977 registered a significant rise of public mistrust in national institutions. Trust in government declined from an 80 percent approval rating in the late 1950s to about 33 percent in 1976. In the business sector approval fell from a level of approximately 70 percent in the late 1950s to 15 percent in 1970. Three out of four people felt that too much power was concentrated in the hands of too few people, that federal officials could not generally be believed,[1] and that far too many people were taking payoffs in exchange for favors. Tax money was wasted and misappropriated, many people felt, and when it came to having a say about how things were run "the little guy did not stand a chance."[2]

This chapter introduces the reader to the problem of FWA in not-for-profit organizations and discusses how it comes about and how institutional controls may be developed and/or strengthened to minimize it. Particular emphasis is given to examining internal controls and describing vulnerability assessment determination.

THE GRACE COMMISSION

Formerly known as the President's Private Sector Survey on Cost Control (PPSSCC), the Grace commission, in the person of J. Peter Grace, has been a vocal critic of the federal government's waste and inefficiency. President Reagan charged the commission with evaluating the government's operations as if it were a private sector enterprise. The commission claimed that $424 billion in yearly savings could be realized if recommended procedures reducing waste and inefficiency were implemented. A number of outrageous examples of inefficiency and waste were circulated to the press. They include: (1) the federal General Services Administration employing seventeen times as many people and needing fourteen times as much space to perform essentially the same tasks as a private sector enterprise; (2) the cost of building a Veterans Administration Hospital bed unit costing $61, 250, or about four times more than a similar bed constructed in the private sector; and (3) a three cent screw costing $91.

While the Grace Commission did much to highlight and to direct public attention to waste and inefficiency in government, it oversimplified the problems it was studying. The methods used in carrying out the study were ad hoc, unsystematic, and difficult to defend. In fact, most of the outrageous examples of waste and inefficiency identified could be explained away for one reason or another. Also, the commission's rationale that private sector production of goods and services is superior to the public sector's capability is not really so simple.[3]

If the charge given to the commission were applied to the W. R. Grace Company, its rating might be no better and perhaps even worse than the public sector's. The 1971 purchase of the Mr. Gasket Company of Brooklyn, Ohio, by the W. R. Grace Company provides a good case in point. Soon after the $17 million company was purchased, many of the experienced middle- and lower-level managers that had "grease under their nails" were dismissed and replaced by MBAs steeped in the Grace management philosophy and perspective.

Ten years after the purchase of the company, the original owner, Joe Hrudka, was offered the opportunity to repurchase the Mr. Gasket Company for $4 million ($13 million less than the original selling price). Within two years after the repurchase, the company was estimated (market value) at slightly over $150 million.[4]

A number of important observations can be made here. Hrudka's re-acquisition of the company brought the immediate rehiring of more than eighty-five employees who were let go by W. R. Grace. A Mr. Gasket official expressed the opinion that it was necessary to rehire these former employees and to dismiss Grace's MBAs because the Grace managers "simply did not know the business." The point was made that there was virtually no matching between job requirements and the experience of the people who were hired to fill them.

The major indictments of the Grace management included the following:

1. It failed to establish effective communication links with suppliers and distributors.
2. It failed to study and understand its competitors.
3. It forced out the people who knew the business when it severed its links with the original owners.
4. It suffered from decision paralysis. Corporate headquarters had to be consulted for the most minute decision.
5. There was a lack of sound and creative ideas about the business. In addition, the time lag for implementation of ideas for new products continued to lengthen.
6. The MBAs, with a push from headquarters, selected a profit level and strove to realize it without understanding the means to reach it.
7. Only items with big profits were pushed. The nickel and dime items were not considered even though this was where the profits were to be made.
8. There was too much preoccupation with time and motion study and too little with finding the right product and the appropriate mix at the appropriate time.

In summary, it can be said that W. R. Grace Company was oblivious to the business environment in which it was operating. It moved too slowly and operated like a rigid or mature bureaucracy in an area that required the ability to act quickly. Grace's cadre of middle-level managers was inappropriate for the time, place, and business. At the end of ten years, experience had not increased, the learning curve had not been smoothed out. Thus W. R. Grace, to forestall the possibility of the business falling apart, was willing to resell for only the worth of the assets.

An important point that might be made here, contrary to J. Peter Grace and others, is that the private sector's supposed productive superiority over the public sector has very little basis in fact. It is not a matter of being public or private that determines efficiency or productivity in the delivery of goods and services. Instead, it is more a matter of having good managers who can motivate workers to produce optimally.

Without question, FWA is a serious problem in the public sector and perhaps to a lesser extent in other not-for-profit organizations. At the federal level of government, the General Accounting Office (GAO) estimates from $5 billion to $50 billion in fraud annually, while Donald Lambro suggests that up to $100 billion is lost due to waste and abuse.[5] As noted earlier, the Grace Commission put the figure at $424 billion. A former Inspector General at the Department of Health, Education and

Welfare (now the Department of Health and Human Services) estimated that as much as $8 billion is lost yearly in that department due to FWA.

The general public feels that government officials waste a large portion of the taxpayers' money. In a 1981 Gallup Poll the public felt that 48 cents out of every federal tax dollar is wasted. Paradoxically, these same people want the government to maintain or increase major programs. A possible explanation for this is that the elimination of waste would reduce spending and make it unnecessary to disturb beneficial programs.[6]

Defining FWA. There is no universal definition of FWA. Sometimes the FWA concept is used interchangeably with terms such as bribery and corruption. Most observers do agree that it involves behavior which violates norms and standards. Obviously, the definition of FWA will be affected by value judgments. Thus the application of FWA should, as far as possible, be context specific. The general attributes that might reasonably be identified with FWA have been summarized as follows:

1. It is a violation of public trust.
2. It is a conversion of public benefit to private ends.
3. It is a perversion of authority and the commission of an unacceptable act.
4. It is a failure to enforce laws, rules, and regulations or to apply sanctions to a given situation.
5. It is the intentional or unintentional misapplication or wasteful use of public resources.[7]

While the general definition and attributes discussed so far are useful, greater specificity is needed if the reader wishes to apply the concept FWA consistently in specific situations.

Fraud involves trickery, cheating, and intentional deception that causes an individual or individuals to give up some lawful rights or ownership of property. There are two kinds of fraud that cause injury: actual fraud and constructive fraud. When someone relies on an individual's intentional misinterpretation of material fact, this is called actual fraud. Constructive fraud is unlike actual fraud in that it is not caused by self-interest or evil design but by the very nature of the act.[8] Fraud is, in essence, an intentional or unintentional illegal and wrongful act employed explicitly for obtaining money or benefit from public programs. The conditions that give rise to fraud have been grouped into three categories: (1) situational pressures, such as heavy losses and high debt; (2) opportunities encouraging fraud, such as inadequate internal controls and poor accounting records; and (3) personal characteristics, such as low moral character and poor credit rating.[9] The common forms and methods used to commit fraud include:

- intentional mistakes, such as arithmetical or clerical errors, for example, purposely omitting an entry or making incorrect calculations

- purposeful misinterpretation of the facts
- the recording of nonexistent transactions
- intentional misallocation of contract costs
- embezzlement and theft by means of deceit and suppression of the truth
- the removal of varying amounts of money from cash funds and registers
- the overcharging of clientele or service recipients while pocketing the difference
- the placement of fictitious names on the payroll
- advances made to nonexistent employees
- kickbacks from suppliers for overpriced goods
- payment for self-completed false invoices
- the taking of agency materials, equipment, and services[10]

Waste most often is comprised of unintentional acts that result in inefficient practices or misapplication of resources, causing increased public costs or reduced benefits to potential recipients.

Abuse involves the violation of agency rules, procedures, and regulations, impairing the effective and efficient implementation of an agency's programs. Acts of abuse typically involve the reduction or denial of goods or services rightfully due to eligible participants. There is an element of ambiguity about abuse because value judgment plays a bigger role here than in the case of fraud. The abusive individual may be described as being ineffective or inefficient, or as misinterpreting policies and program guidelines. Abuse is often more insidious than fraud; therefore it is more difficult to combat.[11]

INTERNAL CONTROL SYSTEMS AND FWA

If fraud, waste, and abuse are to be minimized over the long run, the establishment of a control system that provides information about the accuracy and reliability of an agency's assets is required. The internal control system must assure that the agency's accounting transactions are "accurate and complete and that procedures for detecting malfunctions are effective."[12] An internal control system is made up of a set of procedures and actions which have been designed by the management of an agency to facilitate policy execution and to permit the minimum amount of FWA. It was noted in Chapter 2 that internal controls have two basic elements: (1) administrative control, consisting of procedures and records to ensure the implementation of agency decisions as intended; and (2) accounting control, consisting of procedures concerned with the safeguarding of assets and the reliability of financial records. To ensure reliability, an internal control system requires the establishment of a regular internal audit program to monitor the system, to evaluate its performance, and to provide the agency management with the required feedback. An independent auditor audits the entire internal control system on a yearly basis.

Internal Control as a System of Action. The federal Office of Management and Budget (OMB) requires that each agency carry out an evaluation of its internal control system. An effective system of internal controls needs more than administrative and internal accounting controls. It needs a continuous feedback of information to management indicating how well agency policies and financial information activities are being executed. The internal control system aids management in monitoring policy implementation, maintaining the accuracy of financial records, and reporting on weaknesses and corrective actions that are needed. "By frequently checking agency performance, the internal audit serves to deter fraud, error, waste and abuse in government."[13] While the feedback mechanism is an important factor in minimizing FWA, each agency's overall system of internal control must be audited periodically by independent auditors. Four major components make up the internal control system: administrative controls, internal accounting, internal audits, and external controls. The most critical of these is the system of internal accounting control. It emphasizes the following:[14]

- authorization—to ensure that transactions are executed in accordance with an agency's specified guidelines
- recording—to ensure that transactions are recorded to permit preparation of reports in accordance with generally accepted accounting principles and to maintain accountability over assets
- access to assets—to permit only authorized personnel access to assets
- asset accountability—to compare the record for assets with existing assets from time to time, taking appropriate corrective action when relevant differences occur

"Information on assets, liabilities, revenues and expenditures must be reliable to meet legal demands and to allow investors, stockholders and the public to evaluate the organization properly."[15]

Ideally, internal accounting controls, when properly established, become a network of checks and procedures that act as an important barrier and deterrent to improper conduct. Breach or violation is likely to occur only when management is negligent and fails to effectively monitor and maintain the system. Internal accounting controls may be classified as preventative or detective. Most often they are employed in combination with each other. Preventative controls are implemented prior to the occurrence of an event and may be viewed as instruments of deterrence, while detective controls occur after the event. The preventative controls are preferable, but the typical organization should have both in place. The point should be made that no one type or set of procedures, rules, or organizational controls is applicable to all agencies at all times. The appropriate type of internal controls will depend on the nature of each agency.[16]

Pre-audit as Preventative Check. The pre-audit check is a system which determines the appropriateness of a proposed action before it takes place. For example, purchase orders and vouchers are verified and checked before the orders are sent to vendors; vouchers are carefully reviewed before any payments are made to vendors (suppliers). Among the objectives the pre-audit attempts to achieve are the following:

- ascertain that forms authorizing disbursement of funds are complete and accurate
- determine that requests for payment are in accordance with administrative rules and procedures and comply with statutory requirements and contractual agreements
- determine that appropriations are available for the request for payment
- determine that price and the purchase are reasonable

In the long run an effective system of internal controls is the most useful means for reducing FWA in government (see Figure 19.1). A strong system of internal controls will help to ensure that resources are used in accordance with legal requirements, regulations, and policies. It facilitates the generation of reliable data which are maintained and properly disclosed in reports to aid in safeguarding resources and minimizing their loss due to FWA. Several categories have been used to summarize the general requirements of an internal control system:

- *competent employees* who are provided with clear lines of authority, effective supervision, and technical training
- *appropriate and effective separation of duties* (e.g., separating the custody of asset function from the accounting for asset activity; separating original recording of accounting transactions from posting to the general ledgers; and separating recordkeeping from operational responsibility)
- *proper procedures for authorization* (e.g., preventing those authorizing the purchase of materials from receiving them)
- *adequate documents and records* by requiring that forms be used upon which all transactions are summarized and entered to include purchase orders, subsidiary ledgers, and time cards
- *physical control over assets, records, and forms* to ensure protection against theft, fire, or other damage
- *independent checks on performance* by having someone not responsible for the transactions check or oversee the appropriateness and execution of performance

Electronic Data Processing and Control (EDP). EDP has become an increasingly important part of modern management. Financial management has been especially susceptible to EDP application. In fact, instances of computer-related fraud and abuse have been occurring far more, on the average, than fraud and abuse through conventional methods, both in the

Figure 19.1
OMB Process to Evaluate Internal Controls

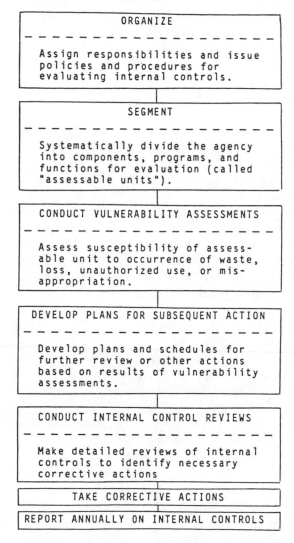

```
┌─────────────────────────────────────────┐
│              ORGANIZE                    │
│ ─ ─ ─ ─ ─ ─ ─ ─ ─ ─ ─ ─ ─ ─ ─ ─ ─ ─ ─  │
│  Assign responsibilities and issue      │
│  policies and procedures for            │
│  evaluating internal controls.          │
└─────────────────────────────────────────┘
┌─────────────────────────────────────────┐
│              SEGMENT                     │
│ ─ ─ ─ ─ ─ ─ ─ ─ ─ ─ ─ ─ ─ ─ ─ ─ ─ ─ ─  │
│  Systematically divide the agency       │
│  into components, programs, and         │
│  functions for evaluation (called       │
│  "assessable units").                   │
└─────────────────────────────────────────┘
┌─────────────────────────────────────────┐
│  CONDUCT VULNERABILITY ASSESSMENTS       │
│ ─ ─ ─ ─ ─ ─ ─ ─ ─ ─ ─ ─ ─ ─ ─ ─ ─ ─ ─  │
│  Assess susceptibility of assess-       │
│  able unit to occurrence of waste,      │
│  loss, unauthorized use, or mis-        │
│  appropriation.                         │
└─────────────────────────────────────────┘
┌─────────────────────────────────────────┐
│  DEVELOP PLANS FOR SUBSEQUENT ACTION     │
│ ─ ─ ─ ─ ─ ─ ─ ─ ─ ─ ─ ─ ─ ─ ─ ─ ─ ─ ─  │
│  Develop plans and schedules for        │
│  further review or other actions        │
│  based on results of vulnerability      │
│  assessments.                           │
└─────────────────────────────────────────┘
┌─────────────────────────────────────────┐
│  CONDUCT INTERNAL CONTROL REVIEWS        │
│ ─ ─ ─ ─ ─ ─ ─ ─ ─ ─ ─ ─ ─ ─ ─ ─ ─ ─ ─  │
│  Make detailed reviews of internal      │
│  controls to identify necessary         │
│  corrective actions                     │
└─────────────────────────────────────────┘
┌─────────────────────────────────────────┐
│       TAKE CORRECTIVE ACTIONS            │
└─────────────────────────────────────────┘
┌─────────────────────────────────────────┐
│  REPORT ANNUALLY ON INTERNAL CONTROLS    │
└─────────────────────────────────────────┘
```

Source: GAO, *Implementation of the Federal Managers' Financial Integrity Act: First Year* (Washington, D.C.: GAO, 1984), p. 3.

not-for-profit sector and in private organizations. In government, because of improper control, programmers and employees who have access to computers have been able to divert large sums of government money for their own use.

While EDP has not changed the purposes or objectives sought by internal controls, it has had significant impact on internal control systems, including the following:

- EDP systems significantly reduce the requirement for clerical employees, limiting the opportunities for segregated functions.
- Information is maintained internally in the machine, thereby retarding the conventional monitoring approach.
- Most transactions, documents, and recordkeeping-related transactions are maintained by the computer, drastically reducing or eliminating the "audit trail."[17]

At the federal level of government, Congress passed the Federal Managers Financial Integrity Act in 1982. The act requires that each agency implement a system of internal accounting and administrative controls consistent with the standards prescribed by the Comptroller General. Particularly noteworthy is the requirement that each agency evaluate its system of internal controls, indicating to what extent it is in conformity with the Comptroller General's standards, and that it submit the report to Congress and the President.

Using the Computer to Combat FWA. The EDP system can also work strategically to aid management in combatting FWA. The computer can be used to assist in detecting fraud, as shown in the following examples:

- identify unusual activities by a purchasing agent suggesting the possibility of fraud. (In this case a number of small identical orders were placed with the same supplier. By means of the sequence of the invoice, the computer revealed that the supplier had few customers and was receiving far more orders than might normally be expected. These computer indicators initiated an investigation which revealed fraud.)[18]
- identify Medicaid and Medicare claims which show a pattern suggesting potential fraud
- match welfare and other recipients to payroll and death records to identify potential abuses
- identify taxpayers who file differing tax returns for state and federal governments

ASSESSING AGENCY VULNERABILITY TO FWA

When making a fraud vulnerability assessment (FVA), an agency's internal control system is the major focus of attention. Vulnerability assessment is predominantly a quantitative systematic technique for measuring an agency's exposure to FWA. In assessing exposure to FWA an agency relies heavily on how well an agency's internal control system is designed to minimize FWA. Close attention to internal controls is likely to improve the reliability of vulnerability assessment. Vulnerability assessment may be viewed essentially as an analysis of the susceptibility of an agency or any component thereof to avoidable loss (including dissipation of assets and unauthorized use or distribution of resources), inaccurate reports and information, unethical or unlawful actions, and other activities that may adversely affect the public image and standing of an organization.

By means of a survey approach, an evaluation of an agency's potential for or vulnerability to FWA can be determined. Note that the emphasis is put on the potential for FWA and not on how existing internal controls actually prevent FWA.[19] FVA is thus an estimate of which units are susceptible to FWA—management, program, activity, project, function, or other units. In Figure 19.2 vulnerability points for auxiliary providers and third party providers are identified from point A to point H. Each vulnerability point carries with it particular risks associated with the program concerned.[20]

In the U.S. Department of Housing and Urban Development, not only are existing systems evaluated for susceptibility to FWA but new and substantially revised programs are subjected to FVA. The vulnerability assessment not only identifies the potential for FWA; it also outlines the "risks and abuses that may occur if adequate management controls are not installed at the 'front end.'"[21] Known past abuse, weaknesses, or breakdown in management controls are clearly identified. The objective is the maintenance of a fraud vulnerability assessment system that permits programs to be managed free from fraud, waste and inefficiency.[22]

The Vulnerability Process. As the first stage in FVA, the structure of the organization should be analyzed in terms of its administrative functions. The organization should be classified according to its various components, as follows:

- programs or functions broken down by subprograms or subfunctions
- the matrix of the organization indicating each department's contribution to the operation of the program
- the degree of independence exercised by the program function
- allocated budget
- relative centralization and decentralization
- personnel assigned to each program
- determination of goals, objectives, and the delivery system
- management sanctions in place
- management incentives in place to motivate sound management action against FWA

Figure 19.2
Program Vulnerability Points

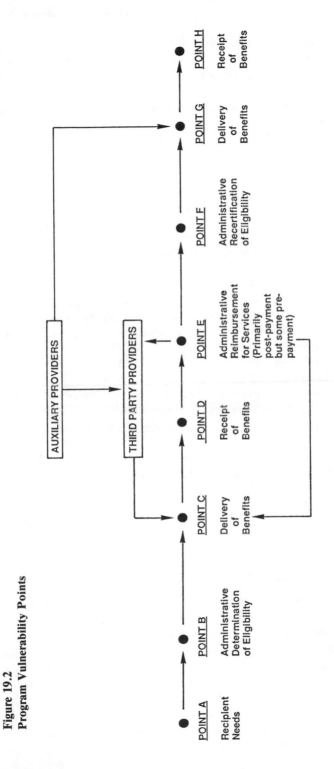

Source: Andrea G. Lang and Robert Bowers, ''Fraud and Abuse,'' in *Government Benefit Programs* (Washington, D.C.: U.S. Department of Justice, LEAA, 1979), p. 19

The degree of centralization and independence is an important factor in carrying out a FVA because it tends to suggest the intensity of supervision that may be present. When programs have multiple locations, it is usual to perform FVA at the different sites.[23]

In stage two, each program and/or responsibility center is evaluated for FVA by considering the factors that lead to FWA, such as inherent riskiness in the functions and in the organizational environment. The important objective at this stage is the development of criteria to produce ranking of the programs' or functions' vulnerability to FWA.[24] The use of the ranking approach has been gaining wide use. Among the agencies employing it are the U.S. Defense Audit Agency, the HUD Inspector General, and GAO in its *Framework for Assessing Job Vulnerability to Ethical Problems.*[25] The Task Force Report on internal controls has suggested a guide (see Figure 19.3) that might be used in vulnerability assessment.

FVA has three main steps:

1. Conduct an analysis of three general control environments. This includes the examination of personnel's competence and integrity; effectiveness of the delegation and communication of authority; overview of the organizational structure; budgeting and reporting practices; and the organizational checks and balances to financial control and internal auditing.
2. Examine the inherent risks, such as outside pressures on the agency, unclear or confusing goals and objectives, budgeting constraints, decentralization, age and life expectancy, and potential problems suggested by prior studies.
3. Make preliminary evaluation of the adequacy of internal controls.[26]

Once these three FVA steps are completed, a determination about vulnerability of the program or function can be made. The results of the FVA provide the input to conduct internal control reviews on each program and administrative function.

The flow process for vulnerability determination employed in the Department of Housing and Urban Development is shown in Figure 19.4.

INCENTIVE MECHANISMS TO MINIMIZE FWA

Though incentive mechanisms are an important factor in the fight against FWA, little has been said about this topic. The establishment of a conducive, accommodative, and effective organizational environment is most desirable. In such an environment effective controls are in place and ethical practices are emphasized and followed at all management levels. In addition, honesty must be viewed as an indispensable asset to the organization. Among the positive practices that should be observed are:[27]

1. Maintenance of an open line of communication with employees
2. Hiring and promoting only competent and trustworthy employees

Figure 19.3
Vulnerability Assessment Grid

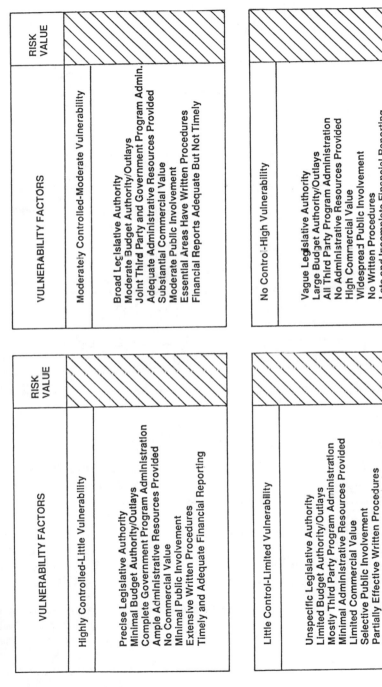

VULNERABILITY FACTORS	RISK VALUE
Highly Controlled-Little Vulnerability	
Precise Legislative Authority Minimal Budget Authority/Outlays Complete Government Program Administration Ample Administrative Resources Provided No Commercial Value Minimal Public Involvement Extensive Written Procedures Timely and Adequate Financial Reporting	

VULNERABILITY FACTORS	RISK VALUE
Moderately Controlled-Moderate Vulnerability	
Broad Legislative Authority Moderate Budget Authority/Outlays Joint Third Party and Government Program Admin. Adequate Administrative Resources Provided Substantial Commercial Value Moderate Public Involvement Essential Areas Have Written Procedures Financial Reports Adequate But Not Timely	

	RISK VALUE
Little Control-Limited Vulnerability	
Unspecific Legislative Authority Limited Budget Authority/Outlays Mostly Third Party Program Administration Minimal Administrative Resources Provided Limited Commercial Value Selective Public Involvement Partially Effective Written Procedures Financial Reports Not Comprehensive	

	RISK VALUE
No Control-High Vulnerability	
Vague Legislative Authority Large Budget Authority/Outlays All Third Party Program Administration No Administrative Resources Provided High Commercial Value Widespread Public Involvement No Written Procedures Late and Incomplete Financial Reporting	

Source: "Federal Executive Reporting on Internal Control—An AGA Study," *Government Accountants Journal* 29, no. 3 (Fall 1980): 16.

Figure 19.4
Fraud Vulnerability Determination

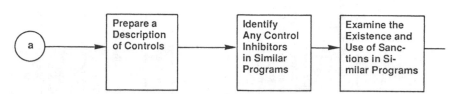

Source: U.S. Department of Housing and Urban Development, *Fraud Vulnerability Assessment Handbook* (Washington, D.C.: HUD, Inspector General's Office, 1980), Appendix 2, Figure 3.

3. Close examination of the work of employees on a continuing basis
4. Regular review and appropriate changes in weak control areas
5. Unannounced inspection tours
6. Thorough investigation of public complaints, tips, and rumors
7. Careful review of budgetary and MIS reports, giving attention to material deviations
8. Clear and early assignment of responsibility
9. Prompt issuance of agency policy

TRAINING PROGRAMS TO COMBAT FWA

The commitment to the fight against FWA has been given the greatest formal acceptance at the federal level of government. All departments and major agencies of the federal government have an Inspector General whose major objective is to minimize or eradicate FWA. There are a number of places throughout the federal government where seminars and specialized training in FWA techniques and approaches can be learned. While training programs on FWA in the government are not yet well organized, some credible efforts have been instituted.

1. The Graduate School of Agriculture conducts a three-day seminar throughout the year from October to September on (a) prevention and detection of FWA, (b) evaluation and report on internal control systems, and (c) internal control in automated systems.
2. The General Accounting Office provides a three-and-one-half-day seminar on fraud awareness for its employees involved in the FWA area.

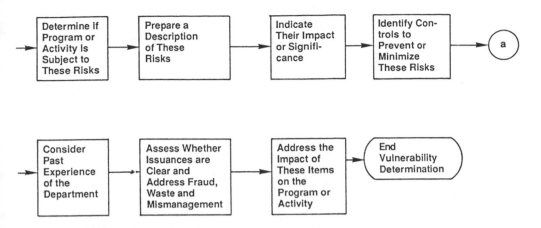

3. The Association of Government Accountants provides, from time to time, a short seminar on financial investigation.

4. The Federal Office of Personnel Management offers a two-day seminar on evaluating, improving, and reporting on internal control in federal agencies.

5. The U.S. Defense Contract Audit Agency provides a self-study course for its auditors on the prevention and detection of fraud, waste, and abuse. Additionally, FWA prevention and detection is stressed in all audit-related training courses.

6. The John Jay School of Criminal Justice offers a Master's of Public Administration Inspector General Program.

CONCLUDING OBSERVATIONS

Special emphasis focused on the comparative efficiency of public versus private agencies indicates that there is very little or no inherent superiority of one over the other. The massive problems that must be faced to combat FWA require creative and innovative leadership.

Estimates of the amount of FWA in government vary depending on who is doing the estimate. Irrespective of the estimates, the public feels that FWA is massive and that governmental officials can not be trusted. Distrust exists not only toward government but extends to other institutions, especially the business community.

The greatest efforts toward eradicating FWA have been devoted to strengthening the internal control system. This includes paying greater attention to internal auditing and to vulnerability assessment of FWA. It is my view that the long-run approach to minimization requires resocialization—a change of the internalized norms and philosophy of public officials.

NOTES

1. Reported in Seymour Lipset, "The Decline of Confidence in American Institutions," *Political Science Quarterly* 98, no. 3 (Fall 1983): 379-98.

2. Michael Johnston, *Political Corruption and Public Policy in America* (Monterey, Calif.: Brooks/Cole Publishing Co., 1982), p. 1.

3. Steven Kelman, "The Grace Commission: How Much Waste in Government?" *Public Interest* (Winter 1985): 62-82.

4. Appeared on CBS' *60 Minutes* July 20, 1985, and interviewed on August 7, 1985, with management of Mr. Gasket Company in Brooklyn, Ohio.

5. See Donald Lambro, *Fat City: How Washington Wastes Your Taxes* (South Bend, Ind.: Regency Gateway Inc., 1980), p. 2.

6. Martin Lipset and William Schneider, *The Confidence Gap: Business, Labor and Government in the Public Mind* (New York: Free Press, 1985), chaps. 1 and 2; also Mark Green and John F. Berry, *The Challenge of Hidden Profits* (New York: William Morrow, 1985), chap. 1.

7. Jerome B. McKinney and Michael Johnston, ed., *Fraud, Waste, and Abuse in Government* (Philadelphia: Institute for the Study of Human Issues, 1986).

8. See *Black's Law Dictionary*, (rev. 4th ed. (St. Paul, Minn.: West Publishing Co., 1968), p. 789.

9. See Steven W. Albrecht et al., *How to Detect and Prevent Business Fraud* (Englewood Cliffs, N.J.: Prentice-Hall, 1982), chaps. 3-5.

10. See Government Accounting Office, *Fraud in Government Programs: How Extensive Is It? How Can It Be Controlled?* vol. I (Washington, D.C.: GAO, 1981), p. 2; Martin Calpin, *Understanding Audits and Audit Reports,* 4th ed. (Ottawa: Canadian Institute of Chartered Accountants, 1984), p. 35; and Pacific Northwest Intergovernmental Audit Forum, *Auditing for Fraud* (Philadelphia: October 1982), pp. 20-21.

11. Andrea G. Lange and Robert Bowers, *Fraud and Abuse in Government Benefit Programs* (Washington, D.C.: U.S. Department of Justice, LEAA, 1979), p. 16.

12. New York State Legislative Commission on Economy and Efficiency in Government, *Preventing Fraud, Waste, Abuse and Error: Internal Control Reform in New York State Government* (Albany: State of New York, June 2, 1982).

13. Ibid., p. 10.

14. Ibid., p. 11.

15. Ibid.

16. Ibid., p. 17.

17. Mark W. Dersmith and Abraham Simon, *Local Government Internal Controls: A Guide for Public Officials* (New York: Council on Municipal Performance, 1983), part 2, pp. 30-31; see also Thomas Whiteside, *Computercapers: Tales of Electronic Thievery, Embezzlement and Fraud* (New York: T. Y. Crowell, 1978).

18. Lawrence B. Sawyer, *The Practice of Modern Auditing* (Altamonte Springs, Fla.: Institute of Internal Auditors Inc., 1981), p. 724.

19. Pacific Northwest Intergovernmental Audit Forum, *Auditing for Fraud,* p. 16.

20. Lange and Bowers, *Fraud and Abuse in Government Benefit Programs;* surveyed were Medicaid, Aid to Families with Dependent Children, vocational

education, food stamps, summer food, service programs for children, CETA, and unemployment insurance.

21. U.S. Department of Housing and Urban Development *Handbook: Fraud Vulnerability Assessment* (Washington: D.C.: Office of Inspector General, 1980).

22. Ibid., pp. 2-4.

23. Paul E. Weisenbach, "Vulnerability Assessment and Internal Controls," *Government Accountants Journal* 33, no. 1 (Spring 1983): 5.

24. Ibid., p. 6.

25. GAO, *Framework for Assessing Job Vulnerability to Ethical Problems* (Washington, D.C.: GAO, 1981), FPCD-82-2.

26. Weisenbach, "Vulnerability Assessment," pp. 6-8.

27. Pacific Northwest Intergovernmental Audit Forum, *Auditing for Fraud*, p. 14.

CHAPTER 20

FINANCIAL ADVISING FUNCTIONS: LOCAL AND OTHER NOT-FOR-PROFIT ORGANIZATIONS

As the financial function has grown more complex, the need for expert financial advice has grown. Over the years a variety of sources has emerged. In the public sector the major sources have been states, civic-minded corporations, professional associations, chambers of commerce, foundations, local universities, and paid-for consultants. While not-for-profit organizations have access to some of the same sources as local government, their main sources of financial advice are the United Way and paid-for consultants.

This chapter presents a brief overview of the advising function of local government and other not-for-profit organizations. The three main provider groups (investment bankers, commercial banks, and independent paid advisors) are examined.

CAPITAL FINANCING

Most local governments seek financial advice when they raise funds for capital financing. The advice is sought either for a specific project or bond sale or for the preparation of a comprehensive financing strategy that involves a complement of services beyond a particular debt issue. It is generally recommended when there is a need for advising services that they be secured at the beginning of the undertaking, especially in the case of a capital investment program. "Early participation in the process permits the advisor to develop (or assist in developing) a comprehensive financing plan that articulates the government's need for capital funds, explains alternative sources and structures of those funds and examines their implications for the future fiscal health of the government."[1]

Involving the advising service early in a debt issue can often increase the financing alternatives available to the governmental unit. The advisor's review of the laws may show existing practices that limit the financing options. Given enough lead time, such limits or impediments (current practices, procedures, or laws) may be removed, permitting sizeable cost savings to the issuer.[2]

TYPES OF ADVISORY FIRMS

There are three main types of firms from which governments can obtain advisory services: investment bankers, commercial banks, and independent consultants. Investment bankers and commercial bankers are typically grouped together in terms of the services they provide. Both provide advisory services as part of their normal business of marketing securities and making loans. Independent advisors do not sell securities, make loans, or underwrite municipal bonds; they sell only their professional services. Most advisory services to governments have been confined to a single area—bond-related financing. In the past, advice on general finance and planning or project feasibility has been more the exception than the rule. However, this has been changing, and to cope with this change many firms have been expanding their capability to respond to this need.

Advisory firms that provide financial advice and underwrite municipal bonds are regulated by the Municipal Securities Rule Making Board (MSRB). Under the MSRB Rule G-23, an underwriter may operate in a dual capacity as a financial advisor on a bond issue and may bid for the same issue if the following conditions are satisfied: (1) the issue is competitive, and (2) the issuer interposes no objections.

The MSRB rules are applied differently to negotiated bond sales. When the underwriter is also acting as financial advisor, Rule G-23 requires that a disclosure be made in writing to the client, indicating the potential for conflict of interest between the two roles. The advisor must resign its financial role before participating in the underwriting activities of the client. This role change has traditionally been viewed with a degree of uneasiness because of the high potential for conflict of interest. In the new role, the underwriter has two clients who have opposite interests. The governmental unit selling the bond wants the lowest interest possible, while the purchaser of the bond wants the highest interest possible. "Since the underwriter is compensated only if the deal goes through, the underwriter is under considerable pressure to make the bonds as marketable as possible to consummate the sale."[3]

DECIDING ON THE TYPE OF FIRM TO BE USED

The selection of a specific type of advisor will depend on a number of factors, such as cost, reliability, experience, and confidence in the integrity of the advice. A number of arguments have been advanced for the different kinds of financial services provided.

- Independent advisors' perspectives tend to be broader in the range of services that are provided. Since advising is the independent providers' primary concern, they can tailor their services and focus their attention on the specific and overall needs of the client. Their role is not limited to debt financing.

- The MSRB does not regulate independent advisors. This means that the governmental unit must thus rely more on firms that have established reputations.

- Investment bankers and commercial banks stress the fact that their size and standing gives them a reputation they must strive to maintain.

- Investment bankers and commercial banks that participate in the underwriting are regulated by the MSRB, which provides a degree of assurance that the organizations are maintaining levels of competency and responsibility.

- Investment bankers and commercial bankers acting in dual capacities as financial advisors and underwriters create a potential for conflict of interest. In addition, since these groups typically participate in many syndicate (group underwriting) cooperative arrangements, they may not be willing to push the interests of a given client in order to maintain good working relationships with fellow bankers with whom they will be collectively involved in future underwriting activities. It may sometimes be necessary to employ financial providers that have integrated services, that is, to permit the financial advisor to act as an underwriter and investment banker. In the case of a negotiated underwriting, the governmental unit or organization deals principally with one investment banker for selling and marketing the bond. This permits the bond counsel to provide "a multi-party advisory role by assisting the issuer, the underwriter, the trustee and the purchaser."[4]

Disadvantages of Independent Service Advice. While there are efficiencies to be gained by using independent advisors, there are also a number of disadvantages:

- Cost must be closely controlled to ensure that it does not exceed comparable in-house targets and to minimize the possibility of permitting fast-talking service providers from dazzling public officials with unneeded services at excessive costs.

- Accountability becomes more difficult since the service provider leaves immediately after performance.

- Standards of quality must be clearly identified—an exceedingly difficult task in most public and not-for-profit organizations.

- Segmented independent financial advice is unwise due to the complicated nature of some financing arrangements. To minimize cost and limit risks, it may be necessary to employ financial providers that have integrated services.

- One-time improvements and ad hoc advice are not likely to be enduring when there is no continuity to ensure that management will carry out recommendations.[5]

SELECTING THE FINANCIAL ADVISORY SERVICE

A preferred method for the selection of a financial advisory service is through the distribution of request for proposals (RFPs) to obtain a wide array of potential firms (see Figure 20.1). This means more than a mere

Figure 20.1
An Action Plan and Simplified Checklist for Obtaining and Using Consulting Services

Step

    1. IDENTIFY OR CONCEPTUALIZE THE SERVICES DESIRED

      [ ] Somebody has an idea, an inspiration, or a problem.
      [ ] Vendor makes a proposal.

    2. IDENTIFY INTERNAL PLAYERS AND OUTLINE THE PROCESS

      [ ] Who will and should participate?
      [ ] Develop a step-by-step agenda.
      [ ] Assign staff to specific tasks and deadlines.

    3. DEFINE THE SCOPE OF SERVICES

      [ ] What do we want and need? When?
      [ ] What will be delivered?
      [ ] What is done for other governments?
      [ ] How will we benefit?
      [ ] What do we do internally; what are our own capabilities?

    4. DETERMINE QUALITY STANDARDS

      [ ] Identify professional standards.
      [ ] How is quality determined and described?
      [ ] How do others define quality?
      [ ] How will we enforce quality standards?
      [ ] Do we need professional help to define quality?

    5. EXPLORE ALTERNATIVE PRICING METHODS

      [ ] Review theoretical options.
      [ ] Which are used in this profession?
      [ ] What is the industry standard in this market?
      [ ] What are our fiscal goals and limitations?

    6. PREPARE A REQUEST FOR PROPOSAL (OR REQUEST FOR INFORMATION)

      [ ] Staff assignments.
      [ ] Quality standards and scope of services.
      [ ] Standard procurement language.
      [ ] Will a contract be prepared using the proposal?
      [ ] Anticipate the evaluation process and state criteria.
      [ ] Require specific information in standard format.
      [ ] Research RFPs used in other jurisdictions.

Source: Girard Miller, Selecting Financial Services for Government (Chicago: Government (Chicago: Government Financial Officers Association, 1984), pp. 37-38.

7. IDENTIFY POTENTIAL VENDORS

[ ] Contact other jurisdictions.
[ ] Contact professional associations.
[ ] Consult the GFOA Directory of Financial Services.
[ ] Pre-qualify or screen if necessary.
[ ] Determine which vendors are inappropriate.

8. DESIGNATE SELECTION COMMITTEE

[ ] Find appropriate players.
[ ] Establish criteria.
[ ] Determine ground rules.
[ ] Review proposals.
[ ] Interview vendors/finalists if needed.

9. FINAL SELECTION

[ ] Is governing body action required?
[ ] Who presents report?
[ ] Can rational criteria overcome political influences?
[ ] Is negotiation appropriate?
[ ] What if governing body looks for different criteria?
[ ] What if proposal exceeds budget?

10. CONTRACTUAL PROVISIONS

[ ] Is a control appropriate?
[ ] Will the RFP and the formal proposal form the basis of the contact?
[ ] Are quality standards and timetables included?
[ ] Is pricing/billing basis clear?

11. IMPLEMENTATION AND ADMINISTRATION

[ ] Who is the government's staff contact person?
[ ] Are progress payments based on performance?
[ ] Will performance be measured?
[ ] Are regular reports provided?
[ ] Who approves payments and maintains files?
[ ] How will "change orders" be controlled?

announcement of the RFP. A comprehensive list of advisory firms may be compiled using aids such as the *Directory of Municipal Bond Dealers of the U.S.,* published by *The Daily Bond Buyer.* The RFP should clearly specify the type and scope of services desired, setting forth the criteria for selection and the method of compensation.

Sometime before the proposals have been reviewed, the governmental unit should clearly identify the criteria to be applied in evaluating the proposals. Among the criteria that should be used are the following: (1) past experience and familiarity of the firm with the financial services to be provided; (2) expertise and experience of staff to direct and implement the project; (3) experience with other governments both in and outside the state; (4) an estimate of the costs of carrying out the project. Once this process is completed, the top two or three applicants are invited to make presentations to provide additional input regarding their familiarity with the substantive matter of the project, to obtain a reading and feel for the personality and caliber of the principals, and to clarify questions and queries that surface in the written proposals.

Compensation of Financial Advisory Service. There is no set or definable system that can be applied in determining an advisor's fee. Any of a number of methods may be used, such as a bond float, an agreed upon amount on an annual basis or an hourly rate, or a percentage of the total dollar amount of the financing related to the advisor's services rendered. While there is no accepted right or wrong way to determine advisory fees, it is generally considered imprudent to tie an advisor's fee to the amount of bonds sold. This may provide the advisor with an incentive to sell bonds at rates that might be higher than otherwise. This method provides no built-in incentive to recommend alternative financing approaches or to postpone sale of the debt or the bonds in a volatile market.

As previously noted, the scope and content of advisory services differ so greatly that it may be hazardous to speak about comparative costs. Surveys in 1979 indicate that bond floatation advisory fees averaged from $1.45 per $1,000 on general obligation bonds of $5-$10 million to $2.60 per $1,000 on revenue bonds. The point has been made that it would be wise for an issuer to exchange informal information with other issuers or to send out RFPs to obtain some realistic ranges of out-of-pocket costs.[6]

THE AVAILABILITY OF DIFFERENT KINDS OF FINANCIAL ADVICE

Though the most important governmental advice sought is financial, it is the least well known of all the services provided to government.[7] Attempts to obtain consistent financial answers about the criteria governmental and other not-for-profit organizations employ in selecting financial service providers seldom meet with much success. The kinds of financial services available from the commercial marketplace, not-for-profit interest group associations, professional associations, universities, other governmental units, and civic-minded corporations are rich and diverse. In fact, it is this diversity that creates a challenge to the public finance professional. A partial list of financial providers aids in demonstrating this point:

- accountants
- auditors
- bankers
- bond counsels
- computer services
- financial advisors
- leasing services
- pension portfolio management advisors
- property appraisers
- risk management consultants

Since finance is so critical, it is important that financial services be carefully chosen because they can have significant impact on the financial condition of an organization. Selecting the most appropriate or best available service is a difficult task in public and other not-for-profit agencies. In public organizations "managers and elected officials are unfamiliar with varying professional standards of quality,"[8] compounding the difficulty of the problem.

PRICING OF FINANCIAL ADVISORY SERVICES

Pricing methods for financial services differ among professional organizations. Table 20.1 shows one possibility for categorizing the different methods.[9]

Table 20.1
Financial Services: Contract Pricing System

Fixed Price Type	Upset Hybrid Fixed Price	Cost Reimbursement
Fixed Fee (Lump Sum)	Guaranteed Maximum Price	Cost Only
Unit Price	Ceilings on Overhead	Cost Plus Fixed Fee
Percentage of Total	Incentive Clauses	Cost Plus Percentage Fee
Fixed Price With Escalator	Penalty Clauses	Loaded Hourly Rate
	Escalation Clauses	

Source: Adapted from Girard Miller, *Selecting Financial Services for Government* (Chicago: Government Finance Officers Association, 1984), p. 17.

Fixed Price or Lump Sum. In this type of contract, the contractor agrees to carry out specifically defined work in a given time period for an agreed upon sum of money. Since there is a single price, this type of contract is viewed as the simplest of all the pricing methods. Note that this method shifts the cost risks to the contractor, because the contractor is paid the agreed upon price regardless of the cost incurred.

Unit Price. This is a variation of the fixed price contract. The contractor agrees to perform a repetitive assignment and bills the client for the unit of work completed. This approach is typically used when the quality or volume of work cannot be easily determined in advance. Unit costing facilitates marginal costing because each additional unit of output cost can be compared with the prior unit.

Percentage of Gross Fees or Revenue. This method is widely used in the financial service industry. It allows fees to be charged as a percentage of the dollar amount of the activity (e.g., a financial advisor may charge $1.65 for every $1,000 of bonds floated). This method has survived because of the imperfect nature of competition and the ability of the service provider to exact charges due to its influence and dominant position.

Fixed Price Contract with Escalation. In those situations where a contract covers a long period, contractors, especially during periods of unstable prices, attempt to protect themselves and limit risk by attaching escalation clauses.

Upset Fixed Price. This pricing system has enjoyed a degree of popularity among public managers. The method allows the contractor to charge on a per unit or per hour basis but is limited by a maximum price that may not be exceeded. When this method is used, the assumption is made that the maximum price will be applied unless favorable conditions occur. In a way, it could be easily argued that the upset or maximum price is really a kind of cost-reimbursement approach with the application of a ceiling or cap.

Cost-Reimbursement Contracts. This approach to contract pricing permits the contractor to be paid for all allowable costs. The approach is premised on the view that prices are determined on the basis of variable costs which cannot be readily identified in advance. The cost-reimbursement method is used when the volume and type of work cannot be easily determined. Effective operation of this pricing procedure requires considerable trust in the contractor. Additionally, there is no built-in incentive for the contractor to control cost or to meet schedule deadlines. Thus reporting and monitoring requirements should be clearly and specifically spelled out.

Cost-Only Reimbursement. This method is acceptable if the quality of the product produced can be maintained. This kind of pricing is based on direct costs and excludes overhead and profit expenses. A contractor may desire such an arrangement to enhance business relationships, keep the services of critical employees, or undercut competition.

Cost-plus-Fixed-Fee. This permits the contractor to carry out agreed upon work within a specified period of time for an amount of money based on itemized costs plus an additional fee known as a fixed fee, which comprises the contractor's cost, overhead, and profit. This method is used in those cases when the work in question cannot be adequately defined. A number of problems may arise in the use of this approach, such as (1) the contractor's rapid completion of work to increase his/her profit ratio without due care being given to quality, and (2) the contractor's obtaining unreasonable profits. To minimize these problems many governmental contractors have required close supervision and ceiling clauses stipulating amounts which the cost may not exceed.

Cost-plus-Percentage. This is sometimes known as the "overhead" pricing system. This method requires that all costs be explicitly defined. An agreed upon percentage of these costs is calculated, generating the fee. This system has a built-in incentive for the contractor to recapture his/her overhead. Thus it is the contractor's intent to include as much expense as possible in the total cost figure. Because of the potential for abuse, this approach is usually avoided or is prohibited in some jurisdictions.

Loaded Hourly Rate. This is the cost-plus-percentage-fee. It is commonly found in public finance agreements. Charges are determined on the basis of labor services. Worker classifications are defined for each function to be performed. A composite hourly rate (including indirect costs) is then assigned to each worker classification. Because overhead costs are built in, there is some incentive to prolong the contract. Like the other reimbursement methods, imposed deadlines and continuing monitoring of work should be followed. Where this method must be used it is desirable to include ceilings.

Cost-plus-Incentive-Fee Contract. This has a built-in factor to reward contractors for controlling costs and to penalize them for cost overruns. This approach typically requires that targets be set: (1) target cost, (2) target fee, (3) minimum and maximum fee, and (4) formula for fee adjustment. The target cost is the contractor's best estimate of the cost required to complete the work. When the contractor controls the hours applied or charged, an incentive is provided that increases the fees. But if cost overruns are generated, a penalty is imposed. The operation of the minimum and maximum fees thus protects both sides from wide price fluctuations.

The incentive method may be applied creatively to enhance the benefits for all concerned. Consultants may be given the incentive to find ways of reducing cost or increasing revenue. Based on the amounts involved, a percentage can then be applied to the amount to reward the consultant. Where such a system is encouraged care should be exercised to minimize abuse. For example, a consultant should not be allowed to obtain a windfall profit from a recommendation that is general knowledge in the industry.

Hybrid Costing. Variations of fixed and cost-reimbursement contracts include the following: (1) The *guaranteed maximum price* establishes a price that a contractor may not exceed. It is very much like the fixed price method discussed earlier. This type of control is common in the public sector because legislative bodies pass appropriations that cannot be legally exceeded. (2) The *ceiling-on-overhead-reimbursement* may be applied to the overhead to recapture types of contracts such as loaded hourly rates and the cost-plus-percentage-fee. (3) *Incentive clauses* incorporate aspects of the fixed price contract. They attempt to motivate contractors toward greater efficiency. Contracts that provide for specific incentives to contractors are seldom found in public and other not-for-profit agencies. (4) *Penalty clause* contracts seek to promote minimum standards of professional quality and timeliness. Typically, a fixed percentage or sum is deducted from the contract for noncompliance. Where this is designed to effect compliance, it may foster output when quality is impaired. (4) *Price escalators (multi-year engagements)* are used when stability in price levels is sought. Most often indices such as the Consumer Price Index (CPI) or the Gross National Product (GNP) price deflator are used to avoid the possibility of contract price negotiation. There are a number of benefits to be gained from price escalators, such as (a) technology changes that can lower cost and help the organization; (b) contractors' benefiting from spiraling costs; and (c) avoidance by the governmental unit of start-up and retraining costs. From the perspective of procurement officials, this approach lacks certainty; thus they feel that prices should be negotiated at a fixed rate at the time the contract is entered into.

PUBLIC AND OTHER NOT-FOR-PROFIT ORGANIZATIONS AS SOURCES OF FINANCIAL ADVICE

Other governmental units can often be a ready source of financial information and assistance to local governments. The type and quantity of services vary among governmental units. At the local level, the state is a major provider of financial advice, both to other state agencies and to local governments. Since local governments are more often in need of financial advice, attention will be focused on this issue.

Advising takes several forms: (1) legally mandated or prescribed financial requirements which the state closely monitors; (2) provision of model financial management practices set forth in a series of reports, booklets, or pamphlets; (3) provision of seminars, lectures, and short courses geographically dispersed throughout the state at regular and convenient times; and (4) a combination of forms 1 through 3.

The state of Pennsylvania emphasizes forms 2 and 3. At regular times throughout the state, seminars, lectures, and short courses are conducted for local officials. Among the written materials that have been developed for local officials are the following:

- *Fiscal Management Handbook* (1981), containing basics on revenue sources, budgeting, bookkeeping, and accounting guidelines and municipal borrowing
- *Purchasing Handbook for Local Government* (1981), discussing desired techniques and practices
- *Auditors' Guide* (1984), acquainting elected auditors with their duties and responsibilities; outlining the scope of an audit and suggesting programs for the audit of various funds; and explaining how to prepare various required fiscal reports
- *Taxation Manual* (1984), containing simplified explanations of the various kinds of local taxes permitted to be levied in the commonwealth
- *Tax Collectors Manual* (1984), providing guidance and assistance to elected tax collectors.

The state of Georgia has emphasized forms 1 and 2. The Institute of Government at the University of Georgia has been a very prolific source of financial information for local officials in the state of Georgia. Among its publications are the following:

- *Getting the Most from Professional Services: Fiscal Advisor* (1979), by Charles K. Coe, containing sample contract provisions, an evaluation checklist, and a brief description of fiscal services provided by advisors, especially on bond issues
- *Getting the Most from Professional Services: Outside Auditor* (1981), providing a brief introduction to the problems facing public officials when searching for an outsider auditor
- *Understanding Risk Management: A Guide for Government* (1980), by Charles K. Coe, containing a comprehensive overview of the risk management field
- *Getting the Most from Professional Services: Computer Selection* (1979), by Charles K. Coe, indicating some basic options that should be considered in selecting a computer
- *A Basic Budget Guide for Small Cities and Counties* (1981), by Arthur Mahor, Jr., containing steps for preparing and adopting a budget in small governmental units

The state of Colorado emphasizes form 1. It provides a comprehensive *Local Government Financial Management Manual* (1985) that is regularly updated, setting forth legal requirements and suggested practices.

Not-for-Profit: Professional Associations. This category comprises a wide spectrum of financial service providers. Only the more prominent are included here.

- *Government Finance Officers Association* (GFOA) publishes a number of handbooks, books, pamphlets, and yearly updates of current research on financial management. To foster better financial reports among local governments, the GFOA awards a Certificate of Conformance to those governmental units that meet the announced reporting criteria.
- *International City Managers Association (ICMA)* provides numerous books, pamphlets, and reports. ICMA publishes books on virtually every area of financial

management; prominent among its publications are the following: *Management Information Service Report (MIS),* monthly, on timely financial topics, the *Financial Monitoring Trend System,* developed (1980) to assist governmental units in evaluating the fiscal health of their communities, and *Guide to Management Improvement Projects in Local Government,* quarterly.

- *Association of Government Accountants (AGA)* provides intermittent reports, books, and pamphlets. The AGA's strength lies perhaps more in its many short, timely seminars and lectures offered especially to financial managers in the Washington, D.C., area.

- *University City Science Center* provides fiscal gap and expenditure trend analysis.

- *Public Technology Incorporated (PTI)* is a cooperative research, development, and technology transfer organization providing services to American cities and counties. It assists local governments in developing and improving their financial management systems to increase efficiency, reduce costs, and improve services. It publishes books and pamphlets, conducts workshops and seminars, and offers consulting advice. It provides technical assistance in the following areas of financial management: (1) information management/office automation; (2) operational effectiveness, revenues and expenditure, forecasting, and user charges and fees. Among PTI's publications are the following: *Contracting Out Public Service to the Private Sector* (1980); *The Economic Recovery Tax Act of 1981: A Municipal Perspective* (1983);*Financing Public Infra-Structure: Policy Options* (1982); and *Improving Productivity Using Work Measurement: A Technical Guide for State and Local Governments* (1977).

Private Corporations and Foundations. The Pittsburgh corporate community, through the Chamber of Commerce, has been successful in providing financial advice to the city of Pittsburgh, Allegheny County, and the Pittsburgh School District in western Pennsylvania. It may perhaps serve as a useful model for other areas in the country.

The relationship established between the two large governmental units (city of Pittsburgh and Allegheny County and the Pittsburgh School District) has been most beneficial, constructive, and creative. The business community and the governmental units reached an operating understanding regarding the disposition that would be made of recommendations resulting from studies carried out on the governmental units' operations. "They agreed on the condition that everyone involved accepted one fundamental provision: that any recommendations made by the business community and accepted by the elected officials must be implemented."[10] Among the projects that the corporate community has carried out are the following:

- *Committee for Progress and Efficiency in Pittsburgh* (COMPEP) examined the city of Pittsburgh's purchasing process and recommended ways that it might be streamlined to more effectively carry out its duties and responsibilities.

- *Committee for Progress in Allegheny County* (COMPAC) was aimed at improving the economy, efficiency, and effectiveness of county government. Three main objectives were sought: (1) to make immediate improvements in the operation of county government; (2) to put in place self-generating enhancements to facilitate change; and (3) to build bridges between county government professionals and business counterparts.

- *Committee for Improvements in the Courts* (COURT) attempted to streamline administrative systems to enhance the efficiency and effectiveness of the courts.

- *Systems Program for Interactive Financial Forecasting* (SPIFF) was developed for the city of Pittsburgh, Allegheny County, and the Pittsburgh Board of Public Education to provide two important capabilities: (1) maintaining and displaying historical data for up to fifty years and permitting it to be organized in tabular form; and (2) providing techniques and methods for projecting revenues and expenditure.[11]

- *Local Government Computer Capability Project* (COGNET) is an instrument to promote better management and intergovernmental cooperation among the 131 municipalities in Allegheny County. COGNET's goal is the development of a computer network to serve the county's eight regional Councils of Governments (COGs) to facilitate sharing of services, capacity building/improving management capability.

  The COGNET project is a follow-up of earlier Pittsburgh Chamber of Commerce municipal involvement in COMPEP, COMPAC, and COURT. The project is tied into the University of Pittsburgh's AT&T campus of the future and the county of the future. This project is the collective effort of five different organizations: (1) the Intergovernmental Cooperation Program based in Pittsburgh, (2) the Pittsburgh Chamber of Commerce as the main resource provider, (3) the University of Pittsburgh, along with (4) Carnegie-Mellon University as the planning, research, and training arm, and (5) Allegheny County as the in-kind provider of administrative support.

  To enhance the project's capability, the Pittsburgh Foundation recently granted COGNET resources to develop a number of internships with students from Carnegie-Mellon University and the University of Pittsburgh. In June 1985 the Pittsburgh Chamber of Commerce received the Prudential Citation of Merit for Private Sector Initiatives for its innovative direction and accomplishments with the COGNET project.

  Three main objectives have been established for the project in the near future: (1) the development of a research proposal to study the organizational impact of COGNET on people; (2) using the project to study the innovation acceptance of the COGNET process; and (3) employing COGNET as an instrument for economic development of Allegheny County.

- *Local Government Financial Forecasting Project* is a computer based in-house long-range financial forecasting capability for the city of Pittsburgh, Allegheny County, and the Pittsburgh Board of Education.

The Ford Foundation. To stimulate and share creative approaches to the operation of state and local government, the Ford Foundation initiated a program called innovation in State and Local Government. The objective is to provide awards to units of government that have successfully applied methods to overcome social and economic problems and improve the quality of life. A $2.5 million grant has been awarded to a committee headed by former Michigan Governor William J. Miller at the John F. Kennedy School of Government at Harvard University to recognize and promote innovative programs. "The goal of the Awards Program is to identify and publicize initiatives that exemplify creative inventive thinking about government, managerial climates that encourage innovations, and particular state and local innovations which are worthy of transfer and replication." Greatest attention will be given to innovation in such areas as families, health care, education, job training, housing, and community neighborhoods.[12]

Municipal and Economy Leagues. These are professional associations and public interest organizations that offer valuable assistance to local governments. The Maine Municipal Association (MMA) provides an example. The MMA is made up of 495 towns and cities. Presently, 490 of the municipalities are dues paying members. The association engages in strategic planning, as it did in 1982 when it carried out a needs analysis of local government to identify areas upon which the MMA should focus attention. A result of the 1982 strategic planning was the strong recommendation that increased financial and consulting services should be provided to member municipalities. This recommendation led to the hiring of a staff to (1) carry out surveys and collect and review member inquiries as a service to members; (2) provide consulting to members on specific financial issues for a nominal (below market) per hour fee; and (3) develop financial workshops and publish articles on current financial events in the association's monthly magazine.

The state of Maine has facilitated the exchange of information on financial management. State agencies in Maine have developed peer-like relationships with local governments. The advantage of this approach manifests itself in situations involving creative state and local problem solving. For example, the Reagan administration signaled its policy intent to reduce funding for waste water treatment facilities. In a cooperative response to minimize the financial uncertainties among local governments, Maine enacted environmental laws tougher than the federal government's and provided increased federal aid to this important program area.

The Economy League of Pittsburgh provides an example of civic-minded corporate leadership support for improved delivery of public goods and services. The league gives advice and assistance to all units of government. Though the League prefers to work with a collective of municipalities, it responds to individual governmental unit calls for assistance. For example, the Allegheny League of Municipalities was recently asked to evaluate the need for a regional bond bank to assist towns and cities in obtaining debt financing. The league has developed a number of handbooks on various financial topics.

Local Universities and Colleges. Most colleges and universities, especially state-supported ones with programs in public administration, provide an array of services and publications to governmental units, often below cost or totally free of charge. Many of these institutions seek agencies that will provide internships for their students.

The Not-for-Profit Sector. The most prolific source of financial advice is private professional associations and United Way–sponsored agencies. For example, in Allegheny County the CPAs' association has been generous with its assistance to not-for-profit agencies. Many of the big accounting and consulting firms sit on not-for-profit agency boards. Most often services are provided gratis or at minimal cost to not-for-profit agencies.

Community Technical Assistance Center (CTAC). This is an example of an agency that was organized to assist not-for-profit agencies. It charges fees according to ability to pay. Among the services CTAC provides are the following: (1) financial management—setting up accounting systems; and (2) computerized accounting, cost-effectiveness analysis, bookkeeping, development of financial reports, budgeting, and financial planning. These services are available to non-profit agencies and community development corporations on a nonpartisan basis in the city of Pittsburgh.

CONCLUDING OBSERVATIONS

Though financial advising has become a very important and strategic function in government and other not-for-profit organizations, little attention was given to it in the literature before the recent appearance of Government Finance Officers Association publications. In the past many governmental units sought financial advice only when they needed to enter the capital markets to borrow funds. This has been changing for many reasons, among them being the many regulations, and complex financial management problems faced by governmental units and other not-for-profit organizations.

Most states have developed varying ways to respond to the increasing need for financial advice, as shown by Georgia, Maine, and Pennsylvania. These efforts cannot, however, meet all of the financial advising requirements of governmental units—thus the need for financial advice from corporations, universities, foundations, and associations.

As can be seen from the Pittsburgh experience, the corporate community can be a forceful and strategic source of creative financial aid to communities.

NOTES

1. West C. Hough and John E. Petersen, "Selection and Use of Financial Advisory Services," *Governmental Finance* 13 (March 1984): 42.
2. Ibid.

3. Ibid., p. 45.

4. Girard Miller, *Selecting Financial Services for Government* (Chicago: Government Finance Officers Association, 1984), p. 9.

5. Ibid.

6. Ibid., pp. 46-47.

7. Miller, p. vii.

8. Ibid.

9. H. Edward Weseman, *Contracting City Services* (Pittsburgh: Innovations Press, 1981), pp. 60-61; Miller, pp. 17-18; Frank M. Alston et al., *Contracting with the Federal Government* (New York: John Wiley and Sons, 1984), pp. 12-14.

10. Edward S. Kiely, "Mobilizing Business Resources for Better Government: Pittsburgh's Learned Executive Experience," *Urban Resources* 1 (Summer 1983): 8.

11. Mellon Institute and Carnegie-Mellon University, *SPIFF User Manual* (Pittsburgh: Pittsburgh Chamber of Commerce, 1985), p. 1.

12. Ford Foundation and Harvard University, "Innovations in State and Local Government" (pamphlet) (Cambridge, Mass.: John F. Kennedy School of Government, Harvard University, n.d.).

BUDGETING AS PROGRAM AND POLICY INSTRUMENT

DECISION UNIT: Crime Prevention

DECISION PACKAGE: Neighbors Watching out for Neighbors

GOALS: To establish, promote, and maintain voluntary
                     neighborhood- organizations which will be alert
                     and report to the police suspicious, unusual
                     activity, unfamiliar or suspicious cars, or
                     suspicious individuals in the neighborhood.

OBJECTIVES: 1. To reduce reported crimes against persons
                        or property by 3% through these
                        organizations.

                     2. To increase arrest and conviction rates by
                        7% as a result of these organizations.

                     3. To encourage increased voluntary neighbor-
                        hood participation in the program on a
                        block-by-block basis.

                     4. To encourage participants to notify the
                        police of unusual activity or suspicious
                        persons or cars in their neighborhood.

                     5. To raise the level of consciousness of
                        residents to be aware of unusual
                        happenings and/or suspicious persons or
                        cars in their neighborhood and to report
                        such to the police.

Source: Adapted from Betty Brooks' assignment in "Budgeting as Program and Policy
Instrument" in the author's course at the University of Pittsburgh, March 8, 1982.

	BUDGET			POSITIONS		
	$15,000			2		

1981 SERVICE LEVEL OPTIONS

		Budget		Positions		Rank	Dept.Rank
S/L	S/L	Cum	S/L	Cum.			
1	$ 7,000	$ 7,000	1	1		4/4	4/13
2	8,000	15,000	1	2		2/4	5/13
3	16,000	31,000	1	3		1/4	7/13
4	5,000	36,000	1	4		3/4	11/13

SERVICE LEVEL NARRATIVE

1. This level would provide the minimum level of service necessary so that the goals and objectives of the program would not be jeopardized or lose their effectiveness. At this level, assistance is provided to residents in order to encourage the organization of voluntary neighborhood groups and to report unusual or suspicious persons, cars, or activities to the police for investigation.

2. This is the current level of service whereby assistance is provided to residents for the creation of voluntary neighborhood organizations. Police officers involved in the program are also available to speak at civic organization meetings to encourage more participation in the program and to discuss with residents possible ways of improving the program.

3. Since there is no juvenile section in the police department, this enhanced level would create an additional position to work specifically on juvenile matters and with the courts.

It would also allow for an "Officer Friendly" program whereby the officer would speak before school children and answer their questions concerning police and law enforcement activities.

4. At this enhanced level the program would be expanded and would focus on training sessions for participants. Specifically, outside consultants would teach residents particular types of behavior to watch out for thereby reducing some unnecessary calls to the police for investigation.

DEMAND

Number of inquiries from residents in the program.

Increased crime rate in the jurisdiction.

Number of requests to speak before civic organizations.

Number of requests from residents to participate in the program.

Number of requests from school officials to help deter juvenile delinquency.

Number of requests from participants for additional training to increase the efficiency of the program.

WORKLOAD

Number of meetings with residents who want to establish voluntary neighborhood organizations.

Number of hours to be spent with residents in establishing these groups.

Number of calls received from participants in this program.

Number of additional neighborhood organizations to be created.

Number of appearances before civic groups.

Number of improvements to be implemented to upgrade the program.

Number of juveniles expected to be arrested and/or adjudicated.

Number of appearances to be made before school children.

Number of hours to be spent in court appearances.

Number of hours to be spent in informal conversations with children outside of the school environment.

Number of training sessions to be held.

Number of hours to be spent in training sessions.

Number of participants in the training sessions.

EFFECTIVENESS

Percentage increase or decrease in requests from residents to participate in the program.

Percentage increase or decrease in suggestions implemented for improving the program.

Percentage increase or decrease in appearances before civic organizations.

Percentage increase or decrease in calls received from participants, responded to and investigated.

Percentage increase or decrease in overall crime rate.

Percentage of residents expressing a feeling of security from crime.

Percentage increase or decrease in juveniles arrested and successfully adjudicated.

Percentage increase or decrease in speaking before school children.

Decrease in adult and juvenile crime rate.

ALTERNATIVE ANALYSIS

Several alternatives are available. The program could be: (1) entirely eliminated; (2) reduced in size; (3) maintained at its current level; (4) merged with another unit; or (5) increased in staff support personnel.

Since there is a need for the program in the community, eliminating it does not seem feasible. Reducing the program is a possibility since residents would continue to benefit from it on a limited basis. Maintaining it at its current level would provide a much needed service and allow visibility for both the program and the police within the community. Merging the program with another unit in the department would cause the program to lose its effectiveness because the amount of staff time required could no longer be given to this activity. Increasing the staff support personnel would allow for the program to be expanded in scope and provide additional services to the residents.

It would thus appear that the best alternative would be to expand the program to include one additional staff position to deal specifically with juvenile matters. The increase in juvenile crimes and the concern by residents would warrant this new position. Furthermore, the program has been well received by residents and could be enhanced with the hiring of an individual to work specifically with juvenile-related problems.

CONSEQUENCES OF NOT FUNDING

It would be detrimental to residents of the community not to fund at least the minimum level of service. As taxpayers, residents would feel that the police department is not serving or meeting their needs if the program is eliminated. Furthermore, they would feel less secure in their homes and neighborhoods if the program is not funded. In addition, the crime rate would continue to rise if residents were denied the opportunity to participate in this important program.

SUGGESTED: RANKING CRITERIA

Minimal new activities that require additional funding.

Minimal increase in personnel.

No additional special training skills required.

No new cars or major equipment purchases.

Favorable towards any outside funding (federal, state, or other) to help support the program.

Potential consequences if services are not provided.

JUSTIFICATION FOR SELECTING SERVICE LEVEL 3

It is recommended that the decision package be funded at Service Level 3 for several reasons. Since there is no juvenile section or juvenile officer in the police department to handle juvenile matters, it would be appropriate to include an additional position in this package. The officer would be speaking frequently to children at school and become better acquainted with them. This would establish rapport among the children, the school, and the community to help alleviate the recent rise in juvenile crimes.

The participants in the voluntary neighborhood program would benefit by knowing that the officer is familiar with where the children live and which ones may have problems that could eventually lead to delinquency. The residents would also feel that their needs are being served because the increase in juvenile crime is serious enough to warrant the hiring of an individual to deal specifically with this problem.

Furthermore, the officer would follow the case from arrest to adjudication for any child who became involved in the juvenile justice system. He/she would also be able to provide insight and input about the child to other police officers, social workers, and/or the court.

PRESENT VALUE FACTORS

Present Value Factors   Table I: Present Value of One Dollar at the End of *n* Years

Year (n)	1%	2%	3%	4%	5%	6%	7%	8%	9%	10%	12%	14%	15%	Year (n)
1	0.990	0.980	0.970	0.962	0.952	0.943	0.935	0.926	0.917	0.909	0.893	0.877	0.870	1
2	0.980	0.961	0.943	0.925	0.907	0.890	0.873	0.857	0.842	0.826	0.797	0.769	0.756	2
3	0.971	0.942	0.915	0.889	0.864	0.840	0.816	0.794	0.772	0.751	0.712	0.675	0.658	3
4	0.961	0.924	0.888	0.855	0.823	0.792	0.763	0.735	0.708	0.683	0.636	0.592	0.572	4
5	0.951	0.906	0.863	0.822	0.784	0.747	0.713	0.681	0.650	0.621	0.567	0.519	0.497	5
6	0.942	0.888	0.837	0.790	0.746	0.705	0.666	0.630	0.596	0.564	0.507	0.456	0.432	6
7	0.933	0.871	0.813	0.760	0.711	0.665	0.623	0.583	0.547	0.513	0.452	0.400	0.376	7
8	0.923	0.853	0.789	0.731	0.677	0.627	0.582	0.540	0.502	0.467	0.404	0.351	0.327	8
9	0.914	0.837	0.766	0.703	0.645	0.592	0.544	0.500	0.460	0.424	0.361	0.308	0.284	9
10	0.905	0.820	0.744	0.676	0.614	0.558	0.508	0.463	0.422	0.386	0.322	0.270	0.247	10
11	0.896	0.804	0.722	0.650	0.585	0.527	0.475	0.429	0.388	0.350	0.287	0.237	0.215	11
12	0.887	0.788	0.701	0.625	0.557	0.497	0.444	0.397	0.356	0.319	0.257	0.208	0.187	12
13	0.879	0.773	0.681	0.601	0.530	0.469	0.415	0.368	0.326	0.290	0.229	0.182	0.163	13
14	0.870	0.758	0.661	0.577	0.505	0.442	0.388	0.340	0.299	0.263	0.205	0.160	0.141	14
15	0.861	0.743	0.642	0.555	0.481	0.417	0.362	0.315	0.275	0.239	0.183	0.140	0.123	15
16	0.853	0.728	0.623	0.534	0.458	0.394	0.339	0.299	0.252	0.218	0.163	0.123	0.107	16
17	0.844	0.714	0.605	0.513	0.436	0.371	0.317	0.270	0.231	0.198	0.146	0.108	0.093	17
18	0.836	0.700	0.587	0.494	0.416	0.350	0.296	0.250	0.212	0.180	0.130	0.095	0.081	18
19	0.828	0.686	0.570	0.475	0.396	0.331	0.277	0.232	0.194	0.164	0.116	0.083	0.070	19
20	0.820	0.673	0.554	0.456	0.377	0.312	0.258	0.215	0.178	0.149	0.104	0.073	0.061	20
21	0.811	0.660	0.538	0.439	0.359	0.294	0.242	0.199	0.164	0.135	0.093	0.064	0.053	21
22	0.803	0.647	0.522	0.422	0.342	0.278	0.226	0.184	0.150	0.123	0.083	0.056	0.046	22
23	0.795	0.634	0.507	0.406	0.326	0.262	0.211	0.170	0.138	0.112	0.074	0.049	0.040	23
24	0.788	0.622	0.492	0.390	0.310	0.247	0.197	0.158	0.126	0.102	0.066	0.043	0.035	24
25	0.780	0.610	0.478	0.375	0.295	0.233	0.184	0.146	0.116	0.092	0.059	0.038	0.030	25

Year (n)	16%	18%	20%	22%	24%	25%	26%	28%	30%	35%	40%	50%	Year (n)
1	0.862	0.847	0.833	0.820	0.806	0.800	0.794	0.781	0.769	0.741	0.714	0.667	1
2	0.743	0.718	0.694	0.672	0.650	0.640	0.630	0.610	0.592	0.549	0.510	0.444	2
3	0.641	0.609	0.579	0.551	0.524	0.512	0.500	0.477	0.455	0.406	0.364	0.296	3
4	0.552	0.516	0.482	0.451	0.423	0.410	0.397	0.373	0.350	0.301	0.260	0.198	4
5	0.476	0.437	0.402	0.370	0.341	0.328	0.315	0.291	0.269	0.223	0.186	0.132	5
6	0.410	0.370	0.333	0.303	0.275	0.262	0.250	0.227	0.207	0.165	0.133	0.088	6
7	0.354	0.314	0.279	0.249	0.222	0.210	0.198	0.178	0.159	0.122	0.095	0.059	7
8	0.305	0.266	0.233	0.204	0.179	0.168	0.157	0.139	0.123	0.091	0.068	0.039	8
9	0.263	0.225	0.194	0.167	0.144	0.134	0.125	0.108	0.094	0.067	0.048	0.026	9
10	0.227	0.191	0.162	0.137	0.116	0.107	0.099	0.085	0.073	0.050	0.035	0.017	10
11	0.195	0.162	0.135	0.112	0.094	0.086	0.079	0.066	0.056	0.037	0.025	0.012	11
12	0.168	0.137	0.112	0.092	0.076	0.069	0.062	0.052	0.043	0.027	0.018	0.008	12
13	0.145	0.116	0.093	0.075	0.061	0.055	0.050	0.040	0.033	0.020	0.013	0.005	13
14	0.125	0.099	0.078	0.062	0.049	0.044	0.039	0.032	0.025	0.015	0.009	0.003	14
15	0.108	0.084	0.065	0.051	0.040	0.035	0.031	0.025	0.020	0.011	0.006	0.002	15
16	0.093	0.071	0.054	0.042	0.032	0.028	0.025	0.019	0.015	0.008	0.005	0.002	16
17	0.080	0.060	0.045	0.034	0.026	0.023	0.020	0.015	0.012	0.006	0.003	0.001	17
18	0.069	0.051	0.038	0.028	0.021	0.018	0.016	0.012	0.009	0.005	0.002	0.001	18
19	0.060	0.043	0.031	0.023	0.017	0.014	0.012	0.009	0.007	0.003	0.002		19
20	0.051	0.037	0.026	0.019	0.014	0.012	0.010	0.007	0.005	0.002	0.001		20
21	0.044	0.031	0.022	0.015	0.011	0.009	0.008	0.006	0.004	0.002	0.001		21
22	0.038	0.026	0.018	0.013	0.009	0.007	0.006	0.004	0.003	0.001	0.001		22
23	0.033	0.022	0.015	0.010	0.007	0.006	0.005	0.003	0.002	0.001			23
24	0.028	0.019	0.013	0.008	0.006	0.005	0.004	0.003	0.002	0.001			24
25	0.024	0.016	0.010	0.007	0.005	0.004	0.003	0.002	0.001	0.001			25

Present Value Factors   Table II: Present Value of One Dollar per Year for *n* Years

Year (*n*)	1%	2%	3%	4%	5%	6%	7%	8%	9%	10%	12%	14%	15%	Year (*n*)
1	0.990	0.980	0.971	0.962	0.952	0.943	0.935	0.926	0.917	0.909	0.893	0.377	0.870	1
2	1.970	1.942	1.914	1.886	1.859	1.833	1.808	1.783	1.759	1.736	1.690	1.647	1.626	2
3	2.941	2.884	2.829	2.775	2.723	2.673	2.624	2.577	2.531	2.487	2.402	2.322	2.283	3
4	3.902	3.808	3.717	3.630	3.546	3.465	3.387	3.312	3.240	3.170	3.037	2.914	2.855	4
5	4.854	4.713	4.580	4.452	4.330	4.212	4.100	3.993	3.890	3.791	3.605	3.433	3.352	5
6	5.796	5.601	5.417	5.242	5.076	4.917	4.767	4.623	4.486	4.355	4.111	3.889	3.785	6
7	6.728	6.472	6.230	6.002	5.786	5.582	5.389	5.206	5.033	4.868	4.564	4.288	4.160	7
8	7.652	7.325	7.020	6.733	6.463	6.210	5.971	5.747	5.535	5.335	4.968	4.639	4.487	8
9	8.566	8.162	7.786	7.435	7.108	6.802	6.515	6.247	5.985	5.759	5.328	4.946	4.772	9
10	9.471	8.983	8.530	8.111	7.722	7.360	7.024	6.710	6.418	6.145	5.650	5.216	5.019	10
11	10.368	9.787	9.253	8.760	8.306	7.887	7.499	7.139	6.805	6.495	5.938	5.453	5.234	11
12	11.255	10.575	9.954	9.385	8.863	8.384	7.943	7.536	7.161	6.814	6.194	5.660	5.421	12
13	12.134	11.348	10.635	9.986	9.394	8.853	8.358	7.904	7.487	7.103	6.424	5.842	5.583	13
14	13.004	12.106	11.296	10.563	9.899	9.295	8.745	8.244	7.786	7.367	6.628	6.002	5.725	14
15	13.865	12.849	11.938	11.118	10.380	9.712	9.108	8.560	8.061	7.606	6.811	6.142	5.847	15
16	14.718	13.578	12.561	11.652	10.838	10.106	9.447	8.851	8.313	7.824	6.974	6.265	5.954	16
17	15.562	14.292	13.166	12.166	11.274	10.477	9.763	9.122	8.544	8.022	7.120	6.373	6.047	17
18	16.398	14.992	13.753	12.659	11.690	10.828	10.059	9.372	8.756	8.201	7.250	6.467	6.128	18
19	17.226	15.678	14.324	13.134	12.085	11.158	10.336	9.604	8.950	8.365	7.366	6.550	6.198	19
20	18.046	16.351	14.877	13.590	12.462	11.470	10.594	9.818	9.129	8.514	7.469	6.623	6.259	20
21	18.857	17.011	15.415	14.029	12.821	11.764	10.836	10.017	9.292	8.649	7.562	6.687	6.313	21
22	19.661	17.658	15.937	14.451	13.163	12.042	11.061	10.201	9.442	8.772	7.645	6.743	6.359	22
23	20.456	18.292	16.444	14.857	13.489	12.303	11.272	10.371	9.580	8.883	7.718	6.792	6.399	23
24	21.244	18.914	16.936	15.247	13.799	12.550	11.469	10.529	9.707	8.985	7.784	6.835	6.434	24
25	22.023	19.523	17.413	15.622	14.094	12.783	11.654	10.675	9.823	9.077	7.843	6.873	6.464	25

Year (*n*)	16%	18%	20%	22%	24%	25%	26%	28%	30%	35%	40%	50%	Year (*n*)
1	0.862	0.848	0.833	0.820	0.807	0.800	0.794	0.781	0.769	0.741	0.714	0.667	1
2	1.605	1.566	1.528	1.492	1.457	1.440	1.424	1.392	1.361	1.289	1.225	1.111	2
3	2.246	2.174	2.107	2.042	1.981	1.952	1.923	1.868	1.816	1.696	1.589	1.407	3
4	2.798	2.690	2.589	2.494	2.404	2.362	2.320	2.241	2.166	1.997	1.849	1.605	4
5	3.274	3.127	2.991	2.864	2.745	2.689	2.635	2.532	2.436	2.220	2.935	1.737	5
6	3.685	3.408	3.326	3.107	3.021	2.951	2.885	2.759	2.643	2.385	2.168	1.824	6
7	4.039	3.812	3.605	3.416	3.242	3.161	3.083	2.937	2.802	2.508	2.263	1.883	7
8	4.344	4.078	3.837	3.619	3.421	3.329	3.241	3.076	2.925	2.598	2.331	1.922	8
9	4.607	4.303	4.031	3.786	3.566	3.463	3.366	3.184	3.019	2.665	2.379	1.948	9
10	4.833	4.494	4.193	3.923	3.682	3.571	3.465	3.269	3.092	2.715	2.414	1.965	10
11	5.029	4.656	4.327	4.035	3.776	3.656	3.544	3.335	3.147	2.752	2.438	1.977	11
12	5.197	4.793	4.439	4.127	3.851	3.725	3.606	3.387	3.190	2.779	2.456	1.985	12
13	5.342	4.910	4.533	4.203	3.912	3.780	3.656	3.427	3.223	2.799	2.469	1.990	13
14	5.468	5.008	4.611	4.265	3.962	3.824	3.695	3.459	3.249	2.814	2.478	1.993	14
15	5.576	5.092	4.676	4.315	4.001	3.859	3.726	3.483	3.268	2.826	2.484	1.995	15
16	5.669	5.162	4.730	4.357	4.033	3.887	3.751	3.503	3.283	2.834	2.489	1.997	16
17	5.749	5.222	4.775	4.391	4.059	3.910	3.771	3.518	3.295	2.840	2.492	1.998	17
18	5.818	5.273	4.812	4.419	4.080	3.928	3.786	3.529	3.304	2.844	2.494	1.999	18
19	5.878	5.316	4.844	4.442	4.097	3.942	3.799	3.539	3.311	2.848	2.496	1.999	19
20	5.929	5.353	4.870	4.460	4.110	3.954	3.808	3.546	3.316	2.850	2.497	1.999	20
21	5.973	5.384	4.891	4.476	4.121	3.963	3.816	3.551	3.320	2.852	2.498	2.000	21
22	6.011	5.410	4.909	4.488	4.130	3.971	3.822	3.556	3.323	2.853	2.499	2.000	22
23	6.044	5.432	4.925	4.499	4.137	3.976	3.827	3.559	3.325	2.854	2.499	2.000	23
24	6.073	5.451	4.937	4.507	4.143	3.981	3.831	3.562	3.327	2.855	2.499	2.000	24
25	6.097	5.467	4.948	4.514	4.147	3.985	3.834	3.564	3.329	2.856	2.499	2.000	25

SELECTED BIBLIOGRAPHY

Albrecht, Steven W., et al. *How to Detect and Prevent Business Fraud.* Englewood Cliffs, N.J.: Prentice-Hall, 1982.

American Public Works Association. *Revenue Short Fall.* Chicago: American Public Works Association, 1981.

Anthony, Robert N., and David W. Young. *Management Control in Nonprofit Organizations.* Homewood, Ill.: Richard D. Irwin and Co., 1984.

Anton, Thomas. *The Politics of State Expenditures in Illinois.* Champaign, Ill.: University of Illinois Press, 1966.

Bahl, Roy. "Estimating Equity and Budgeting Effects of Financial Assumptions." *National Tax Journal* 29 (March 1976): 54-72.

_____. *Financing State and Local Governments in the 1980s.* New York: Oxford University Press, 1984.

Biggs, Charles L., Evan G. Birks, and William Atkins. *Managing the System Development Process.* Englewood Cliffs, N.J.: Prentice-Hall, 1980.

Boskin, Michael J., and Aaron Wildavsky, eds. *The Federal Budget: Economics and Politics.* New Brunswick, N.J.: Transaction Books, 1982.

Brown, Richard E., et al. *Auditing Performance of Government.* New York: John Wiley and Sons, 1982.

Clark, Terry Nichols, and Lorna Crowley Ferguson. *City Money.* New York: Columbia University Press, 1983.

Clark, Terry Nichols, et al. *Financial Handbook for Mayors and City Managers.* New York: Van Nostrand Reinhold Co., 1985.

Coe, Charles K. *Understanding Risk Management.* Athens, Ga.: Institute of Local Government, 1980.

Comptroller General of the United States. *Standards for Audit of Governmental Organizations.* Washington, D.C.: GAO, 1981.

Connors, Tracy D., and Christopher T. Callaghan, eds. *Financial Management in Non-profit Organizations.* New York: AMACOM, 1982.

Cramer, Robert M. "Local Government Expenditure Forecasting." *Governmental Finance.* (November 1978): 4.

Dotsey, Michael. "An Investigation of Cash Management Practices and Their Effects on the Demand for Money." *Economic Review* 70, no. 5 (September/October 1984): 3.

Drebin, Allan R. "Criteria for Performance Measurement in State and Local Government." *Governmental Finance* 10 (December 1980): 4.

Drebin, Allan R., et al. *Objectives of Accounting and Financial Reporting for Governmental Units: A Research Study, Vol. 1.* Chicago: National Council on Governmental Accounting, 1981.

Government Accounting Office. *Federal Capital Budgeting: A Collection of Haphazard Practices.* Washington, D.C.: GAO, 1981.

_____. *Framework for Assessing Job Vulnerability to Ethical Problems.* Washington, D.C.: GAO, 1981.

_____. *Study of Selected Local Procurement Systems Part I.* Washington, D.C.: GAO, 1978.

Green, Mark, and John F. Berry. *The Challenge of Hidden Profits.* New York: William Morrow, 1985.

Hall, John R. *Factors Related to Local Government Use of Performance Measurement.* Washington, D.C.: Urban Institute, April 1978.

Haller, Leon. *Financial Resource Management for Non-profit Organizations.* Englewood Cliffs, N.J.: Prentice-Hall, 1982.

Harper, Charles, et al. *Financial Systems for Community Health Organizations.* Belmont, Calif.: Life Learning Publications, 1981.

Harrell, Rhett D. *Developing a Financial Management Information System for Local Government: The Key Issues.* Washington, D.C.: Government Finance Research, MFOA, 1980.

Hatry, Harry P., and John F. Cotton. *Program Planning for County and City.* Washington, D.C.: George Washington University, January 1967.

Hayes, Frederick O'R., et al. *Linkages: Improving Financial Management in Local Government.* Washington, D.C.: Urban Institute Press, 1982.

Herbert, Leo, et al. *Governmental Accounting and Control.* Monterey, Calif.: Brooks/Cole Publishing Co., 1984.

Hickman, Dale, et al. "Taxing over Debt Limits." *Public Administration Review* 41 (July/August 1981): 445-53.

Hough, West C., and John E. Petersen. "Selection and Use of Financial Advisory Services." *Governmental Finance* 13 (March 1984): 42.

Housley, Charles E., ed. *Hospital Purchasing.* Rockville, MD.: Aspen Systems Corporation, 1983.

Humphrey, Nancy, et al. *The Future of Cincinnati's Capital Plant.* Washington, D.C.: Urban Institute Press, 1979.

Institute for Local Self-Government. *Public Agency Liability: The Law and the Risks; Management, Avoidance and Transfer.* Berkley, Calif.: Institute for Local Government, 1978.

International City Management Association (ICMA). "Planning for Capital Improvements." *MIS* 16, no. 18 (August 1984): 5-8.

Kamensky, John M. "Budgeting for State and Local Infrastructure: Developing a Strategy." *Public Budgeting and Finance* 4, no. 3 (Autumn 1984): 3-17.

Kane, Thomas J. Jr. "Budget Directors View Budget Control." *Public Budgeting and Finance* 2, no. 2 (Summer 1982): 44-47.

Kelman, Steven. "The Grace Commission: How Much Waste in Government?" *Public Interest* (Winter 1985): 62-82.

Kettinger, William J. *Information Resource Management and the Use of Information in Local Government: A Policy Guide*. Columbia, S.C.: University of South Carolina, 1980.

Knezevich, Stephen. *Program Budgeting PPBS*. Berkeley, Calif.: McCutchan Publishing Co., 1973.

Knight, Henry C. *Zero-Based Budgeting Process: A Practical Guide to Evaluation, Implementation and Use*. Hamilton, Ont.: Management Society of Management Accounts of Canada, 1979.

Knighton, Lennis M. "Four Keys to Effectiveness Auditing." *Governmental Finance*, 8, no. 2 (September 1979).

Lange, Andrea G., and Robert Bowers. *Fraud and Abuse in Government Benefit Programs*. Washington, D.C.: U.S. Department of Justice, LEAA, 1979.

Levine, Charles H., ed. *Managing Fiscal Stress*. Chatham, N.J.: Chatham House Publishers, Inc., 1981.

Levine, Charles H., et al. *The Politics of Retrenchment*. Beverly Hills, Calif.: Sage Publications, 1981.

Liner, Charles D. "Projecting Local Government Revenues." *Popular Government*, 43 (Spring 1978): 33-37.

Lipset, Martin, and William Schneider. *The Confidence Gap: Business, Labor and Government in the Public Mind*. New York: Free Press, 1985.

Litechy, Charles R., and Earl R. Wilson. "Systems Development for Small Governments." *Governmental Finance* 10, no. 3 (September 1981): 11-18.

Luksus, Edward J. "Strategic Budgeting: How to Turn Financial Records into Strategic Assets." *Management Review* 70 (March 1981): 44-47.

McCabe, Raymond L. "Electronic Funds Transfer as a Cash Management Tool." *Governmental Finance* 10, no. 4 (December 1981): 9-14.

McKinney, Jerome B. *Understanding ZBB: Promise and Reality*. Chicago: Public Policy Press, 1979.

McKinney, Jerome B., and Lawrence C. Howard. *Public Administration: Balancing Power and Accountability*. Oak Park, Ill.: Moore Publishing Co., 1979.

MacSherry, Cathy Daicuff. "Infrastructure and S & P Credit Rating." *Public Budgeting and Finance* 4, no. 3 (Autumn 1984): 41-45.

Matzer, John, Jr., ed. *Practical Financial Management*. Washington, D.C.: ICMA, 1984.

Mendonsa, Arthur. *Financial Management in Local Government*. Athens, Ga.: Institute of Local Government, University of Georgia, 1969.

Mikesell, John L. *Fiscal Administration*. Homewood, Ill.: Dorsey Press, 1982.

Miller, Girard. *Selecting Financial Services for Government*. Chicago: Government Finance Officers Association, 1984.

Moak, Lennox L., and Albert M. Hillhouse. *Local Government Finance*. Chicago: Municipal Finance Officers Association, 1975.

Moak, Lennox L., and Kathryn W. Killian. *A Manual of Techniques for the Preparation, Consideration, Adoption, and Administraiton of Operating Budgets*. Chicago: Municipal Finance Officers Association, 1963.

Mundt, Barry M., et al. *Managing Public Resources.* Stamford, Conn.: Peat Marwick International, 1982.

Municipal Finance Officers Association, *Governmental Accounting, Auditing and Financial Reporting.* Chicago: Municipal Finance Officers Association, 1980.

National Committee on Governmental Accounting (NCGA). *Statement #1, Governmental Accounting and Financial Reporting Principles.* Chicago: NCGA, 1979.

Neuber, Keith A., et al. *Needs Assessment: A Model for Community Planning.* Beverly Hills, Calif.: Sage Publications, 1975.

Newton, Ken. *Balancing the Books.* Beverly Hills, Calif.: Sage Publications, 1980.

Ontario. Ministry of Intergovernmental Affairs. *Managing Purchasing.* Toronto: Ontario Government Book Store, 1981.

Patitucci, Frank M., and Michael H. Lichtenstein. *Improving Cash Management in Local Government: A Comprehensive Approach.* Chicago: Municipal Finance Officers Association, 1977.

Peger, Hal, and Gerald Lonergner. "Popular Financial Reporting in the Public Sector(?)" *Governmental Finance* (May 1976): 33-38.

Public Securities Association. *Fundamentals of Municipal Bonds.* Rev. ed. New York: Public Security Association, 1982.

Rosenberg, Philip, and C. Wayne Stallings. *An Operating Handbook for Small Cities and Other Government Units.* Chicago: Municipal Finance Officers Association, 1978.

Rubin, Irene S. *Running in the Red State.* Albany, N.Y.: University of New York Press, 1982.

Schick, Allen. *Budget Innovations in the States.* Washington, D.C.: Brookings Institution, 1971.

Sherman, Phyllis. *Basic Risk Management Handbook for Local Government.* Darien, Conn.: Public Risk Management Association, 1983.

Solomon, Ezra, and John J. Pringle. *An Introduction to Financial Management.* 2nd ed. Santa Monica, Calif.: Good Year Publishing Co., 1980.

Steiss, Alan Walter. *Local Government Finance.* Lexington, Mass.: Lexington Books, 1975.

_____. *Management Control in Government.* Lexington, Mass.: Lexington Books, 1981.

United Way. *A "PPBS" Approach to Budgeting Human Service Programs for United Ways.* Alexandria, Va.: United Way of America, 1974.

_____. Budgeting: *A Guide for United Way and Not-for-Profit Service Organizations,* Alexandria, Va.: United Way of America, 1975.

Vinter, Robert D., and Rhea K. Kish. *Budgeting for Not-for-Profit Organizations.* New York: The Free Press, 1984.

Wasserman, Natalie, and Dean G. Phelus, eds. *Risk Management Today.* Washington, D.C.: ICMA, 1985.

Weisenbach, Paul E. "Vulnerability Assessment and Internal Controls." *Government Accountants Journal* 33, no. 1 (Spring 1983): 5-10.

Wildavsky, Aaron. *The Politics of the Budgetary Process.* Boston, Mass.: Little, Brown and Co., 1984.

INDEX

About the Author

JEROME B. McKINNEY is Associate Professor, Graduate School of Public and International Affairs, University of Pittsburgh. He has served as a consultant to government and non-profit agencies and has published books and articles on financial management, including *Understanding ZBB: Promise and Reality*.